Alice in Transmedia
Wonderland

Alice in Transmedia Wonderland

*Curiouser and Curiouser
New Forms of a Children's Classic*

ANNA KÉRCHY

McFarland & Company, Inc., Publishers
Jefferson, North Carolina

LIBRARY OF CONGRESS CATALOGUING-IN-PUBLICATION DATA

Names: Kérchy, Anna, author.
Title: Alice in transmedia wonderland : curiouser and curiouser new forms of a children's classic / Anna Kérchy.
Description: Jefferson, North Carolina : McFarland & Company, Inc., Publishers, 2016. | Includes bibliographical references and index.
Identifiers: LCCN 2016031481 | ISBN 9781476666686 (softcover : acid free paper) ∞
Subjects: LCSH: Carroll, Lewis, 1832–1898.—Characters—Alice. | Carroll, Lewis, 1832–1898.—Adaptations. | Alice (Fictitious character from Carroll)—In mass media.
Classification: LCC PR4611.A73 K57 2016 | DDC 823/.8—dc23
LC record available at https://lccn.loc.gov/2016031481

BRITISH LIBRARY CATALOGUING DATA ARE AVAILABLE

ISBN (print) 978-1-4766-6668-6
ISBN (ebook) 978-1-4766-2616-1

© 2016 Anna Kérchy. All rights reserved

No part of this book may be reproduced or transmitted in any form or by any means, electronic or mechanical, including photocopying or recording, or by any information storage and retrieval system, without permission in writing from the publisher.

Front cover image: Adriana Peliano's "Alicedelic" collage is based on John Tenniel's original colored illustrations fused with surrealist imagery inspired by Salvador Dalí, Marcel Duchamp and M. C. Escher. From *ALICE 150 anos: Aventuras de Alice no País das Maravilhas e Através do Espelho e o que Alice encontrou lá* (Rio de Janeiro, Brazil: Editora Zahar, 2015) (courtesy of the artist and the publisher)

Printed in the United States of America

McFarland & Company, Inc., Publishers
Box 611, Jefferson, North Carolina 28640
www.mcfarlandpub.com

To my children,
Sára, Lilla, Miklós and Vilmos

Table of Contents

Acknowledgments — ix
Preface — 1
Introduction: Adapting Ambiguous Alice — 3

1. Transmedia Wonderland — 27
2. Imaginative Reluctance and the (Meta)fantasy of Girlish Fantasy — 75
3. Picturing the Erotic Girl — 125
4. Embodied Language, Multisensorial Nonsense — 166

Epilogue: Celebrating the 150th Anniversary of Wonderland — 221
Chapter Notes — 229
Bibliography — 239
Index — 253

Acknowledgments

During the writing of this book, in 2014 I was awarded the Bolyai János Research Grant of the Hungarian Academy of Sciences for a three-year research project called *Postmodern Configurations of Victorian Fantasy: The Metamedial Aspects of Lewis Carroll's Iconotextual Poetics*. This study is the first important outcome of this project.

The EJES Book Grant received from the European Society for the Study of English in 2014 granted me access to important resources.

The research grant TÁMOP-4.2.1.D-15/1/KONV-2015–0002, "Establishing higher education service satisfying the needs of knowledge industry in the Southern Great Plain region," supported by the European Union and co-financed by the European Social Fund allowed me to travel to the University of Huelva, Spain, to discuss the changing status of reading in the age of digital culture with the *Bodies in Transit* research group directed by Pilar Cuder Dominguez. I gained inspiration for my first chapter, from this 2015 workshop and the "Adapting Alice" panel of the *IRSCL International Research Society for Children's Literature Congress* on Children's Literature and Media Cultures organized in 2013 in Maastricht, The Netherlands, where I travelled with the help of Balassi Institute's Campus Hungary Mobility Grant (B2/2R/1063).

I had the chance to think and teach about nonsense literature, psychogeography and Alice at two consecutive interdisciplinary international summer schools in Venice, Italy, within the frames of the EU Erasmus Intensive Lifelong Learning Programme, 2013–2014, co-organized with colleagues from the Universities of Milano, Venice, and Warwick, among them Loredana Polezzi, who advised me on untranslatability and cross-cultural readability.

Other academic events which gave considerable impetus to my work include the *Fairy Tale After Angela Carter Conference* at the University of East Anglia in 2009 where I first presented a paper on postmodern Alice adaptations, slightly intimidated and tremendously stimulated by the presence of such outstanding scholars and role models in the audience as Marina Warner and Jack Zipes; the 2010 *Anti-Tales* conference at Glasgow University where I gave a plenary lecture on changing media of enchantment and post/millennial filmic Wonderlands to the invitation of Catriona McAra, my co-editor and partner in crime for the forthcoming EJES journal special issue on feminist interventions into intermedial studies; and the 2012 *The Fairy Tale Vanguard* conference at the University of Ghent, Belgium, where I started to tackle the topic of meta-imagination in the Alice tales and their repurposings.

I owe a lot to the thought-provoking conversations with conference organizers and participants, ever-so-inspiring colleagues like Cristina Bacchilega, Martine Hennard Dutheil De la Rochere, Liliane Louvel, Catriona McAra, Vanessa Joosen, Michelle Ryan

Sautour, Mayako Murai, Björn Sundmark, Stijn Praet, Jessica Tiffin, Virginie Iché, Kiera Vaclavik, Katarina Labudova, Andrea Zittlau, Sabine Coelsch-Foisner, Sarah Herbe, Karin Kukkonen, and Celia Brown.

I cherish good memories of an unprecedented international translation project *Alice in Wonderland in 150 Languages* managed by Jon Lindseth and the Lewis Carroll Society and the *Alice through the Ages Conference* organized in 2015 by the University of Cambridge in celebration of the sesquicentennial anniversary of the initial publication of *Alice in Wonderland*, landmark projects in Carrollian studies I am grateful to have participated in, since they singularly fostered the advance of my book. I am indebted to Enikő Bollobás and Nóra Séllei, who agreed to act as readers to my habilitation dissertation on this theme.

The Institute of English and American Studies of the University of Szeged welcomed my courses on fantastic fiction and cultural imagination, and the Gender Studies research group encouraged my endeavors. I owe thanks to relentless support of Zsazsa Barát, the exciting discussions with Larisa Kocic-Zámbó and Korinna Csetényi, and the curiosity of my students, especially in the seminars "Down the Rabbit Hole: Nonsense Fantasy Variations on Alice in Wonderland" and "Who is Afraid of the Big Bad Wolf? Fairy Tales for Adults."

This book could not have gained its present form without the generosity of admirable artists (Samantha Sweeting, Alan Moore and Melinda Gebbie, Robert Sabuda, Polixeni Papapetrou, Julie Zarate, Zdenko Basic, Balázs Sármai, Jodi Harvey Brown, Dave McKean, P. Craig Russell, Bruce Zinger, nobogfrog, Venilian, Daniel Daekazu Kordek) who let me use their artwork in this volume by means of illustrations to my thoughts. Adriana Peliano generously allowed me to use for a cover image her "alicedelic" collage that perfectly captures the metamorphic nature of Alice I wished to highlight in this book.

Last but not least, I would like to thank my family, my mathematician father who introduced me to the twisted logic of Lewis Carroll and made my childhood memorable with his nonsense language games, my tender-hearted mother, the best performer of the Wonderland Duchess' vicious lullaby, my reiki-savvy sister who gave me Jedi energy whenever I was feeling down, my husband who took me to Disneyland Paris (twice!) and has entertained me with the most wicked sense of humor for the past 15 years, and my kids, Sára, Lilla, Miklós, and Vilmos, with whom we invent each day our own private Wonderland.

Preface

This book traces how a story spills over from one media platform into another, transgressing the confines of the written text towards visual, acoustic, kinetic, and digital new media regimes of representation which all interact in the coproduction of a fictional reality's increasingly elaborate fantasy realm, a transmedia Wonderland realized by/in the ever-expanding corpus of late 20th and early 21st century adaptations of Lewis Carroll's Victorian nonsense fairy-tale fantasies *Alice's Adventures in Wonderland* (1865) and *Through the Looking-Glass, and What Alice Found There* (1871). The aim is to explore the ways in which intermedial shifts employed elicit different modes of enchantment and disenchantment, affect contemporary fantasists' strategies of make-believing, and circumscribe a metafantasy commenting on limits and potentials of the fantasy genre as well as the dys/functioning of imagination. The key words around which the analysis revolves are adaptation, media transition, image-text dynamics, multimedia literacy, (meta)imagination, (dis)enchantment, children's literature, interdisciplinarity, popular culture, and overall Alice as the emblem of the perpetual wonderer/wanderer.

The purpose is to study the functioning of metafantasy in contemporary postmodern adaptations of Carroll's *Alice* tales—I treat as an intertextual, dialogic unit—across a variety of popular media platforms, ranging from novel, cinema, photo, music, comics, pop-up paper craft to iPad application, fanfiction, theme park ride, puppetry, ballet and body-art performance. The twofold aim is to unfold the generic and medial self-reflexivity permeating the iconotextual poetics of verbal and visual (mixed media) nonsense in all forms and eras alike; and to trace audiences' changing attitude to their imaginative agency put on trial by encounters with the Unthinkable and the Unspeakable manifested in many ways, including 3D CGI technology's referentless verisimilitude, the traumatic experience of taboos, childish pretense play, or the philosophical dilemma of imaginative resistance. The focus is on how Alice impersonates unlimited imaginativeness to become a metafictional double-agent who also challenges the limits of our fantasy, the techniques of make-believing, and the ethics of enchantment endowed with an increasing significance in our secularized, disenchanted world. The book argues that the adventurous journey to Wonderland today signifies a metafantasmagoric, metamedial mission urging all to interactively explore the cultural critical stakes of their embodied imaginative experience of making sense of nonsense.

Since Alice in and beyond Wonderland indubitably proves to be an iconic figure with an enduring influence on art and a relentless hold on most of us, numerous academic and non-academic books have embarked on exploring the complexity of her character, and some recent publications do resonate with my own work in which I nevertheless strive to elaborate on their ideas and extend their scope of investigation. A decade after Will Brooker's *Alice's Adventures: Lewis Carroll in Popular Culture* (2005) my analyses scrutinize a subsequent period, mostly focusing on 21st century Alices to uncover the process of remediation while keeping in mind the image-text dynamics Brooker leaves out of focus. Besides elaborating on Jack Zipes' distinction between failed and successful adaptations outlined in his chapter on Alice in film in *Enchanted Screen: The Unknown History of Fairy-Tale Films* (2011), I interpret within a larger, multimedial frame of reference both the visual aspects of Carroll's work tackled in Cristopher Hollingsworth's *Alice Beyond Wonderland: Essays for the Twenty-First Century* (2009), the transformations through print, illustration, film, and song traced by Zoe Jaques and Eugene Giddens' *Lewis Carroll's Alice's Adventures in Wonderland and Through the Looking-Glass: A Publishing History* (2013) and the forms of visual entertainment spectacularly catalogued in Catherine Nichols' *Alice's Wonderland: A Visual Journey through Lewis Carroll's Mad, Mad World* (2014). The goal is to trace transmedia interconnections and metamedial self-reflectivity across a variety of representational methods.

My interdisciplinary analysis of the changing meanings, interpretive strategies and epistemological crisis mirrored by the medial multiplicity of contemporary *Alice* adaptations with of a focus on the functioning of human imagination is much in line with the popular fascination with possibility of thinking impossible thoughts as well as current neuroscientific research on memory, language, and consciousness.[1] The methodology of the iconotextual poetics of image-text dynamics adapted to new media is combined with further fresh research areas such as the philosophy of the mind, poststructuralist language philosophy, the postsemiotics of the embodied subject, and corporeal narratology. The study explores different facets of mediality, concentrating on cutting-edge phenomena such as intermedial interactions, our culture's multimediality, metamedial self-reflectivity, the cycle of remediation, and transmedia storytelling.

Today, when academic societies, Carrollian scholars, researchers of the Victorian era, of children's literature or fantasy fiction, as well as reading groups, fan clubs, cosplayers and aficionados have celebrated the 150th anniversary of the publication of the first edition of *Alice's Adventures in Wonderland* on and off the world wide web all over the globe, the term transmedia storytelling seems a particularly appealing term as the ideal aesthetic platform for an era of collective intelligence. This book studies Carroll's *Alice* tales and their numerous adaptations across a variety of media as interrelated constituents of a gigantic transmedia experience, each contributing in unique ways to an unprecedented elaborate story-world. Transmedia Wonderland provides favorable ground for different interpretive communities—academics and fans, children and adults, artists and audiences, old and new media generations—to enter into fruitful dialogue with each other, and—through familiarizing with a multitude of Alices—gain a better understanding of each other's alternative viewpoints as well as their own creative imagination's relational link-making capacities.

Introduction: Adapting Ambiguous Alice

"doesn't matter which way you go…—so long as i get somewhere"

One of the English canon's best loved and most influential literary works of all time, *Alice's Adventures in Wonderland*, a whimsical nonsense fairy-tale fantasy written by Oxford mathematician Charles Lutwidge Dodgson under the pen name Lewis Carroll, was published on 4 July 1865,[1] with its sequel *Through the Looking-Glass, and What Alice Found There* quick to follow in 1871. The books never ceased to remain in print, appeared in various editions from nursery classic picturebook (e.g., Adams & Oliver's 2012 Baby Lit board book Alice) to critically annotated philosophical guidebook (see Heath's 1974 classic or Gardner's ultimate annotated edition of 2015), have been translated in over 150 languages,[2] inspired innumerable adaptations in an impressive variety of media—including stage and screen, theme park and computer game, pop-up paper craft art and iPad application—and continue to fascinate both scholarly academic and popular cultural imagination ever since. The questions spelt out by Carroll biographer Morton Cohen still prevail: "What is the key to their enchantment, why are they so entertaining and yet so enigmatic? What charm enables them to transcend language as well as national and temporal differences and win their way into the hearts of young and old everywhere and always?" (Cohen 135). What keeps the spirit of Alice alive after all these years? And what makes us so spontaneously turn into armchair travelers ready to unconditionally follow a little girl on her fantastic journeys down a rabbit hole into topsy-turvy worlds underground and to the other side of the mirror, and then way beyond, towards Tideland, Hotel Himmelgarten, Underland, or Tulgey Woods, just to name a few of recent adaptations' reimagined wonderlands.

I believe that Alice's unfailing ability to amaze is due to her fundamental characteristic ambiguity that entails a plethora of interpretive possibilities and hence a rewarding adaptability to multiple mixed media forms which stimulate senses beyond the verbal games establishing the trademark charm of the original books. The aim of my study is to explore this amazing ambiguity through an analysis of popular postmodern post/millennial reconfigurations of Victorian fantasy, with a focus on late 20th century and especially early 21st century adaptations of Lewis Carroll's two Alice tales, a pair of texts I treat as a dialogic, intertextual unit. My main question is how intermedial transitions elicit different modes of enchantment, disenchantment, and re-enchantment which both shape and reflect contemporary fantasists' strategies of make-believing. I contend that adventures get curiouser and curiouser once Alice ventures into Transmedia Wonderland, transgressing the confines of the written text towards visual, acoustic, tactile, kinetic and digital new media regimes of representation. Contemporary adaptations dynamically interact with their Victorian source texts as well as one another to enhance the immersion into an elaborate fictional universe and maximize audience engagement while retelling a story that remains recognizably the same, yet turns radically different with each new retelling.

Once upon a time, in the beginning, Alice was a textual creature inseparable from Charles Dodgson, who immortalized his "infant patron" and child muse, the daughter of the dean of Christ Church College, Alice Liddell, as the fictional Alice in the tales improvised on that much mythified bright summer day's boating trip and in turn was inspired by her to bring into being/publication Lewis Carroll, a public figure and famous writer alter ego of a legendarily reserved private self (Schanoes 35). A "private occasional writing for a particular child" was transformed into "a public text for popular consumption" (Sigler xviii). (The same goes for the sequel that was partly inspired by teaching Alice Liddell the mysteries of the game of chess and, as some speculate, partly by another little girl, Alice Raikes, who gave Carroll a witty response to a riddle on a looking-glass.[3]) However, by today Alice has also matured into an extra-textual cultural phenomenon one can "know" without actually having read the original novels about her adventures. Besides lines like "We are all mad here!" "Why is a raven like a writing desk?" and "Off with her head!" resonating as household terms familiar to most, numerous visual adaptations succeeded to Carroll's original manuscript drawings and Tenniel's by now classic illustrations to permeate popular cultural imagination to such an extent that Alice's figure gained an iconic status as a spectacular emblem of a curious wanderer and wonderer toying with Unknowability in the company of such easily recognizable fantasy figures as the White Rabbit, the Mad Hatter, Humpty Dumpty or the Red Queen.

No matter how contemporary adaptations' intermedial shifts transform the story, *Alice*[4] remains an "interminable fairy tale" as its author called it in his diary (Brustein in Nichols vii). It combines an escapist "pleasure in the fantastic" and a social critical "curiosity about the real" (Warner 1994, xx) with a metafictional commentary about the functioning of our imagination that seeks to change the world to accommodate and stimulate us, while we endlessly struggle metamorphosing both to fit in and transgress its frames (see Zipes 2012, 2). The genre's trademark "poetics of wonder" (Bacchilega 2014, 5) surfaces in Carroll's frequent use of the word "curious" to excite, enchant, and function as "a kind of tocsin awakening us [readers] from our reverie"; but "it isn't the strangeness of Alice's Wonderland that it reminds us of—it's the bizarre incomprehensibility of our own" (Brooker 98). The absurdities of our commonsensical consensus reality are presented in a hilarious, fantastic way in topsy-turvy worlds refusing logic and moralization: the confrontation with authority figures becomes bold rebellion, the perplexing difficulties of communication result in nonsense language games, and the identity crises border on grotesque masquerade. Chaos terrifying well-socialized adults is reinterpreted from a child's perspective as unlimited play. The greatest ambiguity of all resides in the enrapturement by Wonderland that is equally delightful and shocking, and—in the eyes of Alice, whom we identify with—more and more of a customary surprise.

Carroll's[5] classic *Alice* novels are distinguished by an ambiguous generic hybridity that creatively mingles fairy tale and nonsense fantasy with gothic horror, political satire, sociocritical allegory, literary pastiche, language philosophical arguments, games of symbolic logic, photography theory, ethical insights related to children's rights and representation, encoded love letter, thought-provoking paradox and infantile gibberish among others to provide, via an "inter-generational epiphany" (Self in Brooker 97), "abstract and concrete" "meaning and enjoyment" to child and adult readers alike (Ennis in Zipes 2000, 12). This book aims to demonstrate how this narrative structural complexity enables a free play of multiple meanings which motivate contemporary popular adaptations to focus on different layers of the above significations. Different uses of the genres are exploited in a variety of media platforms all contributing to the unfolding of the story in individual ways. Creative reinterpretations record and resolve their own era's specific cultural anxieties, struggles, desires and dreams, while amply proving the versatility and mutability of Alice's story across time, space and discourse.

An inherent ambiguity is involved in the adaptation process itself. While each reinterpretation's indebtedness to the source-text is clearly recognizable, the familiarity with the original is not a prerequisite of making sense of the new artwork that should be comprehensible and enjoyable independently on its own right. The capacity to interface the two versions might nevertheless "enrich our reading of a transformation" (Frus and Williams 4). Since the fragmentary, dream-like, sequential structure of the two Alice novels[6] easily allows episodes to be rearranged, omitted, added or even merged into one single story, most adaptations mix Alice's chance encounters in Wonderland and beyond the Looking-Glass[7] to create a quest of their own making. The heroine's originally purposeless meandering is usually reorganized along the lines of a goal she must reach, ranging from the modest wish to get back home to the ambitious mission of saving Wonderland. Again, the ability to distinguish the two original storylines does not necessarily affect readerly pleasures. "Trajectories of adaptation become divorced from the original as they [intertextually] build upon one another," with John Tenniel's Victorian illustrations or Walt Disney's musical animation becoming a source for adaptations at least as significant as Carroll's own originals which come to function as "conceptual framework for larger tropes of dreaming, fantasy, drug-taking, childhood fears, or heroic belligerence" while Alice's character often gets conflated with rebellious girl child fantasist twin-sisters Dorothy from *The Wizard of Oz* and Wendy from *Peter Pan* (Jaques and Giddens 201, 206).

Carroll's literary nonsense, a most self-reflective genre that strategically "fuses disguise, masquerade and imposture" (Reynolds 50) strangely forecasts the transformative effects of future tributes' inevitable misinterpretations of his text. Alice's identity crisis constituting the kernel of the narrative is enhanced by the wondrous creatures repeatedly misidentifying her as Mary Ann, Mabel, a serpent, a volcano, a blossom with untidy petals, or a fabulous monster. Ironically, many adaptations' largely modified Alices stay true to their foremother in so far as they must face replicas of these misrecognitions. Gilbert Adair's Alice is mistaken for a comet, Jeff Noon's for a lice, Angela Carter's for an alchemical homunculus, Tim Burton's and American McGee's for the heroic savior of Wonderland, Neil Gaiman's for the normativized Caroline instead of the unique Coraline. Alice's multifaceted, mutable character "in a constant process of becoming" (Sigler xiv) is indeed difficult to grasp, even for herself.[8]

Literal (mimetic, referential), metaphorical (poetic) and rhetorical (metafictional) interpretations alternate throughout attempts to make sense of nonsense. Child readers nearly automatically suspend their disbelief to interpret Alice's make-believe tale in a literal way as an alternative reality, as consistently incongruous fictional worlds, where a little girl can shrink tiny and grow enormous by pure chance or at her own will, where even the most eerie may come true and should be accepted as natural simply on accounts of being elsewhere. Literalizing also takes part of a serious biographically and cultural-historically contextualizing decoding process. Referential or mimetic interpretations of Carroll scholars strive to detect the real nature of the relationship between the author and the muse, while endlessly speculating about the Alice Liddell-riddle, missing diary pages and hidden emotions shaping the subtext, or who claim to discover in fictionalized form anxieties related to Victorian socio-cultural phenomena ranging from shocking technological innovations to restraining bourgeois codes of conduct. Yet Alice remains an imaginary surface upon whom historically changing desires and fears are projected by means of metaphorical readings, which associate with the mythified character abstractions, even whole philosophies, self-reflexive meta-takes on real-life phenomena. In the eyes of the fellow Victorians she is the embodiment of the mystified, idealized Dreamchild, for the surrealists a traveler of dreamscapes and an alchemist of the word, for the 1960s' countercultures a rebel toying with hallucinogenic experiments, for Freudians the agent of infantile drives and neurotic fantasies, for feminists an empowering alternative for claustrophobic, domestic narratives of feminine helplessness, and for postmodernist scholars a language philosopher and ideology-critique challenging regimes of truth and rule-bound discourse to celebrate the transgressive, ludic aspects of speaking and being. We might speculate that "the Alice books' enduring power and appeal may very well lie in the fact that, like dreams, they *can* mean whatever readers *need* them to mean" (Sigler xiv).

The *Annotated Alice*—first published in 1959, with a *More Annotated Alice* to follow in 1990, and a combined, definitive anniversary edition in 2015—remains the ultimate reference book of all Carroll scholars. The editor, mathematician, logician and cultural critic Martin Gardner, provides thorough annotations to the text allowing for mimetic readings grounded in a socio-cultural contextualization deemed a fundamental prerequisite for the comprehension of the oeuvre. Gardner suggests that the *Alice* books constitute a "very curious, complicated kind of nonsense" (Gardner xiii) with multiple layers and a connotative richness that today can only be grasped by contemporary readers willing to embark on a background research. One should explore firstly meanings which used to be evident for the 19th century British audience but have been forgotten by now, secondly witticisms or side-winks comprehensible only to Carroll's fellow residents at Oxford, and thirdly even private jokes understood just by the lovely daughters of Dean Liddell. The most important implication, I believe, is that the uncovering of real-life phenomena at the root of fiction includes tackling the fantasies shared by the people involved in the creation of the text: referential readings may attempt at remembrance of metaphors past, of emotions, impressions and imaginings fueling the story. Whereas Gardner claims that devoid of these para-, inter-, sub-textual information the *Alice* books remain incomprehensible (uninteresting for adults and frightening for children), I would take the side of C.S. Lewis (1952) arguing that the "unknown," "'unknowable" facet of the fantasies is enough to fascinate readers of all ages. In Lewis' words, "fairy land arouses a longing for [the reader] knows not what. It stirs and troubles him (to his life-long enrichment) with the dim sense of something beyond his reach and, far from dulling or emptying the actual world, gives it a new dimension of depth" (29–30). Hence, ravishing reinterpretations may emerge while disregarding authorial intentions, biographical data or cultural surrounding, too, simply stimulated by the endless meaning-generating capacity of literary nonsense fairy-tale fantasy masquerading in the guise of meaninglessness.

Carroll's Alice tales excel in *literary nonsense* filled with conversations which resemble and are decoded as language, as meaningful communication, yet their intelligibility becomes dubious, defamiliarized for the implied reader heroine who grows increasingly uncertain about the viability of the conventional representational and interpretive strategies meant to make sense of them. Nonsense requires its recipients to exercise an inventive linguistic creativity, to make self-corrections, re-readings and playful deconstructions, while exchanging primary (normal, literal, denotative) meanings for supplementary (less obvious, figurative, allusive, poetic) ones or vice versa, succeeding to Humpty Dumptian claims of "that's not what I meant" (Carroll 221, 224). I contend that the reader's balancing between a surplus and a void of meanings during the mis/interpretation of nonsense is driven by the same "desire to reinhabit a beloved story" and to create for the source text an unprecedented meaning in new form (Wells-Lasagne and Hudelet 2) as any actual adaptation project. Eventually, one of the aims of this book is to trace the shapeshiftings of literary nonsense which result from the adaptations' media transitions: the first chapter analyzes how *visual nonsense* turns language games into pictorial puns and surprising images and explores the *technological enhancement of nonsensification* (in iPad app and 3D CGI imagery), the second chapter studies how *imaginative nonsense* plays with the oscillation between a reluctance and a willingness to fantasize, the third chapter tackles how *erotic nonsense* emerges in the ambiguous meanings attributed to the girl child nude in post–Freudian times' retro-Victorian art, and chapter four is devoted to the study of how *embodied nonsense* allows the representation of the body to reanimate the signification process by embracing fleshly traces of the unspeakable and the unimaginable.

The Alice tales' "adaptogenic" quality (Groensteen in Hutcheon 15) can be traced by a close reading of the genesis and evolution of the original source-text itself that reveals how Carroll's numerous revisions have basically paraphrased the same story with subtractions, contractions, extensions, and variations throughout three decades which kept him preoccupied with various adapting practices targeted at his own work. First, with a shift of communicational and medial channel, he transformed his oral narrative, improvised on a rowing excursion with the Liddell girls up the Isis on 4 July 1862, into a written fairy tale decorated by his own drawings, completed under the title *Alice's Adventures Under Ground* in 1863. Then, he expanded the adventures with new episodes ("Pig and Pepper" and "A Mad Tea Party"), changed the title to *Alice's Adventures in Wonderland*, commissioned professional Punch cartoonist John Tenniel to illustrate the manuscript, and—encouraged by George MacDonald—had it published by Macmillan to send a presentation copy to Alice on 4 July 1865, exactly three years after the ominous boating trip. A few years later he exploited readers' familiarity with his curious wandering heroine and in a sequel invented a new quest for her in *Through the Looking-Glass and What Alice Found There* illustrated by Tenniel and published in December 1872. He contributed to a medial transposition that turned the first novel into a theatrical production in Henry Savile Clarke's Christmas 1886 play on 23 December—he agreed to the dramatization on condition the play omitted any form of "coarseness" along with the slapstick harlequinade popular in pantomimes, and used old airs for songs (Nichols 40). In the same year he had the facsimile edition of his original *Under Ground* manuscript published, and he also commented on the theatre performance from a critical metaperspective in his essay "Alice on the Stage" (1887). His 1890 *The Nursery Alice* abbreviated the Wonderland adventures and enhanced the story with color illustrations, kinesthetic interactive experience, and revived oral pleasures to make it suitable for early- or pre-readers. Keen to promote his books, he published "Puzzles from Wonderland" in the December 1870 issue of *Aunt Judy's Magazine* as a sort of an appetizer for his impending sequel, and in 1871 collaborated with composer William Boyd, who set to music some verses of *Looking-Glass* (Jaques 56). Carroll also worked on various commercial enterprises which helped to market his books and expanded fans' fantasy experience with tie-in products such as the Wonderland postage stamp case or a biscuit tin decorated by characters from *Looking-Glass*.

Although Carroll was bitter about the proliferation of his Victorian contemporaries' imitative rewritings of the visit to Wonderland theme he claimed as his own but he himself strategically exploited the creative powers of adaptation. In *Sylvie and Bruno* he opined: "Perhaps the hardest thing in all literature—at least I have found it so: by no voluntary effort can I accomplish it: I have to take it as it comes—is to write anything original. And perhaps the easiest is, when once an original line has been struck out, to follow it up, and to write any amount more to the same tune" (Carroll xxxvi in Sigler xviii). In the case of the *Alice* tales, a variety of manuscript versions, revisions, different print edition stand in dialogue with each other and create what Bryant calls a "fluid text" (in Hutcheon 170).

Instances of intertextual fluidity abound in Carroll's fantasies. First, the boundaries of Alice's story worlds, Wonderland and Looking-Glass realm blur, so the two volumes constitute a dialogic unit of Genettian hypotext that almost necessarily elicits further variants, adaptations which con/fuse the two books' episodes, characters and puns "selected, abridged, and rearranged [at whim] as the acts of a television variety program of the 1950s, held together only by Alice's abiding presence" (Leitch 185) within a single new retelling, mostly under the simplified title *Alice in Wonderland*. (In postmodern adaptations, the biographical myth of author and muse, of Lewis Carroll and Alice Liddell's creative partnership are also often mingled within the retelling of the story they coproduced, to further nuance fictional adventures with a metanarrative layer.)

Second, the humor of the Alice tales partly springs from subversive intertextual reappropriations of earlier literary classics: parodic pastiches of didactic verse taught to Victorian schoolchildren (from Isaac Watts' rhyme about the busy bee praising the virtue of diligence to Oliver Smith's *Little Goody Two Shoes* whose heroine—possibly inspiring Carroll's Duchess—is so fond of moralizing that even the death of a pet dormouse gives her a pretext for a lecture on the uncertainty of life and the necessity to be prepared for death [Leach 91, Kelly 32]), repurposings of well-known nursery rhymes (e.g., Humpty Dumpty, The Lion and the Unicorn) as well as mock Anglo-Saxon poetry presented in the nonsense stanzas of "Jabberwocky" (that has generated countless parodies ever since including "Chapatiwocky" [about Indian cuisine], "Jabberstocky" [about Wall Street trading], "Wockyjabber" [about integral solving] [Lim 2014], as well as "Der Jammerwoch" and "Iabrivokaveda" [a faked German balladistic and a proto-Indo-European original] [Sundmark 26]).

Thirdly, the *Alice* tales can be interpreted as picturebooks in so far as the illustrations constitute an integral part of narrative meanings. The interaction between word and image will necessarily contribute to the textual fluidity by setting up, in Hillis Miller's words, an "oscillation or shimmering of meaning in which neither element is prior to the other, since the pictures are about the text, and the text is about the pictures" (in Hancher 113). Interpretations vary depending on the different meanings added to the text by Carroll's original illustrations, Tenniel's line drawings (updated from one volume to the other to make the heroine's dress contemporaneous with the readers' [Nières 198]) which eventually eclipsed Carroll's to become canonical, and all future artists' revisionings of Wonderland.

Thus, Carroll's Alice tales build on an "extended intertextual engagement with a source text, and creative interpretive acts of appropriation" (Hutcheon 8): a sequel engaging with a prequel, parodies engaging with the canon, images engaging with the text, multiple repurposings engaging with the "original" oral version meet the criteria of Linda Hutcheon's above definition of the adaptation process. However, these Carrollian remakes are also much in line with Walter Benjamin's idea on storytelling as "the art of repeating stories" too (1969, 90)—an assumption Alice must face during her fall down the rabbit hole that marks her entry into the storyworld that takes place between bookshelves, maps, and images as if locating her intertextually amidst stories told, untold, and awaiting further retellings.

This book embarks to analyze adaptations of Lewis Carroll's *Alice* tales, focusing on contemporary understandings and uses of Alice's character circulating in late 20th century and early 21st century globalized popular culture. The adaptations I consider are acknowledged, extended, creative transpositions of an original artwork recognizable by virtue of the wondering wanderer heroine and the atmosphere of her curious adventures. They revisit the source text without subserviently replicating it, they "bring together the comfort of ritual and recognition with the delight of surprise and novelty, involve both memory and change, and combine narrative persistence with material variation" (Hutcheon 173). Alternately called "repurposings" (Bolter and Grusin 45), "expansions" (Rabinowitz 247), "creative revisions" (Kérchy 2011a, 67), "creative transformations" (Jaques and Giddens 200), "creative reanimations" (Hutcheon 8), they never fail to remake, alter, and adjust the adapted story to preserve it for posterity while enhancing its "evolution" to fit new times, different places, and changing audience expectations (Stam 3). The shift of medium, frame, or context involved in the adaptations studied here entails a change in the mode of engagement and enchantment with the text and both reflects and shapes the specific era's interpretive community's attitude to the imaginativeness emblematized by the figure of Alice, who guarantees that the original "artwork's spirit is conveyed" (Hutcheon 10).

Far from being regarded as inferior imitations of the original, adaptations will be interpreted as part of an intertextual web where each element—old and new and newer: Carroll's variations on the original, the variety of adaptations produced by posterity, and for the knowing reader even the metatexts of academic critical reception, reviews, or fanfiction—stand in a dialogic relation with one another, contributing to a dynamic modification of meanings. The hierarchical superiority based on the chronology of publication is challenged by a dynamic oscillation between the significations generated by the source and the adaptation. For instance, first impressions might be decisive as the adaptation is possibly the version the reader/spectator encounters first and will regard as the original in her subjective view, but echoes of memory traces of *Alice* permeating the cultural imaginary or the individual order of re-experiencing an artwork might also be influential.

This book primarily concentrates on *Alice* adaptations created in English and circulated within the Anglo-American context but in the case of the few artworks produced in languages other than English (Jan Svankmajer's Czech puppet film) the translation into English adds yet another layer of adaptation to the complex interpretive experience. While Walter Benjamin argues that translation, instead of copying, paraphrasing or reproducing some fixed nontextual meaning allows us to see in different ways the original text that already "bears in itself all possible translations and gets richer with each additional reading-rewriting" (2005, 17), Susan Bassnett calls translation a transaction between text and languages, an "act of both inter-cultural and inter-temporal communication" (9) and Martine Hennard Dutheil de la Rochère insists upon "the agency of the translator as mediator and re-creator" (3). In line with this turn in translation studies Lawrence Venuti draws a clear-cut analogy between translation and adaptation as creative derivative methods which "inscribe an interpretation that inevitably varies the form and meaning" of a de- and re-contextualized source text (29). This analogy is especially relevant for my research since I study *Alice* adaptations from the viewpoint of a non-native speaker heavily influenced by a first childhood experience of the source text in Hungarian language and illustrations which remain the original versions for me, thereby rendering all my succeeding academic readings of Carroll and Tenniel's English classic necessarily palimpsestic. For me, the Cheshire Cat is inseparable from the figure of the grinning wooden dog, a literalized embodiment of the Hungarian metaphorical idiom "to giggle/grin like a *wooden dog*" (vigyorog, mint a fakutya")—in which the wooden dog ("fakutya") is an archaic term for a sledge making a screeching sound like laughter on ice and/or for a boot-horn shaped like a smile—featuring in the translation domesticated for Hungarian readers by Dezső Kosztolányi (1935) revised by Tibor Szobotka (1958) as well as Tamás Szecskó's illustrations to the seventeen editions of Szobotka's modernized text version.

My analysis of contemporary retellings, revisions and remediations explores multivocal means to reinterpret and relocate the same source text. Highlighting Alice as a "shapeshifter and mediumbreaker" (Greenhill 3) I argue for a lateral coexistence of multiple versions which destabilize the authority of the original and create a choir of alternative Alices. In line with the performative word magic of the Carrollian universe where the name Alice is supposed to be identical with Alice-hood itself, our presuppositions (based on prior readings or knowledge of the original) influence the meanings we attribute to adaptations which are evaluated conforming to the expectations towards an Alice type story.

Carolyn Sigler summarizes the constituents of "the Alice type story" as follows: a typically polite, articulate, and assertive heroine; a transition from the "real" waking life to a fantasy dream world; rapid shifts in identity, appearance, and location; an episodic structure centering on encounters with nonhuman fantasy creatures or characters based on nursery rhymes; nonsense language, verse parodies, songs; an awakening to the real world generally portrayed as domestic; and a clear acknowledgment of indebtedness to Carroll through dedication, apology, mock-denial of influence, or other textual, intertextual reference (xvii). Certainly an adaptation does not have to include all these features in order to be recognizable, nor does it necessarily have to include media change. It is sufficient to pick just a few story elements—"themes, events, world, characters, motivation, points of view, consequences, context, symbols, imagery" (Hutcheon 10)—to get a convincing and creative variation of the adapted heterocosm. The mature, empowered action heroines of many postmillennial adaptations—from Syfy channel's judo sensei to Burton's armored warrior—

are far from the loving, gentle, courteous girl child Carroll originally invented, however the unrestrained curiosity and the brave "acceptance of the wildest impossibilities with all that utter trust that only dreamers know" (Carroll 1887 in Kelly 225) retained from the original character concept are sufficient personality traits for audiences to identify Alice's figure.

Amidst the wide yet necessarily inexhaustive range of *Alice* adaptations I study here all sorts of adapting strategies occur. Closest to the fidelity criteria, *Alice for the iPad* (2010) reproduces Carroll and Tenniel's text and image in their integrity but the adaptation to a different medium nuances meanings by technologically enhancing the original with animated illustrations which facilitate an even livelier readerly interactivity. Robert Sabuda's pop-up book *Alice* (2003) revisits the original text in an abridged form with new illustrations inspired by Tenniel. Scottish Ballet's *Alice* performance (2011) reimagines the trademark story elements such as the fall down the rabbit hole and the whole crew of oddball Wonderland creatures framed within a fictionalized account of Dodgson's photographic activity that becomes a major plot device of a renewed story. American McGee's Alice computer game (2000) toys with a trequel inventing new adventures for an Alice traumatized by the death of her parents in a house fire caused by her imaginary visits to dream realms. Neil Gaiman's *Coraline* (2002) at the other end of the scale pays a less obvious but still recognizable tribute to Alice by making a little girl's journey to a curious dream realm and her succeeding identity crisis the major narrative leitmotifs. Intertextual allusions might be as subtle as the heroine's reading a book entitled *Alice's Adventures in Wonderland* we only get a quick glimpse of as in the film *Tideland* directed by Terry Gilliam (2005).

Alice is perhaps the easiest to access in literary adaptations which do not involve any radical media transition. As Björn Sundmark points out, "in the decades following *Wonderland* and *Looking-Glass*, the impact of Alice made itself felt primarily through the emulations of other writers." Carroll himself complained after the publication of his first Alice novel that "something like a dozen story-books have appeared, on identically the same pattern. The path I timidly explored … is now a beaten highroad: all the way-side flowers have long ago been trampled into the dust" (Sundmark 10). *Alternative Alices: Visions and Revisions of Lewis Carroll's Alice Books* (1997), edited by Carolyn Sigler, introduces "the most original," "extraordinarily coherent, creative, critical responses" to the *Alice* novels of the almost 200 literary imitations, revisions, parodies produced between 1869 and 1930. The Wonderland themes, motifs and structures are recycled for different ends by the four major types of *Alice* stories distinguished by Sigler: sentimental, subversive, didactic, and political parodic rewritings illustrate "how fantasies were read, reinscribed, or resized in the late 19th and early 20th centuries" in "alternately enchanting, experimental, satiric, and subversive" manners (xi).

The *Alice* books did not only provide a favorable ground of experimentation for Victorian authors' didactic, parodic or political rewritings collected in Sigler's anthology but have remained a rich source of inspiration for (post)modern tributes available in two remarkable volumes. In *Fantastic Alice: New Stories from Wonderland* (1995), edited by Margaret Weiss, "today's masters of modern fantasy" further explore the wonderful world of "Alice and her inspired creator" in "brilliantly original new stories" (ix). In Richard Peabody's collection *Alice Redux: New Stories of Alice, Lewis and Wonderland* (2005) contemporary writers revisit the wondrous "world of controversy and speculation" to reconnect with their own childlike fantasies and provocatively mock modern morality, let their imagination be "sparked by the Alice and Lewis relationship," "'gyre and gymble' with Carroll's muse, characters, times, and persona to discover truths and unravel riddles personal and profound, silly and sensational" (xiv), to "return to pinafore days of yesterday before lost innocence when the road to Wonderland was reached by simply turning the pages in a book" (xvi). The texts chose one of what Helen Pilinovsky calls "the three primary paths for retelling Alice": they either continue the original adventures in a Victorian setting, or update into more contemporary circumstances Alice's childish struggle in the perplexing world of adults, or diverge from their surroundings to focus on her maturation (Pilinovksy 176). Kathleen Blake (1974) greets among critical responses to Alice and Carroll, the cheerful, playful "Heiterkeit Alice" besides the aggressive "Malice Alice" and the victimized "Angst Alice." However, an episodic dream structure, a playful use of symbolic nonsense language, metamorphic motifs, and a foregrounding of interactivity, of ambiguous open endings which all enable varied and contradictory readings also prove to be efficient grounds for Alice adaptations.

Juliet Dusinberre's *Alice to the Lighthouse: Children's Books and Radical Experiments in Art* (1999) revealed the revolutionary change Carroll's *Alice* tales initiated in writing for and about children and the enormous impact they had on subsequent children's writers (Stevenson, Kipling, Nesbit, Hodgson Burnett and Twain), and more importantly on high literary modernism. Artists like Virginia Woolf addressed adult audiences but, adopting the Carrollian ars poetica, "celebrated writing as play rather than preaching," challenging the "mastery over language, structure, vision, morals, characters and readers" alike. Alice holds a strong attraction for postmodern writers too, who have produced quite a few imaginative and highly self-reflective revisions. These gems include Jeff Noon's *Automated Alice* (1996), a dystopian steampunk fantasy about Alice and her doll Celia, who follow Great Aunt's parrot through a grandfather clock to get lost and try to solve a murder mystery in a future Manchester city ruled by chaos theory, jazz music and Carrollian puns and puzzles, and inhabited by human-machine-animal hybrid Newmonians, Alice's termite-driven, robot "twin twister," the Automated Alice of the title, Captain Ramshackle, a Badgerman and Randomologist, and a Crow-woman scientist Professor Gladys Chrowdingler, who puts cats in boxes that may or may not turn them invisible. In Jonathan Lethem's satirical science fiction *As She Climbed Across the Table* (1997) Alice is a particle physicist obsessed with a wormhole named Lack who gives the author pretext to reflect on philosophical issues pertaining to quantum physics, deconstruction, and human interaction with artificial intelligence. Bryan Talbot's graphic novel *Alice in Sunderland* (2007) explores the links between Lewis Carroll and the Sunderland area, tackling themes of history, myth and storytelling, while documenting local legends such as that of the monkey hanged in Hartlepool or the Lambton Worm that possibly inspired Carroll's monstrous Jabberwock. Most recently, Gregory Maguire's *After Alice* (2015) traces the adventures of three characters who set out in search of missing Alice and freedom: her sickly friend Ada tumbles down the rabbit hole to be liberated in the subterranean nonsense realm from the confines of her waking life and the iron corset meant to correct her crooked spine, her teenage sister Lydia struggles, during her pursuit, with coming-of-age in an adult world ruled by strict mores of Victorian England, while Siam, a runaway slave child traveling with an American accompanying Darwin, falls through the looking-glass into a Wonderland where his racial difference will cease to matter. Along the same lines, Vanessa Tait, the great-granddaughter of the original Alice explores the mysteries of the self while denying Alice the heroine status in *The Looking Glass House* (2015) by recreating the events surrounding the genesis of Wonderland from the perspective of the governess of the Liddell family.

Despite the difficulty of transplanting to the primarily visual medium of cinema the nonsense language games, logical ambiguities, and verbal enchantment so characteristic of Wonderland, Carroll's tales have lent themselves well to *film adaptations* from the very youth of motion picture industry keen on "turning for inspiration and development to the substantial literature of childhood" (Street xix-xx). The first cinematic revision of *Alice*, a ten-minute-long moving image sketch directed by Cecil Hepworth and Percy Stow in 1903 was among the first silent movies ever, screened only a year after Georges Mélies' legendary *Voyage to the Moon* inspired by Jules Verne's fantastic fiction entered cinemas, and just five years after Carroll's death.

In Kara Manning's compelling wording, "like the slices of Looking-Glass plum-cake that 'always join on again,' Alice and film constantly reconnect, showing how Carroll's classic is perfectly fitted for a technology that did not yet exist at the time of its creation" (156). In Manning's view a proto-cinematic multimodal quality permeates the Alice books. The original editions as material objects akin to the proto-cinematic optical toys (often called philosophical toys) so popular in nineteenth-century households, the stories preoccupied with governing and arresting motion, and especially the narrativization of a temporally, spatially, and logically ambiguous statuary motion (i.e., moving and remaining still simultaneously) all prepared the Victorians for motion pictures which indeed granted the illusion of mobility for a stationary observer (Manning 156, Manning 2013).

Critical consensus now claims that moving-image adaptations should not be simplistically evaluated along the lines of fidelity to the literary source-text and the mythical primacy of words as origins of images (Street 1984, Wojcik-Andrews 2000, Brooker 2005, 200). A simple reason of the necessary challenging of hierarchization may be that today's audiences often engage with remediated versions first and do not experience the new work as adaptation (Hutcheon xv). For many, Disney's Wonderland animation remains the ultimate classic based on the primacy of the childhood experience while the box office success of Tim Burton's tech-savvy 3D adaptation he called an "extension" (Ryder 2009) allegedly boosted the sales of Carroll's original novels. The post/modernist tendency of the cinematic adaptation's relying on a multitude of preceding hypotexts, paratexts, and adoptions across different media instead of one single particular source-text ensures that the number of "duplications" which subserviently perpetuate the original's canonical form, plot or moral is indubitably surpassed by the "critical revisions" which subvert the story by incorporating new values, perspectives, aesthetics or politics to it (Zipes 1994, 8–9), or "creative revisions" which "rather gain inspiration from the original, to reimagine the same fantasy patterns with a different manifest dream content" (Kérchy in McAra-Calvin 2011, 67). Pauline Greenhill and Sidney Matrix agree with Robert Stam that the range of cinematic adaptations extends far beyond homage or critique to include film rewritings, resuscitations, resignifications, or even "cannibalizations" of literary or oral texts, to correct, echo, and experiment with the original story (2004, 25 in 13).

Film adaptations' intertextual indebtedness, interestingly, also signifies a return to the very archaic origins of the fairy tale genre distinguished by a proliferation of anonymous, orally transmitted versions, "a myriad of indeterminate intervening retellings" (Stephens and McCallum in Zipes 2000, 161), none of them authoritative, or "the original." When Maria Tatar talks about the "extraordinary cultural elasticity" of fairy tales which, even when recited verbatim from a book, rarely turn repetitive, since every new voice puts a new inflection on each episode, she offers just another synonym for the inherent adaptability of the genre.[9] And so is the case with the "expansive range and imaginative play" of *Alice* adaptations: each new revision of her fairy-tale fantasy story "seems to recharge its power, making it crackle and hiss with renewed narrative energy" (Greenhill and Matrix 2).

Another fundamental feature of fairy tales, the traditional collective intent to please and instruct *mixed-aged audiences*, arises in the case of many cinematic adaptations of *Alice* which belong to the ambiguous generic category of family movie blurred with the genre of children's film that is alternatively regarded as a work designed for, about, or by children, frequently an adaptation of a children's literary classic. Tim Burton's 2010 3D CGI enhanced *Alice* adaptation featured on the International Movie Data Base as a "live-action family adventure film" rated PG (Parental Guidance advised)[10] by the Motion Picture Association of America "for fantasy action/violence involving scary images and situations, and for a smoking caterpillar." Yet, it may not be so far from fairy tale classics and Carrollian fantasies as one would presume on first seeing the film's classification since many of the originals are full of explicit violence, social critical commentary and sexual innuendo themselves. Bengt Holbek's catalogue of the similarities between the fairy tale genre and contemporary live-action fairy-tale films also lays emphasis on their intergenerational aspect. Children may listen but are not the primary audience of this popular cultural exchange between adults: skilled specialist storytellers on one side and "the lower strata of traditional communities" with different male and female repertoires on the other (Holbek 1998, 405 in Greenhill-Matrix 4). As a result of the dual spectatorship of post-millennial fairy tale fantasy film, the in-between audience segment of young adults nearly necessarily becomes "the new IT market for film producers seeking to capitalize on the hype surrounding everything magical or supernatural" (Enzerink 2011).

The question of a double audience address is particularly exciting in the case of Carroll's *Alice* tales full of philosophical contents difficult to access for children and a whimsical playfulness excluded from adult reality. G.K. Chesterton opined that children "are far better employed making mud-pies" than reading the complex Carrollian text (Kelly 14), while Peter Heath author of *Philosopher's Alice: The Thinking Man's Guide to a Misunderstood Nursery Classic* (1974) downright declared that "it is especially children who have the smallest chance of understanding what [the Alice tales] are about" (3). Virginia Woolf agreed that the Alice stories are not written for children but are "the only books" in which mature readers can become children: curious, heartless, ruthless, and passionate (82). On the contrary, for Morton Cohen Wonderland is "a survival course" offering the power "to triumph over childlike confusion and fear" (139) a fantastic thematization of the struggles of growing up. In other critics' view Alice is an emblem of eternal childhood identified with the resilience and "high-spirited courage of little girls amidst harsh circumstances" (Kali 255), a rebellious rejection of adult authority and a vindication of the rights of the child to self-assertion (Leach 92, Kelly 35), or a mythic figure of "self-control, perseverance, bravery, and a mature good sense" (Rackin in Sigler xiii), respectively.

Carroll himself seems to have been aware of the duality of the audience attracted by his stories—in a way similar to many other Victorian fairy tale fantasies. His preface in *The Nursery Alice* (1890) does not only stratify the community of his interpreters by addressing mothers who will read the tale to their children listening to Alice's adventures (distinguishing between parents and offspring, readers and listeners, buyers and consumers of the book) but also extends his readership by fully eliminating age limits and assuming to have reached the "child-like" English reading populace in its integrity.[11]

Yet another reason of the easy contemporary adaptability of the *Alice* tales to mixed age audiences relates to the infantilization today's consumers are accustomed to by the acceleration of the commodification of fantasy lamented by numerous fairy tale scholars. In Jack Zipes' view, *Alice*'s filmic adaptations now do not only face us with those disturbing psychic contents of childhood we recall yet repress in adult representations (2011, 302) but the protagonist perplexedness in a Kafkaesque world reflects the "onrush of postmodern conditions" (295), a familiar unfamiliarity confronting contemporary consumers of culture. As Claudia Springer reminds us, the rapid-fire ever-changing language that bombards Alice with elusive meanings and simulated realities recalls discourses of advertising, while her confusion resonates with circuitous, labyrinthine postmodern architecture and the MTV-style fast-paced manipulation of space, time, and logic (Springer in Zipes 294). Therefore, instead of being just charming children's stories or tales of teenage terror, Alice adaptations record the anxiety of a timeless "desire to impose stability on a turbulent world," a dream shared by fantasists of Postmodern and Victorian times too. Both eras experience an epistemological crisis, as ages characterized by an increasing mechanization, industrialization, economic, philosophical, social upheaval, as well as cultural redefinitions of child and adult identities, and an escalating doubt and apprehension about the future (Sigler xv).

Carroll's Alice novels are truly paradoxical in so far as their *timeless* message concerning the *ephemeral* nature of meanings calls to be *constantly updated* to be kept alive for future generations. The books are "in a limbo," as Jan Susina says (2010, 144). As pieces of children's literature they are "neither fully dead nor fully alive texts," to use Peter Hunt's terminology, for three reasons. They are mostly sustained by adults (critically interested scholars or adapting artists realizing their contemporary, (post)modern Zeitgeist in Victorian Wonderlands); their representation of a nineteenth-century, British, upper-middle class, white, able-bodied girl child hardly fits the rapidly changing social, historical concept of childhood; and though they are enjoyed by some children but their popularity on a global scale does not live up to the success of more easily accessible children's classics such as *Winnie the Pooh*, *The Little Prince* or *Pinocchio*. As attested by *Wonderland*'s bright red cloth binding Carroll ordered from Macmillan on accounts of its being "the most attractive to childish eyes" (Carroll 71 in Sundmark 109), *Alice* was initially written and marketed for children. But it was subsequently picked up by a wider educated adult audience who could have been implicitly addressed from the beginning by Carroll's commission of Tenniel, the best-known political cartoonist of his day whose illustrations foregrounded "the politico-allegorical, satirical drift of the narrative" as well as by the subtitle to the preface of *Nursery Alice*: "ADDRESSED TO ANY MOTHER" (Sundmark 109, 168).

On the other hand, the contemporary relevance of *Alice* is due to its fitting the increasingly popular genre of "crossover fiction" that enjoys commercial success, media attention and increased critical legitimacy as a result of declarably existing in-between or above literary age categories. (Recent examples range from double editions of J.K. Rowling's *Harry*

Potter series and Pullman's *His Dark Materials* trilogy to dark fantasies as *Hunger Games* or the *Twilight* sagas). Various recent editions of *Alice* with radically different cover aesthetic, illustration design, or book concept clearly made the choice to target either at a child/juvenile *or* a more mature adult readership. At one end of the spectrum we find Helen Oxenbury's cheerful fairy tale illustrations of a light hearted Alice with a short sundress, unkempt hair, and a bunny friend, a fresh vision that "washed the page clean of all puberty allegory, political satire, death traps and dilemmas of identity" (Brooker 116) popular in reprints from 1995 to the present; not to mention the plethora of abridged picturebook versions for pre-readers including pop-up, touch-and-feel, coloring and board books. At the other extreme, the 2012 cloth-bound exclusive art book Penguin classic decorated by Yayoi Kusama's abstract pop art reduces Wonderland to a surrealist vision of polka dots to satisfy the acquired taste of mature readers, while Camille Rose Garcia's 2010 pen and ink watercolors reimagine a bold Alice on a bad trip, exaggerating Tenniel to invest Wonderland with a dark goth sensibility and a mean psychedelic feel sprung from the sixties' hallucinogenic countercultures. These examples show how Alice has become canonized as a "crossover picturebook" (Beckett 2012) for all ages.

I believe that the analysis of *Alice*'s contemporary adaptations across a variety of media serves multiple purposes. Examining the changing place of children's literature within today's shifting media ecologies allows us, on the one hand, to critically reflect upon the common marketing strategy of "family entertainment" pieces which commercialize imagination for a mixed-age, intergenerational, homogenized mass of passive consumers and to welcome those provocatively subversive artistic gambits which refuse to participate in the ideological colonizations of children's imagination and create original revisions against the mainstream. On the other hand, we can explore how the new imaginative and imaging practices of new media circumscribing new (ways of relating to) fictional realities tie in with a reinterpretation of notions of children's fiction, childhood, childlikeness and child-loving and the revisioning of the Child as a fragile fetish in our cultural imagery. Eventually, at the heart of change we recognize a sense of continuity. Alice's adventures never cease to epitomize intergenerationally and interculturally shared experience of childhood Gillian Beer identifies with growing pains, learning to read and write, frustrations by being hushed by adults, and an irrepressible curiosity and enchantment pertaining to the plentiful of unknown things in the world (Beer 2015). Emerging generations remodel childhood with reference to past cultural molds, the most ground-breaking ideas are driven by the refashioning of former patterns of thoughts and fantasies, new media challenge old media while paying a tribute to them. I believe that the most decisive permanent feature permeating fictional (re)formulations of Wonderland throughout the ages is an invitation to interactivity, self-reflexivity, and playfulness, a (tongue-in-cheek) toying with the idea of "becoming-children."

As Yan Wu, Kerry Mallan and Roderick McGillis's recent title suggests, *(Re)imagining the World* is particularly intriguing in the case of children's literature that most frequently does not (only) offer a mimetic representation of the world but rather urges an imaginative construction of non-existent but possible worlds. It hence opens up political vistas by exploring innovative models for remapping and reshaping our lived realities along the lines of an empathic consideration of other's, imaginative, new perspectives of perceiving the world. An escape to possible worlds of fantastic realities faces us with "the imaginative responsibility of confronting the world as we know it or as it might be or even as it might have been" (xi). Along the same lines, in this book, I shall disclose the process of "(re)imagining" as a non-linear movement across and between different times, spaces, and media to analyze how books read, films watched and games played by/for/about children can renew the ways we think of our past, present, and future. Accordingly, all fictional journeys to Wonderland and through the Looking-Glass offer the finest education by fantasy since they invite us to consider "multiple ways of knowing: curiosity, creativity, pleasure, and imagination as the bedrock of reason in its most exalted form" (Wu, Mallan, McGillis xii).

Carroll's Alice tales are memorably timeless children's classics because they are based on fantasy worlds dreamt into being by a child character whose adventures end in both parts with her waking up to a reality where she can relive wonders by courtesy of the magical skill of storytelling she grows to master, inspiring readers to make up stories of their own "*ad infinitum*" (Sundmark 176). The changing meanings attributed to Alice's character throughout the ages neatly reflect the current cultural status imaginativeness holds at a given socio-historical milieu, ranging from associations with infantile innocence, perverted pathology, to artistic experimentation, or empathic ethical responsibility. Even minor instances of updatings prove to be revelatory concerning the era's ways of commodifying, controlling, or containing the ever-so celebrated fantasy. Disney's animation claims to deliberately go against Carrollians and classics to "make a 1940 or 1945 version right up to date with fantasy and imagination" identified with screwball logic, musical fun and the company's trademark magic. Ralph Steadman's illustrations to a 1967 edition move Wonderland to the realm of popular entertainment by depicting the Cheshire Cat as the "ideal TV announcer whose smile remains as the rest of the program fades out" and turning the Drink me! bottle into a bottle of Coca-Cola. Unsuk Chin's 2007 opera (libretto by David Henry Hwang and Unsuk Chin) refers to contemporary Chinese Zeitgeist by having the Dormouse insert Mickey Mouse, Mao, and Marx into the list of words beginning with the letter M (Nichols 28, 49, 111). Grégoire Guillemin's "The Secret Life of Superheroes" paints Alice in mundane situations as a real 21st century girl, text-messaging on her iPhone, fingering tranquillizers, or shaving her armpit, reduced to disembodied abstraction on ill-framed selfies of minor fragments of her body—glimpses of her blonde hair, hairband or blue dress—a set of signifiers just sufficient in identifying her Alice-hood while performing an ironic "dedisneyfication."

This book reveals how in numerous contemporary adaptations Alice's childish imaginative agency gains a variety of strategic significations way beyond the character's infantile self-pleasing or the author's compensatory self-consolation. It is alternatively interpreted as an ontological necessity, a mode of empathic relationality to others, an evolutionary given and a means of survival, a self-healing, therapeutic and problem-solving mechanism, and overall a dynamic process conjoining make-believe and disbelief, psychic automatism and intellectual creativity, dream and logic, solidarity and autonomy. Most importantly, in the light of the Alice tales, imagination does not only mean an ability of creatively forming images and sensations unperceived before (as in 'making-up' things), but refers to a fundamental faculty through which human beings empathically attempt to 'make sense of' the world and themselves, by curiously and caringly considering a plethora of potential viewpoints, accepting the occasionally nonsensical, irrational functioning of the marvelous multiplicity of being. Alice's fantasy thus challenges the culturally biased, dispassionately rationalistic common sense of normativized 'mature' truth. This is what fairy tale scholar Jack Zipes regards as Carroll's most important contribution to children's literature and literary fairy tales: "his Alice books serve[d] to liberate the fairy tale from moralism and encouraged young readers to think for themselves and question the accepted morals of the adult world" (73).

Alice's inventiveness in 'dreaming to being' an alternative reality full of wonders and surprises while resting assured of her weird adventures' safety and the certainty to find her way back home upon awakening resonates with the "funcanny" experience in which today's immensely popular postmodernist genre of "children's gothic" fiction (see Jackson, Coats, McGillis 2008) is deeply rooted. The enchantment by escapist pleasures easy to identify with coincides with a strictly logical trial of the limits of one's imaginative agency.

In addition, the making of Wonderland proves to be a communal effort subverting the engendering of imagination whereby traditionally a passive female muse is presumed to inspire a creative male artist. I undertake to reveal how Alice's girlish fantasy functions as a major creative engine behind Carroll's polyphonic oeuvre and argue that numerous contemporary Alice rewritings also result from the creative partnership of a canonized artist and a clandestine female co-author, as in the case of Jan Švankmajer and Eva Švankmajerova's, Tom Waits and Kathleen Brennan's, Alan Moore and Melinda Gebbie's, Polixeni and Olympia Papapetrou's amorous cooperations.

Furthermore, the 21st century audience's fascination with Alice's character can be likely explained by the attractivity of the "incredible powers of distraction" (Kelly 20). Carroll grants his heroine with and practically all postmillennial adaptations preserve, "as if to demonstrate that the mind has remarkable defenses against the panic inherent in human condition" experienced particularly vividly in our own uncertain times. Like forgetting is a part of remembering, the Carrollian Alice's absent-mindedness, apparently prosaic politeness and adultish common sense are paradoxical parts of her *imaginativeness* contributing to her admirable resilience. Despite her predilection of death jokes, during her fall down the rabbit hole she daydreams of marmalade instead of mortality, and in the pool of tears ponders about the proper way of addressing a mouse instead of fearing the prospect of drowning (Kelly 20). Her acting mature and her occasional adultish pedantry—criticized by Kincaid (1992)—can be just a part of her childish pretense play. Imagination is never idealized yet fills Wonderland with optimism and hope besides madness.

Wandering/wondering Alice celebrates the affirmative world-making capacity of children's fantasy, pleasure, and desire in unidealized yet more positive aspects often disavowed by Freudian psychoanalysis concentrating on deprivation and lack. She is the embodiment of the child called by psychologist Adam Phillips the curious "beast in the nursery" "who can be deranged by hope and anticipation—by ice cream," who has "an unwilled relish for sensuous experience which often unsettles the adults, who like to call it affection," and who has "a passionate love of life, a curiosity about life, which for some reason isn't always easy to sustain," and a desire to make stories that "make interest" beyond the colonizing narratives of (hetero)normativity (Phillips 19 in Bruhm and Hurley xx). Our wondering about Alice's wondering is a crystallization of our curiosity about this curiosity.

If the figure of Alice is an agent of metafantasy and metamediality who offers a critical commentary on the dynamic interaction of artistic media and creative imagination, her journeys to Wonderland across a variety of media invite to an interdisciplinary exploration of human imaginative faculty, of the limits of fantasy, of techniques of make-believing and of the modes and ethics of enchantment endowed with a special importance in our secularized, 'disenchanted' world. Enchantment is a result of imaginative willingness that is not necessarily automatically generated by Alice's incredible imaginary adventures. Some of Carroll's contemporaries found his story an "amusingly written" "glorious artistic treasure" "full of humor," others believed "this stiff, overwrought story" might be "more puzzling than enchanting" for children (as an *Atheneum* reviewer wrote in 1886), while today's critical consensus seems to suggest that its timeless appeal to young readers is due the "underlying message" that a child may "emerge unscathed and wiser" from the unfamiliar world of adults governed by unfathomable rules she must navigate throughout her coming of age (Nichols 3). Enchantment—a sense of wonder found in the out of the ordinary features of the fairy-tale fantasy world—is posited by these opinions in the service of comfort, didacticism, spiritual elevation and moral improvement along the lines of Bettelheim's (1976) or Tolkien's (1947) understanding of the term. In the Alice tales, enchantment fulfills this conservative, restorative, curative function paradoxically, through the anarchic destabilization of order, meaning and embodiment. In a topsy-turvy world everyone can act mad without fatal consequences. Nonsense works much like Freudian jokes (1989) or the Bakhtinian carnivalesque (1984) in so far as it creates surprise effects with the predictable outcome of psychological enrichment by the therapeutic release of energies used for the repression of disturbing psychic contents. A more postmodernist aspect of enchantment concerns the fascination with the functioning of (meta)fantasy, the belief in the incredible, and the imaginability of the unimaginable. The prominent role the immersive and the meta- experience of enchantment play side-by-side in postmillennial Alice adaptations reflects the current ambiguous socio-cultural status of dis/enchantment in connection with fantasy, arts, and mediality.

According to Marie-Laure Ryan, the adequate analysis of any adaptation demands the consideration of how narrative power draws upon its specific *mediality*: the semiotics of each media must be scrutinized along with "the senses they address, their spatio-temporal extension, their signs' materiality, their cultural role and methods of production/distribution" (Ryan 2004, 18–19 in Bacchilega 36). In the first place, I wish to argue that way before postmillennial transmedia adaptations, Carroll's *Alice* tales decorated by John Tenniel's drawings should be interpreted, already, as *plurimedial* books in which illustrations are at least as prominent to the overall narrative meaning as the words with which they are in a "dialectical relationship" (Leitch 186). The collaboration's curious "iconotextual" (Louvel 2011) (con)fusions between verbal and visual regimes of representation—including the figurative picturesque metaphoricity of language-games, "telling" images functioning as plot vehicles, vanguardist graphic design, and typographical tricks—constitute a real challenge to adapting intents. These border crossings involve *metamedial* implications by testing representational confines as well as boundaries of imaginability and speakability (as in the ambiguous imagetext of the Jabberwock/y mingling mirrorwriting, nonsense poem, and the illustration's grotesque visualization of a "thingless name"). Regarding Hutcheon's distinction between media that tell (literature), media that show (visual arts), and media that involve audiences physically (video games, theme park rides) (xiv), all three modes of engagement coexist in Carroll and Tenniel's *multimedial* masterworks. Besides requiring verbal mastery and a visual literacy increasingly important in postmodernist digital culture too, the *Alice* tales originally designed to be published in Victorian gift book format naturally foregrounded the physicality and performativity of the reading experience. Nonsense language games' activation of multisensory registers of signification has generated the carnal embodiment of signification resulting from synesthetic sensations, transverbal vocal play, language's rhythmicality, musicality, and the priority of sound over sense. The simple time sequential operation of reading was disrupted by the unique materiality of the book as a spatial object coupled with typographical symbols of spatial/cognitive transition in the form of strategically placed asterisk patterns (* * *) which indicate section breaks, possibly refer to Alice's unattested sounds, words, exclamations of surprise, and denote motion, her shrinkings, growings, and crossings of brooks separating squares on the chessboard landscape beyond the Looking-Glass, through which she flees the entrapment within verbal/visual discourse. The ambiguous pictoriality of words is enhanced by the "artistic chirography" (Gardner 35) of *picture poem* or *figured verse*, a "visual analogue of poetic onomatopoeia" like the tale that takes the form of the mouse's tail it describes, or the message the enlarged Alice writes to her left foot by means of a 'footnote' embedded within but pointing beyond the boundaries of the text, while verbal and visual pun neatly conjoin. The interpreter's kinesthetic, tactile interactivity served as a corporeal contribution to meaning formation. The narrative tells, shows/hides, and interacts when the reader's single flip of the page back and forth induces an optical illusion whereby the Cheshire Cat disappears with only its grin remaining behind (on the page beneath the one where its shown in its full bodily integrity), whereas Alice contemplating the cat becomes lost amidst the text, and disappears "overwritten by words" beneath the grin (Wong 146).

However, these seemingly insurmountable challenges the traditionally hand-held *Alice* books impose on postmillennial *new media adaptations* end up supporting a sense of continuity as regards reading practices which are presumed to have radically changed from the nineteenth century to the present. The similarities shed light on how the interactive agency attributed to the interpreter as a co-creator of Wonderland has been recycled and updated from Victorian to Postmodern times. The e-book, iPad application, or online digital novelized versions of Alice digitalize the printed page but maintain the tactile experience in a naturalized form enabled by the technological enhancement of the onscreen reading process whereby the text is controlled by our tapping on touchpads. We find analogue historical examples for the audience's direct physical involvement in Alice's adventures and the making (up) of wondrous lands through the readers' tactile agency in Carroll's vanguardist book design. For instance, upon the entry into the Looking-Glass World, Alice is moved to the other side of the mirror by the turning of the page. This calculated corporeal interaction is reinforced both verbally and visually by the layout of the text abruptly disrupted mid-sentence on one page and continued on the next one ("In another moment Alice was through … the glass."), and by the inventive doubling and reversal of the illustration (showing the recto and verso of the same image of Alice crossing the mirror). As Mou-Lan Wong argues, Tenniel's illustrations of Alice's huge hands intervening in many Wonderland scenes—clutching the Red Queen and then the kitten—"visually emulate the reader's hand holding the *Alice* book—hands that are present and active in the reader's peripheral vision throughout the reading process," "large, powerful, and actively involved in the movement from one world to another" (148). When the iPad application, the 3D CGI cinema or online social media manifestations of creative fandom insist on expanding on the literary experience by the story's mobilization through audience involvement (encouraging you to shake the device, put on 3D glasses, or post photographic records of your DIY cosplay on Facebook), they use new multimedia technology to revisit the same idea of an interactive performative potential nested at the heart of the original literary work conceived from the beginning as a playable (narrative) space.

In fact, as Hutcheon suggests, our postmillennial postmodernist predilection of remediation is a habit inherited from the Victorians who were fond of adapting "just about everything—and in just about every possible direction; the stories of poems, novels, plays, operas, paintings, songs, dances, and *tableaux vivants* ... from one medium to another and then back again" (xi). Remediations are far from deteriorating the original—in a way lamented by Walter Benjamin in his classic essay on the artwork's loss of aura in the age of mechanical reproduction (1936, 1972). On the contrary, with a Darwinian metaphor so dear to the Victorians, as means of evolution and survival, adaptations are odd mutants which parasitically "suck the life out their hosts but also help their source text survive, adapt to changing environments and tastes and to new medium with distinct industrial demands, commercial pressures, censorship taboos, and aesthetic norms" (Stam 3).

New media forms often openly acknowledge the inspiration they gain from earlier analogue media: *Alice for the iPad* refers to itself as a pop-up book for the twenty-first century, American McGee's PC game Alice recycles Carroll's photographs as background props to the story world design, and Burton's 3D CGI movie turns Tenniel's Victorian drawing a pivotal point of the plotline. Cutting-edge digital technologies (from computer graphics to virtual reality to theme parks) never fully separate from earlier media for an entirely new set of aesthetic and cultural principles but throughout a process of "remediation" (Bolter and Grusin 2000) they rather refashion, rival, and pay homage to their analogue predecessors (novels, drawings, photos, or films) which have also remediated one another once each on their turn. Today, new media versions coexist with alternative Alice adaptations across a variety of old media from modern ballet dance to experimental rock music, surrealist puppetry, carnal performance art, therapeutic photomontage, feminist philosophical manifesto, fashion advertisement or tourist attraction which all aim to expand the story and augment the interactive potential of the implied fantasist recipient in a manner worthy of the Victorian original. Alice's cultural (and economic) value increases with repeated repurposings.

If adaptation signifies the retelling of a story in different media, the way adaptations interact with one another, using multiple media platforms to unfold a story world denote what Henry Jenkins calls a "transmedia expansion" of Wonderland's complex fictional world that encourages interpreters to drill deeper into ambiguous meanings generated by nonsensical playfulness, gaps, excesses and additions foregrounded by numerous retellings which can each stand on their own but provide a richer experience together. "Extensions" facilitate "additive comprehension" in so far as they make the story more immersive by adding new pieces of information which invite us to revise our understanding of the fictional reality as a whole, and by toying with insatiable curiosity maximize audience engagement. They might offer insight into characters, motifs, unelaborated plotlines, bridge events, fill in gaps or resolve excesses in the unfolding of the story, flash out unknown aspects of the imaginary world, add a greater sense of realism and augment fantastic effects, too. According to Jenkins, transmedia storytelling both divides and unites audiences. Extensions may create different points of entry for different audience segments to expand the potential market for an artwork. The extensions' connection with each other and the original master text and their functioning as a collective incentive to readers to continue to interact with the story world larger than the single story also illustrate the collective production and circulation of communal knowledge within a networked society. In fact, much like in a single franchise, where key bits of information are conveyed through a variety of media, each revealing new bits and pieces about the complex functioning of a fictional universe (as *The Matrix* live action films, animated shorts, comic book stories, and video games), *Alice* adaptations in old and new media are in a relentless dialogue with each other, and constitute an intricate web functioning according to the logic of transmedia storytelling. "Integral elements of fiction get dispersed systematically across multiple delivery channels for the purpose of creating a unified and coordinated entertainment experience [where] each medium makes its own unique contribution to the unfolding of the story" (Jenkins 2007). On the one hand, Carroll's narrative ceases to be the single source or ur-text where one can turn to gain all of the information needed to comprehend the postmillennial meaning of the Alice experience or Wonderland universe. On the other, postmodernist adaptations even the most loosely related to Carroll's original novels like Burton's, Gilliam's or Selick's Alice films function in a palimpsestic manner, interconnected with modernist predecessors and Victorian "others" (Sadoff and Kucich xi)[12] with nods to the Alice of Disney cartoons, Tenniel drawings and Carrollian child-photography among others. The Alice fandom implies a cult following of all the adaptations, speculations about key story information, and a multiplication of creative retellings of the story in fans' individual ways.

Matt Hanson identifies a fictive world's extension into multiple media and "advanced moving image" formats with the modern narrative condition of "screen bleed" he believes to be proliferating because today's digital media consumers' immersion in 3D worlds entails the need for all-encompassing mythologies multimedially involving contemporary audiences in "interactive online worlds, where each strand of narrative offers a new dimensional layer" (47). Different types of transmediatization targeting the expansion of a story world include: the segmentation of an idea into multiple installments and media within one single work (digital novel and educational tool *Inanimate Alice* (2005) uses text, audio, video, special effects and gaming to deliver a narrative in an interactive way, playing with the evolution of formats, from still to moving image to 3D game, within the progression of the story), the proliferation of tie-in products and events related to one story (Scottish Ballet's 2011 adaptation complemented the dance performance with further interrelated Wonderland-themed multimedial initiatives ranging from a parkour project called the Hatter's Garden to a photography competition, a costume exhibition, a tea party, and special label editions of wine as tie-in merchandise meant to elaborate the story world's feel), or the spreading of the same story multiplied across different media platforms (Coraline coexists on the pages of Neil Gaiman's novel (2002), Henry Selick's animation film (2008), Bruno Coulais's gibberish soundtrack to the film, Russell Craig's graphic novel (2008), and most recently MCC Theater's Off Broadway musical performance (2009), too, not to mention the abundant fan art reappropriations on online social media networks like deviantart.com).

Unified transmedia experience entails an illuminating diversity instead of homogeneity because each media "adds a new cultural layer, supporting more diverse ways of communicating, thinking, feeling, and creating than existed before." Dis/located in a heterogeneous network of meanings each media "disrupts old patterns, requiring us collectively and individually to actively work through what roles different forms of media are going to play in or lives" (Jenkins, Clinton, McWilliams 11), in what ways they are going to mediate reality while foregrounding interactivity, intermediality and connectivity, and how "new technologies extend our senses outside us into the social world, [to make] new sense ratios occur among all of our senses in that particular culture" (McLuhan 41).

This book scrutinizes postmodernist Alice adaptations with the aim to explore how the intermedial shifts accompanying the transmission of a literary text to a visual plane and to digital new media or alternative analogue media forms bring about changes in contemporary, 21st century audiences' predominant perceptive, cognitive, imaginative modalities of experience decisive of interpretive strategies making sense of reality and make-believing fictionality. The goal is to find out how media change elicits different modes of enchantment, disenchantment and reenchantment in metafantasies commenting on the limits and potentials of the fantasy genre as well as the dys/functioning of imagination, and how these prove to be both representative and formative of postmillennial fantasists' cultural anxieties, dreams and yearnings. Adaptations' intent to update a classic for one's own era results in media transitions' emphasizing certain meanings of the ambiguous original and eliminating others in a revisionary process that "affects people's sense of what is possible" (Bacchilega 7), thinkable, imageable, or imaginable—and in the case of nonsense fantasies even tackles what is impossible, unsayable, and unimaginable.

Chapter 1 focuses on Alice as a verbose visual product after the "pictorial turn" and metamedial imagetext (Mitchell 1995) adaptations. First, the evolution of *Alice* as an interactive iconotext (Louvel 2011) is traced through the analysis of 21st century pop-up book adaptations of Alice (Zdanko Basic and Harriet Castor 2010, Benjamin Lacombe 2010, Su Blackwell 2007, Robert Sabuda 2003) and the most recent adventures in digital media as realized by the Alice for the iPad application (2010) and a born digital novel called *Inanimate Alice* (2005).

A double reading of Disneyfied Alices provides examples for a debilitating commodification of fantasy and for a metafictional liberation of creative imaginative agency, too. Case-studies of a variety of Disney Studio products include the most influential "all-cartoon musical wonderfilm" from 1951, the unjustly forgotten 1920s' *Alice Comedies* animation series, and the latest 3D CGI family movie collaboration with Tim Burton in 2010 with a sequel coming up in 2016. After criticizing Disney's commodification and taming of female fantasy (Ross 2000, Zipes 1994), the Jabberwock/y's subversive potential is highlighted, as this memorable specimen of iconotextual monstrosity, a hybrid embodiment of verbal and visual nonsense is haunting beyond the realm of the imaginable and the speakable like an irresistible agent of subversion in Carroll, Tenniel, and Disney alike. While spectators are sucked in the *Alice Comedies* with the help of visual metalepsis that blurs the boundaries of the fictional and actual world to allow mutually exclusive realities to mix, the teenage Alice in Burton's Underland identifies, through a metafictional mise-en-abyme, with the imaginary alter ego of Carroll's title character, Tenniel's picture of the mythical knight slaying the Jabberwock. Thus, she turns the iconotextual original 'truly fictionalized' within the filmic revision's factualized alternate reality to reinforce the primacy of the adaptation that gains credibility on account of the indubitable master-mythological veracity of the source.

Finally, a focus on changing media of enchantment adapts narratological considerations to the cinematic medium, reading filmic image as text to scrutinize the metafictional trope of "reading images" and "(co)authoring pictures" in Disney and Burton's new media Alice collaboration. The adaptation's emphasis shifts from the original language games to visual means of creating nonsense effects to strategically charm movie audiences by raising epistemological questions and subverting representational codes and strategies. Despite a postmodernist self-reflectivity, the hyperrealistic simulation of wonders through the 3D computer-generated imagery enables enchantment to predominate disenchantment as Wonderland's trademark ambiguity is gained—instead of the original's *discursive* subversion (Carroll's subtle literary, philosophical, socio-critical allusions)—from the cinematic technologies' *spec(tac)ular* powers apt to authentically re/produce the unimaginable.

Chapter 2 explores notions of imaginative reluctance and the (meta)fantasy of infantile fantasy through the challenging example of *Tideland*, Mitch Cullin's poor-girl fiction novel (2000) adapted onto screen by Terry Gilliam's poetic horror fantasy (2005). After a discussion of the artist's self-portrait as a dreamgirlchild ready to make-believe the marvelous multiplicity of being, nonsense is revealed as a vital engine of child-like thinking, while infantile imagination becomes celebrated as a psychic automatism of the *homo imaginans* that can be strategically turned into an ethically and epistemologically exemplary empathic endeavor. Still there are moments from when on one does not wish to dream along with Alice any longer. Adults experience imaginative resistance (Szabó Gendler 2000) upon facing and attempting to interpret trauma as tragedy or fantasy, logical and ethical Impossibilities, as well as the dizzying vertigo of Many Worlds Postulate, a simultaneous coexistence of multiple parallel realities' potentialities, emerging in practically all *Alice* adaptations.

Further aspects of imaginative dis/engagement are activated by curious *Coraline*'s adventures mapped in novelistic (Neil Gaiman, 2002), animation (Henry Selick, 2009) and comics (Russell Craig, 2008) form. Children's Gothic genre toys with a daring daughter's fantasies of a monstrous Other Mother and reinterprets the *Alice* tales along the lines of a girl's adventure story in which the disintegration of the nuclear family, of sweet home, and of delimiting stereotypes of docile femininity or childhood serve grounds for tremulous anxiety and wishful fantasizing, too. Gothic doublings provide social criticism about the patriarchal constraints imposed upon women's agency and empowering self-expression. Like Alice, subverting all the girl character stereotypes popularized by Victorian children's books by refusing to enact the girl angel fated for tragic downfall or an early death, the impossibly virtuous little lady, or the naughty girl eventually reformed in response to heavy adult pressure (Leach in Phillips 89), Coraline embarks on a quest for herself through boldly facing the otherness lurking within the selfsame. Her "psychonarration" "conveys the unconscious, the vague, the unuttered feelings by finding an adequate linguistic expressions for them" (Cohn 21–46, Nikolajeva 180) in a variety of media each creating in a different way the illusion of a "transparent mind," using the engendered voice and mental imagery as a camouflage and a trick device in inventing one's own story.

Finally, 'imagination run out of control,' the fascination and fright caused by frenzied fantasy, and the meanings of madness in participatory culture come into view through two very different but equally successful, widely transmediatized products: American McGee's Alice computer games (2000, 2010) and the *Once upon a Time (in Wonderland)* ABC TV franchise launched in 2013, one reframing Wonderland within the psychological thriller, the other the family adventure romance genre. Both generated innumerable spin-offs, including "official" novelizations, picture- and photobooks, collectibles, and even more predominantly fan communities' interactive contributions ranging from online forum discussions, fanfiction, graphic fan art, fan videos to cosplay performance and makeup tutorial and DIY gadgets. All set out from a narrative zero point assuming that Alice's adventures start out in a lunatic asylum where her unrestrained imagination both led her and eventually can release her from.

Chapter 3 deals with a taboo breaking topic that touches upon nearly transcultural sensibilities of our times: the iconographic limits and potentials of picturing the erotic girl. After briefly tracing how the authorial figure of Lewis Carroll "fathering" *Alice* has been largely over-sexualized by posterity in spite of his canonization as a children's classic, the section explores contemporary fictionalizations of Carroll's and Alice's desires, examining how today's adaptations "reload" Wonderland adventures with erotic (dis)contents by projecting upon the title-character—situated in an intensely intimate connection with storytelling—collective cultural fantasies of liberation from sexual, linguistic, representational restraints. A variety of media forms fall under scrutiny here, including lyrical biografiction about Alice and her photographer, as illustrated by Katie Roiphe's novel *Still She Haunts Me* (2001) and Stephanie Bolster's *White Stones* poems (1998), the cinematic thematization of the grown-up *Dreamchild*'s forgetful senile desires in Gavin Millar's film (1985), a metafictional commentary on photography's mythmaking quality in the Scottish Ballet's *Alice* performance (2011), and contemporary photographic challenges to the fossilized picturing of mirror images of Carroll's Alice and Alice's Carroll by Polixeni Papapetrou's *Wonderland* (2004) vibrated by maternal erotica and David O'Kane's demythologizing project (2005) questioning the identification of seeing with believing in his digital-collage simulation of a stolen kiss between author and muse which, ironically, quickly got viral on the internet as an authentic visual proof of Carroll's pedophilia.

The final section analyzes radically revolutionary repurposings of children's literature, and Alice's fairy-tale fantasy adventures in particular. Melinda Gebbie and Alan Moore's *Lost Girls* graphic novel trilogy (2006) is "stripping kiddie-lit" (Kidd 2007) for the sake of forging a pro-porn feminist agenda that uses comics imagetext for therapeutic purposes to heal childhood sexual traumas and explore women's erotic agency. The feminist graphic novel scrutinizes the ideological stakes of fictionalizing girls' sexuality.

Chapter 4 explores Wonderland focusing on embodied language and multisensorially stimulating nonsense as the fundamental constituents of its pleasurably perplexing atmosphere. A trio of late twentieth century Alice adaptations demonstrate the fusion of postmodernist, Neo-Victorian, and embodied storytelling strategies and via a sequence of interrelated medial transitions entail a transmedia storytelling experience: Carroll's *Alice* is revisited by a Czech puppet animation that inspires a philosophically charged, English short story that calls forth an American poetic novelistic tribute, on its turn.

Jan Švankmajer and Eva Švankmajerova's puppet movie *Something from Alice* (1987) fuses little girls' imaginativeness with surrealist anti-aesthetics, hermeticist esoterism, Eastern European politics, and the philosophy of object-oriented ontology in a unique cinema of *anatomo-(in)animation* distinguished by a haptic aurality addressing kinesthetic spectators (Sobchack 2004). Angela Carter's "Alice in Prague or the Curious Room" (1990) a literary homage dedicated to the Švankmajers' *Alice* film foregrounds the embodied voice of/in image and text along the lines of revolutionary "isms," major intellectual movements such as mannerism, surrealism, postmodernism, even magical realism which challenge the limits of knowability and imaginability and test the reliability of language and reality models in a Wonderland turned Curiosity Cabinet and an anatomy theatre of the speaking subject. Rikki Ducornet's *Jade Cabinet* (1994) inspired by Carter's *Alice* story and the Carroll myth scrutinizes various modes of telling stories ranging from fabulation, misremembering, myth-making to historicization while focusing on the quest for a perfect primal language intertwined with the longing for Etheria, an Alice alter ego and a Carrollian muse emblematizing the transverbal beauty of art. A musicality bursting representational frames appears even more explicitly in Tom Waits' 2002 album *Alice* co-written with partner Kathleen Brennan for an "art musical" theatrical play directed and designed by Robert Wilson that combines musicalized linguistic grotesqueries with heartbroken melodies of a biofiction centered on impossible intergenerational desire and with tunes of Victorian low cultural entertainment matching Wonderland's grotesqueries. Finally, conventional, clichéd representational practices get reanimated ('reincarnated'!) by the "somatization of semiosis" (Brooks 1993), the uncanny return of the formerly repressed, 'unspeakable' carnality, invading the signification process with the use of embodied kinetic nonsense, incarnated voice, and materialized metaphors in 21st century repurposings: Samantha Sweeting's immediately contemporary carnal performances and taxidermy art, the Royal Ballet's 2011 gracefully grotesque *Alice* choreography, and culinary adventures devised by the cookbook *Alice Eats Wonderland* and star chef Heston Blumenthal.

1

Transmedia Wonderland

"and what is the use of a book, without pictures or conversation?"

Metamedial Adaptations After the Pictorial Turn

The visualization of *Alice* has always constituted a veritable challenge for illustrators, film-makers, graphic designers, and visual artists of all kinds because the literary stature earned by the dream-like narrative structure, nonsensical wordplay and ambiguous meanings of Carroll's Victorian fairy-tale fantasy novels proved ever so difficult to translate into visual media. Nevertheless, since Gertrude Thomson's cover art for *Nursery Alice* first reimagining John Tenniel's classic drawings, a filmic revision of the book in 1903 in Cecil Hepworth and Percy Stow's ten-minutes-long silent movie only five years after Carroll's death, or José de Creeft's 1959 huge bronze sculpture in New York's Central Park inviting children to climb, touch and crawl into a Wonderland scene cast in bronze, visual adaptations have pervaded cultural imagination to such an extent that Alice ceases to be simply read as a heroine of children's literature. Her enigmatic charm prevails, but she is no longer inseparable from Carroll's bizarre literary bricolage of fairy tale, nonsense fantasy, and gothic horror, that so perplexingly fused social-critical allegory, political satire, literary parody, philosophical language-games, playfully thought-provoking paradox and infantile gibberish to provide "abstract and concrete" "meaning and enjoyment" to child and adult readers alike (Ennis in Zipes 2000, 12). Today, Alice is rather regarded as a visual product sprung from the "magical world" of Walt Disney, Tim Burton, American McGee, or Hello Kitty, and associated with the animation, the 3D CGI family movie, the computer game, the cosplay persona, the girly gadgets, or the theme park entertainment, respectively—and an increasing spectacularization, unanimously.

The popularity of spectacular moving image resuscitations of Carroll's fiction can be explained by a major characteristic of any adaptation: an aim to "update" a classic canonized artwork by adjusting it to the cultural conditions, social meanings, and horizon of aesthetic expectations of one's own historical era. The adapting artist seeks to maintain or revive contemporaneous audiences' interest in the story she endeavors to repeat in an innovative yet accessible way, while taking into consideration major epistemological crises and paradigm shifts that affect how thinking and sentient human beings make sense of their existence, its dilemmas, and representational possibilities.

The late twentieth century's most important paradigm shift has been indubitably what iconographer cultural critiques refer to as the *pictorial* or *iconic turn*. This "problem of the twenty-first century" is marked by an extension and diversification of visual culture, and a massive self-reflective preoccupation with pictures and images as primary means of communication, information, but also of control and "fantastification" (see Kiss 2002) which result in an increasing dependence on and incredulity in images peaking in our postmillennial times. In an era of simulation (Baudrillard 1981) and a society of spectacle (Debord 1967) lives and social relations are determined by illusory images and a challenging visual literacy one can neither live without nor fully rely upon. A characteristically postmodernist ambiguity invades the regime of visuality: images are regarded to be all-pervasively influential but also unreliable and deconstructable. The pictorial equally provokes enchantment and disbelief. Besides anxious hesitation, there are benefits to the increasing skepticism about the visibility and decipherability of—original or final—ultimate meanings. The gradual diminishing of the naïve fidelity critical approach that insisted on the adaptation's responsibility to truthfully replicate the initially intended, canonically justified "authentic" meaning of the source-text is complemented by an insistence on polyphonic plural perspectives of 'untruthful' revisions.

Another consensual gesture of post-structuralist semioticians' theoretization of the image after the pictorial turn is the emphasis on any symbolical signifier's inherent involvement in a dynamic *intermedial* interaction with various other technologies of communication. The welcoming of the grafting of visuality onto verbality and vice versa motivated the introduction of the notion of "imagetext" WJT Mitchell described as a "dialectical trope" that "resists stabilization as a binary opposition, shifting and transforming itself from one conceptual level to another, and shuttling between relations of contrariety and identity, difference and sameness" (in Nelson-Shiff 57). Liliane Louvel outlined a similar theoretical agenda in her *Poetics of Iconotext*[1] (2011) in pursuit of a systematic study of intricate interactions rooted in the complex crossover between the literary and the pictorial form to trace "the infinite dialogue between two heterogeneous media in a position of equality" (113).

Along these lines, this chapter explores a variety of interactions between verbal and pictorial means of representation which conjoin to conceive complex imagetextual meanings. First, I study how *picturebooks*—both in retrograde pop-up and technologically advanced iPad application format—urge audiences to alternately read pictures and picture texts via a tactics Louvel calls "*voyure*," a portmanteau of contemplative *la lecture* (reading) and rebellious *la vision* (seeing) akin with transgressive voyeurism. Then, the Jabberwock/y is revealed as a memorable specimen of imagetextual monstrosity, a hybrid embodiment of verbal and visual nonsense haunting beyond the realm of the imaginable and the speakable. Finally, adapting narratological considerations to the cinematic medium allows us to scrutinize the metafictional trope of "reading filmic images" and "(co)authoring pictures" in Walt Disney's and Tim Burton's *Alice*-adaptations, with a focus on changing media of enchantment as well as elaborate metafictional devices such as metalepsis that allows for the transgression of the boundaries between narrative levels, media planes or logically distinct worlds' realities/fictionalities.

The ongoing intermedial interaction between aspects of the imagetext necessarily stimulates a *metamedial metafictionality* given that the different representational modes do not only complement, contradict, and subvert each other, but also self-referentially shed light on the very process and mode of imagetextual construction, foregrounding the constructedness (and deconstructable potential) of the fictional universe. As Louvel puts it, if artworks represent the world and also signify the way we perceive and conceive of it, this inherent self-reflectivity is enhanced by the image that functions as "the eye of/in the text" (109) mirroring—in an analogical or oxymoronic manner—artistic creativity itself, hence operating as a remarkable metamedial device. Even if the contemporary imagetexts at the kernel of my analysis have a visual quality allowing us to look back on our ways of seeing, it is important to note that visuality's predomination over verbal representational practices might be misleading, since, all so-called visual media involve other senses (tactile, auditory, and even olfactory impressions) which turn all media, from the standpoint of sensory modality "mixed media" (see Mitchell 2005, 257). The transmedia storytelling described by Jenkins is in a way a byproduct of this mixed mediatization as the literary textual original loses its (chronological, canonical, generic) priority to be extended by multiple interconnected media platforms constituting a coherently heterogeneous artistic experience.

Metafictionality functions by today as a household term that is nevertheless in need of constant revision: I refer to it as a narrative strategy that is just as postmodern as Victorian, just as much popular as elitist, just as much pleasing as alienating. The first seminal theoretical works by Patricia Waugh (1980) and Linda Hutcheon (1984) saw metafictionality as the symptom of a *Zeitgeist*, suggesting that the self-reflective questioning of consciousness, rationality and reality emerged as an intellectual response given to the specific stimuli of twentieth century socio-cultural and epistemological changes initiated by the modernist challenge of the Cartesian transparency of meaning via ludic destabilizations of hegemonies and proliferations of polysemic potentialities that came to fundamentally define the postmodern era. Certainly, metafictionality characterizes practically all the contemporary adaptations I am dealing with in this book. However, metafictionality is not a uniquely postmodernist phenomenon. Already Carroll's late nineteenth-century fiction makes a vanguardist use of self-referentiality in its most complicated forms as metafantasy and metaimagination. Neither should we restrictively categorize metafictionality as a sophisticated, academic-theoretically informed rhetorical and political strategy of the intellectual elite[2] because its versions proliferate in mass cultural practice too, ranging from the generic conventions of traditional fairy tales to marketing strategies of audience involvement activated by popular animated feature-films. Metafictional instances of intratextual self-awareness abounding in Carroll's original literary fairy-tale fantasies are further enhanced by the intertextual dialogical process: the adaptations engage with the source-text to expose themselves as reiterations of fictional illusions. Nor does metafictionality uniquely entail destabilization. Postmodern narratology celebrates how any metafiction draws attention to itself as a work of art(ifice) so as to offer its audiences a self-reflective point-of-view that enables them to adopt an active co-authorial positionality, entering into productive play with malleable meanings of a "blissfully writerly/writable" (Barthes 1975), "revolutionarily poetic" (Kristeva 1984), "open" (Eco 1989) imagetext.

Jack Zipes regards metafictionality as the marker of quality recycling. He distinguishes between two ways of inviting to imagine, two uses of enchantment applied by fairy-tale films. While some want to "titillate," immerse in idealized dream-realms, and guarantee happy endings to compensate for discomforts of our social realities; others provide more difficult joys by "wanting to compel us to engage with open eyes all those haunting dilemmas that cause existential and social problems" (2010, xii).[3] An infantile, oblivious, escapist indulging in fantasies is contrasted with a more mature, politically self-conscious, bifocal meta-perspective that keeps an eye on reality while fantasizing and strategically using imaginative agency as a means to critically reflect on and ameliorate social reality.

A similar evaluative gradation of fantasizing appears in Zipes' critical reflections on the Disney film-industry as a major formative force of contemporary popular cultural imaginaries. Accordingly, spectators' individual phantasms, utopian dreams and subversive hopes are presumably threatened to be ensnared and engulfed homogenized by the Disney animations' shallow scopophiliac pleasures, falsely promising images, and ready-made clichés governed by the exclusionary proprietary ownership of the brand name, the ideological and commercial interests of the company. Numerous cultural critics associate the calculated magic of the "Disney Princess Industry" (Pilinovsky 2011) with a "degenerate utopia" (Marin 1977), where simplistic plotlines and oppressive narrative closures propagate the prevailing power regimes' value systems. The good versus bad dichotomies avoiding ambiguities, the teleologically progressive reconciliation of conflicts by moral improvement, and the cleansing of evil or the elimination of ambiguities for the sake of happily-ever-after endings transmit capitalist, patriarchal, colonialist and a fundamentally normative "petit bourgeois"[4] ideology, with the aim to maintain the political *status quo* and discourage social transformation (Bell, Haas & Sells 1995, Budd & Kirsch 2005, Giroux & Pollock 2010, Zipes 1995, 2011, 25–26).

According to this argument, throughout the trickiest form of ideological containment even transcultural myths of omnipotent magic, childhood innocence, and especially creative imagination are turned into commodity in the eyes of transfixed audiences. In fact, imaginative productivity proves to be such a luring product that it functions most efficiently as a clandestine means of ideological interpellation, offering spectators identificatory positions promising co-creative potentials of dreaming along a Wonderland of one's own, that actually conforms with hegemonically prescribed scenarios of social control.[5]

Although theoretically I agree with the need for the critique of the commodification of fantasy, but I think that the argumentation cited above needs to be nuanced. In practice it is nearly impossible (and perhaps also senseless) to attempt to set up a binary, exclusionary categorization, to distinguish between purely escapist versus purely political artistic imaginings, between authentic, individual, subversive dreams versus contained, calculated, ideologically-infiltrated fake-phantasms. I think that these two functions and modes of fantasizing tend to blur and dynamically interact with each other in more conservative and revolutionary artwork alike, not to mention that their activation is largely dependent on individual interpretive choices, too.

A fine example for this heterogeneous interaction might be the mainstream mass media corporation the Walt Disney Company's and avant-garde independent filmmaker Tim Burton's working relationship. Burton is commonly referred to as "a potent counter-mage to Hollywood's syrupy adaptations of fairy tales" (Ray 218) whose "dark, magical, twisted cinematic fantasies" established his trademark "manic gothic," grotesque "highly personal visions" by affirmatively deviating from the cuter and cleaner feel of Disney-animations (Tiffin 148). Burton's trademark style is often originated in the beginning of his career spent with "dungeon-days slaving as an underappreciated cartoonist for the Disney studios" that refused to release his early attempts at rebellious fables (Ray 2010, 198). Even if this opposition sounds tempting, as all dichotomies do, I think we should also take into consideration the overlappings, parallels, and inspirations in the Disney-Burton connection. It was the Disney Studios that funded Burton's training at the California Institute of Arts, and it was Burton who decided to cooperate with Disney throughout his latest filmic fantasies, including the 2010 *Alice in Wonderland*. Even if 'Wonderland in Disney style' can occasionally be criticized for a debilitating commodification and control of fantasy, on other instances it manages to metafictionally liberate the powers of creative imagination. Although the Burton adaptation's cinematic plotline is yoked by a teleological *Bildungsroman* plot inherited from the Disney Princess animations' stereotypical scenario suppressing the originally much more chaotically episodic Carrollian nonsensical narrative structure, his Alice is still an action heroine empowered by her intermedially motivated self-recognition as implied reader and co-author of the imaginary realm she inhabits. The Disney-Burton coproduction fantasy's spectacular entertainment fails to reproduce Carroll's original witty word magic, but the 3D CGI technology's dazzling eye-candies offer visual equivalents to language games' verbal virtuosity. The media of stimulating nonsense-effects changes but the enchantment prevails: 19th and the 21st century audiences share a surprised wonder upon facing challenges of representational modes and interpretive strategies. Hence, instead of unproblematically celebrating the subversive unmaking of ideologically controlled "old patterns of thought" or universally condemning their conservative reinforcement I argue—in a Foucaultian vein (1980)—for a necessary coexistence, and a complex intermedial conjoining, of limits and transgression.

I argue that throughout the transmediatization of the Carroll corpus, the two Alice tales tendentiously merge into one to become endlessly complemented by further 'updated' adventures. Alice's iconic figure functions as a best-selling franchise that conveys new information intended by adapting artists yet remains charged with residual meanings of earlier remakes, too. In the end, all adaptation is about reimagining, palimpsestic overwriting without erasure. To introduce an intermedial analogy, the original acts as the sheet music and any remake does not only play an individual performance, an inspired, improvisative variation on the same theme, but also puts his/her annotations there in the sheet for posterity to see and improvise upon. My semiological investigations of contemporary repurposings of the Alice tales explore if the intermedial shifts accompanying the transmission of a literary text to mixed media effectuate different modes of dis/enchantment by virtue of a variety of means, from 3D CGI live-action animation's predictably unreliable computer digitalized visual medium that depicts mimetically with a photorealistic accuracy what has never been to pop-up picturebooks' and new media iPad apps' architectural whimsy expanding the embodied spatial experience of the story world, transforming nonsense discourse into tangible, playable paper craft or reading-turned-game on the digital screen.

The working hypothesis I undertake to prove is that the change in media is never absolute or exclusionary, for both the Victorian and postmodern eras are characterized by an inter/multi-medial con/fusion, where different media—as diverse means of representation and interpretation—complement instead of substituting one another. An early example is Henry Saville Clarke's 1886 "musical dream play" stage adaptation of Carroll's novel, a theatricalization assisted by the author that used proto-cinematic means of magic lantern slides to enhance the Wonderland experience. A careful examination of the changing place of the children's book classics about Alice's adventures within shifting media ecologies today—from Victorian picturebook to pop-up paper-artwork, iPad application, and 3D

CGI animation—provides a perfect illustration to Henry Jenkins' and David Thornburn's argument in so far as it reveals that "media transition is always a mix of tradition and innovation, an accretive process in which emerging and established [visual/verbal] systems interact, shift, and collude with one another" (2003, x). Today's Alice is a poster child of remediation (Bolter & Grusin 2000), a retrofuturist character who challenges "the modernist myth of the new" by proving that the innovativeness of digital technologies of new visual media (the World Wide Web, virtual reality, or computer graphics) are largely indebted to earlier media (perspective painting, photography, film, or television), traditions they strategically "refashion" just like these earlier media have refashioned one another previously. Thus, the authentic cultural significance, aesthetic value and ideological complexity of contemporary artworks are achieved by virtue of their inherently multi-layered, palimpsestic, hence metanarrative, metamedial quality as the story peels off the page and into the real world.

Interactive Imagetexts from Pop-Up Books to iPad Apps

Retro Paper Art Wonderlands

Carroll's Alice tales have been designed from the beginnings as illustrated books, as attested by the title-character's very first line, a rhetorical question "And what is the use of a book, without pictures or conversation?" (11) that functions by means of a metafictional inquiry conjoining visuality and verbality as co-dependent components of fictional adventures in Wonderlands collaboratively produced by author and illustrator. We tend to associate the Alice novels with immense visual powers, a "voyeuristic theme" of "an unplanned sight-seeing trip through a marvelously strange country" (Greenacre in Kelly 2011, 60), "a tour of *Ripley's Believe it or Not?!* where one bizarre spectacle follows one another" (Kelly 60). Yet, Carroll gives hardly any precise physical description of his characters or settings. The few paltry details we learn about Alice's appearance, that she has long, straight hair, shiny shoes, a skirt, small hands, and bright eyes, turn her into a "nondescript Everygirl" (Kelly 1982, 55). This verbal omission, as a gap left open for readers' imagination, could be considered to be a reason of the text's immense appeal for numerous future adaptations, but Alice's looks are actually depicted pictorially in great details on 25 of Carroll's 37 drawings decorating the first hand-written text-version of the 1863 original manuscript.

Carroll was a highly visual storyteller with manyfold scopophiliac interests: he was a pioneering photographer of children (he entertained his underage models with tales and riddles throughout the long sittings), he illustrated the stories he improvised for his child friends "by pencil or ink drawings as he went along" (Hargreaves 274, Green in Phillips 1977, 14), and he carefully designed and decorated the hundreds of rebus-letters sent to them. (Susina calls *Wonderland* "nothing more than an elaborately illustrated letter" [2001, 15]). When Carroll invited the chief cartoonist for *Punch*, Sir John Tenniel to provide a more refined pictorial form to his fantasies, the artist's 42 wood-engraved drawings were prepared under the personal supervision, and in line with the meticulous instructions of the author who bombarded his famous illustrator with suggestions and criticism throughout their prickly but fruitful collaborative partnership. The importance attributed to the illus-

"The Queen's Croquet Ground," Lewis Carroll's illustration to the original manuscript of *Alice's Adventures Under Ground* (held and digitized by the British Library. 1864. Ink on paper. British Library. Add MS: 46700 [f. 26r]).

trations is shown by the fact that the first print run of 2000 copies in 1865 was destroyed at the perfectionist creators' request because they were dissatisfied with the images' "disgraceful printing" (Ray 1991, 116), and the book was reprinted in 1866.[6] The careful coordination of text and illustration was designed together by Carroll, Tenniel, and the publisher Macmillan (Hancher 120). A technique called "padding" used verbal insertions to manage the appropriate placement of illustrations and to guarantee that Tenniel's drawings did not constitute separate panels but were rather integrated into the text, making the "image linger so enticingly within the peripheral vision that it seems to be effortlessly incorporated into the reading process" (Carroll 2008, 6, see in Susina 2010, 82, Wong 138).

Besides Carroll's preoccupation with the materiality of the book-object, the attention he paid to engaging the interpreter's embodied self through tactile, motile corporeal sensations fostering interactivity with the imagetext made him a precursor to postmodern attempts at invigorating texts. In *Nursery Alice*, a simple bracketed instruction, an apparently primitive attempt at interactivity, literally sets the story in motion, when the narrative voice comments on the White Rabbit as follows: "So the poor thing was as frightened as frightened could be. (Don't you see how he's trembling? Just shake the book a little, from side to side, and you'll soon see him tremble.)" (3). This exact innovative means of enhancing audience-interaction is recycled some 120 years later by the iPad book-app: upon the requested shaking of the device new media technology offers an on-screen animated moving image realization of our initial mental imaging of the movement (trembling) thematized in the story (and reenacted by cooperative readers). Carroll's *The Wonderland Postage-Stamp Case* (1889) included paper-engineering feats called "pictorial surprises." The outer cover's chromolithographic image by Tenniel of Alice holding the Duchess's crying baby—an illustration absent from Carroll's book—was replaced by an image of Alice holding the pig, when one

John Tenniel, "The Caucus Race. Alice meets the Dodo." In Lewis Carroll, *Alice's Adventures in Wonderland* (London: Macmillan, 1865). Wood engraving by Thomas Dalziel.

took hold of the stamp case within and pulled it out. Yet, curiously, no pop-up book version of Alice's adventures ever appeared in Carroll's life. Pioneering German illustrator-author Lothar Meggendorfer's first movable toy books featuring dissolving discs and pull-down panoramas reached England later in the 1890s, and Carroll's legendary insistence on high quality craftsmanship likely scared off all designers who could have ventured to collaborate with him on such a book art project (Susina 2010, 146).

The beginning of the 21st century, however, abounds in celebrations of the Carrollian creative genius (and of the Carroll-Tenniel collaboration) in eye-pleasing pop-up books which play with a spatial extension and dynamic mobilization of the story[7] realized in three-dimensional, movable paper craft format distinguished by an "architectural whimsy and transfixing tactility" (Popova 1). Carroll's original illustrated book (where the text can exist independently) is transformed into picture storybook (text and image are equally important in Sabuda and Basic), wordless picture narrative (Lacombe's double spread sequence) and exhibit book (Blackwell's paper craft) characterized by a vast spectrum of interrelations between words and pictures complementing, enhancing, deviating, contradicting and counterpointing each other. The iconotextual dynamics is complicated by the latent intertext of Carroll's novel as a source-text of all the adaptations, as well as by the nondescript and undisplayed registers, those gaps of visual and verbal narrative which challenge representational confines, tease readers/spectators imagination, and elicit a multitude of ambiguous interpretations preserving the true spirit of Wonderland. The varieties of stimulating iconotextual counterpoints catalogued by Maria Nikolajeva and Carole Scott include counterpoint in address (verbal and visual gaps are filled differently by children and adults), counterpoint in style, modality, or perspective (a pseudo-realistic story is told as truthful from the child's point of view while pictures detail fantastic qualities in celebration of infantile imagination) and counterpoint of metafictive nature (words describing the unimaginable and images depicting the unspeakable) (24–25). In the following I shall analyze the most remarkable postmillennial specimen of these interactive book artworks.

The mobilization of the story is maximalized in a spectacular manner in Benjamin Lacombe's *Il était une fois… (Once Upon a Time…)* (2010), a pop-up book in pop surrealist style, filled with mobile paper art decoupage structures. According to Jean Perrot's explicatory postface annexed to the end of the picturebook, the "relief images" the artist "imagines and draws" to life "open and close the secrets of a superb vision" as the "architecture of the album vividly constructs the sense of reading." As in any pop-up book, with the turning of the page the image made of unfolding paper literally pops up, gaining three-dimensional form, and entertains the child with the surprising feel as if the book was coming to life. Moreover, the readers' leafing revivifies a play with stasis and dynamics on each page: we witness how Alice contemplatively leans back in a bed of painted roses as a cascade of half-animated play cards are swirling around her, Little Red Riding Hood rests peacefully amidst the wolf's jaws ravenously gaping wide, and a comatose Sleeping Beauty is surrounded by a luxuriously sprawling vegetation of tangled thorns and a violently erupting phallic needle. Perrot's 'adult reading' acclaims the disturbing, mysterious strangeness lurking in the heroines' dispassionate glances that mask "the drama of eternal feminine suffering." However, one must also note the infantile ludic aspect of the pop-up book that allow readers to generate a certain sense of freedom and *joie de vivre* by providing a relative liberation and momentary delights to these heroines. With the turning of the page Madame Butterfly spreads her wings, Wendy flies away with Peter Pan, and Alice can play hide-and-seek beneath the pack of cards on loose.

Lacombe's picturebook is entirely composed of large format, double-page-sized, deliciously colored mobile plates, condensing in purely pictorial form, without textual intrusion, the "profound, sublimated meaning" of a selection of classic fairy tales. Visuality predominates the work through metapictorial means, illustrating Perrot's assumption that picturebooks, by virtue of their very genre "cast a look at their readers." While the white rabbit's bulging eyes burn bright reflecting a red Venetian lantern's light, Alice's recurring image is marked by her enigmatic, brooding, upwards gaze directed beyond the picture-frame, pointing outside the page, further down the story lane, or out of the reach of her fictional reality.

Alice is a crucial character of the book because of her singularly multiple appearance, too. She takes part in the cover page's *mise-en-abyme* design where she is encircled by miniature versions of the very book she inhabits and we read. She features on the title page lost in the Wonderland forest, on the already mentioned full color plate with a halo of cards embracing her. She is there on the last textual commentary page, too, resting on a giant mushroom. Additional references to her adventures include the book's promotional video organized by a "follow the white rabbit" from page to page leitmotif, as well as a tagline introducing the book as "a collection of children's classic through a fantastic journey to extraordinary *Wonderlands*."

The most interesting out of these appearances is certainly the cover art where Alice's peculiar, curious and introspective, but overall visionary and meditative gaze is focusing not on the multitude of mini cover art *images* but on the single line of *text* belonging to the primary corpus of the picturebook, the title spelling out the words: "Once upon a time." This gaze is truly revelatory concerning the imagetext qualities of the work. Alice concentrates on the traditionally set, ritualistic initial line of fairy tales so as to dreamily speculate about the continuation of the story. But instead of the expected verbal narrative follow-up we get its condensed pictorial version, in the form of hallucinatory images that on the one hand provide *déjà-vu* reiterations of the intertextually familiar, hence soothing storylines and on the other hand present troubling, dramatic episodes instead of idyllic happy endings. The similarity between the *mise-en-abyme* multitude of 'cover art images within cover art image' and the traditional first phrase of fairy tales (circulating in oral tradition to initiate with the same opening line a multiplicity of versions) resides in the sequentiality that appears to reoccur infinitely—just like Alice's figure migrating haunting between the pages of the book.

The intermedial shifts result in an appeal to readers to integrate unconscious, associative mechanisms within their interpretive approaches. Just how playful the free flow of meanings should be is indicated by the only word in the Alice plate: JOKER inscribed on a card conventionally decorated by a fool or a clown, and personified in Lacombe by the relentlessly grinning Cheshire Cat who embodies the "impertinence escaping habitual rules of reading" (Perrot 19).

Lacombe's picturebook is an exciting adaptation because it combines the picturing of astonishingly critical moments of (non)being with the safe knowledge that everything will turn out to be just fine (conforming to the rules of functioning of the fairy tale, even if that final happiness is beyond the scope of visibility, representation, and the interests of the unconventional picturebook retellings of classics). These are coupled with surprise effects enhancing the physically self-conscious, carnivalesque *grand guignol* of *commedia dell'arte* laughter, as well as an awareness of the storytelling's own illusionism, theatricality, its staged and restageable nature, and an insistence on the spectacularity of texts and the narrativity of images—a curious dynamics Lacombe keeps exploring in his illustrations to the 2015 French edition of *Wonderland*.

Robert Sabuda's 2003 *Alice's Adventures in Wonderland: A Pop-Up Book Adaptation of Lewis Carroll's Classic* presents an abridged text version faithful to Carroll's original story (though unfortunately devoid of the nonsense poems). The multitude of mobile illustrations clearly pay an homage to Tenniel's classic style that is nevertheless rendered more vibrant by the pop-up artist's trademark vivid colors, thick black outlines, and paper engineering feats. Paper artwork special effects include an amazing variety of pop ups, pull down/ups, flap tabs, multifaceted foil, and touch-and-feel fur figurines. The overall impression is that of a text embraced or engulfed by a more predominant imagery. The large pop-up paper sculptures of emblematic Wonderland scenes and sites (of a clearing by the woods with Wonderland characters camouflaged in the branches, the White Rabbit's house, the Duchess' kitchen, the Mad Tea Party, the Queen's Croquet Ground, and the Courtroom with Alice on Trial) occupy most of each double-page, while the verbal narrative is reduced to a secondary role, with the story's being summarized in smaller fold-out booklet format disposed to the edge or corner of each picture plate, taking up about a fourth or less of the place assigned for the visual design.

Textual, visual, and tactile stimulation cleverly conjoin in this book described on the blurb as "a pop up to read and admire again and again." Furthermore readers become engaged in an exciting experience of spatial location, dislocation, and external and internal mobility, too. At the very beginning, an origami paper craft structure directly addresses its audience to "open me," "pull me up and look inside" so as to unfold into three-dimensional form a five-story-high bookshelf that offers to reader-voyeurs, through a glance into a neo-Victorian peep-show, a vivid feel of Alice's fall. (This is a vision that both Tenniel and Carroll refused to pictorially represent perhaps for fear of drawing a too obvious distinctive line between dream and waking life.)

The fall seems to be strategically prolonged, as Alice's hyperactive figure is kept in perpetual motion on the pages of Sabuda's work. First, the static posture of her reading sister is contrasted with the rushing by of Alice hurrying with flowing hair, flying skirt, and a feet in the air, in the direction of the rabbit hole and further on, off the picture-plate towards new adventures to come up on the next pages. Her energetic corporeal moves—swimming, shrinking, or growing—emerge in mobile paper art form (decorating the story booklet embedded folded within the pop-up book) and match the bizarre activities performed by the outlandish Wonderland creatures: the Caterpillar's smoking, the Cheshire Cat's dis/appearing, the Dormouse's plunging into a teapot, the Mock Turtle's sobbing, the White Rabbit's blowing the trumpet, the Jury's falling out of the box, and the baby's transforming into a pig. (The baby/pig mobile image is an inventively animated version of one Carroll's early paper-engineering feat to his *The Wonderland Postage-Stamp Case*.) The final moving paper-sculpture of Alice plays with multiple meanings on various grounds. It merges into one image two separate actions: Alice waking up, raising her head from the pillow of her arms on the return from her curious dream, *and* her unfolding and folding her arms to embrace her sister, who stands by her side. But the final storyline, complementing the image with text, undermines the promise of an eventual rest upon the completion of the quest entertained by the visual narrative. It emphatically spells out Alice's constant being on the move: "So Alice got up and ran off, *thinking while she ran* what a wonderful dream it had been." Vagrant wanderlust and a self-reflective contemplation thereof, instead of being mutually exclusive experiences, constitute equally important personality markers of the protagonist.

Sabuda's Alice never stops to face readers and establish eye-contact with us, readers, she is rather ever-so busily passing by from one page to another, freely absorbed in her Wonderland journey. Just how much the adventures leave a vivid impression on this highly empathic young traveler is demonstrated by the wide array of feelings crossing her face alternating between joy, surprise, annoyance, fear, concentrated effort, or anger. These are

Robert Sabuda, from *Alice's Adventures in Wonderland: A Pop-Up Book Adaptation of Lewis Carroll's Classic* (New York: Little Simon and Schuster, 2003) (courtesy of the artist).

affects surfacing without any textual reference, readable merely from the paper-cut visualization that cleverly combines motion (mobility) and emotion (sensitivity, excitability, affective responsiveness) as Alice's primary personality markers. Interestingly, this combination bears a hard-scientific basis. Recent neurophilosophical research on embodied cognition—how the body shapes mental activity—discovered a causal link between motion and emotion. Apparently, it is not only thinking that involves creating mental simulations of bodily experiences, but also bodily movements influence the rate, intensity, and speed of thinking during the recollection of emotional memories. Traces of this interaction lurk in linguistic expressions, such as spatial metaphors of emotions, too (Casasantro and Dijkstra 2010, Kövecses 2000). Accordingly, her "feeling *down* in the dumps" or "spirits soaring *up*on the top of the world" surface in Alice's facial expressions, physical movements, the turns of events in the plotline, as well as the verbal colloquialisms evoked in readers. Moreover, the recognition about our bodily maneuvers' affecting our way of thinking might have particularly exciting implications in the case of pop-up books inviting readers to pull, push, and pet the pages, to invigorate textual meanings with the help of *moveable* paper-art crafts, throughout an emphatically embodied reading experience.

Another remarkable, modernized and condensed pop-up retelling of Carroll's classic is *Lewis Carroll's Alice's Adventures in Wonderland* retold by Harriet Castor and illustrated by Zdanko Basic published in 2010 timed to coincide with the widely anticipated release of Tim Burton's Alice-film from the Disney Studios. In the mock-subtitle on the cover page the luring voice of the personified book directly addresses readers with an irresistible invitation to "Open me for curiouser and curiouser surprises!" Indeed, the book is enhanced with an impressive variety of paper-craft extra features, such as pull-down tabs that make Alice grow and the Cheshire Cat disappear, doors on flaps and magical cupboards that can be opened to show all manners of curious things, and pop-up still-lives like the very last one of the courtroom trial. This latter scene is revisited by all pop-up adaptations likely because of its spectacularly staging the main Carrollian idea about the overthrowing of all logical rules of the game (of life, self, and narrative) emblematized by the pack of playing cards jumping to life to stumble, scatter and fall.

The book also performs an exciting visual play with the extension of spatial dimensions through rudimentary implementations of optical illusions via banal but clever *trompe l'oeil* effects. Beneath/behind a tiny door we find a forced-perspective garden Alice wants to reach that appears to recede in the distance. The wall of the hall Alice reaches after her fall to soon undergo in this very place her first diminutive metamorphosis is decorated, graffiti-like, by realistically nonsensical, chaotic kids' doodles and scribblings which constitute a surprising counterpoint to the main illustration-plotline's gracefully refined, eerily elegant painterly style. Most characteristically, abundant montages, superimposing and embedding images over/in one another, fill the pages with a plethora of tiny little details, such as keys that vanish and reappear at different places, migrating between different scenes or visual

Zdenko Basic and Harriet Castor, from *Lewis Carroll's Alice's Adventures in Wonderland*, a pop-up book (New York: Barron's Educational Series, 2010) (courtesy Zdenko Basic).

clues referring to the Carrollian arch-text's language-games, like the minuscule rocking-horse-flies scattered all over the changing Wonderland landscape. These images-within-images cunningly challenge the figurative element's conventional supremacy over the presumably purely decorative, atmosphere-setting, secondary background. They highlight the relativity of our points of views and multifocal perspectivism's capacity to enrich textual significations. They also make an intriguing commentary on subtextual and paratextual meanings breaking the boundaries of narrative frames, while conjoining visual and linguistic registers. Such is the case of the final interactive imagetextual riddle whereby the keys decorated with letters when put by readers in the adequate order spell out the solution to how to get to Wonderland. (The enigmatic answer is "In your dreams.")

Despite its visual inventiveness and abridged retelling delighting the youngest, the primary target audience of Castor and Basic's pop-up Alice tale are not so much pre-readers but rather early or even young adult readers who can decipher and decode the multitude of embedded texts proliferating as typographically pleasing, interaction-inducing footnotes to Carroll's original hypotext. Among texts-within-texts we find curious messages creatively integrated 'domesticated' within the double-page illustrations' Wonderland visions. These include the Duchess's letter to the White Rabbit flying out of the window of the house burst by Alice's sudden growth, the Mad Hatter's favorite song decorating a kite tied to the March Hare's chair at the Mad Tea Party, the correspondence of the Two of Spades and the Head Gardener delivered by one of the personified playing cards rushing through the Queen's croquet ground, or the Duchess's lullaby stabbed with a silver fork on a barrel surrounded by scattered kitchen utensils placed in the corner of the kitchen where she is reluctantly nursing her baby. These odd messages are authored by and addressed to fictional characters, and belong within the fictional reality of the wondrous alternate universe beneath the rabbit hole, so that Alice (and us, all passer-byes) acts only as chance witness to them.

However, further embedded notes directly target Alice and the implied reader pre-identified as a curious tourist visiting Wonderland whose culture-shock might be prevented with the help of didactic instructions and practical advice meant to ease the troubles caused by this strange realm's unusual customs, routines, and rules of functioning. These include advice from the Caterpillar, notes to the organizers of a Caucus Race, a Mushroom Booklet that helps Alice to regain her normal size, and a summary of useful things Alice has learnt from empirical evidence gained in her waking life. The White Rabbit's guide to Wonderland attached to the inner side of the cover page is full of helpful suggestions for confused visitors: "Be alert, flexible, polite, and prepared! Do not have definite expectations before you start the journey!" We gain answers to dilemmas like "How do I get to Wonderland? What can I do there?," information about political system, school curriculum, local food and safety advice, as well as a full list of a Dos and Don'ts. The latter, including lines like "Do try to say what you mean and mean what you say at all times. This may save you from getting into trouble. On the other hand, it may not" mockingly illustrates the illusoriness of the knowability of Wonderland with the help of extra nonsensical language games.

Moreover, the pseudo tour-guides mark the rationalization of mad illogic along the lines of cultural difference. They never impose hegemonic standards of normativity and regimes of truth upon otherness, and instead of fearing uncertainty and ambiguities, rather celebrate the enriching potential of heterogeneous alterities and cultural diversity. They constitute a genuinely Carrollian *and* postmodern gesture. Cultural critical statements gain a fictional form in the shape of the numerous public announcement-like guides, notes, maps, road signs, and memoranda, complementing more intimate messages, as letters, riddles, and song lyrics which all recycle, rejuvenate and extend the Carrollian text (within the Bašić-Castor imagetext) while being invested with special meta-, inter-, and hypertextual significance. These texts-within-texts speak to, about, and in place of another text—or rather relate to a *plurality* of other texts: the main plot frame narrative, Carroll's original, and the visual storyline. Bašić's picturing Alice falling down the deep, deep rabbit hole surrounded by infinite bookshelves (and maps) provides a self-reflective visual commentary on the narrative transformations the pop-up adaptation necessarily performs throughout its intermedial translation, interactive extension and hypertextual elaboration of the source-text.

Pop-up books belong to playable media. As Andrea Schwenke-Wylie points out, handheld, metamorphic paper-engineering art foregrounds the materiality of the book and creates a self-reflexive awareness of the reading process by considerably slowing it down because of the many details hidden under the movable flaps and tabs. The tangibly palimpsestic pop-up books hold a singular metafictional potential. Since these imagetexts cannot be understood at a single glance, their deciphering requires numerous revisitings, and illustrates the wondrous mutability, the labyrinthine structure, the intermedial imbroglio of the story, and in the case of Alice adaptations "the irresistible elasticity of fairy tale" (Tatar). The pop-up book's metamorphic quality—albeit largely deprived of its metafictional charge—functions as a major source of inspiration and, technologically speaking, even a forerunner to the iPad book application marked by a shift from textuality to tactile intimacy and a "hacking of rules of classic storytelling" (Schwenke-Wylie 2013).

Adventures in digital media: *Alice for the iPad* and *Inanimate Alice digital novelized*

Within Gérard Genette's typology of narratological devices of transtextuality—emerging within, outside, and in-between books that form a part of the mediation between book(s), author, reader, and publisher—illustrations qualify as *paratexts* which form a frame and fringe to the text. However, Jan Susina also calls attention to the *hypertextual* nature of illustrations which constitute visual texts derived from and "grafted in" the verbal text they accompany (Genette 1997, 5). Still, considering Tenniel's drawings to be hypertexts that complement the arch-text of Carroll's writing does not imply a hierarchical ordering of these two media. In fact, the entire Wonderland book, as Susina convincingly argues, can be regarded as a "proto-hypertext" that self-consciously refers to previous texts with poem-parodies and carefully combines synchronized images and texts in a fundamentally inter(image)textual system that breaks the sequentiality of the reading and viewing experience, while offering multiple imagetextual entrances and exits (145). The most important lesson we learn here is that hypertext is not limited to the technology of the digital realm, multimedia cyberspace, or enhanced DVDs: "a desk, whether organized or not, is essentially a hypertext, if the user can link all the pieces together" (Susina 2010, 142).

Nevertheless, Susina updates Alice's initial, metafictional question to the postmodern new media digital age, and deems it important to inquire: "What is the use of a book, even if it is full of pictures and conversations, if it lacks sound, animation, and links?" (2010,

144). Apparently, Susina nostalgically takes side with Carroll and Tenniel's proto-hypertext, and criticizes early multimedial hypertext versions of *Alice* for making the text less accessible than a print version. By renouncing of the illustrations, Project Gutenberg's online electronic text truncates original imagetextual meanings and turns lines pointing out of the text towards images straightaway incomprehensible, leaving readers ponder where to look when reading: "If you don't know what a gryphon is, look at the image." CD ROMs' educational interactive games did not only misplace or entirely omit illustrations and ignore typographical play, but also, by their very genre, undermined the original Carrollian attempt to create non-didactic children's literature. The most recent digital hypertextual adaption, the Alice for the iPad application,[8] issued right after the publication of Susina's *The Place of Lewis Carroll in Children's Literature* (2010), aims to resolve the above shortcomings and makes use of new media technology in creatively innovative hypertexts which nevertheless preserve a certain degree of textual sincerity and a resulting aura of authenticity.

Alice in Wonderland digitally remastered for the iPad became an instant hit upon its release by Atomic Antelope in the Spring of 2010 and was unanimously heralded by critiques as "the cleverest iPad book yet (that) blows away by an interactive book design" incorporating animation like no other eBook to date" (CNET), an application that "reinvents reading" (TheHuffingtonPost.com), "enhances children's literature on the device" (MacLife.com), and provides a prophetic "glimpse of the future of digital reading" (BBC.co.uk) to "irk luddites" with its sumptuous full screen, interactive artwork (*The Sunday Times*). Certainly, the critical acclaim responded just as much to the new technology as to the iPad book itself, and was largely based on the assumption that 'the application can do stuff that paper books cannot.'

iPad e-book-apps for kids can indeed do more than simply display static pages. They enhance the classic printed book format's original visual stimuli with a variety of spatial, mobile, tactile, auditory experiences which can all be enjoyed at the user's will and whim by virtue of the added value of the interactive multimedia technology. Among the most frequently mentioned advantages of digital editions—besides convenience, selection, and portability—we find the "expansion on literary experience" brought about by the full screen physics modeling, the touch-or tilt-powered extras, the incorporated animation, 3D imagery, voice acting and sound effects which are all meant to add an unprecedented level of vitality and engagement to the text. Apple iTunes website's product description addresses intended audiences with an appealing summary of the things users can make the text do:

> Tilt your iPad to make Alice grow big as a house, or shrink to just six inches tall. Throw tarts at the Queen of Hearts—they realistically bounce off her. Witness the Cheshire Cat disappear, and help the Caterpillar smoke his hookah pipe. Play with the White Rabbit's pocket watch that swings and bounces, help Alice swim through pool of tears, swipe your finger and hand out sweets that bounce and collide with the magical talking Dodo. This wonderful book includes hundreds of pages and amazing animated scenes. Watch as full screen physics modeling brings illustrations to life. [http://itunes.apple.com/alice.ipad].

The interactive book design offers a multisensory experience, investing the reading process with conjoint user-activated acoustic, ocular, and tactile pleasures. For example, a royal fanfare toot of the White Rabbit's trombone takes you to the index and settings if you tap the Cheshire Cat at the bottom of each page, but you can also make the feline figure disappear and vanish by touching a specific part of the screen.

However, the greatest fascination likely comes from the spatial magic introduced by the application. Besides more conventional illustrative means to create effects of spatial dimension and geographical plasticity (when Alice peeps in the little door leading to Wonderland she sees a beautiful landscape, a glass observatory in the distance, and the receding rim of the horizon), space appears as a malleable material for mobility-induced play. Some animations are equipped with gravity awareness and sensitivity to the movement of the iPad due to an inbuilt accelerometer device. Hence a simple tilt of the iPad or a finger tug can make the Caucus Race comfits bounce and drop, the red rose petals dreamily swirl, soar and fall, the Drink-Me-bottle float like a balloon. The Cheshire Cat's head bobs, the pocket watch swings, and Alice undergoes her memorable bodily changes, shrinking and growing as we move (with) her. With the help of these new digital technologies users can literally invade, conquer, and modify the fictional (and virtual) *space*. They are provided with an embodied simulation of Alice's metamorphic corporeal experiences, and become fully endowed with her wondrous capacity to stretch physical boundaries and reach spatial pleasures resulting from the extension and the boundlessness of the weightless yet powerful body-in-space.

Moreover, the small size of the intricate, interactive e-book-artwork on the iPad screen might stimulate our imagination in specific ways—considerably differing from the gigantic 3D IMAX cinema screen's effect—by inviting us to draw *closer* and create an intimate space. This forward movement entails a specifically attentive mental and imaginative activity, examining minute details, as if through a kind of magnifying glass, "imbuing our experience of the object with an almost hallucinatory quality and a visceral physicality" (Rugoff 14), increasingly forgetful of the size of the gulf separating us from the fictional reality's realm.[9] As the empathic, embodied experience of moving along with the image/text enables readers' creative, corporeal cooperation in the ludic meanings-(de)formations of Carrollian fantasizings, we witness a technological enhancement of nonsensification.

Even if *Alice for the iPad* undertakes to technologically update and even surpass the readerly delights offered by the traditional printed book, both the abridged 52 page bedtime edition and the 250 pages-long full story mode (as well as the simplified iPhone app) clearly acknowledge the digital versions' undeniable indebtedness to Carroll and Tenniel's original analogue imagetext. The colophon's production notes in the front matter—"Alice for the iPad designed by Chris Stevens, coding by Ben Roberts. *Alice in Wonderland* hand-built by Atomic Antelope based on the work Lewis Carroll and John Tenniel, an original digital edition"—pay homage to Wonderland's founding fathers (most of the illustrations, animated or not, are still Tenniel's, and the text remains Carroll's in its integrity). But they also vindicate the status of originality for the digital adaptation, and strangely claim a certain kinship with the printed book artwork as a carefully crafted physical object through adding the label "hand-built" to the e-publication details. This labeling is very much in line with how Chris Stevens, co-founder of Atomic Antelope coins *Alice for the iPad* a "super-modern, digital take on the pop-up book format enhanced for a Blade Runner generation," and how critics echoing his ideas associate the daring design of Apple's new platform with "a pop-up book for the 21st century."

Paradoxically, the marketing of a supermodern commodity (iPad app) takes place via its connection with a somewhat obsolete printed artform (pop-up book). The reasons for that might be manifold ranging from the similarity between the embodied spatial experimentations of the two modes of telling stories to the strategic augmentation of affective reactions and odd temporal confusions through adding the feel of nostalgia for the past to the amazed surprise at the future. Even more likely is an attempt to acquire a level of authenticity that the app's parchment-like page design (an ancient edition's digital remastering) already toys with by suggesting that the virtually simulated wear-and-tear of the physical book is a sure sign of its having been widely read and enjoyed—hence of historicity, knowingness, precious personal, literary, educative value.[10]

Despite the amusingly anachronistic chronological inconsistency resulting from the new media recycling the old, we also notice a certain sense of temporal and medial continuity. Medial transition seems never fully finite or exclusive, the new e-book format does not entirely take over the role of the old printed page, and replacement coexists with replication, modification with miming, so that different imagetextual modes come to co-exist side-by-side. This is a perfect illustration of media critics Bolter and Grusin's notion of remediation (2000): the new media of our digital age achieve their cultural significance by simultaneously paying homage to and rivaling earlier media. iPad storyteller Joe Sabia in his *Ted Talks* lecture (2011) on the technology of storytelling praised Lothar Meggendorfer the maker of the first pop-up book for revolutionizing the traditional book format and creating a bold new technology for storytelling. Sabia's talk—a metastory on the art and technology of storytelling, self-designated as a "meshing [of] viral video and new display technologies with old-fashioned narrative"—argued for the necessary evolution of the practical, technical devices that each generation invents to tell stories of its own, and a logical continuity between historically succeeding forms of popular narrative entertainment. In his words, storytellers were "channeling Meggendorfer's spirit" when they moved opera to vaudeville, radio news to radio theatre, film to film in motion, to film in sound, color, 3D, on VHS, DVD, and iPad. Ways of storytelling evolve but the same stories are recycled with a difference in a form that proves to be telling of the given era's narrators and listeners.

The question is what the iPad e-book application's digital, virtual format might be telling about contemporary readership, our current notions of children's literature, and our social(izing) strategies of subject formation. Technological sophistication has its downsides. The slow close-reading literary experience and the challenging interpretive process looking for the multitude of layers of meaning embedded in the Tenniel-Carroll imagetext risk being turned into a shallow, instantly-gratifying, interactive game burdened by what Slavoj Žižek calls in his *Sublime Object of Ideology* (1989) the "compulsory idiotic pleasure of consumption." Readers turned "users" seek fleeting delights in interactive multimedia technology that turns the reading experience into a gaming adventure overshadowing the pleasures of the written text. A single line of advertisement for *Alice for the iPad* encapsulates the superficial purpose of the book-turned-consumer-product: "The perfect interactive story for entertaining kids on a car journey." Child-readers, marginalized in the back seat of the car, risk turning into solitary users of the app functioning as agents plugged in an information system who might lose opportunities to communicate, expand in language, relate to other readers, and share the literary experience.

Less paranoid critical readings, like David Marshall's urge to acknowledge the hybrid new subjectivities generated by the interactive functions of new media which allow individuals to become so-called "prosumers" or "producers" who browse through media contents to make sensible choices that prove to be transformative of the meanings to be generated. Nevertheless even Marshall seems to admit some superficiality to new media interactions: "surfers" are involved in a surface engagement with content and a distracted, distanced playfulness; "players" are governed by the predetermined objectives of the particular game; "lurkers" watch and listen anonymously without any productive participation (2004, 25–6).

Even if the "produsers" of *Alice for the iPad* enjoy a certain degree of interactive agency, their liberty is minimalized. It is restricted to the range of options included in the game design, the decision between the "play" or "read only" functions—the first being a more likely, calculable choice as the one encapsulating the very essence of the app. The greatest limitation is reading experience's being reduced to playground fun as the physical pleasure of tapping the screen to produce multimedia effects (via features more often distracting from the story than enhancing its comprehension) predominate the more complex intellectual challenge to make sense of imagetextual meanings by relying upon one's own creativity and imagination.[11] *Alice for the iPad* creators' defensive argument—"kids who would have never read *Alice* as a traditional book might pick it up on the iPad instead of staring at Grand Theft Auto" (Stevens in Disham 12)—locates the app as a transitional medium in-between passive video-gaming and active reading. But the potential promise to move underage audiences towards a more sophisticated pastime is undermined by the technological given that makes engagement with the application likely predominate over the engagement with the story, and the resulting question "How much does the pleasure provided by the app's animated imagetext have to do with the reading experience of Carroll's original *Alice*?"

Moreover the physical pleasures of e-books do not last. They cannot be passed on to family and friends, they cannot be inherited, collected, caressed or creased, and hence they cease to matter as unique physical objects, precious personal belongings, beautiful, tangible, leafable, vulnerable artefacts with private histories, lasting memories and a visceral material reality of their own the old printed books used to be/have. Josh Catone's 2013 article on "Why printed books will never die" neatly sums up the "pro-print-and-paper" arguments. The electronic text-design, no matter how eye-pleasing, evokes an ethereal ephemerality of "temporary pixels" as opposed to the "more robust experience" of a hardcover edition's physical beauty. Digitality is about the *contents* (not the looks or form), as users pay for the right to access data but never actually own an e-book as a unique, individual possession. Despite the multisensory stimulation an iPad e-book app offers, the most basic physical experience of the printed book as a material object—with a specific smell, texture, weight, feel (not to mention the distinctive binding, cover image, type, illustration, each with a personal and paratextual significance of its own that might modify imagetextual meanings)—is still deeply missed. Because of these differences, Michael Agresta envisions a whole new status for paper books in the digital-age future, suggesting that they will surpass being textual vessels and will only survive as art: well-designed, high-quality, collectible gift books rivaling the paintings "hanging beside them on the walls for beauty, expense, and 'aura'" (Catone 2013).

In fact today's so-called "book sculptures" already pre-embody this vision. Su Blackwell's unique, fairy-tale- and folklore-inspired paper-craft scenes are created from images and pages cut out and folded from vintage old books and mounted three-dimensional diorama-like on the top of an opened book. They deliberately use printed paper as a classic, ephemeral, delicate medium to test its storytelling abilities to represent timeless feelings of wonder and melancholy. As the artist claims on her website, paper-cutting "employs irreversible, destructive processes to reflect on the precariousness of the world we inhabit and the fragility of our life, dreams and ambitions." It dwells in a spatial play—that has been used by pop-up book and iPad formats too—so that compositions seem to release characters and landscapes that "have been trapped inside the book all this time." Blackwell's lost little girl cut-out figurines, including Alice, are helped "to discover something, or perhaps escape from something" "leaning towards [spectator-readers] on their way to somewhere"[12] (Blackwell 2013). Similarly, book sculptor Jodi Harvey-Brown praises the interactive spatial dynamism of the genre, claiming that paper art allows for an immediate, intimate encounter of readers and their beloved fictional characters who "come out of the pages to show us their stories" as book art lends a communally sharable, objective visibility to the make-believe worlds "books pull us into" (2012). The artists cuts up the text of the canonized novel to create 3D visual delight by building sculptures from the paper slips to attribute a brand new, performative function to the book. First, the cut out pages offer a live enactment of Carroll's fragmented narrative and postmodern interpretations' dissemination of meanings. Second, the very experience of reading is reevaluated along the lines of affectivity: instead of a linear, rational word-by-word progress, we make sense of book art by letting our thoughts idly wander, spontaneously recognizing and cherishing the paper-folded Wonderland scenes which provide spatial models for how mental images take shape in the reader's consciousness, and hence hold a metaimaginative significance, too.

For a book-sculptor, printed paper bears a visible memory because of its malleability to the hand (Blackwell 2013). Likewise, for average readers the attraction of the printed book lies in the memorial function it might fulfill, allowing us to add (and abandon) side notes, dog-ears, sequels, and intertexts embodied in trivial physical memorabilia such as notes, letters, tickets to and in-between the original pages, turning with these personal contributions the book in question into a personal autobiographical artifact of our own.[13] What makes the traditional printed book appealing for nostalgic readers is its very anatomy and physical structure. The blank space of the margin where one's own handwritten comments and opinions can be annexed to the main text, the gaps between the pages where further personal textual/visual belongings can be inserted, the momentary silence during the turning of a page where further thoughts and actions can come to mind. These constitute a place for the unsaid and the unseen that is left up to the reader to be said and seen, imagined and lived in his/her own particular ways, words, and visions which should all complement the original narrative with their own specific meanings. (My own paperback copy of *Annotated Alice* contains several Wonderland-themed, hand-made bookmarks decorated with my children's drawings from various years which—by means of personal textual addendums—neatly document their growing up along with their changing imaginative reflections on Wonderland, and turn the leafing of this book into an invaluable, one-of-kind readerly experience.)

It is this specific material, memorial surplus of print and paper editions that the Alice for the iPad e-book application lacks and attempts to compensate for by various means. Its page-design imitates the look of a parchment- or manuscript-like old book weary of use (with each pages' edges soiled on its way down the rabbit hole, possibly trampled by a multitude of undecipherable, muddy foot- and fingerprints). It embeds bits of calligraphical handwriting (Alice's Right Footnote, the Mouse's Tale) within the typographically undistinguished e-text format. It also employs an option to have with a finger-swipe virtual pages

Jodi Harvey Brown, "The Mad Hatter's Tea Party," book sculpture, 2015 (© www.jodiharvey-brown.com, courtesy of the artist).

curl and not just slide, as if to simulate the traditional reading experience. *Alice for the iPad*'s self-identification in promotional marketing material as a technologically enhanced version of the traditional "craftsmanship" of bookmakers, ink illustrators, paper sculptors, and oral storytellers, and the makers' alleged aim to preserve kinship, sensitivity, and fidelity to the original media they recycle (see Stevens 2010) appear to be similarly compensatory gestures. An extra emphasis falls on turning e-books into a supplementary (and not a substitutive) art form that is meant to mime printed books' strategies responsible for the real fun of reading, like offering enough space for readers to create their own mental images through striking the appropriate balance between text and illustration, rhetorics and aesthetics, between the pleasure of *reading* the narrative and *watching* its pictorial animation (Martellaro 2012).

These imagetextual solutions, in search of the right balance between readerly and spectatorial simulation, constitute the most rewarding components of *Alice for the iPad*. On page four, the White Rabbit's pocket watch swings on a chain hung onto the lower curve of the capital letter "S," while the rabbit itself contemplating an immobile, miniature version of the same pocket watch, on Tenniel's original portrait in colored *Nursery Alice* style, hides in the hole shaped by the capital letter "O." The two letters read together spell out the word "SO" by means of initials to the second sentence of the novel: "SO she was considering, in her own mind (as well as she could, for the hot day made her feel very sleepy and stupid), whether the pleasure of making a daisy-chain would be worth the trouble of getting up and picking the daisies, when suddenly a White Rabbit with pink eyes ran close by her." This first animated page of *Alice for the iPad* provides a complex intermedial experience. We read a text about Alice's seeing and picturing things, first in her mind's eyes throughout her daydreamy mental image-making concerning an option to play with daisies, and then due to the actual ocular surprise caused by the rabbit's sudden appearance launching the Wonderland adventures. On both instances readers take part in a meta-imaginative agency imagining Alice imagining. But readers also see on the same page the two pocket watches showing the passing of time, the smaller one hidden *inside*, and the larger swinging *beyond* the text, *mise-en-abyme*-like duplicating each other. The pocket watches seem to *metapictorially* mock philosopher Lessing's classic 18th century assumption about the mutually exclusive categorization of artforms where the narrative art's preeminence lies in communicating temporal flow, and visual art's excellence in displaying spatial dimensions. Here, reversing these traditional functions of "poetry as an art of time" and "painting as an art of space" (Lessing 1766),[14] the animated image shows time in motion and the verbal text creates the space for Wonderland's fictional reality.

The previous, first page of *Alice for the iPad* also revives excitingly the original image-textual dynamics. It features, along with the first line of the novel, a detail of Gertrude Thomson's 1890 cover-image to *Nursery Alice* where Alice is sleeping with a picturebook opened by her side. However, text and image clearly contradict each other: in the narrative Alice complains about the uselessness of her sister's unillustrated book, but the illustration shows a vividly decorated copy, that rather reminds us of the book Alice will plan to write/draw (or will have written/drawn!) about her Wonderland adventures. Moreover, where Wonderland creatures (Gryphon, Mock turtle, Pig baby, White Rabbit, Mouse) emanate amidst floating clouds from the sleeping Alice figure's dream in the original Thomson-cover, we find here, in their place, above Alice, the simple text on the iPad screen. Thus, the emphasis falls on the nonsensical confrontation of dreamer (image) and dreamt (text). The metafictional awareness of necessary intermedial confusions is increased. Users are eventually attracted by the promise of imaginative agency granted by the iPad app's technologically enhanced means of textual co-productivity.

The most recent electronic media adaptation of Wonderland adventures, a born-digital novel entitled *Inanimate Alice* (dir. Kate Pullinger and Chris Joseph, prod. Ian Harper, 2005-) is only vaguely inspired by Carroll's original but it nevertheless brings the interactive, multimodal, metafictional capabilities—implied in the source-text—to the full. The planned story arc embraces a total of ten episodes (five have been released so far) which narrate in a technologically-enhanced near future cataclysmic episodes from young Alice's life (from age eight to her twenties). She repeatedly struggles with the experience of getting lost amidst incomprehensibly alien, absurd circumstances and tries to find her way out by virtue of her own and her readers/viewers' imaginativeness. Alice is an emerging storyteller, a would-be computer-game designer accompanied on her intercontinental vagaries by an imaginary digital friend, Brad she created for herself. Fictitious Brad signifies for fictional Alice the same that Alice does for the real-life reader/viewer who actually animates her throughout the transmedia storytelling sessions which require audience interaction with a combination of text, sound, music, art imagery and games on crucial narrative turning points. Although it has been initially designed as entertainment, *Inanimate Alice* now works as an efficient digital literacy resource (particularly popular in the United States and Australia) intent on expanding learning opportunities. It helps youngsters develop a variety of faculties, including problem solving literacy (solving puzzles, building bridges, or engaging in pretense play, they experience trial and error, and learn to adopt new strategies), cultural literacy (guided discovery lessons on the cultures of countries represented enhances the ability to understand different worldviews), social-emotional literacy (Alice as a lonely child who must face threatening situations facilitates forming emotional bonds with the character and opens up opportunities for conversations about students' own feelings) (see Levasseur 2011, Warren, Wakefield, Mills 2013, Felming 2013). Teen audiences are taught to recognize the stakes of their imaginative decisions and take responsibility over them, to understand global citizenship and transcultural online subjectivities, to repurpose and remix multimodal representations through games and puzzles. Eventually it allows them to co-create new contents (sequels, fresh episodes, own story-versions) either by filling in the gaps or developing new strands of their own making. *Inanimate Alice* is a pioneering gambit in so far as it has been conceived as a "reading-from-the-screen experience" (available on devices capable of running Flash Player) targeting the "'always on' digital generation'" and hence completely lacks a hand-held printed counterpart. Alice connects technologies while avoiding material(ity) gone obsolete.

Cognitive neuroscientist argue that today's reading practices adapt to the technological, digital age: readers growing up in a world of screens must process an accelerating amount of information distributed on online media platforms with "hyperlinked texts, videos alongside words and interactivity everywhere, our brains form shortcuts to deal with it all—scanning, searching for key words, scrolling up and down quickly" (Rosenwald 2014). As a result, a bi-literate brain evolves that learns to alternate between superficial skimming and in-depth processing, the traditionally deep, immersive slow reading circuitry developed over several millennia and required for the comprehension of 19th century novels is competing with (if not overwhelmed by) fast-paced touching, clicking, pushing, linking, liking, scrolling and jumping through texts ingrained in us throughout daily habits of digesting the torrent of online stories.

Much of this is true, yet bi-literacy is not necessarily an entirely new phenomenon: readers of plurimedial artworks such as Carroll and Tenniel's Alice picturebooks must alternate between different styles of reading to grasp meanings of words and images in their complexity. How attention is divided between verbal and visual content is a matter of individual attitude or choice: pre-readers will focus longer on illustrations and just scan through the text for familiar letters or words, and there is surely a difference between early readers spelling as a laborious pioneering adventure in search for narrative pleasures and a mature re-readings' meticulous textual analysis.

An online hypertext's reading permits arbitrary jumps in the text and extensive information change by allowing "impatient cultural consumers," as if with a remote control in hand, to "zap" from one source of information to another, at their own discretion. Yet this "methodological paradigm shift" induced by contemporary new media digitalization—resulting in the fragmentation of a text deprived of its boundaries—is not unprecedented either, but may bear radical continuities with the past's so archaic analogue textual phenomena as manuscript culture's marginalia (Szőnyi 230). Fragmentation, a necessary outcome of any hypertext, also characterizes the original Carrollian narrative's episodic, non-(con)sequential, illogical structure and finds its print precedent in annotated, critical editions like Martin Gardner's seminal *The Annotated Alice* in which critical commentaries organized on the page margins allow readers to edit the (para)text and challenge the chronological order of events/reading conforming to their individual preferences.

According to Jan Susina, the *Alice* tales are beloved material of multimedia transformations because of the perceived malleability, the dual audience and the collectible status of the texts (2010, 145). I believe that the characteristic of malleability entails another major attractive feature for medial revisions: namely "metafictionalizability" that lures reader-spectators into the fictional realm with the promise of an active involvement in its making. Commodifying and more creative uses of metafictionality clash in popular moving image adaptations of the Alice tales.

Disneyfied Alices: Commodifying or Stimulating Imaginative Agency?

Metafictionality as a Marketing Strategy and the Framing of Female Fantasy

Stephens and McCallum's assertion made at the turn of the millennium (in Zipes 2000, 160) still prevails: the reception of fairy tale fantasies have been heavily influenced by the proliferation of moving image adaptations in the past decades. Children nowadays are likely to first encounter literary classics mediated by the popular film industry, in the interpretation of media moguls like the Walt Disney Company that also become the first to familiarize young spectators with metafictionality: a playful, self-reflexive, or ironic disclosure of the artistic constructedness of fictional reality. What was originally an inherent generic quality of the socially-subversive fairy-tale fantasy and a rhetorical device of postmodernist narrative has been turned into a marketing strategy that puts on sale the creative imagination as its major commodity. I shall discuss frustrating, oppressive as well as potentially inspiring, liberating effects of Disney's commodification of multimedial metaimaginative capacities, especially the representation of female fantasizing, in animated Alice-adaptations, first focusing on the former, more obvious, debilitating effects.

The simplest cinematic uses of metafictionality emerge in the Disney animated feature-films *Winnie the Pooh* (1959), *Beauty and the Beast* (1977), and *Sleeping Beauty* (1991). These—similar to many other cinematic adaptations of classic tales for children—feature in their first shots the opening up of a book as an authentic portal that can guarantee the entry into the fictional realm through invoking the archaic act of storytelling, with the voice-over narration emphasizing the oral origins and the retellability of the tale.[15]

In a more complex manner, the 1951 Disney "all-cartoon musical wonderfilm" adaptation *Alice in Wonderland* starts with Alice's governess-like sister reading out a book and Alice listening to her, as the camera contrasts their different point of views and their differing textual belongings. Alice balancing high on a tree branch embodies fantasy, adventures, a greater horizon of expectations while the sister neatly seated in the meadow below her is short-sighted by the boring history book she is immersed in. An intermedially complex metanarrative celebration of visuality is performed when the title-character, an animated *picture* herself, fantasizes about making a "world of my own" in which every book would be nothing but *pictures*, and "nothing would be what it is and everything would be what it is not." The sister's irritated response to Alice's pondering "Nonsense!" is just as much a realization of how the little girl's line provides an adequate definition of the literary nonsense genre, as well as a commentary on the difficulties involved in the filmic adaptation's intermedial shift necessarily distorting original meanings. Nevertheless, the exclamation as a tongue-in-cheek aside works only extradiegetically for the spectators, whereas the sister remains surely unaware of its metafictional implications.

Another typical metafictional imagetext interaction surfaces on occasions when the primordial subtext lurking beneath the visual adaptation is materialized in the form of a book or a scripture the alternate cinematic reality's characters (usually including the Alice-alter ego figure) are reading or enacting. This might be a book literally entitled *Alice in Wonderland* (as in the more radically avant-garde artistic postmodern revisions, Terry Gilliam's *Tideland* [2005] or Guillermo del Toro's *Pan's Labyrinth* [2006]) or a manuscript like the Disney-sponsored 2010 Tim Burton *Alice in Wonderland* movie's Wonderland scrolls, an oraculum-compendium-calendar that featured the novel's original, most famous illustration of the monstrous Jabberwock by Victorian artist John Tenniel. Burton's recycling of Tenniel's addendum to Carroll, on the one hand, accelerates the metafictional imagetext dynamics by embedding a major paratext, an image (complementing a novelistic text) into/within cinematic moving image medium, and on the other, significantly calls attention to the extremely visual nature of the Carrollian text, and to the inherent textuality of the filmic image.

In the above examples, the most obvious and accessible goal of the Disney Studios' appropriating self-reflectivity and metafictionality is to lure the reader-spectator into the fictional realm with the promise of an active involvement in its making. Disney has been frequently condemned by cultural critics for tendentiously distorting with its patriarchal, capitalist narrative-formula the universal

Alice from the trailer of Walt Disney's *Alice in Wonderland* (1951).

human values embedded in folk and fairy tales' archetypal structure and characterization, so as to fit the specific socio-historical conditions and ideological interests propagated by the cultural industry of the production's own era (Stephens and McCallum 160; Pilinovsky 17–33, Zipes 2012). Throughout this process, as scrutinous scholarly studies notice, imagination (and in particular female imagination!) is encouraged only to be punished by guilt, and to reward a compulsory return to realism and a reality perpetuating ideologies of prevailing hegemonic power structures, regimes of patriarchy, colonialism, capitalism, or consumerism (see Ross 2000, 210,[16] 2004, Zipes 1994). As Deborah Ross notes, Disney corporation's rendering the liberating power of fantasy itself a major commodity incites a nearly trade-mark internal contradiction of imagination and control, provoking an "ambiguity that at its best ultimately resolves into a connected and complex worldview that embraces difference and spontaneity, but at its worst produces confusion and anxiety" (Ross 2004, 54).

Ross very justly points out that Disney's first animated Alice is alternatively rendered depressed or hysteric by the "menacing gang of wonders" called to life by her own imagination—like the Mad Tea-Party's wildly proliferating live crockery, the broom-headed dog-creature who dusts all paths away, or the flexible flamingo croquet-bat tickling her to prevent her from winning over the Red Queen. It is the Tulgey Woods episode that evokes most clearly the Carrollian-Tenniellian nonsensical spirit with its unique creatures made from surprising combinations of mundane objects (telephone ducks, drum-and-cymbal frogs, and a bird with a birdcage stomach containing two smaller live birds) but the heroine's ultimate fright and flight of these oddities makes the same episode also harshly contradict and undermine "Carroll's radical investment in the power of wonder [that] frees Alice's imagination from the constraints of her assumed social and gendered position in realist terms." Reduced to a tiny, frustrated, forlorn figure lost in a large, dark or chaotic frame, accompanied by "self-lacerating musical laments," Disney's animated Alice chides herself weeping for her own curiosity, impatience, and for always getting in trouble. Her sad song "I give myself good advice (but I very seldom follow it)" utterly deforms the meaning of the original line. In Carroll, Alice is frustrated at her inability to reach the key to the Wonderland garden she wants to explore, while in Disney she cries tormented by the desire to get back home, to safe inactivity. According to Ross, when Alice "reaches the limits of her fear of imagination," and "rejects all this nonsense" she "abandons her fantasy of power and excitement," "undoes herself and her whole story," as she is "anxious to get back home for a cup of tea and to write a book about it, [only because] writing a story seems much safer than living one." Thus, her eventual creative authorship seems to be more of the result of an intimidated escape from the "terrors of the unconscious," a compensatory, paranoid, neurotic activity, and a passive compromise with picture-less books rather than a celebratory agency. Her quest is not completed by her "awakening self-confidence" but is interrupted by her willful waking up and a return to her dull "feminine" reality's perpetually infantilized, domestic passivity. Disney's Alice willingly renounces of the mad "dream that alone, to Carroll, made reality tolerable" and submits herself to the control and protection of the sane, adult, rational world (Ross 219, 32).[17]

I believe that it is truly telling that Disney subtitles this 1951 Alice-animation an "all cartoon *musical* wonderfilm," since the frustration of/by the plotline so neatly encapsulated by Ross, in fact, presents a schizophrenic clash between major themes of the era's most popular artistic genre, the Hollywood Musical. The Golden Age Hollywood Musical propagates fundamental ideological values of the American dream: independent and pioneering spirit, a safe moral home, and women's duty to become caring, docile, mothering, homemakers. The Carrollian tales about the nonsensical adventures of a girl child fantasist clearly fail to fit the Disney Princess Saga's classist heterosexual romance formula and evoke the American dream of self-making. Yet the adaptation hastens to reinforce conservative Protestant values and prevent gender-trouble by depriving the protagonist of any male privileges and instead chaperoning her back to the safe, homely, feminine realm.

As Susina pointed out, Walt Disney himself regarded Alice 'his problem-child': the story was full of what he called "a whimsy terribly tough to transfer to screen," the animation adaptation struggled with an annoying competition from the start, and initially failed to bring the expected financial and critical success. (It became the most popular film adaptation ever-made only much later on.) Disney's idea was to preserve Carroll's spirit by fusing his "funny lines" with screwball comedy, visual gags, and no less than 23 songs he believed would appeal to his American target audience. Yet, in a 1964 interview Disney eventually confessed that although he liked Tenniel' drawings which "seem to have been created for translation into screen but could never get Carroll's story," and found the Alice figure flawed for not being sympathetic enough, perhaps because of the studio's too careful normativization of nonsense (Susina 2015).

Even if this Alice animation does have its subversive moments, I shall turn to in a later part of my analysis, but in general, critics see it in a tremendously, and perhaps unjustly exclusively, negative light. Jack Zipes condemns Disney's fairy-tale adaptation on three grounds, for its being: irrelevant (a "Hollywood musical that has more fluff than substance"), stupidly pedantic ("takes all the life out of the comic antics and song and dance routines"), and silly and infantile ("a helpless blonde girl who does not learn to help herself," "papier-mâché, cuddly one-dimensional creatures" that are merely decorative and lack the intriguing complexity of Carrollian enigmas) (2011, 297). Donald Thomas locates Disney's Alice "touched by the vulgar assertiveness of Lolita" closer "to the culture of popcorn and bubble-gum than to the genius of either Dodgson or Tenniel" (in Brooker 206). Will Brooker regrets the reduction of the "dry irony of Carroll's prose to a soppy heroine in a blandly stereotyped English pastoral and Tenniel's detailed creatures to crude slapstick cartoons," the sanitization of morbid violent elements in favor of family fun, and the substitution of wild, parodic rhymes by over sugared songs to be taken at face value (208). Jan Susina argues for a loss of the Carrollian spirit in Disney's adventures driven by the heroine's desire to get back home, a moralizing she takes over from the Duchess missing from the movie, and a curiosity associated with dangers which turn her passive in the face of nonsense, waiting to be rescued or yearning for safe homeliness (2015). Interestingly, all the above critical voices imply that the distortion of the textual original has been effectuated by a medial shift, visualization conjoint with consumerization, emblematized by the emphasis on "decorativeness," "popcorn," "family cartoon fun," and the application of Hollywood plotlines like "Ozification." Even the very few critics who hail the nonconformist, counter-cultural, creative powers of Disney-Alice's fantasies—like Douglas Brode, who regards her as a "progenitor of the flower-power hippie girl"—imagine her imaginative freedom to be necessarily limited and ideologically contained: she "foreshadows every straight girl who went crooked over drugs and *lived to regret it*"[18] and "realizes a happy medium between woman's reactionary life and *brief flirtations with cultural revolution*" (Brode 24, emphasis mine).

Ironically, even Disneyland theme park's animation-based *Alice in Wonderland* dark ride (first opened in 1958) includes mild versions of popular metafictional device that tease imagination only to control or suppress it. The entrance is decorated by the page of a book, and the alienation or estrangement effect is evoked when vehicles exit the Queen's courtroom and before heading back to the last attraction the Mad Tea Party, leave the ride-building and descend by people waiting in line for the show. This sort of exit is a rare occurrence in a non-thrill ride at Disney Park, and Walt Disney presumably claimed that he regretted making the Alice-theme rides[19]—the former complemented by the Mad Hatter's spinning tea-cups ride—"because it lacked a connection to the audience's hearts." Whereas alienation in the traditional Beckettian sense aimed to prevent the audience from passive submersion into fictional delights for the sake of heightening their critical self-awareness, this ride reinforces visitors' collective self-identity as consumers queuing for a popular-cultural fantasy product that demands for a "strict parental supervision of participating children," and ends with the explosion of the unbirthday cake with a dynamite candle that makes the vehicles "escape back" to the reality from where they have started out the ride.

Disney's latest cinematic revisiting of the Alice-theme in cooperation with director Tim Burton operates with a story that likely disillusions fans of Burton's trade-mark quirky dark fantasies and Carroll's crazily calculated cacophony alike. It embraces a didactic, faux-moralizing *Bildungs*-plotline,[20] peaking in a simplistic finale that celebrates a dubiously post-feminist girl power strangely combined with entrepreneurial, pro-capitalist, colonizing might and a touch of Oedipal desire. The heroine's maturing into rationality signifies that she neither submits to her wealthy, pedantic suitor representing the Victorian marriage market nor to the luring but escapist Wonderland fantasies. Instead she pragmatically decides to undertake her father's business and embark on oceanic trade routes towards China, a locus of exoticized, wondrous otherness, and financially motivated adventures with the trading company that becomes the scriptwriter Linda Woolverton's[21] rather down-to-earth "metaphor for life" (Woolverton in Callaghan 2011). Despite Alice's farewell "futterwacken jig" dance, an homage to the anarchist Mad Hatter's crazy feat, rationality triumphs over fantasy. The heroine adapts to the domesticated (pseudo)feminism of Disney princesses, like Belle, Mulan, Rapunzel, or Merida, who "fight for their dreams" while carefully respecting the Disneyfied fairy tale's strict narrative structures and a closure organized by a teleologically uniformizing coming-of-age, a heteronormative patriarchal family romance, a bourgeois class hegemony, and a docile delimiting of all rebellious feminine tendencies. Even if this adaptation's Alice is—as Zipes described her—a strong-willed young woman with an inquisitive and critical mind, an independent spirit, a sense of humor, and valiance in battle, "more tomboy than petite comatose princess," who is "not looking for a mate but herself" (Zipes 2011, 302) still the scenario of a self-reflective female self-fulfillment is never brought to its full realization. A sense of the Hollywood sentimental melodrama is lurking in implications of the Hatter's impossible crush on Alice—Woolverton's original script included a clear romance line with two kisses that got eventually eliminated to remain within the safe frames of family entertainment. A simplistically unambiguous the Good wins over the Bad battle scene reinforces a "symmetrical sense of ultimate justice, lightened by an essentially comic vision" (emblematized by the futterwacken jig) (Tiffin 2008, 148), while the finale is tainted with classist, colonialist fantasies whereby Alice's dreams come true in a mundane form, as she "becomes a rich businesswoman to live off the Chinese" (Zipes 302).

The media-mogul seems to appropriate the originally ideology-critical, artistically sophisticated narrative strategy of metafictionality in the service of box-office success. Entertainment purposes gradually diminish the philosophical, political potentials of "baring the fictional and linguistic device"[22] constituting the imaginary textual universe. Predictable, sanitized scenarios cheat with illusory, "narcissistic pleasures"[23] of a creative authorship promised to the viewers but in reality usurped by the filmmaker Disney, who undersigned his family name turned brand name as a sign of ownership over the product.[24]

The same narcissistic authorship emerges in the Disney Bros Studios' earliest silent Laugh-o-Gram animated cartoon short ventures inspired by Carroll's classic that actually brought the company into being. *Alice's Adventures in Cartoonland* later known as the *Alice Comedies Series* produced in 57 episodes between 1922 and 1927 about a live-action little girl's (Virginia Davis, followed by Margie Gay, and Lois Hardwick) adventures in an animated landscape. (It was advertised as: "Kid comedies with cartoons coordinated into the action. A distinct novelty.") The series' trademark narratological device that has a lot to do with its instant success is the masterful use of *metalepsis*—originally a rhetorical trope introduced by Gérard Genette, here transmedially employed as a tool of animation. Through *metalepsis* the boundaries of the fictional and actual world are transgressed, "glanced, travelled or transported across," two mutually exclusive realities mix, and the spectator gains an impression of being fully 'sipped' within the story or of actors/animations stepping out off the screen, as the 'fourth wall' of the filmic imaginative space (separating the audience's reality and the on-screen fantasy) collapses (see Feyersinger 2010, Kukkonen and Klimek 2011, 1).

On these metaleptic occasions the animator's extradiegetic hand arbitrarily and literally reaches into the diegesis of his creations to manipulate the course of cinematic actions by altering something, erasing or drawing from/within the visual narrative. For example, in *Alice Chops the Suey* (1925) Alice escapes the Chinese rats chasing her by jumping into an inkwell that is removed by the artist's hand entering the scene, leaving the rats gesture angrily at off-screen space. In another, perhaps even more surprising episode, Alice's animated companion Julius the Cat flees by building a ladder from the question marks emerging in his own thought-bubbles. These cartoon speech-balloons indicate his unformulated ideas and unspoken emotions as fascinating visual traces of trans-/pre-verbality.

Besides the cinematic author's *deus-ex-machina* manual interventions into the on-screen story, another recurring form of metalepsis occurs in the *Alice Comedies* when the real little girl enacting Alice steps into the animated world, while the live-action frame narrative undergoes a sudden transition to cartoon usually brought about by a dream sequence—much in line with Carroll's original idea conceptualizing life as a playful dream. In an explicitly metafictional scenario disclosing and destabilizing the process of the making-of-the-movie, the first episode, *Alice's Wonderland* (1923) shows Alice's visit to a cartoon studio where she curiously watches cartoons being created and come to life. In her succeeding dream that night of being in the cartoon world, she plays with all the cartoon characters until wild lions break free from a cage and chase her down a cliff and out of the story.

Alice (Virginia Davis) in *Alice's Wonderland*, also known as *Alice in Slumberland*, from the Laugh-O-Gram series, 1922–1923 Disney Cartoons. Animation by Hugh Harman, Rudolf Ising, Ubb Iwerks and Carman Maxwell. The Alice Comedies saw 57 episodes between 1923 and 1927.

One could perhaps assume that it is a sign of Alice's passivity, objectification and limited imaginative agency that the shift from life-action to cartoon-animation is consistently effectuated by a dream sequence resulting of Alice falling asleep and losing consciousness because of fatigue, bedtime, or even because of being knocked on the head and resulting hallucinations. However, it is noteworthy that in the animated dream-scenes all the alternate universes and characters are projections and creative inventions of Alice's own mind. On the other occasions, like in *Alice's Wild West Show* (1925), the little girl emerges even more explicitly as an active author of her own making. She copes with her unruly kid audience, and makes them behave by presenting her imaginary heroic adventures (about winning over similarly unruly cowboy gangs) to them, and does not hesitate to stand up for her storytelling rights by beating up a big fat boy who is making fun of her tall-tale. Sometimes she seems to directly address spectators with her story, so that her gaze looking out of the screen blurs and bridges the ontological difference between fictional-filmic and real-life spaces. In another self-reflexive scene, in *Alice Solves the Puzzle* (1925) Alice struggles with a crossword puzzle, fends off the crossword-thief cartoon-bear Bootleg Pete, and eventually solves the puzzle, triumphantly crying "I've got it!," penciling in the elusive, final missing words, "The End," which also signify the filmic closure.

These scenes perfectly stage *metalepsis* as a "paradoxical contamination between the world of telling and the world of the told." Alice "takes hold of (telling) by changing narrative level," her "deliberate transgression of the [syntactic and semantic] threshold of embedding [and of representation]" produces an effect of "the mixture of humor and the fantastic" and "functions as a figure of creative imagination" involving beholders in a thought-provoking border-crossing between universes that "points toward a theory of fiction" (Genette in Pier 2013).[25] As J.P.Telotte stresses, the above transitional scenes prominently thematize the Disney-pattern at the core of the studio's work. They foreground the relentlessly negotiated link between the real and the fantastic realms, suggesting the importance of the latter to the former, while revealing its (the filmic space's) constructedness through the insertion of a live-action character into the animated world (334). According to Telotte, the developing house style known as the "illusion of life" transcends the "life-like illusion" on accounts of "let[ting] *us* enter into that fantasy space, as if we were being invited to go down the rabbit hole, to undertake the same sort of liminal exploration as Lewis Carroll's Alice, to participate in a 'life of illusion,'" "a world that, through its artistry, argues for its own reality on its own terms," in Cholodenko's words "not illusion as unreal but as real unreal" (in Telotte 335). The metaleptic trick marks not only a decisive step for Disney animation and an attractive new filmic possibility, but also a vanguardist use of metafictionality put in the service of the celebration of imaginative agency.

Disney's *Alice Comedies* seem to carefully avoid fidelity to *Wonderland* or *Looking-Glass* motifs. However, besides larger themes of dreaming, fantasy, and encounters with strange creatures (Jaques and Telotte 204), the surrealist and transgressive generic qualities of cartoons—which persistently invoke representationality and realist conventions only to defy them (Ross 217)—are much in line with Carroll's rebellious reliance on the fairy-tale fantasy tradition. We can recognize his visionary recycling and breaking of rigid narrative codes aimed to arouse critical awareness and a philosophical sensitivity concerning culturally-constructed truth values and stable identities, and to activate a playful proliferation of meanings.

Jabberwock/y's Subversive Potentials in Disney's Earliest and Latest Alice Adaptation

In Carroll's novel, Alice first encounters in the inverted world behind the Looking-Glass the "Jabberwocky" nonsense poem scripted in a mirror-writing she initially decodes as a strange picture-language she cannot read, since the words turned topsy-turvy, from right to left/wrong are perceived by her more as non-figurative images than linguistic signs. For Alice the Kcowrebbaj/Jabberwock, whom she never actually meets, remains a "name without a thing," a referentless signifier, a grotesque (image-)textual product that never gains a fleshly physical embodiment but its overarching presence invades the fantastic diegetic universe like the ghostly aura of its absent author. Accordingly, what fascinates and frustrates Alice is not so much the un/vincibility of the unseen mythical predator but the overall in/comprehensibility of the nonsensical discourse about it. The strange lines of the embedded poem—starting with the emblematic sentence: "Twas brillig, and the slithy toves/ Did gyre and gimble in the wabe;/ All mimsy were the borogoves,/ And the mome raths outgrabe." (155)—evoke in Alice a reaction that mirrors the readerly response to the fictional frame-text in which she features as a protagonist: "'It seems very pretty,' [...] 'but it's *rather* hard to understand!' [...] 'Somehow it seems to fill my head with ideas–only I don't exactly know what they are!'" (156). What is at stake here is the manageability and enjoyability of the textual monstrosity of nonsensical representation testing the limits of imaginability. This uncertainty prevails in a visual form in Tenniel's drawing that remains one of a kind, the only and still decisive depiction we have of the enigmatic monster that earns the status of metafictional imagetext. Readers' imagination is teased by the literary nonsensical ambiguity of this "whiffling," "burbling" creature with "jaws that bite" and "claws that clash." What has been in the poetic text "a name without a thing," a referentless signifier, an indefinable, faceless, formless enemy keeps its ambiguity in pictorial form too. Tenniel pays visual homage to the literary text's potential inspirations of legendary, mythological, and scientific origins. His Jabberwock is a degenerate mutant, a dead-end on the Darwinian evolutionary scale, a grotesque parody of monstrosity, a hybrid like nonsense discourse's portmanteau word coinages: it fuses features of a dragon, a griffin, a dinosaur, an insect, and the Lambton Worm, all dressed in a petit-bourgeois checkered waistcoat. Initially planned as a frontispiece to *Looking-Glass*, it became relegated to the middle of chapter one to calm the mothers of prospective readers who feared that this "too terrible monster" would "alarm nervous and imaginative children['s]" fantasies (Gardner in Carroll 163), as the embodiment of the Unimaginable itself.[26]

The Jabberwock preserves its mysterious unimaginability and does not show up in the classic 1951 Disney animated adaptation *Alice in Wonderland*,[27] but we do find an illustration of its intended appearance in *Walt Disney's Alice in Wonderland Meets the White Rabbit*, a volume of the Little Golden Book storybook series. It is depicted as a nonantagonistic, kind, and rather comic dragon-like creature with burning eyes, a stovepipe-nose, fuzzy orange hair, an extra hand on the end of its tail, dressed in a single green glove and a slightly outgrown yellow waistcoat. On this same illustration Alice encounters another strange being who forms the other half of the rhyme in the little (mock)prose-poem accompanying the image: the Cheshire Cat "who faded in an out of sight" as the Jabberwock's "eyes flamed in the night," as the caption says.

While the Jabberwock character got removed from the final, 1951 Disney animation version, it is his mysterious, mischievous, pink and purple striped, and permanently grinning companion, the Cheshire Cat, who eventually comes to recite the first and last stanzas of the classic Jabberwocky poem.[28] The Cheshire Cat, a trickster figure, a guide, and agent of metamorphosis who disappears, reappears, and even disintegrates or decapitates itself at whim, challenging laws of gravity, rationality, and etiquette alike, becomes an embodiment of imagetextual intermedial transitions. Tellingly, the Cheshire Cat appears first in Tulgey Woods where the multitude of contradictory road signs pinned on trees signal the invasion of visuality by textuality (as in the case of the imperatively overwritten Eat me!/Drink me!-cookies), a textuality that defies and decomposes common sense. Similarly, in the presentation of the Cat lurking in Tulgey Woods the Jabberwocky is transformed into a little song, whereby the rhythmic, melodic, vocal qualities of musicalized discourse (music as discourse) predominate linguistic signification.

The Disney Cheshire Cat's riddles can be interpreted as verbal equivalents of his visually stunning moves, ranging from acrobatic feats to teleportation. Its grandest riddle "We are all mad here!" also functions as a *meta-line* that discloses the certainty of uncertainty, the awareness of the unreliability of representation in a hyperspectacularized realm. The Cat acts as a guide to deconstruction. When Alice is lost in Tulgey Woods, her feline companion opens up the filmic space to reveal a hidden door in a tree trunk, a secret passageway

John Tenniel, "The Jabberwocky," illustration in Lewis Carroll, *Through the Looking-Glass, and What Alice Found There* (London: Macmillan, 1871).

that leads her to the next stage of her journey, the Queen's Croquet Ground. At the final trial scene the cat repeats Alice's insults which outrage the Queen and lead to the climactic chase and the protagonist's perplexed return back home.

In a highly symbolic vein, when the Cheshire Cat vanishes, only its eyeballs or grin remain behind alternatively, as if to mock notions of (Un)imaginability and (Un)speakability. Its verbal and visual ungraspability are encapsulated in the line: "You may have noticed that I'm not all there myself." In fact, when Disney's Alice looks upon the Cheshire Cat, who is swinging on a high branch in Tulgey Woods singing the Jabberwocky nonsense poem, her body posture is the same as that of Tenniel's original illustration of the beamish boy knight facing the mythical beast Jabberwock and later that of Tenniel's drawing of Alice conversing with the Eggman Humpty Dumpty, who explains the meaning of the nonsense poem about the Jabberwock to her and attempts to help her defeat textual monstrosity. An ambiguous figure, the Jabberwocky-chanting Cheshire Cat embodies the very spirit of the 'magical anti-magical' world of Disney's Alice-animation: it offers and refuses guidance (to strange wonders and the right road home alike), it makes Alice laugh and cry, while it teases, appeases, and oversees her imagination.

In Disney's 1951 Wonderland there is just one other agent of bodily, logical, and medial transformation similar to the shape-shifting Cheshire Cat and the nonsensical Jabberwock. The Caterpillar (whose name is etymologically akin with the Cat's) addresses verbal inquiries to Alice which take visual forms in the puffs of smoke released from his hookah, which literally rub her nose in the dilemma of identity-crisis, and stick on her shoes preventing her from getting away without an answer. Alice is led to the Caterpillar by the sound of his inarticulate song "A-E-I-O-U" and the trail of exhaled smoke clouds that take the shape of the vowels themselves. The Caterpillar's question "Who are you?" appears in smoke in capitalized, abbreviated, mock-phonetic transcript, in letter-homonym counterparts to the original words as "O R U?," and his other linguistic utterances also take pictorial form: the word "not" is symbolized by the smoke form of a "knot" and "why" by a simple question mark. Disney's visual puns efficiently replace Carroll's nonsense language-games, facing spectators with multimedial ambiguities involved in the interpretation process, hence offering intellectual pleasures of self-reflectivity in the guise of easy entertainment.

In the 2010 computer-animated, live-action family fantasy film *Alice in Wonderland* directed by Tim Burton, written by Linda Woolverton, and released by Walt Disney the Jabberwock gains the spectacular physical form of an arch-enemy. Represented as a dragon, very similar to Tenniel's original illustration (with wings, forked tongue, lightning-breath, burning eyes, low voice) it proves to be the Red Queen's monstrous pet and her dictatorial rule's major weapon that Alice must fight with the mythical Vorpal Sword to save Underland. Throughout a verbal increase of filmic tension, the Jabberwock is much talked about before it eventually appears on screen to constitute one of the highlights of the 3D CGI movie's stunning visual effects.

It first shows up in a disturbing flash-back memory of the Mad Hatter Tarrant Hightopp from which we learn that the monstrous beast burnt down the native village and destroyed the entire clan of the Hatter on the Horrevendush Day, and accordingly is culpable for driving him mad. The Jabberwock is metonymically evoked in this vision of the fatal fire and of the origins of mental breakdown when the Hatter runs out of words while describing the terrors of the past: the unimaginable images of total destruction stand in the place of unspeakable traumas. In the light of these events, the Hatter's eerie reciting of Carroll's "Jabberwocky" nonsense poem seems to signify a failed verbal attempt at coping with ideas and emotions related to this psychological wound that eludes criteria of meaningfulness. The Hatter half-mumbles to himself in an incomprehensible gibberish, a maniac voice and a strange Scottish brogue accent[29] to which he switches from his "sweet lilting English lisp" (Bye 10) whenever he undergoes the splitting of his personality before his mad fits. His mesmerizingly monotonous monologue attests that tragedy is always necessarily interpreted as nonsensical and unspeakable: as if in a ritualistic mourning chant, rhyme, rhythm and repetition, and the material surplus of his incarnated voice predominate over sense. Besides meta-representational realizations of the misbehavior of language and the ambiguity of (verbal and/or visual) common sense, we face the other major literary technique of the nonsensification of sense here. This foregrounding of the sensory, lived, embodied experience of discourse, the corporeal, physical nature of the signifying activity is called by Brooks the *somatization of semiosis* (1993, 8), and associated by Kristeva with a *revolutionary poeticity* (see 1984) whereby the sounds and shapes of words may produce decisive surplus-meanings. Indeed, as Bye suggests, the soliloquist Hatter belongs with Burton's recurring otherworldly, revolutionary, "sad clown" figures—like Joker, Beetlejuice or Willy Wonka— who must battle with their inner demons as well as the external oppressive regimes, and "must struggle to express themselves creatively in a hostile or uncomprehending environment" (13). Joker communicates via aggression, Beetlejuice via bio-exorcist haunting, Willy Wonka via chocolate fantasies, whereas the Hatter's insanity—acting as a protective shield against the interiorized pains of mourning, the hunger for revenge, and the Queen's external torture too—surface in his fabulous hat making skills, a final, crazy futterwhacken jig dance, and his gibberish nonsense speech. His crazy sentences, like "You ran out on them to save your own skin, you guddler's scuttish pilgar-lickering, shukm-juggling sluking urpal. Bar lom muck egg brimni!" a line addressed to Chessur (the Cheshire Cat) match his memorable reciting of "Jabberwocky."

However, this poetic madman's rare verbal (oral-auditory) curiosities are likely not the ones moviegoers will associate with the Burtonian Wonderland, since this adaptation unfortunately does not make much use of Carrollian language games. The nonsensical Jabberwock/y as recounted by the Mad Hatter turns into a post-traumatic stress disorder symptom of a tortured action hero instead of a playfully-provocatively unjustifiable *action gratuite* of a ravishing eccentric that it used to be in the original. It belongs to the disillusioning Burtonian project of rationalization—whereby the director wanted to give some "emotional grounding" to his version by making each character "indicate some mental weirdness that [anyone] goes through" (Burton 2009).

Still, despite the film-makers inappropriate insistence on comprehensibility, the "Jabberwocky" nonsense poem plays a prominent role in organizing the filmic structure. It provides the basis for a quest and rite of passage story in which Alice must find the Vorpal sword and her 'true' heroic self to defeat the evil and tyrannical Red Queen by slaying her monstrous pet-dragon, the Jabberwock. Moreover, in Burton—like in the many metafictionally playful children's films mentioned before—the original image-text of Carroll's poem and (especially) the accompanying Tenniel-illustration appear embedded within the cinematic adaptation as a decisive reading and prophetic vision apt to change the protagonist's fate and choices by initiating an exciting play of belief and disbelief, in fantasy and reality.

Accordingly, in the first part of Burton's film Alice refutes Wonderland as a phantasmagoric make-believe devalued as Underland, a nightmare she would rather wake up from. As the strange inhabitants say, she has lost her "muchness,"[30] her ability to believe in the authenticity of their fictional realm, and her belonging with them. However, by virtue of an implied readerly identification, she finally accepts the heroic place assigned to her, upon discovering that the famed Underland scrolls are decorated with the picture of a dragon-slaying knight slightly reminiscent of and clearly identified with her by locals.[31] She willingly enters a deeper layer of fiction-within-fiction, as the protagonist of an embedded nonsense anti-tale(within-tale) in Wonderland's legend about the beamish Childe fighting the monstrous Jabberwock on a glorious, "frabjous" day—intra-textually decodable as the mythical messiah from the Underland scrolls and extra-textually recognizable as a Joan of Arc-like[32] feminist action hero re-embodying Tenniel's original illustration to Carroll's novel. Via this recognition, a fictive realm is suddenly perceived as true while mythology gets reinterpreted as history and Alice moves from a debilitating skepticism to an empowering belief in Wonderland and herself, too.

Like in other adaptations where Carroll's novel appears as a book the filmic protagonist reads, the Burton movie's 'real life' heroine, Victorian, bourgeois, teenage Alice identifies with the imaginary alter ego (the mythical knight/Tenniel picture) of the title-character of the Carroll-novel, and thus turns the (image)textual original 'truly fictionalized' within the filmic revision's factualized alternate reality. By virtue of a simultaneous homage and destabilization, the adaptation's fictional reality earns a primacy over the original's. Yet, the original (image)text invoked in the moving image adaptation also owns a certain indubitable master-mythological veracity that allows for the reinforcement of the credibility of revisioned fantasy's reality status.

Alice's first ocular self-(mis)-recognition on witnessing the scrolls is reinforced by a performative speech act upon the final triumphant fight with the Jabberwock. The fully armed and armored Alice, besides authentically embodying and enacting the Tenniel illustration's knight, also reads herself out loud into the story. She states in her voice-over narration, as if by a magical

nobogfrog, "In Arms with Alice," fan art inspired by Tim Burton's *Alice's Adventures in Wonderland*, ink on paper, 2016 (courtesy of the artist, Deviantart.com).

incantation, that her capacity and willingness to believe impossible things (as many as six, before breakfast; and even impossibilities as her being the savior of Wonderland[33]) allows her to defeat the monster. (Again monstrosity here might refer just as much to the flesh-and-blood dragon as the nonsensical (il)logic of Wonderland.) Thus, she calls to life Wonderland on verbal-visual-auditory planes (actualizes the image-text-sound interaction), and affirms fictionality's credibility and her own agency as a character, reader and author of her own story. Imaginativeness appears as a question of determination, practice, and will like in the original where the Queen advised Alice to exercise believing impossible things half-an-hour each day until she can "believe as many as six impossible things breakfast" like she did at her age (210).[34] However, Burton's Alice affirmatively masters the imaginative agency Carroll's heroine was uncertain about. Still, both in the source text and the adaptation, fantasy emerges as an acquirable skill, dependent on the capacity to believe in believing, and a matter of self-confidence and survival, too.

Paradoxically, the oscillation between imaginative willingness and reluctance initiated by the above intermedial shifts and fusions does not stop here. Alice's intratextual mythologization via Carroll's and Tenniel's image-textual evidence attests her predestination to heroism in fantasy realms she finds increasingly credible. But it will eventually result in her rejecting her belonging to the daily reality of Victorian England on her return, arguing that its bourgeois customs and conventions—corset wearing and polite small talk dictated by the prevailing etiquette—are impossible phantasmagorias she is unwilling to believe in or identify with. She rejects her era's social codes of conduct as communal fantasies in the name of proto-feminist pragmatism for the sake of a private mythology that idealistically allows her to follow and realize dreams of her own, in the footsteps of her inventor, adventurer father. (In fact, this fantasist anti-conventionalism already lurks there in the original Tenniel illustration that mockingly dresses up the nonsensical monster to be slain in a neat bourgeois waistcoat, as if to highlight the inseparability and perhaps interdependence of fantasizing and realism.)

The multi-layered conjoining of fact and fiction is further emphasized by the illustrations complementing Tenniel's iconic cover-image to the Oraculum Scroll. Conceptual designer artist Dermot Power's drawings remain largely off-screen and feature only in the Blue Ray edition menu, but their sequential, comic strip-like depiction of events mirrors the Carrollian narrative's hallucinatory loose, episodic structure, while neatly blurring distinct fantasy-layers by featuring side-by-side a succession of characters from different textual registers. On the Oraculum Scroll we spot side by side the White Knight who never shows up in the film but clearly embodies an alter ego of the author Carroll, diegetic agents like Humpty Dumpty, the Mad Hatter, and the dragon-slaying action-heroine Alice, along with the prophetic apparition of a trades-ship on which she will sail away on her return from Underland, in (and out of) her otherworldly reality.

The stakes of Alice's vacillation between Underland and her fictional reality (as well as the Carrollian Wonderland and our world, necessarily invoked in spectators' minds) reside in the questions: Which is the world she can inhabit the most comfortably and emperoweringly in her own fashion? Can she creatively shape her own story(world) to her liking? These are metafictional dilemmas Jack Zipes calls "questions of the battle over the narrative" (2011, 301). Alice's balancing between imaginative willingness and reluctance, enchantment and disenchantment results from the fact that she can never be fully overwhelmed by anything in Underland because she has been there many times before in her childhood dreams and assumes that these are fantasies of her own making she can/should gain control of. Her metaperspectivism teases the audience with the following existential philosophical dilemmas worthy of the Postmodern Zeitgeist: "Can we control our dreams? Can a young woman write her own narrative? Can we humans who have become caricatures of humans in today's society of the spectacle in which commercials, advertisements, and other media influences invade our lives, determine the plot and narrative of our lives?" (Zipes 2011, 302)

Although Zipes, in the end, regards the hesitation involved in these questions in a positive light and acclaims the Burton-Disney filmic collaboration for allocating more creative liberty to Alice's figure than the Carroll-Tenniel original did, but the answers are far from being self-evident. Susan Bye formulates another approach to the same dilemma in her Education Resource Kit entitled "Approaches to Alice in Wonderland" prepared for a 2010 Tim Burton exhibition in Melbourne organized by MoMA as follows: "What has happened to the sprightly little girl who managed the nonsense world of Wonderland with such aplomb?" The film tackles this question about the process—or even the consequences—of growing up and about a world that takes a brave, bold child and turns her into a timid and uncertain woman who feels unable to control her destiny." (4)

On the basis of Bye's analysis we may also recognize the sarcastic, self-ironic side of the filmic metanarrative. The originally pretty garden of cheerfully talking live flowers turned into a shadowy, tangled, sepia-toned landscape overgrown by wildly abandoned vegetation, as well as the grown-up Alice's paler, thinner and less substantial adult self imply that the adaptation is just "a faded copy, or perhaps the ghost, of the original" story, its ludic adventures, and of its vivacious, robust little girl protagonist (who embodies the "lost self" Alice's quest aims to reunite with) (10). The grotesque cruelty with which the defenseless cute animals are treated (a frog is executed for stealing tarts, a pig is tread on by means of a footrest, tiny monkeys are forced to hold heavy furniture supporting the Queen—each echoing the Carrollian abuse of flamingos as mallets, and hedgehogs as balls) exercise a similar metafictional effect as they subversively recontextualize cuteness in a negative way so as to "cast doubt on the whole aesthetic of innocence that underpins the vision of childhood that drives so much cinema" (Bye 15). This systematic contrasting of ideal and lived realities, of visions and revisions only goes to show that the Burtonian Wonderland-sequel's vision is not so saccharine or idealistic as one would perhaps expect from a Disney production at first sight. Burton's singularly pragmatic Alice slays the dragon of nonsense—literally and symbolically too—to leave behind both Underland's daydreams and Victorian England's pedantry as insubstantial, insignificant fantasies, be they grounded in individual make-belief or social consensus. Burton's Alice, this no nonsense girl uses imagination for empowerment instead of escapism or self-restriction.

Changing Media of Enchantment: Tim Burton's 3D CGI Visual Nonsense

Tim Burton's films certainly qualify as *auteur* cinema. They consistently reflect the director's personal creative vision marked by a deeply rooted multimedial metafictionality resulting from the antagonism involved in "a macabre sense of childhood *images* of violence and horror cushioned by a fable-like unreality of con*text* and simplicity of *narrative*" (Tiffin 2008, 148, emphasis mine), as well as a postmodernist, self-reflective interest in storytelling (folk lore, myth magic), and a clash of imaginative and realist dimensions—with the relentless celebration of the supremacy of the former over the latter.

Imaginative world-making is a common feature of all artistic cinematic productions. Instead of a servile mimesis or an impassive mirroring of our phenomenal reality, moving-image representations have always aimed at constructively creating a brand new cinematic reality inhabited by fantasmatically conceived beings and things organized and mobilized by different, technologically simulated rules of functioning. Filmic fantasies never aim to be authentic copies of the real; the alternative universe on the silver-screen operates independently, makes sense on its own, without needing to rely on (constant comparisons with) commonsensical standards of the actual life-world. A non-mimetic, non-referential, non-realistic, and fully fictitious truthfulness or verisimilitude founds the basis of the film's possible world. As Marina Warner puts it, the fairy-tale fantasy "becomes a tool for thought, a multicolored skein of images with which to think about the real, both reiterating and shaping the real in restructured narratives, reassembled images" (1994, 17 in Greenhil-Matrix 5). It is challenging to explore how in recent specimens of this filmic genre the fictional reality's fictitious realism interacts with the 3D computer technology's digitally enhanced life-likeness, and to study the effects of this interaction upon spectators' dis/belief, dis/enchantment, and imaginative liberation or debilitation.

Critics unanimously agree that the introduction of 3D computer animation into cinematic technologies signifies a profound transformation in the nature of visuality. It is comparable to the radical shift from medieval imagery towards Renaissance perspectivism (Crary 1 in Manovich 1997, 5), to Victorians' preoccupation with stopping motion (in photography) gradually turning towards attempts at mobilizing images (in proto-cinematic devices: optical toys, filoscopes, magic lanterns, then eventually movie screens) (Manning 167), and in general to early cineastes' fascination by the celluloid world of moving pictures where fantastical beings temporarily do become real (see Marcus 2003). According to Lev Manovich the most crucial concern of 3D animation technology—from educational, advertising, business, military, science, and entertainment perspectives alike—is the "progression towards realism," the ability to simulate authentically (in fast high-quality rendering) in space and movement alike, three-dimensional images of existent and imagined objects and environments in a photorealistic way virtually indistinguishable from live action motion picture photography, in such a complex and visually rich form as if they were real scenes.

However, "this realism is qualitatively different from the realism of optically based image technologies (photography, film), for the simulated reality is not indexically related to the existing world" (Manovich 1997, 5). The fact that the synthetic 3D animated image does not necessarily have to correlate with a real-life referent, opens the way for a realistic fantastification of the real. 3D animated moving images owe their synthetic quality to the ambiguous nature of "synthetic realism" that simultaneously aims to simulate "the perceptual properties of real life objects and environments" and to simulate "the codes of traditional cinematography" (Manovich 1992, 13). This signifies, at once, the reproduction of the presence of an actual lived reality that has possibly never ever been, and the reproduction of the re-presentational conventions of a cinematic art intent on creating new fictional realities of its own making.

This meta-awareness of syntheticity is counterbalanced by the illusion of interactivity, of the penetrability of the filmic space offered to spectators. Mark Salisbury's visual companion to Burton and Disney's 3D Alice-movie impressively captures the feel of this interactive sensation upon describing the cinematic Wonderland-journey's rich and dense visual landscapes with occasional expanses of the sky as follows: "there are definite moments in the film, where we let it breathe, where the frame opens up" (83). This 3D experience stages the culmination of French film theoretician André Bazin's 1946 vision of "Total Cinema," a "total cinematic realism" (17): a complete representation of reality through the reconstruction of a perfect illusion of the outside world in sound, color, and relief. Bazin regarded the perfection of the filmic illusionistic techniques sustaining reality effects as the highest stage the evolution of cinematographic technology could reach, yet he also maintained that cinematic realism is not borne from scientific, economical, industrial advancements, but rather derives from the artistic human being's 'innate,' idealist desire to reproduce the "real" world around us in perfect detail. Bazin's notion of total cinematic realism was (unaware) of a fundamentally paradoxical quality: a mechanical effort to objectively recreate the world unburdened by the artist's subjective interpretations or the ravages of time, it was also regarded as a pre-technological "drive" (Duckworth 1), an idealistic dream naturally embedded in the human mind (explained with a poetic metaphor as "the myth of Icarus [that] had to wait on the internal combustion engine before descending from the Platonic heavens. But it had dwelt in the soul of everyman since he first thought about birds" [Bazin 22]). Bazin's claim must stand corrected here: cinema is a tool for the reproduction of reality as much as it is a tool of fantasy and dreams, and if there is a human drive for naturalistic realism it must conjoin with a drive for imaginative storytelling, too. However, I believe that Bazin's antagonistic assumptions about cinematic realism's being a technologically enhanced organic beginning and endpoint of cinema, as well as an objective visualization of a subjective idea do not necessarily result from the logical flaws of his theory, but rather reflect the fundamental ambiguity of the filmic medium. This ambiguity is most remarkably present in 3D CGI, fairy-tale fantasy, *auteurial* cinema that provides a life-like representation of a fictional, make-believe reality, puts a realistic technology in the service of realizing fantasmatic mental images; and hence metafictionally problematizes any visionary artistic attempt at (re)constructing the real. The fact that today's two most powerful users of 3D animation are Hollywood and Pentagon proves the intricate interconnections of fantastification and realism, by disclosing that the technology can be equally put to the service of both seemingly contradictory representational modes.

Film critics unanimously regretted the Disneyfication of Burton's Alice: *The Guardian*'s March 2010 reviews wrote on the "fail[ure of] a spellbinding movie *tale-teller*" in a "curiously flat," "lifeless reimagining" with a "mediocre script," (French 2010) "tepid dialogue," "weak characterization," and "a dull, weightless fantasy world" (Bradshaw 2010). But even the strictest spectators had to admit somewhat reluctantly that the "brilliant visual art," the "highly distinctive," (Bradshaw 2010) "vivid imagery," the "dazzling, gothic set design, and lavish costumes" (Brooks-Barnes 2010) made the film "seducing [like a] peacock spreading its fantastic plumage," "a pleasure to regard" as one "gawp[ed] at the sensual beauty of it all" (Brooks-Barnes 2010).

Director Burton claimed that his connection with Carroll's tales is primarily based on the imagery "that has stayed with [him] since [he] first flicked through a copy of *Alice in Wonderland*, and continues to intrigue and haunt and fascinate [him] today" either "through the beautiful drawings of all the great illustrators whose renditions of Carroll's classic creations [he] referred to while making his film or via the multitude of references to Alice in contemporary music videos" (Salisbury 1, Bye 6). The film's Academy Award winning costume designer Colleen Atwood also openly acknowledged on numerous occasions her indebtedness to Tenniel's and Carroll's original illustrations, while composer Danny Elfman, who scored nearly all of Burton's films, "infusing the fantastical visuals with lush symphonic orchestrations," recalls how the picture of Alice's elongated neck initiated his lifelong obsession with physical anomalies and the nightmarish, freakish feel permeating all his soundtracks (Hart 2010).

Besides the nostalgic tribute paid to past artistic visions of Alice's first Victorian illustrators (Carroll, Tenniel, and Arthur Rackham), another dominant visual intertext lurks in the multiple references to the producer's brand, most clearly manifested in the trademark Disneyland Magic Kingdom Castle easily recognizable in each Underland queen's palace. This can qualify as a cunning use of what Maltby calls a "commercial intertextuality" or "commodified aestheticism" that permeates most of contemporary high-budget Hollywood movies and allows the cinematic fictional reality to become an advertising space targeting a demographically desirable audience with the "placement of consumer products defended not only as budgetary instruments but as a form of *capitalist realism*." Similarly to Maltby's examples of the Teenage Mutant Ninja Turtles eating Domino's Pizza in several cartoon episodes to make both themselves and the pizza more credible or of McDonald's Happy Meals's little plastic replicas of animation characters "extending the entertainment experience," the Magic Kingdom Castle–like Underland palaces serve to connect on- and off-screen realities. They support the filmic plotline centered on Alice's hesitation about the reality-status of Underland and confirm the veracity of the Burtonian diegesis by evoking in spectators the real-life referent of the make-believe palaces. At the same time, they reinforce the fantastification of Disneyland as an authentic realm of magic where all dreams can come true with a little imagination and money to spare (Maltby 27 in Neale and Smith).

Eventually, from a paranoid critical perspective, the filmic medium adheres to a fundamentally ideological functioning. As Jean-Louis Comolli's materialist reading of the history of cinematic technology suggests, the silver screen as a "social machine" sustains the "ideology of the real" through commodifying the visible world, and "'objectively' reduplicating the 'real' itself conceived as specular reflection" to propagate the illusion that these are the phenomenal (commodity) forms which constitute the social 'real' rather than the 'invisible' to the eye relations of productions (Comolli 133 in Manovich 1992, 12). Conforming to this logic, any metafictional filmic move works as an ideology-critical gesture disclosing the functioning of this illusory realism and realistic illusionism.

I believe that it is precisely these simulated, pseudo-realistic images' stunning visuality that lets enchantment finally win over unimaginativeness throughout the reception of the Burton-Disney coproduction. Although the counter-fantasy realm's clearly postmodernist, self-reflective metanarrativity quite likely distances, defamiliarizes and destabilizes the alternate universe's fictional reality via the multiple *mise-en-abyme*s of images and texts I analyzed above, imaginative willingness still prevails as an overall effect. Alice is initially unable to remember and unwilling to believe in her childhood's Wonderland devalued as Underland, and after having completed her mission in the realm down the rabbit-hole, she abandons it to accomplish the frame-story's rationalistic project of feminist and colonial empowerment. However, her skepticism is counterbalanced by the spectators' ravishment by the photorealistic simulation of wonders through the 3D CGI (computer-generated imagery) cinematic technique that enables enchantment to predominate disenchantment. In place of the subtle literary, philosophical, socio-critical allusions taking place on the Carrollian original's *discursive* plane, the filmic adaptation's amazing ambiguity is gained from its *visual* powers.

Nevertheless, the visual adaptation is not so far from the literary original as we would first presume: for the celebration of the 3D CGI spectacular visual *style*'s supremacy over the plotline-*contents*' dramaturgic sophistication can be regarded as the cinematic equivalent of literary nonsense's celebration of "sound's supremacy over sense," a stress on the *how* instead of the *what* of sense-making, Jean-Jacques Lecercle finds decisive of the genre of literary nonsense (1994, 2–3). The means are still prioritized to the end, the form still predominates the content, only transmitted to a different medium, shifting the emphasis from the verbal to the visual representational plane.

In Burton, the nonsensical enchantment is primarily not of verbal origin, it does not restrictively result from the Mad Hatter's demented discourse, his recurring, unanswerable riddles, nor the perplexing indecipherability of the Jabberwocky poem. These serve only to complement and maximize the Hatter's insane, psychedelic *looks*, his puzzling *image* that constitutes the peak of ocular nonsensification—and that has become, accordingly, in trailers, movie posters, and advertisements, the trademark of this latest improbable world of Alice. The Mad Hatter is a computer graphically distorted, digitally manipulated live action character whose unnaturally exaggerated facial features, enormously enlarged, impossibly electric green eyes, crazy clownish flaming hairstyle, strangely twisted movements and unnatural mask-like or over-exaggerated mimics—equally reminiscent of puppets, silent-movie stars, or demented maniacs—clearly defamiliarize his humanity, by courtesy of the CGI technology. Thus, the Hatter's looks and speech both reach a familiar unfamiliarity and an unfamiliar familiarity, and an overall uncanny nonsensical effect. Paradoxically, however, the Hatter's positive persona as a helping figure who protects the humanistic values against the Red Queen's ruthless terror also invites to a spectatorial identification, and thus, to the internalization of his spectacular otherness.

The familiarization of the unfamiliar is a trademark strategy of Burton's cinematic art that "uses classic folklore, gothic horror, and science fiction themes to rely on audience recognition in response to such narratives" (Tiffin 149), and hence grounds his unusually quirky, dark, distanced fantasies in the mundanely ordinary and the metaphysically universal, presumably well-known by all. The Burtonian imagery appeals to our visual literacy and collective cultural imagination in a calculated cacophonic way. The pleasures of the familiar are combined with the excitement of the unexpected throughout a self-reflective play with the audience's horizon of expectations. For example, the Hatter is not only a CGI-de/formed double of Burton's favorite actor, Johnny Depp—it is him, but unrecognizable—but by cinéphiles he is also recognized as a fusion of Depp's earlier roles, intertextually melting Edward Scissorhands, Ichabod Crane, Willy Wonka, Jack Sparrow, J. M. Barrie, and Sweeney Todd into the Hatter's character.[35] The outcome is a proliferating postmodernist patchwork, a camp collage of visual nonsense. Certain scenes of fantasy-fragments and filmic crossovers pay a tribute to previous visual adaptations ranging from Dali's surrealistic phantasmagorias, Annie Leibovitz's Wonderland fashion photos, and Disney's sweet children's classic to the eerie Victorian paintings of Arthur Rackham, an Alice-illustrator succeeding to Tenniel in the 1907 edition, whose one-time home Burton uses today as his office.

Other scenes consistently use eclectic extra- and inter-(image)textual allusions and borrowings to invite a multifocal interpretive perspective combining referentiality with symbolicity to resist fixed meanings. Alice—clearly detached from the muse Alice Liddell's figure—deconstructively combines Tenniel's chivalric Childe, dragon-slayer St George, visionary St Anthony and heroic Joan of Arc and, in a somewhat baffling-way, earns her name from Charles Kingsley (though spelt as Alice Kingsleigh), author of Victorian science-inspired fantasy best-seller, the visionary *The Water Babies: A Fairy Tale for a Land Baby* (1863), while she is equally associated with the film-theme-song's performer, Avril Lavigne, pop-icon of teenage rebellion, who plays an Alice-alter ego in her music video. While one of Alice's side-kicks, the mighty dormouse warrior resembles the *Chronicles of Narnia's* Reepicheep; the Red Queen mockingly recalls Queen Elizabeth from the *Blackadder* series and Bette Davis's Elizabeth I; the White Queen is a mixture of star-chef Nigella's dark double who cooks with human body parts such as Butter Fingers, of a punk spirited Debbie Harry, an ethereal Dan Flavin, a glamorous and graceful Greta Garbo, and Glinda the Good Witch on hallucinogens—as Burton affirms in a *Daily Telegraph* interview (Salisbury 2010). The pseudo-rationalistic framing is familiar from the *Wizard of Oz,* and an old, "black-and-white photo of a family having tea during the Second World War with London, disheveled, in the background" (Burton in Salisbury 2010) is also among the major inspirations of the macabre Underland atmosphere. Among Burton's eclectic range of inter(image)textual cinematic allusions film-scholars likely admire his repurposing of the German Expressionistic movie style surfacing in the contrasting of shadow and light effects, or the matching of characters' moral, psychic corruption with their abnormal bodily deformations (the Red Queen's monstrously large head) (Bye 17). But the director never aims at artsy elitism: his homage turns into pastiche as canonically acclaimed artistic modes (expressionist horror) are combined with more mundane popular entertainment forms (cartoon-style jokiness) to reach an overall grotesque effect accessible to all.

The above characteristics attest just what a peculiar interpretive positionality is offered to spectators of the Burton-Disney Alice adaptation who must equally rely on their visual literacy as well as their sub-conscious memory impressions to make an integral sense of the movie. On the one hand, we must face the recognition that both literary and visual nonsense—in particular through their use of metafictionality and inter(image)textuality as major devices in creating other worlds (Tiffin 2006)—require recipients, along with the fictionally implied reader/spectator Alice, to exercise an inventive interpretive creativity, to make self-corrections, re-readings/re-visions and playful deconstructions, while exchanging primary (normal, literal, denotative, original) meanings for supplementary (less obvious, figurative, poetic, intertextual/ intermedial) ones or vice versa, succeeding to Humpty Dumptian claims/realizations of "that's not what I meant" (Carroll 221, 224). On the other hand, Alice's strange world belongs to a "well-established visual tradition" and evokes a sense of reassuring familiarity. Michael Hancher proved that Victorian readers have been granted "frequent previews of Wonderland" in Tenniel's well-known political cartoons drawn for *Punch* magazine he later recycled in bits and pieces for his illustrations to Carroll's books. Similarly, contemporary audiences are aware of our overexposure to the Alice iconography in novel consumer-oriented contexts' postmodern repurposings, ranging from IBM advertisements to sexy Halloween costumes (Hancher 29) which, mingled with vague childhood memories of the Alice tales, constitute a simultaneously pleasing and provoking sub-conscious *déjà-vu* experience, and contribute to the calculably imminent success of any adaptation. Moreover, Ken Hanke suggests that Burton's being influenced by visual adaptations—especially in the moving image form, rather than the original novels—is not a sign of his "disloyalty to ur-texts" but a proof of his work providing prime examples of "new media texts" (I would say new media imagetexts) that rely on subjective (re)interpretations of a "memory half-informed" by intermedial impulses rather than consciously revisionary decisions (Hanke 2000 xvii in Ray 207–9). It is noteworthy that the new media experience of "half-information" akin with the 3D CGI's "looking-as-if" clearly communicate the nonsensical feel of "almost-thereness" Carroll was so intent in reaching.

In Wonderland's CGI realm, everything *looks like* a very vivid-surrealistic-dream version of our own mundane reality where nothing is exactly as it seems. The protagonist experiences spectacular shrinkings and growings but remains the same Alice, whose self-identity is nevertheless constantly doubted by everyone around her. She *looks* like Alice, but she cannot be truly her since "she seems to have lost her muchness" (Burton 2010). This nonsensical line also amply portrays the moviegoers' bewilderment upon their inability to precisely locate what is 'wrong' (out of order/ out of focus) with Wonderland's CGI characters despite their striking lifelikeness. The computer digitally manipulated live action characters, these half-human, half-animation figures *feel* real—"it looks like they have a soul" as the director says in the DVD's extras (Burton featurette 2010)—but spectators, like the filmic Alice, do not precisely *know* what sense to make out of them. In this respect their CGI effects' visual nonsense functions in a very similar way to the Jabberwocky poem's literary nonsense: "they somehow seem to fill heads with ideas—only one doesn't exactly know what they are!" (Carroll 156). More specifically, the CGI animated live action hybrid characters—fusing human and technologically enhanced features—recall the Carrollian portmanteau, neologisms melting two distinct word-entities into one new, undecidable meaning, 'hailing the logic of uncertainty' (Wolff 2008). In fact, *literary nonsense* can be defined as any discursive claim, written text or act of symbolization that resembles, and is decoded as language, as meaningful communication, yet its intelligibility becomes dubious, defamiliarized along with our conventional representational and interpretive strategies meant to make sense of it. This is exactly what makes the reception of 3D CGI cinema so very challenging.

Consequently, I wish to argue here that the Carrollian literary nonsense's foregrounding of the malfunctioning of language is cinematically translated into the troubling of the transparency of visual meaning and representation, as Burton creates *visual nonsense* by exploiting on multiple levels the fundamental ambiguity of the 3D, computer graphically animated/live action fantasy filmic image(text).

Firstly, the conjoining of live action reality's footage and computer graphic simulation creates a hybrid alternate fantasy world in which the numerous digital effects—the movie was shot in 90% on green screen, with a footage of 2000 digital shots (Salisbury 2010)—

distort the actors' actual physical appearances (like the size of the Queen's enormous head, the height of alternatively tiny or giant Alice, or the Hatter's impossibly electric green eyes). Live action CGI animation's sophisticated means also provide to the fully animated fantastic characters the human personalities of the real-life actors who lend them their voices. (E.g. the Cheshire Cat dubbed by Stephen Fry gains his iconic sarcastic persona though Fry never appears on screen in person.) Through multiplications of digitally manipulated real-life characters (like the twins Tweedledee and Tweedledum enacted by the same actor Matt Lucas or the 'clone-army' of identical playing cards) copies of copies are created—and thus enter into a total play with our fantasizing faculties, by questioning the reality status and the very origin of the credible original.

Secondly, our imaginative confusion is further augmented by a perplexing conjoining of the marvelously horroristic fairy-tale fantasy genre's radical *anti-realism* with the computer technology's *hyper-realism*, an all too vivid photo-realism brought to the extreme, that is coupled with the contrast of the historical veracity of the story-frame's authentic Victorian setting and the embedded fantasy story's Carroll-inspired, nonsensical, once-upon-a-time and far-far-away neverwhere. To make Alice in 3D with the help of digital creative processes Burton departs from his trademark cinematic magic making technologies, and renounces of "his preference for physically crafted imaginary worlds and hand-made special effects" (Bye 20). And yet the new media territory he explores preserves its distinctively Burtonesque aura on accounts of mixing the green screen motion capture and the digital animation with live action characters. The result is a haunted, hallucinatory, automated, mechanical simulation-effect that nevertheless still brings "the heart and soul" of the real(istic) "human element" into the computer world (Bonham-Carter in Bye 20).

Thirdly, with the 3D CGI technology the spectatorial gaze is increasingly controlled by the new (mixed-)media's visual literacy that precisely directs our attention, trains us where and how to look. But we also witness a strange destabilization as on-lookers are deprived of a neat separation and a safe distancing of imaginative possibilities through a metamorphic overlap between capricious fantasy and calculable reality.

Fourthly, 3D CGI technology allows for a total immersion in the filmic alternate fantasy-reality and a full identification with its imaginary creatures, events and (il)logic, since it simultaneously enchants and stupefies both adults and children by visibly attributing an 'actual' life-like verisimilitude to the Impossible (Wonderland) 'that has never been.' It turns the 'Unimaginable' visible, feasible and credible via a computer digital technologically simulated blurring of the make-believe fantastic and our real world. Yet, simultaneously, as a major technological means of Burton's visual nonsense 3D CGI also incites metatextual recognitions concerning the misbehavior of representation, shifting the focus from the *what* on the *how* of image/sense-making, while foregrounding the unnaturally all-too-natural and visionarily over-fantastificated "texture of images." The defamiliarization and denaturalization of images, and our alienation from them—paradoxically conjoined with the above mentioned blissfully immersive identificatory mechanisms—is nearly necessarily provoked by the act of putting on the special glasses which allow moviegoers to see the 3D effects, while accompanying their spectatorial pleasure with a physical weight reminiscent of the constructedness of images, texts and stories. This might perfectly illustrate what Mitchell means when he argues that the essence of the pictorial turn is not a "return to naive mimesis" but a "postlinguistic, postsemiotic rediscovery of the picture as a complex interplay of visuality, apparatus, institutions, discourse, bodies, and figurality" (Mitchell 1995, 16).

The tension between imaginative willingness and reluctance is never fully resolved—neither for Burton's Alice whose adventures "validate Wonderland as real [memory and not the dream she had believed it to be] just as she is also moving into adulthood and leaving it behind," nor for the spectators who accompany her on her "dual journey" (Callaghan 2011). Cunningly enough, the question here is not whether Wonderland exists (according to the filmic scenario, it certainly does, regardless of all beliefs), but whether one chooses to believe in it, and whether one chooses to live (in) it. In a playfully nonsensical yet strictly logical manner, the affirmative answer to the former dilemma does not contradict the refusal of the latter option. It is the very possibility of choosing (or rejecting) fantasy that makes reality tolerable.

With regards to the coexistence of imaginativeness and incredulity there is a significant parallel between Carroll's Victorian and Burton's postmodernist era. According to a recurring nonsensical guideline to Wonderland one can and should believe impossible things—with practice believe as many as six impossible things before breakfast as Carroll's Queen does and recommends Alice to do (Carroll 210). "The only way to achieve the impossible is to believe it to be possible," Burton adds somewhat didactically in a recurring line equally uttered by Alice's father soothing his daughter after her nightmare, the Mad Hatter pondering about the interconnectedness of reality and illusion, and eventually Alice triumphing over the Jabberwock. This line also reflects the epistemological crisis shared by late 19th century Victorian and the post-millennial eras. In Carroll's times, the bourgeois public was stupefied by reading morning newspapers' accounts of impossibilities (Wullschläger 43–44), like the invention of photography, the mass print-production of popular novels, the building of the British Museum, an enormous storehouse of pictures, or the opening of the spectacular Crystal Palace World Fair. Burton's postmillennial generation, on its turn, first incredulously gapes at, then gradually gets used to visual impossibilities, such as witnessing worldwide live-real-time-broadcasts or computer simulated, photo-realistic reconstructions of History-making catastrophes on televised and online broadcasts, or circumscribing identities on the basis of photo-shopped, speculative doubles of celebrities, internet avatars, and inventively compiled Facebook profiles. Apart from the loss of faith in the transparency of images and texts, the two eras are identical, as Henry Jenkins and David Thornburn argue, in their resulting self-conscious awareness of change and an apocalyptic rhetoric simultaneously envisioning "a technological utopia where emerging communication systems foster participatory democracy" and a culture of chaos, instability and corruption through the commodification of information by technological changes annihilating more reliable old media (x). According to Jenkins and Thornburn, the transitions witnessed by the Victorian era—amply recorded in John Stuart Mill's "The Spirit of the Age"—sufficiently attest that there is no need to fear the possibly radically innovative (media)changes brought about by the digital revolution. As Deborah L Spar claims, "technological change follows a cycle of innovation and experimentation, commercialization and diffusion, creative anarchy and institutionalization" (in Jenkins and Thornburn x). During media transition, the new system rarely ever obliterates *essentially* its predecessor to *fully* take on its function while consigning the older form to waste and oblivion. New media are more likely to coexist, often reinventing, rejuvenating, and mutually inspiring one another.

The above is illustrated by Kara Manning's interpretive take: Burton's 3D CGI piece as a retro/neo-Victorian revision sheds light on the visionary futurism of the original novel, foregrounding how it anticipates the future and reflects upon the past by turning cultural historical turning points of technological change into elaborate narrative patterns. Carroll's pair of *Alice* tales represent important stages in the development of motion picture technology: the transition from photographical ventures to arrest motion (surfacing in the struggle to find "the right size" in *Wonderland*) towards more explicitly cinematic gambits to actively engage in motion (manifest in the struggle to find "the right place" on the chessboard beyond the Looking-Glass). Burton moves from the traditional cinematographic depiction of the opening scene's stagnant, nineteenth-century garden party to much more revolutionary, hybridized techniques used to create "a dynamic, vibrant, and three-dimensional Wonderland, into which the viewer feels plunged along with Alice" (Manning 173). Both imagetexts, Carroll's and Burton's alike, seem to materially participate in the development of emerging new media technologies on accounts of prophetically foreseeing and attempting to satisfy their times' collective desires to blur boundaries between spectator and spectacle, perception and participation, observation and imagination.

Burton's 3D CGI filmic extravaganza inspired by Carroll's and Tenniel's classic imagetext instead of obliterating the original, rather stimulated book sales of 'the novel behind the blockbuster movie.'[36] The postmodern Alice is marked by an increasing complexity of co-authorship: it is Burton's re/vision of Woolverton's re/reading of Tenniel's view of Carroll's

Venlian, "Let's Hat the World." Fan artwork made for the "Picture Yourself in Wonderland" contest on DeviantArt, 2010 (courtesy of the artist, venlian.deviantart.com.

Alice.[37] The inevitable proliferation and destabilization of the imagetext is illustrated by the fact that besides the numerous visual (book)guides to the film, a novelization of Burton's movie has been published in a movie tie-in book edition by T. T. Sutherland entitled *Disney: Alice in Wonderland (Based on the motion picture directed by Tim Burton)* (2010) that was meant to textually promote the film's visibility but also stands as a work in its own right. In an endless process of imagetextual recycling we move from novel to illustration to script to moving image to movie tie-in novelization.

This proves that the intermedial shifts accompanying the transmission of word to image, or vice versa, quite likely result in a literal animation of any text, even if interpretive attitudes might need to be adjusted to the media in question, in order to be able to appreciate 'original' literary classics' (visual) adaptations which seem less efficient at first sight. One might also argue that the question concerning the similarity and difference of visual and verbal media (of dis/enchantment) is just as unanswerable as the Mad Hatter's famous riddle attempting a comparison of the raven and the writing desk in Carroll's original non-sensical wordplay. Tellingly, the riddle "Why is a raven like a writing desk?" (Carroll 73) was intended to remain unresolved in the book but later triggered numerous answers. Some solutions were based on *verbal* play: most famously the answer "Because Poe wrote on both," Aldous Huxley's witty response "Because there's a *b* in both, and because there's an *n* in neither," and Carroll's own afterthought in the preface to the 1896 edition, "Because it can produce a few notes, tho they are *very* flat; and it is nevar put with the wrong end in front!" where "never" was misspelt with an "a" to read as "raven" backwards, and was often hypercorrected by proofreaders ignoring the pun (Cohen in Carroll 75, Susina 2001, 16–17). It is noteworthy that in order to realize the *verbal* error, the pun of misspelling you have to perceive the text visually too: *seeing* is a token of visual comprehension. Other solutions were based on more explicit *visual* play: for Jan Susina the tall, black-cloaked reverend Dodgson leaning over his writing-desk in his somber clerical outfit reminds of a raven, while the quick action of his hands compiling hundreds of letters, riddles, and language games resemble "the motion of flapping wings" (2001, 18); as the fantasy world he creates allows his imagination to fly free. When Burton's Hatter admits that he "hasn't got the slightest idea" about the answer to this riddle he keeps on repeating throughout the film, Alice reassures him with a line her father comforted her with in her childhood when she was troubled by recurring dreams of Underland: "You are entirely bonkers. But I'll tell you a secret. All the best people are." The conjoining of two paradigmatic Carrollian phrases, the riddle on the raven and the Cheshire Cat's "We are all mad here!" allow for a celebration of the enchantment by undecidability and unnameability as communal experience of fantasist dreamers' whose unlimited imaginativeness turns them into saviors of Wonderland. Eventually, the nonsensical riddle makes us aware of the paradoxical tension between the simultaneous necessity of misinterpretations and the impossibility of meaninglessness, as well as the inevitably ambiguous interplay between words and images toying with the Unspeakable and the Unimaginable—and serving by means of a common basis of Carrollian and Burtonian fantasies' intermedial strategies of make-believing (non)sense.

2

Imaginative Reluctance and the (Meta)fantasy of Girlish Fantasy

"why, sometimes i've believed as many as six impossible things before breakfast."

The Artist as Dreamgirlchild Meets the Disbelieving Spectator in Terry Gilliam's Poetic Horror Cinema

Terry Gilliam's 2005 fantasy thriller movie *Tideland* based on Mitch Cullin's 2000 cult novel of the same title was advertised for its theatrical release with filmmaker David Cronenberg's label, "a poetic horror film." Indeed, both the original novel and the filmic adaptation offer a unique celebration of the poetry of horror and the horror of poetry. As for the poetry of horror, *Tideland* reveals how the radical unspeakability of the incomprehensibly absurd or the repulsively dreadful—foregrounding both the fragility and the magnitude of being—evokes a cognitive and affective confusion that belongs to the register of the cathartic sublime experience. As for the horror of poetry, *Tideland* celebrates, from a meta-perspective, imagination as an artistic agency invested with an astonishing capacity to transform even the most terrible lived experience into creative aesthetic delight—reminding us of the beauty of life even in its most miserable manifestations.

Tideland's first-person narrator, focalizer, nine-and-a-half-year-old little Jeliza-Rose (Jodelle Ferland), following the fatal methadone-overdose of her mother (Jennifer Tilly), flees from L.A. to a remote corner of bleak rural Texas with her drug-addicted, burnt-out, ex-rock-star father (Jeff Bridges), who soon dies of a golden heroin shot, and abandons his disturbed daughter all alone in an isolated, rundown farmhouse called What Rocks. She spends here a solitary summer, embarking on increasingly dark, surrealistic, mostly imagined adventures, sinking deeper and deeper into her childish fantasy life that distorts her terrible reality by misconceiving her infortunes as marvels, in an attempt to unconsciously make up for her unbearable sorrows and fears. Jeliza-Rose's nightmarish reality is invigorated by the twisted world of her daydreams inspired by her favorite and only read, *Alice's Adventures in Wonderland*, and peopled by imaginary, fictionalized creatures worthy of Carroll's classic. Her make-believe company consists of faerial fireflies, villainous squirrels, nocturnal bogman, and disfigured, dismembered Barbie doll heads she wears on her fingertips and personifies ventriloquized as her alter egos and best friends, whom she accidentally drops into a deep-deep rabbit hole. The real-life freakish figures of her surroundings belong in her fantasies to a bizarre invented family: her father's drugged, delirious, then deceased body, later on taxidermied by his ex-lover, neighboring Dell (Janet McTeer), is cuddled by the little girl as an oversized ragdoll or a surrogate fur-parent of psychologist Harlow's monkey experiments, while the glass eyed, half-blind, bee-phobic 'ghost-lady' Dell, in her black robe and gauze mask, frightens and fascinates like infantile fantasies of the bad mother and witch, and Dell's mentally challenged, epileptic, Quasimodo-like brother, Dickens (Brendon Fletcher) is called by Jeliza-Rose her sweet captain and husband. The deserted, delusionary world Cullin and Gilliam create for this Alice living in a curious claustrophobic cottage amidst the infinite yellow sea of swaying Johnson grass is a space, where the infantile phantasmagorias supersede the barren consensus-reality of socially constructed common sense, to create a perplexing fantasy realm with a nonsensical truth value of its own right.

Besides the sophisticated aesthetic and philosophical interpretive potentials, this pair of dark meta-narrative adaptations of the *Wonderland* plot offers a feat of poetic horrific fantasy attributed to *children*, more specifically a *little girl*, who serves by means of a fictional self-portrait for the adult male author. In this respect Cullin and Gilliam are like their forefather, Carroll for whom Alice was just as much an inspiring muse and an ideal reader, as a mirror-image of his fantasist authorial alter-ego. The grown-up artistic imagination of Carroll, Cullin and Gilliam attributes to infantile fantasy a subversive "omnipotential" to challenge the culturally biased, dispassionately rationalistic common sense of normativized "mature" truth, by envisioning nonsense as a vital engine of childish or child-like way of thinking—nothing to do with mental deficiency, psychic imbalance, or aimless *l'art-pour-l'art* bravado—a psychic automatism of the *homo imaginans* that can be strategically turned into an ethically and epistemologically exemplary endeavor to empathically embrace the wonderful, often self-contradictory, and unconceivable diversity of being.

Although a continuity can be traced between Victorian and postmodern artistic conceptions of the 'savage innocent' infantile fantasy, the common adult readerly evaluation of children's capacity to imagine the Unimaginable becomes increasingly complicated as its 19th century idealizing admiration is complemented by a 21st century irritation and incredulity. Contemporary adult audience's anxious concern with the Alice figure's unconstrained imaginative and empathic faculty is not so much a sign of heightened skepti-

Julie Zarate, "Jeliza-Rose: Homage to Terry Gilliam," 20 × 24 inches, oil on canvas, Director's Cut Exhibition, 2010. A perfect illustration of intermedial transition: a painting of a film still (of actress Jodelle Ferland) from a cinematic adaptation of a novel inspired by a literary classic. Zarate's homage to Gilliam's homage to Cullin's homage to Carroll (courtesy of the artist).

cism, but a result of reinterpreting the former virtue of sensibility as an endangering vulnerability that threatens with the destabilization of the safely fixed self and meaning. In a grimmer, secularized, postmodern worldview, dreamers no longer experience flashes of otherworldly wisdom and kindness under a benevolent divine protection the Victorians believed in, but delusionary fantasies shaped by manipulative ideologies ranging from consumerism to patriarchal hegemony, and haunted by irrepressible personal and cultural traumas.[1]

The case of meta-imagination or embedded imagination, when readers are invited to imagine another person imagining something, is a particularly fertile ground of research because it sheds light on the diversity of imaginative practices including daydreaming, dreaming, enacting pretense play, (mis)remembering, speculating 'what if' scenarios alternative to the reality constituted by actualized possibility, or considering, from a multifocal perspective, others' experience of the kaleidoscopic consensus-reality. It reveals the complex interplay of imaginative reluctance and willingness by simultaneously focusing on multiple distinct imaginative agencies: that of the fictional girl child fantasist, that of her adult author who conceives the Alice figure as an embodied metaphor of an idealized version of his own imagination, and that of the reader/spectator who is puzzled, if not intimidated, by these intimate imaginary doublings and interactions.

In line with James Kincaid's and Jacqueline Rose's assumptions about childhood's being a cultural myth, an empty category filled with ideological meanings defined by adult desires and anxieties projected onto it, an analysis of what adult readers are ready or resistant to imagine about children's imagination proves to be telling of who we are, who we (make)believe ourselves to be. The beliefs about children—as Gilliam says in connection with *Tideland*—provide a litmus test showing how people perceive the world and how secure they are about themselves (Gilliam in Stubbs 2005). The conclusions drawn do not only enhance our understanding of the fictional realms of the nonsense fantasy genre, but have trans-literary, material implications too; because the world of imagination may change the world. As Szabó Gendler argues in *The Architecture of Imagination* (2006) edited by Nichols, "when we imagine, we draw on our ordinary conceptual repertoire and habits of appraisal, and as the result of imagining, we may find ourselves with novel insights about, and changed perspectives on, the actual world," too (150–1).

My main questions here are: Whose dreams imagine to life Alice's figure? How do the childish specificities of the imagination of Alice as a Dreamchild call to life Wonderland? Are there moments from when on recipients do not wish to dream along with Alice any longer? Why do we tend to believe that the Humean insight on "whatever is imaginable is possible" holds just as much promising as threatening potentials?

Gilliam's Girlish Make-Believing the Marvelous Multiplicity of Being

In his 2007 filmic foreword to *Tideland*, Terry Gilliam confesses that he believes many cinemagoers will hate the movie, others will love it, and some just will not know what to think about it for precisely the same reason. His filmic adaptation of Cullin's Alice-rewrite loosely inspired by Carroll's classic is shocking because of the innocence of the child protagonist through whose eyes all the bizarre adventures are seen. The film unconditionally adopts an infantile point of view that is ignorant of fear, prejudice and preconceptions resulting from socialization, and remains determined by a systematic non-differentiation between normal and abnormal, possible and impossible, rational and nonsensical. In little Jeliza-Rose's world, the most corrupted, taboo-transgressing deviations, pedophilia, necrophilia, or substance abuse ("silly-kissing" with a young retarded man, administering a heroine injection to one's parent, or snuggling daddy's corpse) can coexist unproblematically side by side with sugary-sweet childish fantasies (the antropomorphization of dolls, waiting for Prince Charming, or belonging to a loving nuclear family) as parts of the very same daydreams. Her fantasy rejects objective value judgments, embraces emotionally comforting, imaginatively inspiring subjective views, and turns hellish chaos into heavenly play by aiming to share fantasies with/of everyone, and to lovingly understand all against all odds. Without delimitations by final, conclusive meanings, she is ready to accept uncertainty, ambiguity, nonsense, or unknowing.

Gilliam stressed that for a full apprehension of the movie you should "try to forget everything you've learnt as an adult, the things that limit your view of the world … try to rediscover what it was like to be a child, with a sense of wonder and innocence, and don't forget to laugh." In his view, critics outraged by the "gruesome awfulness" of his movie never looked beyond the "ugly surface" of the story, and failed to realize that *Tideland* was meant to show "how wonderful the world is" if we dare to look at it "the way it really is." Wonderfulness is not so much an inherent quality of the world, but an outcome of the particularly sensible and resilient interpretive consciousness perceiving it. As Gilliam claimed in a 2003 interview with Salman Rushdie, the adoption of children's unbiased, imaginative worldview could enable all to explore the rich diversity of the harshest existence instead of sanitized, simulated, censored versions of reality mediated by television's lies we are trained, "hammered" to accept as truth.

According to this argument, the ideologically filtered, technologically manipulated reality communicated by mass media (from news broadcasts' computer generated visual reconstructions of US's Middle-East military maneuvers, from the Gulf War to the War in Afghanistan, to the false dreams of whiter teeth or thicker toilet paper propagated by advertisements) can be regarded as more fictionalized and less authentic, less truthful representations of our world than the self-consciously "magical realist" fiction of Gilliam's art movie which tries "to expand our worldview" by illuminating that the world is "not a naturalistic place," and more of a weird opera than a kitchen-sink drama (Gilliam in Rushdie 2003). Postmodern philosophy's crucial metaphor—popularized by the 1999 blockbuster Wachowski-movie *Matrix*—Baudrillard's *desert* of referentless (hyper)reality governed by an ideologically-, technologically-fabricated, systematically calculated copy superseding the original (to become a truth in its own right in a society of spectacle pervaded by all-invasive simulation) is contrasted here with the classic Carrollian leitmotif of Wonderland. This unpredictable and playful, *jungle*-like microcosm—including a garden of talking flowers, woods where things lose their names, and a seashore inhabited by mock-mythological creatures—symbolizes children's unrestrained imaginative potential to understand that "the world is a million possible things" (Gilliam in Rushdie 2003), way beyond just one communally authorized and authenticated version of reality.

It is small wonder that Gilliam identifies with the imaginative child character rebelling against consensual common sense reality, given that he has always been a filmmaker keen on challenging Hollywood mainstream cinema with mad fantasies which thematized a desire to escape through all means, and in particular through creative imagination's "smart, witty, or funny craziness," the "dumb brutish craziness" of our "awkwardly ordered society" (Matthews 1996, Gilliam 2006). *Tideland* itself can be seen as a sort of counter reaction or antidote to another—"visually and in spirit very different"—film Gilliam made in the same year, *The Brothers Grimm* that the director recalls, despite its box-office success, as a bitter experience due to the producers' unimaginative delimitation of his creative ideas.[2] The philosophical, cultural-political critical charge of Gilliam's anti- and meta-fantasies indubitably spans over his entire oeuvre, from *Brazil*'s (1985) impossible quest for a dream-woman amidst a buffoonishly depicted dystopian, totalitarian regime controlling dreams, to the melancholic yet obstinate belief in imagination's obsolete magical powers, providing self-fulfilling enlightenment, to win over gratifying ignorance in *The Imaginarium of Dr. Parnassus* (2009). As Keith James Hamel observes, Gilliam's movies provide Quijotean revisions of sociologist Max Weber's concept of the "iron cage" (or the "steel-hard shell") of modern rationality that traps citizens of Western capitalist societies in systems based purely on teleological efficiency, rational calculation, and bureaucratized state control, in "the polar night of icy darkness" fully deprived of imaginative agency (Weber xvi in Hamel 2004).

Gilliam finds pure hearted childish irrationality to be an adequate metaphor for his artistic liberties. But why does he opt for a cross-gender self-identification, by drawing his ideal fictional self-portrait in Jeliza-Rose, and why does he emphatically claim in his filmic foreword (Gilliam 2006) that the inner child he discovered within himself, at 64, throughout the making of *Tideland* turned out to be a little *girl*?

Gilliam's choice could be simply justified by the fact that Carroll's original dreamchild was a little girl too. By means of strategic anachronism, the 21st century director aims to avoid childhood's denigration by its modernist Freudian sexualization, through revindicating its worship in terms of romantic Wordsworthian sensibility, and embracing the typical, late 19th century, adult, middle-class, male artists' nostalgic attitude to mythified, idyllic girlhood, and an Alice figure whose natural and innocent, imaginative worldview is presumed to be radically separate from the corruption of adult life. Gilliam's explicit emphasis on the significance of childish imagination in his filmic *Alice* rewrite directs our attention to the meta-imaginative essence of Carroll's tales, where the dreamchild is always tackled in connection with the adult dreamer who calls her into being as a dreamer herself. Via a controversial subversion, the Romantic trope of innocent child as sentimentalized victim—highly influential ever since (see Steel 2012) as in the popular television trope "Too Good for this Evil World"– gets placed in a postmodernist metafictionally self-reflective frame whereby she is endowed with an imaginative agency that saves her innocence from victimization on the narrative level of the plotline. It is another question whether her turning into a symbolical embodiment, a materialized metaphor or a fictionalized self-portrait might stand for another form of authorial abuse…

The Dreamchild's Imagination:
Empathy, Therapy, Daydream

Contemporary audiences often interpret Alice's adventures in terms of a grotesque, desperate struggle against the fatal absurdity of existence, and as such an inadequate, psychologically troubling, confusing reading for children. Yet within her troubled fictional reality, *Tideland*'s Jeliza-Rose, a fan of the book, consoles herself by identifying with the protagonist of the Carrollian Wonderland's prefatory verse: a "*dreamchild* moving through a land/ of *wonders* wild and new/ In *friendly* chat with bird or beast" (7). She idealizes her terrible surroundings, turns boredom and anxiety into an adventure she finds comfort in, and befriends her monstrous acquaintances. As a result, this postmodern Alice is a perfect incarnation of Carroll's original character concept, the *dreamchild* described by her "foster-father" in "Alice on the Stage" (1887) as "loving as a dog," "gentle as a fawn," "courteous to all, high or low, grand or grotesque, King or Caterpillar, even as though she were herself a King's daughter," "wildly curious," "then trustful, *ready to accept the wildest impossibilities with all that utter trust that only dreamers know*" in this fatally cruel, hostile and dangerous world (Carroll 1887 in Kelly 225). The dreamchild's most important characteristic is her imagination described in terms of emotional interpersonal relations, and more specifically the trust with which she—like all dreamers—relates to the world. The original, fairy-tale-like microfantasy spheres turn more realistic and gruesome, but not less imaginative in Gilliam's filmic adaptation, as Jeliza-Rose, with an open-hearted attentiveness, strives to understand fellow fantasists: neighbor Dell's taxidermist attempts to freeze-frame passing time, mentally challenged Dickens' fight against the train he believes to be a monster-shark (a fantasmatic equivalent of the Jabberwock), and her drugged, delirious daddy's "special vacations" to the Jutland Bog-men. Via a challenging *mise-en-abyme*, audiences are invited to imagine the Alice-character imagining others' imaginings, during her dreaming, day-dreaming, enacting pretense play, and considering differing views of multiple perspectives of a kaleidoscopic, fictionalizable consensus-reality.

The *Looking-Glass* episode of the encounter with the Fawn from "the wood where things have no name"—that represents in Carroll's original an edenic site of prelapsarian direct communication and unbiased relationality with ephemeral satiety—gets a paradigmatically disturbing tint in Cullin's *Tideland* by illustrating how trusting fantasizing seems an impossible, quasi-heroic gambit in a world governed by mistrust and cruelty. The abandoned, feral-child-like Jeliza-Rose is peeing naked outside the farmhouse in the grass, when she spots a doe and begins briefly fantasizing about their becoming friends, running races and sleeping together. Then she notices that the doe has a broken leg, so likely already knows pain and fear, and is doomed to leave her alone. Although, the contact of the girl and the fawn is extremely fragile, non-verbal, not even tactile, involving only a quick meeting of glances, a momentary perception of each other's presence, still it is clear that Jeliza-Rose considers relating trustfully and loving to the fellow wild being. Her fancy of their shared intimacy originates not so much from the little experience of human care she had in her life before, but more of her imaginative affinity, and her tendency to familiarize herself with her surroundings, no matter how dangerous or curious they are. (Animal lure prevails in the Gilliam adaptation's tagline: "The squirrels made it seem less lonely.")

However, Jeliza-Rose's satiety is not akin to a Rousseaudian innocent ignorance but springs from a daring imaginativeness reinterpreting potential sources of anxieties as adventures. Hers is not a creative "willing suspension of disbelief," but more of an automatic activation of a spontaneous credulous acceptance of all things strange. Hers is an "imagination against all odds" that proves to be a saving grace of humanity cast in a fundamentally hostile environment. Those uncorrupted by socialization excel in this innate feat of crisis-management: as Gilliam (2007) puts it, "children are resilient, when you drop them, they bounce."

Like for Alice,[3] sin and sorrow remain oddly meaningless concepts for Jeliza-Rose because they belong to her everydays, and constitute an inherent part of the milieu she considers familiar, reassuring, homey. She is much like the child in Freud's essay on the *uncanny* for whom the life-like puppet she personifies as the animated inanimate—a par excellence antagonist of any adult horror production—seems comforting because she ignores the socially set boundaries between being and non-being, animation and stasis, identity and otherness, sanity and madness, dream and reality, etc. (categorical distinctions socialized grown-ups believe the puppet coming to life violates). Jeliza-Rose is a provocative figure because for her the Freudian *unheimlich* (1919) or the Kristevian *abject* (1982)— denoting troubling psychic contents, related to primary fears and desires concerning our vulnerable corporeality, which should have remained hidden, repressed in the unconscious, but still come to light, surface to consciousness—are meaningless, nonsensical categories. Deprived of the bar of repression, every thing (every state of being—amidst the marvelous multiplicity and diversity of being[s]) has an equal right to gain and preserve a visible, remarkable existence. Their homeliness is just a matter of perspective, hence no reason for fear. Gilliam's *Alice* adaptation introduces us to the uncanny space of a child's mind that is paradoxically unable to make sense of uncanniness. As Steel points out, adult minds are frustrated by the feeling of helplessness provoked by the intellectual uncertainty about the living/dead in-between status of animated puppets. For mature spectators, the doll-heads Jeliza-Rose impersonates calls forth the idea of the double as a harbinger of our mortality, yet for the little girl their uncanniness is a source of comfort, apt to ease the loneliness of a bright mind seeking company in the *other* always already lurking within the self-same (Steel 37).

From a child's perspective, most of the world is characterized by a relative strangeness and unfamiliarity, because of the scarce empirical evidence the child has gathered by means of relational points of reference that could explain the constituents and complex rules of being. Difficulties arise in distinguishing between possible and impossible, such as the existence of a rhinoceros and a unicorn: since one has not ever encountered either of them, both seem equally feasible and wondrous. Similarly, since Jeliza-Rose has no prior experience and presupposition of a non-dysfunctional family—and no belonging with a community setting the norm for such thing—any invention of hers might pass as a family. Thus, in a way, even the impossible becomes possible. Accordingly, the meal they have after cleansing the house together is a mock-ritualistic occasion (accompanied by Gospel music!) that both festively celebrates the founding of a nuclear family and provides the parody of this convention of domestic bliss. Demented Dell as "stern matriarch," the father's corpse as "paternal hierarchy propped at the head of the table" (Steel 32) and orphaned Jeliza-Rose with disabled Dickens as their subservient children are incongruent elements constituting a faulty whole. When this make-believe family nevertheless appears in the little girl's daydreams as a valid variant of the "they lived happily ever after" narrative scenario,—a cliché conventionally identified with a life-story's normatively idealized accomplishment— one cannot help noticing the ideology-criticism concerning the socially prescribed nature of fantasies.[4]

Mike Watts notices in the little girl's quickly passing, flaring emotions the affective economy of soap opera melodramas that Jeliza-Rose seems to self-consciously toy with: in one paradigmatic scene of Gilliam's film she accidentally bites her lips during a fancy-dress pretense play, and at the site of her own blood drops she pathetically and histrionically flings herself back in a faked swoon exclaiming "I'm Dying! Oh no! I can't go on, I must go on!" while gazing at herself in mirror and all of a sudden ventriloquizing a doctor's voice "You'll survive" to respond straight away in her own voice "Thank you doctor. You have given me hope." Clearly, her ability to survive is sustained by the therapeutic potential of her fantasy, her capacity to imaginatively reinvent catastrophes and cures, constantly displacing pain and danger into the realm of fictionality where it will keep lurking but without provoking fear on her part. Gilliam might have had this in mind when he called Jeliza-Rose "the real predator here" (in Watt 212). Not only does she control and manipulate reality through pretense play but she also metafictionally preys on spectators' expectations of normality shockingly subverting them by imaginatively turning horror film tropes (disfigured neighbor lady, haunted house, decaying mummified corpse) into Grand Guignol (Steel 32) in fervid "pictures of vision, verve, and no self-restraint" (Watt 211).[5]

No matter how extremely the *madness* (dis)organizing Wonderland defies common sense, it is never identical with rage, but serves as a practical way of escaping in the face of an incomprehensible environment. Despite fleeting moments of anger and sorrow, the Alice character never allows herself to be engulfed by total despair; minor irritations quickly distract her from major tragedies. For Jeliza-Rose, running out of peanut butter seems a more vital problem than mourning her deceased daddy, just like Alice seems more preoccupied with the contents of the shelves—holding jam jars!—down the rabbit hole than the possibly fatal consequences of her fall.

Jeliza-Rose's wondrous speech acts recall *sleep-talking* in a delusional dream, without waiting for a response, without willing to transmit an ultimate message, just enacting imaginary personas to sublimate daytime frustrations. As Bennett observes, in connection with Gilliam's movie, the girl child's mumbling to herself in an infinite monologue voices a "kid-stream-of-consciousness" (2006).[6] Jeliza-Rose's strange self-fictionalizing soliloquies also recall the infantile *crib-talk*'s proto-narrative. The child creates a malleable fictionalized reality that fuses actual past and imaginary events, future (mock)realities and present parallel possibilities, stories recited and invented, pseudo-interactions with make-believe characters via an uncontrolled language-use brought into action for the sake of easing daytime anxieties and understanding the world, as well as compensating, correcting it. Given that it is Alice's dream, she possibly functions as a somniloquist narrator-focalizer who voices all fictional figures to become an implied author herself responsible for shaping her own story.

Despite the risk of miscommunication and miscomprehension haunting her journey, the Alice character's *talking to herself* out loud can be considered a form of nonsensical verbal self-pleasuring. Her solitary speech acts, not addressed to others, disregard normativized communicative purposes and interactive value, do not aim at negotiating for the message's communal consensual meaningfulness, and remain completely liberated from codes of conversational politeness, and in particular the submissiveness and silence demanded from minors in customary social interactions. Talking to oneself constitutes a narcissistic verbal-vocal self-contemplation in one's own looking-glass, where playing with the voice enacts and resolves potential threats to or facets of the child's malleable identity, exploiting the self-affirmative potential of imagination. Jeliza-Rose's imaginary friends, the four dismembered Barbie doll-heads, she wears on her fingertips and impersonates in distinctively ventriloquized voices, represent different aspects of her psyche: Sateen Lips is fearful and timid, the ugly Glitter Gal is kindhearted and desperately lonely, Mustique is beautiful, curious, courageous, aggressive, and enacts the voice of the dead bad mother before she/it disappears, dropped down a rabbit-hole, by means of a (self)punishment perhaps.

Both the ventriloquization and the silencing of doll-heads can be diagnosed as compensatory "speechless acts" characteristic of "unheard" neglected children deprived of possibilities of verbalization and attentive listening, consequently hindered in the discursive constitution of their self-identity and in the resulting self-reflective understanding of their reality. Moreover, Jeliza-Rose's illogical infantile claim "If no one can hear me, I must have become invisible." attests her discursive failure's necessary coincidence with an assumed exclusion from the sphere of visibility, acknowledgment, and empowerment. With a twist on the maxim "Seeing is believing," remaining unheard and unseen entails disbelief, disregard, a quasi non-existence extratextually reflected by the spectators' imaginative reluctance to believe what they see as the fictional girl's reality.

Still her solitary polyphonic voice-change allows Jeliza-Rose to reimagine her identity as a playground where contradictory components of her fundamentally flexible self may come to pass in (day)dreams of her own making. In Cullin's poetic novel the little girl's first person voice ponders about her fleeting fancies being proofs of her existence elsewhere:

> I never heard the breath leave my body. Before sleep, the last sound to fill my ears was the beating of my heart, and I knew I was slipping past the tideland, going beneath the ocean and sinking away from What Rocks. The afternoon light had faded above; maybe the waves had curled high enough to extinguish the sun. And in that far-flung region of my imagination, I tried understanding the exact circumstances that brought me to Texas instead of Denmark, but nothing presented itself. I knew only that I'd been on my own since that first night in the back country, and that I'd fled Los Angeles after my mother turned blue. Then I saw myself swimming through a vast underwater wilderness, going deeper and deeper, like a penny tossed into the Hundred Year Ocean—or Alice falling very slowly in the rabbit-hole, looking about, wondering what was going to happen next [139].

Much in line with the postmodern obsession with uncertainty, the monologue[7] focuses not even on dreaming itself, but upon the very last, transitional, seemingly suspended moment before falling asleep (— that also emblematizes the mythified final moment before the 'eternal sleep' of death, before the awakening to a different mode of existence). This last moment before falling asleep is like Alice's fall, apparently never coming to an end or a beginning, hovering in-between wakefulness and sleep, remembering and forgetting, perception and cognition and fantastification, condensing past, present and potential, parallel realities. The experience of this moment is valid to the integrity of *Tide/Wonder-land*'s lucid-dreamlike universe, where the (day)dreaming Jeliza-Rose/Alice experiences an awareness of a multiplicity of simultaneous fantasies, coexisting alternative reality-versions as possibilities awaiting to be brought to actual realization, and transforming, shifting into each other, as the sleeper re-imagines them floating in-between.

Carroll shared the Victorian fascination with psychic states combining extreme mental excitement and quiescence (reverie, meditation) which could presumably reveal for the "inner eye" of imagination, often to the seemingly sleeping subject, things physically unavailable to sensory perception. He was particularly ravished by theories about mind-voyaging in altered states of consciousness, especially the "trance-like" (following the "ordinary" and the "eerie" states), whereby, unconscious of actuality, apparently asleep, one could leave behind earthly toils and "migrate into fairyland" (Warner 2006, 205–220). This interest in self-reflexive dream states—in which you watch yourself live through certain adventures, without the least suspicion of unreality, and then have the time over again to live it in a different, but equally life-like way (Warner 207)—was thematized by the Alice tales and has been found problematic by a significant number of waking-life audience members. The inconsistencies, incompleteness, and incertitudes characterizing these dream states are most often judged to be irritating. In fact, it is surprising to see—among a plethora of favorable criticism—the similarity between Victorian and postmodern critics' condemnatory reactions. The lament of Carroll's 19th century contemporary in *Atheneum* journal claims: "This is a dream story; but who can, in cold blood, manufacture a dream, with all its loops and ties, and loose threads, and entanglements, and inconsistencies, and passages which lead to Nothing at the end of which Sleep's most diligent pilgrim never arrives? Any real child more puzzled than enchanted by this story" (in Kelly 12). In a similar vein, today's film-reviewers assess Gilliam's Carroll revision as a "morbid mindbender," a "kinky cross" of *Psycho, Alice in Wonderland* (blackfilmwww, 2006) and William Burroughs (*Philadelphia Review*, 2005), "uncomfortable to watch," a "Frankenstein-like dream sequence" (Rottentomatoeswww 2006), a "fever dream" of "Alice in Nightmareland" (*Fipresci.com*, 2005) allowing an "entry at your own risk" to a "extremely unpleasant," "hallucinatory," "diseased Lewis Carroll universe" (*Chicago Reader*, 2006), "mostly an endless, pointless drone with characters like bacteria and dialogue like an untuned radio" (New York Post, 2006). In the last part of this chapter I wish to examine reasons of this atemporal dissatisfaction permeating the reception of the *Alice* tales and their adaptations by asking how and why can meta-imagination entail a certain sense of incredulity, an unwillingness to imagine somebody's willingness to imagine something in, or, in this case, a downright refusal to believe in Alice's make-believing Wonderland.

Adult's Imaginative Reluctance

In *Tideland* imagination and incredulity, enchantment and disillusion fluctuate like ebb and tide, dream and awakening, periodically exchanging each other. With the metaphorical tide, the infantile imagination of innocent Jeliza-Rose, eerily intertwined with mentally disabled Dickens' delusions, define the rule of the day. During their childish games, the high Johnson grass becomes the Hundred Year Ocean where they swim hand-in-hand with hair floating on waves or in a diving outfit including goggles and flappers; an overturned deserted school-bus by the railways transforms into a submarine; trains turn into giant killer-sharks to be ruthlessly hunted down; and houses can sink in sorrow. When the ebb of momentary rationalistic recognition comes, Jeliza-Rose meekly admits to herself about Dickens that "he isn't really a captain, or a prisoner or anything" (Gilliam), and that "It's not just a dream, [and] You're pretty stupid if you can't see that" (Cullin 116) while the spectator/reader comes to the shocking realization that it was probably the imbecile young man who accidentally drove the school-bus in front of the train. In the film's literally explosive finale, Dickens, playing sea-captain, blows up with his secret dynamite the nightly passenger train mistaken for a monster-shark. Just like in a false awakening, the reality that invades the fantasies with a blast bears definitely nightmarish qualities, freeze-framing the tragedy within the hallucinatory image of a dream-rose.[8]

Strangely, this final horrifying scene, with the inarticulately screaming injured scattered around the wreck in the pitch-dark prairie illuminated by flames, seems to offer Jeliza-Rose her happy ending. A kind lady comes to her rescue, believing her to be a victim from the train-accident too, and in her long-desired maternal embrace, the little-girl-lost is finally found, comforted by the tangerines she is fed and is addressed the question we have been desiring to ask throughout the entire movie: "are you OK?" Instead of answering, however, Jeliza-Rose ponders out loud, calling the fireflies dancing in the flames her friends who "have names." Thus, she appears to symbolically abandon the a-semiotic space of the fantastic Carrollian "woods where things have no names," no reality-status, and no enworlded self-identity, so that she can finally reach for a unanimously nameable, solidly conceivable consensus-reality. However, the final shots' cinematic focus suggests otherwise: the close-up of Jeliza-Rose's eyes (dis)appearing in the starry sky, while watching us watching, foregrounds meta-narratively the instability and relativity of our spectatorial interpretive positionalities, simultaneously located within real and fictional realms; re/creating fantasies from within a lived reality marked by a radical unknowability, and fraught with imagination that fictionalizes us in each other's dreams. In the end, the postmodern Alice's gaze fading into the night sky embodies a nonsensical, magical realist view-point required to be enacted for the entry into Wonderland: we must close our eyes, otherwise we will not see anything.

Gilliam associates the difficult catharsis *Tideland* holds with the experience of the "purgatory" (Gilliam 2005, DVD extras), a transitional place—largely the creation of Medieval Christian imagination—where those who die in a state of grace are believed to be prepared for an entry into the sublime sphere of the final salvation. The purgatory, as a temporary locus between Heaven and Hell, conjoining purification and punishment, hope and suffering, adequately symbolizes a series of 'suspended animation states': (1) Gilliam's mid-way between the ideologically influenced Hollywood dream-industry and the more revolutionary liberal (l'art-pour-l')art cinema; (2) the Alice figure's never-coming-of-age counter-narrative balancing between innocent child- and experienced adult-hood; (3) a rationalizing interpretive attempt to make sense of illogical infantile fantasy; (4) the half-dream between unconscious sleep and self-reflective awakening; (5) the Carrollian rub of knowing the world is evil and loving it just so. The audience's automatic reaction to *Tideland*, a common sense rationalization in terms of culturally ready-made, exclusionary stereotypes, is regarded as a forgivable sin that can be redeemed for anyone ready to open up to the film's revelative, alternative worldview defined by the focalizer little girl's childish wonder.[9]

The identification of infantile imaginativeness with a trusting relationality to others also has an exciting spiritual, religious connotation within the context of a Victorian literary trend. Locating *Tideland* in this tradition, as a retro-Victorian meta-narrative, might facilitate the comprehension of the oeuvre for contemporary audiences revolted by Gilliam's and Cullin's apparently twisted distortion of ideas of divine benevolence and Christian kindness. Late 19th century novels are characterized by a predilection for the metaphorical transformation of child character into a potential Christ figure whose sacrifice is an inevitable outcome of a prototypical narrative plotline that sentimentally aestheticizes the poor innocents' suffering for the sake of soul-cleansing artistic delights. The Dickensian fixation with the pure orphan child dying a premature death certainly can be regarded as a means to compensate for the adult sorrow felt over the ephemeral, fleeting nature of childhood innocence: the fictionally freeze-framed archetypal *puer aeternus* figure never grows old, and keeps her childish immaculacy in our memories forever.[10]

However, the fictional child martyr can even gain relative empowerment and autonomy upon enacting the stock character of an *orphan ingénue*, free from parental control, capable to fend for oneself, possibly develop a moral character, rise out of misery, or seek a surrogate family, but also ready to become a parent of her/himself, bravely facing an apparently heartless wide world all alone. Alice's struggle to keep her sense of self in unnerving dreamscapes without parental protection or guidance certainly approaches her to the *orphan ingénue*, as Kelly opines (13). Yet Auerbach is also right on arguing that Alice lacks any real character development because of her personality's oddly static quality that results from her unchanging innocence, a typical attribute of the Victorian pure, puerile, poor girl stereotype. The notion of solitary, static struggle (often without real opponents besides herself) finely encapsulates the paradoxical nature of Alice's adventures.

Of course the political message might not be that easy to grasp in a genre still designated as "poor girls' fiction" by means of a generic label that features on the title page of Cullin's novel, attesting his homage to the literary tradition built on sentiments highly troubling by contemporary standards. Cullin's choice of the name Dickens for his mentally deranged character, who is somehow both an involuntary perpetrator and victim of pedophilia, is a twisted form of cultural tribute cum critical commentary on the all pervasive, possibly perverse preoccupation with children within the literary legacy of actual novelist Charles Dickens.

Moreover, *Tideland*'s predominantly socio-realist framing of the abused, disadvantaged child archetype—apart from a brief dream sequence in the movie, and a few obviously poetic (metaphorical) passages in the novel—is complemented by a total detachment from framing value judgments that could act as signposts calming our need for normalcy. These destabilize the spectators' ravishment by the Alice figure's unlimited imaginative capacities, and tarnish the illusorily safe, self-enclosed, fictitious sphere of the intertextually summoned fairy-tale fantasy make-believe. Consequently—as several negative reviews attest—infantile imaginativeness is more likely to be devalued in rationalistic, (pseudo)scientific terms, as a pathological compensation resulting from the inability to deal with psychologically traumatizing experience. The empathic identification with others' feelings, thoughts, and fantasies is interpreted as a schizoid, psychotic thought-disturbance, involving a loss of contact with reality. Hence, the Wonderlandish slogan "we are all mad here" comes to imply a nihilistic existential crisis, a collective fury of disordered, delusionary minds prevented from living a sane and safe, 'normal' life. The originally playful literary nonsense becomes traumatic and tragic when turned real on the level of lived experience. Forgetful of the fairy-tale fantasy source-/inter-text (rendered explicit by the allusions to *Alice*) the first automatic audience-response to *Tideland* is likely predominated by the gut-reaction of horror instead of the appreciation of the work's poetic qualities. And even if one manages to surpass a referential reading, and equally consider both constituents of the mixed-genre "fantasy thriller," recognizing mimetic and metaphorical representational layers alike, the artistic experience remains highly ambiguous.

It is as if we felt the possibility of human happiness amidst utter destruction and desolation inappropriate. Witnessing the deserted Jeliza-Rose's heartfelt smile is just as perplexing as reading in survivor testimonies about the fleeting joys Holocaust victims had in the inhuman hell of the Nazi concentration camps. We experience a clash between the 'matter of fact,' realistic, detached depiction of tragedies and the 'matter of fantasy' (even a 'matter of survival') transformation of them into a more livable sur-reality to avoid psychic breakdown. This conflict is all the more disturbing given that the suffering-surviving narrator focalizer, in her first-hand account, seems to be fully aware of the duality between insupportable reality and therapeutic fantastification. Just like the World War II extermination camp inmates told each other imaginary recipes of marvelous meals to soothe their hunger while precisely knowing that they are in the terminal stages of starving to death (see Vasvary), Jeliza-Rose's make-believe adventures in her Tide/Wonderland are punctuated by momentary recognitions—encapsulated in her equally valid tentative assertions: "this is just a dream," "this isn't just a dream"—concerning the dangerous material stakes of her lived reality and the potentially traumatizing physical consequences of her share of collective fantasizings. As she says, "I tried sending psychic messages to [the doll-head] Classique—wake up now, wake up, I'm in trouble—but she was dreaming of Eskimo Pies. I was on my own. And my father relaxed in Denmark. He wouldn't help even if my mother was choking me, even if she was ripping my head off. So I waited" (Cullin 58).

Foregrounding the elaborate self-reflective (meta)imaginative agency, *Tideland* reveals the haunting similarity between young children's pretense play and the compulsive fantasies trauma patients enact by means of cognitive self-defense. In a bizarre world taken for granted, the frustratingly incalculable course of events can be changed by nothing but fantasizing. The most nonsensical daydreams provide a certain sense of safety and mastery over a reality turned palimpsestic (both fictitious and real). In Jeliza-Rose's world, lived, literalized *nonsense-as-tragedy* refers to ultimately inconceivable, insupportable personal or social traumas. The death of her father, the loss of reason, the evilness of her mother, the social marginalization, and extreme poverty she must experience, all belong to the realm of incomprehensible. As such they can only gain meaning via mythologizing interpretations of a protective fictionalization whereby traumatic reality is imaginatively transfunctionalized into a soothing sur-reality governed by *nonsense-as-fantasy*.

Psychoanalytically inspired, postmodern philosopher Slavoj Žižek—in his cultural critique of eye-witnesses comparing the 9/11 WTC terror attacks to their earlier fantasmatic-cinematic experience of catastrophe movies—uses a Lacanian terminology to describe the traumatic kernel as the repressed and returning "Real." The object of anxiety *par excellence*, the Real exceeds symbolization: faced with it all words cease and all categories fail. It eludes the integration into (what we experience as) reality. (Re)embodied as the Unimaginable Impossible itself, It can be sustained only fictionalized, as a "nightmarish apparition," an "unreal spectre," a "spectacular semblance," a "reality transfunctionalized through fantasy" (Žižek 18–20). I believe that it is much in line with these Žižekian assumptions, that the political parodies of *Alice* published during both World Wars found the nonsensical emptying of meanings to be an appropriate expression of their chaotic era's cultural traumas, as exemplified by *Adolf in Blunderland*'s rewriting of the Jabberwocky: "Twas danzig and the swastikoves/ Did heil and hittle in the reich. All nazi were the linden groves, / And the neu-raths julestreich" (Booker 78). Furthermore, Žižek provides another example for the odd human capacity to present truth/reality as false/fantasy (in a way that goes beyond the simple animalistic survival-instinct to present what is false as true, like in mimicry). He analyzes Roberto Benigni's film *Life Is Beautiful* in which an Italian Jewish father strategically tries to shield his little son from the atrocities of Auschwitz by creating a "maternally protective web of fantasies," pretending that whatever goes on in the camp is just part of a competitive game where the winner "gets to see an American tank" in the end. In both cases—9/11 and World War II—fantasy's Janus-faced nature is revealed: it is simultaneously pacifying through an imaginary scenario enabling us to endure an abysmal loss constitutive of our subjectivity, yet disturbs through its being inassimilable to reality.

The ambiguity of *Tideland*'s Alice figure neatly surfaces if we compare her with Žižek's examples. Her perception of reality in a fictional mode is neither fully an effect of compulsive psychic automatism (as in the case of the terrified passersby near the Twin Towers' blast) nor fully a conscious strategy to shield others (as in the case of Benigni's father figure who fictionally fights back the Holocaust to spare his son), but rather a combination of both relationalities to the Unimaginable. Moreover, her protective fantasizing pretense play serves as a solitary ludic means of maternally taking care of herself, and thus perplexes spectators by fusing infantile and pathological modes of make-believing. Yet again we witness an exciting postmodern revival of a Victorian idea surfacing in the complex understanding of the child as a "naïve innocent, living in a world of wonder and mythological fancy," and an anxious, "animalistic product of a savage past" haunted by her pre-history (Shuttleworth 2010).

The simultaneous presence of the inconsistent experiences of trauma-as-tragedy and trauma-as-fantasy—in other words, the discrepancy between the social realistic and the fairy-tale fantastic rendering of 'poor girls fiction'—can be mapped out on the level of clashing but conjoint referential/mimetic/literal vs. metaphorical meanings. These provoke a cognitive and emotive dissonance that is acted out within the realm of the human body. In *Tideland*, the trope of imagination is indeed the literalized, materialized metaphor invested with corporeal stakes. A "somatized semiosis" (see Brooks 1993) takes place as our gut-reaction of recoiling with repugnance at the sight of the abject materiality is coupled with the sophisticated deciphering of visual puns. I will just mention a few examples for this phenomenon.

First, the hungry Jeliza-Rose's peanut buttered palm covered with crawling ants recalls the famous shot from Buñuel and Dalí's legendary surrealist movie *An Andalusian Dog* (1929) literally visualizing at once two metaphorical expressions. Firstly, the French phrase "to have ants in the palms" means "itching to kill," a symptomatic surfacing of frustrations; secondly the experience of having ants under the skin refers to "a feeling of a hand going to sleep," and thus becomes the very metonymy of surrealistic automatic writing beyond calculation, logic, politeness or plotting. Both denote repressed corporeal presence's troubling return to representation.

My second example is Gilliam's homage to Andrew Wyeth's famous 1948 painting *Christina's World* depicting a paralyzed young woman lying on the ground in a wheat-field, crawling towards a farmhouse in the distance. The Wyethian landscape, Tideland uncannily recalls, is frequently interpreted as a topographical sublimation of "physical grandeur, psychic pain," spiritual solitude, a dwelling of "the eloquence in things left unsaid, the static electricity of gestures repressed" (Corliss 48). This transitional state in-between immobility (physical entrapment by an anatomical frame) and metamorphosis (the dynamically changing thoughts, drives, desires moving) evokes the very experience of *almost-there-ness* that characterizes Alice's suspended fall and endless Wonder/Tide-landian wanderings. Moreover, what is visualized here is the hypnagogic state's sleep-paralysis when on the brink of sleep one distortedly misperceives the body as fatally immobile and unmovable, constituting a counterpoint to the lucid dream's hallucinative mental hyperactivity flux. We are heading towards transdiscursive realms of pre/half-dream conditions, when, in the moments before falling asleep or awakening, already or yet unable to open our eyes to reality, the unspoken hovers on the tip of the tongue.

Thirdly, the abandoned old farm-house, Jeliza-Rose dwells at, takes the shape of a decomposing body, re-embodied in Gilliam's imagination "decaying and rotting inside (as a) smoker's lung." The house is in a strange organic relation with the barren landscape outside, so that Jeliza-Rose's "getting out of that house, and running and playing and leaping and then getting back inside" is like breathing in and out heavily all the time (Gilliam 2005), endowing the narrative with a corporeal rhythm. Moreover, the house is a hauntingly maternal space: as in a fairy tale, it belonged to the late grandmother, emerging in Dickens' fragmented reminiscences as a witch-like figure, who used to be "silly-kissing" with the mentally disabled boy and was crushed to death when pushed down the stairs by him. This ominous atmosphere is augmented by the director's way of presenting the farmhouse by using the trademark low-angle, distanced camera shot familiar from another maternally haunted place, the iconic Bates Motel from Hitchcock's horror *Psycho* (1960). In a wickedly infantile Russian-doll structure, the farm-house serves as a crypt of the taxidermied paternal corpse that becomes, on its turn, a burial ground for the dismembered dolls the daughter hides inside his belly during his anatomical preparation. The doll-heads, enacting the daughter's doubles, clearly literalize-visualize metaphorical expressions of identity crisis, such as losing one's mind, "not having hearts only heads" (as Jeliza-Rose scornfully says), and even the Carrollian Red Queen's famous line, "Off with her head!"

Carroll's original *Alice* tales are often interpreted in terms of a witty allegorical critique of the prevailing social system's unequal distribution of power that affects a variety of hierarchically organized relationalities. Unequal ties between monarch and subject, bourgeois and laborer, conformist and revolutionary, teacher and pupil, adult and child, male artist and female muse, historian and fantasist, logician and illusionist, etc., determine, as Humpty Dumpty recognizes, who is "to be master over meanings," who is to control validated interpretations of reality. *Tideland* functions as a postmodern meta-narrative in so far as it adequately reveals what happens when the extended metaphor's symbolism is decoded literalized and limited by a (socio)realistic representational frame into one single referentially readable denotation. With the undoing of the clandestine critical subtext (subversive because presumably unintelligible for the monomaniac authority bounded by a restricted meaning codified as truth), the rebellious playfulness of poetic ambiguity is eradicated, and only disillusioning sorrow remains behind. After all an extremely literalized Wonderland with real drug addiction (in place of the fabulous, smoking caterpillar), real maternal violence (in place of a harmlessly ferocious Red Queen), and real insanity (instead of a comically Mad Hatter) is not so much fun anymore.

The metanarrative implications, the minimization of fantasy elements, the unreliability of the junkie-baby narrator-focalizer, her failure to make discrete binary oppositions necessary for well-being, the unjust miseries she pleasantly undergoes, and the ambiguous filmic conclusion that does not resolve the tension sustained throughout the narrative all fail to comply with criteria of "affective meaningfulness" (Egan 6). *Tideland* induces emotional engagement by inviting us to imagine "what it would be like to live like Jeliza-Rose," but we do not know how to feel, and how to feel about feeling so, because of the lack of moral signposts (as the clear distinction between good/right vs. bad/wrong or a terminal conflict-resolution by reward/sympathy and punishment/condemnation) provoke in the spectator a psychological discomfort and a resulting so-called "imaginative resistance." This unwilling response is theoretized by Walton and Szabó Gendler (in Nichols 2006, 137–175) who claim that imagination is an ethically restrained faculty. Socially normativized, cultured recipients are likely reluctant to be immersed in any fictional realm that leaves dubiously unpunished or even justifies violations of trans-culturally sustained, fundamental human values and moral laws deemed worthy of unanimous respect in life and art alike. *Tideland*'s thematization of ultimate taboo topics such as the neglect and endangerment of a minor, substance abuse assisted by a child, necrophilia, pedophilia, molestation of/by a mentally impaired person, or a terrorist attack against public transportation certainly qualify, conforming to these standards, as immoral acts. Terrified by their real-life stakes and consequences, we are reluctant to accept these deviant acts as fictional—as if even their fictionalization, metaphorization would entail their justification—and rather perform a compulsively referential and compensatorily moralizing reading. This referential, over-literalizing interpretation functions on a meta-narrative plane too: we take the invitation to *imagine* a claim as true in a story-world (e.g., Jeliza-Rose is happy) simultaneously as an invitation to *believe* some corresponding claim about the actual world (e.g., child-abuse is unproblematic). It results in what Szabó Gendler calls the "problem of imaginative impropriety." The story's unfortunate chain of events leading to the abuse and abandonment of a little girl, who insists on her being happy amidst the chaos and destruction overwhelming her, is regarded by most spectators/readers to be so terrible that the "possible world" circumscribed in the diegesis is identified as fatally nonsensical, impossible, and unthinkable. It is as if the imaginative involvement in a fantasy sphere implied a complicitness and responsibility over its phenomena and logic on the part of readers and spectators too (and not only the author calling the given fictional reality into being). We feel that it is somehow not right to engage in certain (immoral) imaginings, which also activate certain (immoral) "behavioral dispositions and affective propensities" (Szabó Gendler 150).

Szabó Gendler differentiates between conceptually impossible, factual inaccuracies which, nevertheless, can be imagined and morally dubious, evaluative inaccuracies (where the judgment of manners and the sentiments of approbation contradict our standard normativized spectrum of what is desirable and undesirable) which could, but *won't* be imagined.[11] Accordingly, while artists can freely direct our imagination to contemplate the strangest scenarios as fictionally true—talking animals, animate playing cards, travel through time or between fantasy-scapes, alchemy domesticated as good science, shape-shifting, etc., nothing is impossible—but they have much less freedom in manipulating our normativized moral assessments. It is difficult to conceive a fictional reality where murder or pain afflicted on the innocent is judged as a praiseworthy, noble, charming, or admirable act. Our imaginative barriers are immediately activated on being faced with what we could call *ethical nonsense*.

I contend that *Tideland*'s postmodern *Alice* adaptation attests that—if we wish to gain a comprehensive understanding of how 'Alice-as-the-implied-reader' makes sense of her impossible surroundings—*ethical nonsense* is a term worth to be considered to complement the categories *tolerable, ordinary nonsense* and *intolerable, logical nonsense* introduced by George A. Dunn and Brian McDonald in *Alice in Wonderland and Philosophy* (2010).

In their view, *ordinary nonsense* is imaginable and tolerable because it involves twisted laws of nature which surprise us but can be mastered with a little trial and error, once we are ready to discard our earlier preconceptions based on empirical evidence gained from our own world, and accept these unexpected nonsense phenomena as part and parcel of a fictional reality of an alternate universe, practically inexistent in our world, but logically possible elsewhere, underground or on the other side of the looking-glass. Therefore, you only have to walk backwards to reach your end; if you eat one side of the mushroom you will shrink, the other side, you will grow; once you address animals politely they will likely answer. These are the types of nonsensical impossibilities Alice, as the cooperative implied reader, acquires knowledgeable skills at, experiments with, and eventually, once familiarized with their differential rules of functioning, learns to enjoy, too.

Yet on the other hand, as Dunn and McDonald opine, Carrollian Wonderlands also feature *logical impossibilities* mostly on the level of relations of abstract ideas—and not the matters of (fictional) facts—which prove to be intolerable because they impose insurmountable obstacles to our imaginative agency, they fundamentally and inherently contradict our operation of thought. This type of nonsense is not just about a fantastic change in our phenomenological experience due to changeable but graspable, and logically feasible modified wondrous conditions, but implies mental impossibilities. We cannot imagine *any* alternate universe in which 2 + 2 would not equal 4, in which a married bachelor or a square circle could exist, or the meaning and truth-value of a word could be uniquely defined at the speaker's whim, with total disrespect of the surrounding world's reality. Although this type of incredible logical impossibility certainly overabounds in Wonderland, we must also note that it mostly occurs not on the level of actual (fictional) phenomena, but on the level of ideas Alice is invited to entertain without being forced to accept. She ponders about falling without ever reaching the ground, considers having more tea when she had none, and is puzzled by the possibility of individual mastery over consensual language.

The genuine incredibility and madness of Gilliam's *Tideland* originates from the audience's meta-imaginative reluctance. Spectators find it thoroughly uncomfortable to fantasize about an unjust fictional reality where an innocent little girl must suffer. Nevertheless, it is even more uncomfortable to identify with the Alice figure's fictitious worldview since her cheerful, trusting, and empathic attitude seems an inappropriate, unfit reaction to the dark reality she should suffer from conforming to our normative, rationalistic moral standards. At the death of her mother—an event regarded in our cultural imagination to be the most traumatic experience, the unspeakable impossible brought real—Jeliza-Rose is rejoicing over the chance to eat up all of her greedy junkie mommy's hidden candies and chocolate bars and consoles her father with the promise of the pair of them finally getting to travel to daddy's drug-dream realm, a spooky make-believe version of Scandinavian Jutland. Spectators' emotional unease, cognitive dissonance, and general stupefaction come from the inability to share Jeliza-Rose's simple joys, and the reluctance to empathize with a fundamentally empathic fictional figure. Even Jeliza-Rose's characteristic shy little giggle sounds more provocative than pleasurable since it accompanies extremely bizarre activities like when she curiously listens to her stomach-growl she misinterprets as a sign of her pregnancy from "silly-kissing" with her mentally disabled young-man friend, or when she joyfully prepares her father's heroine-shot by means of a pacifying daily routine just as if she was preparing a cup of tea or a light snack.

One might encounter enormous difficulties on trying to reinterpret imagination in terms of a trusting relationality. Both in original and adaptation, the Alice figure does her best to understand all the manic phantasmagorias of the strange characters she meets throughout her journey and to acknowledge them as equally feasible and respectable reality-versions each (from the Red Queen's harmless threats of decapitation or the Mad Hatter's fighting Time in Carroll, to Dell's taxidermia craze or Dickens's hunt for the killer shark-train in Gilliam). Still, most often, her tolerant attempts are not admired as feats of a particularly open-hearted character but are disgustedly attributed to the twisted fantasy of her maker blamed for inventing the most heartbreaking fictional reality ever, inviting spectators to identify with the tormented yet unbelievably happy protagonist. The condemnatory reviews calling *Tideland* "gruesomely awful" (*Entertainment Weekly*), "creepy, exploitive, and self-indulgent" (*New York Times*), an "extremely unpleasant" "diseased" and "risky," "morbid mindbender" (*Chicago Reader*) attest how in the film's odd case the empathy with an empathic person qualifies as an immoral perverse delight.

These negative critics do not only miss the point of Gilliam's outstanding artistic agenda, but also prove to be telling of our culture's normative definitions of the criteria of happiness, the prescriptive social scenarios of well-being, and the hegemonic logic of help that presupposes one's value judgments to be superior to others, relying on the assumption that one can know better what serves good for others who are expected to be grateful for the assistance given (often unasked for) to make their life more satisfactory. Gilliam's artistic message reminds of a witticism from Oscar Wilde, especially from his *Soul of a Man under Socialism* (1891): it suggests that it might be much easier to express a cheap, charitable, self-pleasing sympathy with others' suffering than to have sympathy with thought (about the limits of empathy), while the altruistic virtue of helping the poor may prevent from carrying out the ultimate aim to create a society where there is no poverty at all. *Tideland*'s celebration of the fabulous diversity of being as perceived by the non-differential childish worldview renders the privileged mainstream standards of satisfaction seem shallow, nonsensical, if not meaningless.

We marvel at Jeliza-Rose's ubiquity in a multitude of strange *dreams* she attributes to the individual imaginative activities of Tideland's weird inhabitants. She hopes to make contact with them through consciously dreaming herself into their fantasies, hence coming to (non)being in multiple parallel elsewheres, many worlds emerging as potential homes for all of them, destabilized in their positionalities of dreamer and dreamt. The leitmotif of Jeliza-Rose dreaming herself into non/being in others' dreams permeates the visionary imagery of Gilliam's film and is explicitly spelt out in the poetic asides of Cullin's text. She has nightmares about herself dwelling in the paternal phantasmagoria of the Bog Man, who materialized in her bedroom "a noose encircled his neck, drawn at the windpipe, coiling like a snake on his chest and tried suffocating me with a pillow (and) a look of affliction" on his face (11), about the junkie mother's "warm, dreamy, carefree bubble (that) had become a void" (30), about Dell's obsessions with bees, "birds and rabbits, and children hiding under the bushes, and bad things happening under the sun" (114), as well as infantile "spooky dreams" sprung from her grandmother's memories haunting the house, and from Dickens's fantasies of animalistic predators and apocalyptic annihilation, embodied by "squirrels all over my bedroom, in my bed, gone totally nuts, tangling themselves in my hair, sinking those big yellow teeth deep in my scalp, tearing at everything" (38). And she also has sweet dreams of "trains, of Eskimo Pies and old men dancing with bears" (56), of flight, Classique getting a real brain, and Mom burning bright, dreams she attributes to her beloved doll-heads who, when hypnotized, will dream about her, too, without waking up until she says so, without knowing where she is going, ever (56).

For Jeliza-Rose, dreams are ambiguous sites of surrender and control, hiding places of comfortable absent-mindedness and loci of re/creative agency. These utopian elsewheres hold the potential to turn into "a dream come true" which eventually can be denigrated by stating "It is just a dream." Actual Foucauldian heterotopiac spaces of otherness (1967), they are neither here nor there, surpassing beyond and containing within all earthly geographical locations, spots of physical and psychic ex-stasis like one's presence/absence on the other side of the looking-glass, in one's mirror-reflection, throughout a telephone conversation, or, in this case, in a mind game of others. Numerous references to dream work—25 passages on the whole in Cullin's novel and a dreamy/nightmarish atmosphere permeating Gilliam's movie—pay tribute to the Carrollian *Alice* tales' dream frame and their philosophical relativization of dream and waking life as radically indistinguishable states of being or nonbeing—in line with the Taoist philosophical koan, evoked in the epilogue to *Looking-Glass*, on our never knowing if our lives are not just dreams we make up or other dreamers call into being. The redundancy of Jeliza-Rose dreaming about doll heads dreaming about her—evocative of the Carrollian fantasy of a child fantasizing about an adulthood filled with fantasies of childhood (or of Alice fantasizing about the White King fantasizing about her)—reveals that dwelling in others' dreams is a way of circumscribing a relational mode of identity. The prospective explorative function of imagination tracing the potential selves one might inhabit implies seeking oneself by mapping the directions in which one might move towards others. For the little girl, dreamy longing always has to do with belonging.

> And lying with my father, I prayed for food and somewhere safe to hide. I imagined those cities at the bottom of the ocean, those castles and families—that's where I belonged. Classique would probably meet me there, so would Dickens and Cut 'N Style. My father was already dreaming himself there, I felt certain. And if I could only dream myself there too. If I could shut my eyes and try hard enough, I might find myself waking inside his dream.
>
> If I tried hard enough, if I closed my eyes and held my breath—if I tried hard enough [139].

Paradoxically, the journey to the depth of the unconscious is a matter of trying hard enough; to dream with the intention to get in touch with others' dreams depends on the efficiency of one's creative agency. The Gilliam movie's final meta-scene faces spectators with a close-up of Jeliza-Rose's eyes looking at them fading into the moonlit sky to disappear as just a pair of a billion of twinkling stars. This is a wonderfully poetic visual metaphor modeling the interpretation process of any artwork. Jeliza-Rose's eyes represent her creative consciousness responsible for sense making, meaning formation, hence the cognitive realization, the imaginative animation of a fictional reality latently vegetating in the text as a mere potentiality up until her casting her eyes upon on it to mentally (psychically and physically) engage with the artwork and make her meaning manifest in it. However her view/her meaning will be just one out of an infinite variety of possible significations, which all will keep shining bright on the horizon of expectations/interpretations as uncountable co-existing interpretive possibilities, all having the chance to be actualized, spectacularized into a more dominant (visible, readable) meaning that will make on its turn all other meaning-potentialities fade back into the night sky of the shadowy unread, the temporarily meaningless. The point of twinkling stars—symbolizing the interpreter's eyes opening wide and shutting closed on meanings—is the simultaneous coexistence of multiple, possibly contradictory yet equally valid interpretive perspectives and the celebration of the dynamic ambiguity of polysemic significations.

Coraline's Gothic Adventures across Media: A Tomboy Daughter's Fantasies of a Monstrous Mother

Children's literature initially emerged in largely didactic forms in the 18th century as a counter-reaction to the horrifying and immoral 'adult' genre of Gothic fiction (Townshend 16). Yet one of the first pieces of children's literature young readers today still recognize as a children's book, *Alice's Adventures in Wonderland*, mocked precisely the "morals and manners" of those instructive tales for children which were designed to take Gothic fiction's place (Jackson, Coats, McGillis 3). Although Carroll's *Alice* tales did not become Gothic texts per se, they recycled a fair amount of Gothic generic features, most prominently the destabilization of the boundary between waking life and nightmarish fantasy tormenting the dreamer with the fear of losing one's way, mind, and self-identity. As the introduction of *The Gothic in Children's Literature. Haunting the Borders* encapsulates:

> When the genre of didactic narrative is turned back on itself, and indeed turned upside down and inside out, the result is not a return to the Gothic stories children used to read before children's literature was invented, but the beginning of a new children's literature tradition, the tradition to which all subsequent children's literature belongs [Jackson, Coats, McGillis 3].

Accordingly, the Gothic genre was rejuvenated by means of its multiple subversions. While *classic Gothic* novels penned by male authors deal with "masculine plots of transgression of social taboos by an excessive male will," in the *female Gothic* counter-tradition the formerly heroic male transgressor turns into the villain, a patriarch, abbot or despot with an authoritarian reach who "usurps the great house and threatens with death, rape" or entrapment the heroine who often reflects ironically upon her situation within the confines of her gender and genre (Marinovich-Resch 258). The explicitly feminist project of *female neo-Gothic* writings aims to reveal that the happy ending of marriage, the accomplishment of the family romance plot as a reward at the end of the gothic heroine's quest is indeed a male fantasy interiorized by earlier protagonists but rejected by their increasingly independent successors. A popular subgenre of female neo-gothic fiction, *homely Gothic*, instead of haunted castles in faraway lands, relocates the scene of mysterious events to one's own home, normally a primary comfort zone that suddenly appears defamiliarized as radically alien, and potentially threatening to the inhabitant's safety or sanity.

A primary technique of provoking the pleasurable discomfort characteristic of this genre is the *uncanny* (*unheimlich*) or the 'homely unhomely' described by Freud in 1919 as a cognitive dissonance, an emotional ambiguity, and a perceptual flaw resulting from a vague impression of the return of the repressed that should have remained hidden but comes to light, confusing feelings of foreignness and familiarity. It questions "our sense of ontological certainty about the world through the seeming appearance of phenomena that we *know* cannot exist, or the disappearance of phenomena that we *know* must" (Zolkover 70). A popular example for the *uncanny* all can relate to is the childhood experience when at night the well-known furniture of the kid's bedroom is suddenly seen transformed into predatory monsters. The child *knows* it is an armchair she is peeping at from underneath her blanket but she *imagines*, and even occasionally and temporarily *believes* it to be a monster. Moreover, as Freud suggests, children's sense of the uncanny is particularly complex because of the incomplete process of their socialization's psychic repressive mechanisms, and their partial embracement of the animistic system of beliefs, organizing most fairy tales. This makes them joyously personify throughout daytime play the same toys they dread in nocturnal fantasies about the inanimate coming to life.

It is the deeply disturbing, infantile, night-time experience that becomes a titillating literary adventure and a dominant mode of enjoyment fictionally framed in the form of safe or pretended fear in *children's Gothic novels* which enjoy an ever growing popularity today. The lure of the genre can be attributed to the fact that it addresses those common childhood anxieties which fail to reach the level of conscious verbalization: "fear of sounds in the night, fear of monsters under the bed, fear of a certain space (the basement or the attic), fear of the house catching fire, fear of intruders" all linked to the primary trauma of the separation from the first womb-home (Coats 80). Taken to the extreme, children's Gothic texts lend these fears a concrete embodiment in the form of abject monsters and evil villains which allow young readers to get some degree of control via a safe (narrative) play with fear fused with empowerment, relief, and even laughter.

Despite the unsettling nature of the Carrollian universe, it is a comforting realization that the strangest adventures are after all products of Alice's own fantasy. As a result, villains of Wonderland and the Looking-Glass World, the Red Queen and the Jabberwock, provoke merriment upon enacting pent-up aggressive impulses but leave the dreamer physically and psychically intact since everything is contained within her (sub)consciousness. In a similar vein, in Neil Gaiman's *Coraline*, a gothic tale for children and young adults, I will interpret in the following as a contemporary twin-text of Alice's adventures, the little heroine persecuted by household horrors including a monstrous replica of her own mother can choose to act as an explorer and not a victim to the circumstances, thus turning a tale of terror into a tricky girl's adventure story.

Coraline provides plenty of perfect fictional illustrations to the Freudian theory of the uncanny. In the following passage a visceral horror of the unhomely home quickly transforms into an amazed marvel at the heroine's absurdly mistaking a mundane object for a mysteriously unidentifiable, terrifying thing and then, with the turning of the page, intermedially shifts into a comic relief visually represented by Dave McKean's illustration of a half-laughing, half-gaping rat with a tail in the shape of a question mark holding a huge black key. The text thematizing the fast reconsideration of meanings and the image toying with symbols of knowledge de/formation (key, question mark) refer to the inherent self-reflexivity of any narrativization of the uncanny experience.

> Coraline took a deep breath and stepped into the darkness, where strange voices whispered and distant winds howled. She became certain that there was something in the dark behind her: something very old and very slow. Her heart beat so hard and so loudly she was scared it would burst out of her chest. She closed her eyes against the dark. Eventually she bumped into something, and opened her eyes, startled. She had bumped into an armchair, in her drawing room. The open doorway behind her was blocked by rough red bricks. She was home [59].

Gaiman's *Coraline* (2002)—adapted into animated motion picture by Henry Selick (2009) and a graphic novel by Russell P. Craig (2008)—is a children's Gothic novel written for a recommended readership of over eight-years-old about an adventurous little girl, who abandons her parents because they are too preoccupied with their own work to entertain her, and explores through a secret door of their house, an *Other* house inhabited by an apparently much more attentive and alluring *Other* mother (and father). The *Other* mother eventually turns out to be a witch-like figure who wants to replace Coraline's eyes with buttons, "eat her up," and "steal her soul," and threatens with fully engulfing her by an eternal childhood that keeps her forever blind, undifferentiated, and passive under the Beldam's suffocating guardianship. Coraline courageously fights her, saves the souls of abducted ghost children and gains back her real, imperfect but loving parents and most importantly, with them, her freedom.

In Gaiman's view, this is not a tale about fear but about bravery (ix), a story that matches—according to the epigraph to *Coraline*—Chesterton's understanding of fairy tales which are "more than true: not because they tell us that dragons exist, but because they tell us that dragons can be beaten." Gaiman's poetic preface to a 2009 edition of the novel locates the celebration of imaginativeness at the heart of children's gothic genre he simply calls "scary fiction."

> And scary fiction... ...that should be the tapping of the twig on the window, late at night, when you're alone in the house. The way that shadows slide, amended by imagination, and the whisper of something that may only be the wind.... A world in which there are monsters, and ghosts, and things that want to steal your heart is a world in which there angels and dreams and, above all, a world in which there is hope [Gaiman 2009, viii].

Besides the imaginative curious heroines' simultaneous existence in two worlds (dream/waking life, this/other world) and their optimistic belief in the possibility to find the way back home no matter how far one wanders we find numerous similarities between Coraline's and Alice's tales. The two little girls' adventures start out from a boredom that allows them to explore their own separate selves and their possible desires, including the desire for a fantastic world where one can never be bored. This eventually turns out to be a frightening realm because with all desires fulfilled one can no longer have desires there either (Phillips in Coats 86). In the fashion of portal quest fantasies they go through openings (a secret door, a rabbit hole and mirrors) to reach a magical land where they meet talking animals (a rabbit/ rats), get orientation from a feline companion voicing their own thoughts (Cheshire Cat/ nameless cat), fight a dominant female figure (Queen of Hearts/ Other Mother), experience physical metamorphosis (shrinkings and growings/ doubling and disintegration), revel in oral pleasures (Eat Me! cookies/ food as self-assertion [see Keeling and Pollard 2012]) undergo severe identity crisis (Coraline is repeatedly called Caroline, Alice is mistaken for Mary Ann, Mabel and a serpent among others), and in the end find a new sense of life rediscovering the interesting excitement of consensus reality.

Both in *Alice* and *Coraline* the textual narrative exists in a symbiosis with the visual illustrations—created by John Tenniel and Dave McKean respectively—which complement and nuance the story world. The ambiguous feel generated by the duplicitous meanings of the uncanny phenomena in the text (doubled worlds, split selves, vague anxieties, etc.) resonate with the hybridity of the genre that fuses incompatibles such as children's fiction and gothic horror, fairy tales (functioning according to internally coherent rules of magic) and fantasies (framed by the protagonists' dreams, hallucinations, and imaginings suggestive of the rational explanation of the supernatural realized as a product of an emotional disturbance [Nikolajeva in Gooding 393]). The tales provoke different readerly reactions in dual audiences, likely scaring adults protective of their offsprings' vulnerable psyches but entertaining children who interpret the stories as pure adventures (Gaiman 2009, vii).

Even the psychoanalytical interpretations of Carroll's and Gaiman's texts mirror each other: two phobias Freud relates to the uncanny experience are the fear of being buried alive and the fear of losing one's eyes(sight). Both can be easily connected to the most memorable iconic episodes of the two tales: Alice's fall down the rabbit hole into the belly of the Earth underground and Coraline's struggle against the Other Mother who wants to sew buttons in place of her eyes because "she wants something to love [...] *and* something to eat as well" (79). As child psychologist Melanie Klein argues, these anxieties are immediately associated with the infantile trauma of children yearning to speak yet too often hushed by parents, and the resulting fear of being deprived of one's own voice, the fear of losing the words and meanings necessary for the construction of a self-identity and for the conception of a story in one's own fashion. These fears translate metaphorically into the horror of being cannibalistically consumed by the parental mouth[12] opening up to speak in place of the child who is imaginarily devoured by the gaping jaws, the vagina of the witch mother or the guts of the wolf father. The infantile dread of becoming unseen

Dave McKean, illustration for Neil Gaiman's *Coraline* (London: Bloomsbury, 2002) (courtesy of the artist).

and unheard is a common trope of fairy tales, but it also holds exciting implications in the realm of children's literature authored by adults who speak in the name of the child characters they invent.

Another similarity between Coraline and Alice is that they are both point of view characters whose perspective provides a filter to the events taking place in the narrative. Besides learning about the heroines' conscious thoughts, feelings, and actions infiltrating and shaping the story, Gaiman's and Carroll's adoption of a writerly mode called by Dorrit Cohn "psychonarration" allows readers to get a glimpse at the girl focalizers' "transparent minds." The metaimaginative stories foreground the functioning of their unconscious psychic processes too through narrative strategies designed to "convey the unconscious, the vague, the unuttered feelings by finding an adequate linguistic expressions for them" (Cohn 21–46, Nikolajeva 180). Maria Nikolajeva's study of narrative constructions of subjectivity in contemporary juvenile prose finds the use of psychonarration sophisticated yet ethically problematic. The narrated monologue of a child character's stream of consciousness may express in an elaborate way the inner world of the young protagonist but the adult author hence crafts a subtle poetic language to skillfully imitate a character's perceptions while actually articulating emotions *of/for* the child who feels but is unable to express sensations because of lacking the appropriate language to articulate them (182, 185).

Psychonarration's dialogical juxtaposition of the agencies of narrating and experiencing self (narrator and character, adult and child) appears in an even more complex manner throughout Coraline's experience of transitional states, in between dreaming and awakening, or daydreaming, fantasizing, and a pretense play that toys with the idea of I as another, strategically forgetful of who one is, or the I as No One dwelling in a paradoxical state of non-being apart from the awareness of fantasizing awareness itself. These ambiguous instances of the simultaneously intense awareness and oblivion of the self confuse adult discursive means of self-reflection taken to the level of meta-fantasy with specifically childish experiences of hypersensitivity and a *joy of being alive* where the awareness of being is more sensorial than cognitive. (A perfect illustration for the embodied experience of this transitional state: "Coraline walked up the stairs one step at a time, heading back to her own flat. She was aware of the marbles clicking in her pocket, aware of the stone with a hole in it, aware of the cat pressing itself against her" [146]).

Thus, Nikolajeva's claim is no longer valid here: psychonarration does not only make use of an adult language the child character would not yet logically master, but also benefits from a childish experience the adult no longer has access to. It is this mutual interaction that succeeds in convincingly wording complex transverbal experience and makes the text so challenging to decode. In the following passage, for example, it is truly difficult to tell apart the narrator's and Coraline's stream of consciousness registering fleeting glimpses of the unspeakable.

> CORALINE WAS WOKEN BY the midmorning sun, full on her face.
>
> For a moment she felt utterly dislocated. She did not know where she was; she was not entirely sure *who* she was. It is astonishing just how much of what we are can be tied to the beds we wake up in the morning, and it is astonishing how fragile that can be.
>
> Sometimes Coraline would forget who she was while she was daydreaming that she was exploring the Arctic, or the Amazon rain forest, or Darkest Africa, and it was not until someone tapped her on the shoulder or said her name that Coraline would come back from a million miles away with a start, and all in a fraction of a second have to remember who she was, and what her name was, and that she was even there at all.

Now there was sun on her face, and she was Coraline Jones. Yes. And then the green and pinkness of the room she was in, and the rustling of a large painted paper butterfly as it fluttered and beat its way about the ceiling, told her where she had woken up [81].

Like in *Alice*, in many instances in *Coraline* the psychonarration belongs to the egocentric speech of child talking to herself that is transcribed in the novel as a quoted interior monologue. However, when the omniscient narrator's comments intervene in the child's monologue the discrepancy created between the two voices distinguished by a cognitive difference is not so much didactic, as Nikolajeva would suggest (175), but rather produces a humorous effect that alleviates the horrific quality of the text. Instead of figural representation lapsing into authorial discourse governed by the knowing narrator making value judgments and fun of the ignorant character (Nikolajeva 180), it is the character herself who seems to self-ironically comment upon her passing inaptitude she eventually manages to overcome. As follows, in *Alice* and *Coraline* we find matching passages where the psychonarration oscillates between soliloquy uttered out loud, unspoken thoughts, and subconscious psychic contents which are paraphrased in the third person singular not to deride the heroine's cognitive or emotive deficiency but, on the contrary, to provide insight into her personality growth. This implies her capacity to mature into a female adventurer explorer who fights her fears and—by facing the unimaginable and critically commenting upon its credibility as well as on the reliability of her own perspective—to mature into an autonomous interpreter and a storyteller of her own making too.

"It seems very pretty," [Alice] said when she had finished it [reading the poem about the monstrous Jabberwock], "but it's *rather* hard to understand!" (You see she didn't like to confess, ever to herself, that she couldn't make it out at all.) "Somehow it seems to fill my head with ideas—only I don't exactly know what they are! However, SOMEBODY killed SOMETHING: that's clear, at any rate –" (156)

Coraline took a deep breath. "I'm not afraid," she told herself. "I'm not." She did not believe herself, but she scrambled up onto the old stage, fingers sinking into the rotting wood as she pulled herself up. [...] Coraline hesitated. She did not want to approach the thing. [...] *Perhaps there are no souls hidden in here,* she thought. *Perhaps I can just leave and go somewhere else.* [...] Coraline walked slowly across the damp stage, trying to make as little noise as she could, afraid that, if she disturbed the thing in the sac, it would open its eyes, and see her, and then.... But there was nothing that she could think of as scary as having it look at her. Her heart pounded in her chest. She took another step forward [118].

Coraline and Alice are skeptical fantasists in so far as disbelief and an awareness of potential unimaginability are implanted at the core of their imaginative agency. (E.g., "it seems to fill my head with ideas—only I don't exactly know what," "there was nothing that she could think of as scary.") Since they are also highly self-reflective meta-fantasists, their stories easily lend themselves to a reading where the nightmarish figures of the Red Queen and the Other Mother are produced by the loquacious would-be-storyteller little girl heroines' own imagination as embodiments of the fearful linguistic deprivation endangering their authorial autonomy (symbolized by the threat of decapitation and enucleation). In psychoanalytical terms this silencing at the heart of the text results from a maternal engulfment one equally dreads and desires as a fall back into a quiescent preverbal state of non-differentiation preceding ego formation concomitant with an immediate satisfaction of desires which do not need to be verbalized. Both novels can be read as girls' coming-of-age stories fantastically fictionalizing (pre)teen's emotional turmoil, the metamorphic shapeshifting of adolescent bodies and especially the painful confrontation with monstrous mothers, rival females in a developmental stage the child self is reluctant to reach or leave behind.

The girl's dream of a perfect mother's unlimited love turned into a nightmare fits the agenda of children's gothic fiction: "scary appetites are put to their proper place" by taking wishes to a hyperbolic extreme that reveals their absurdity (Coats 78). In Coraline's case it turns out that her hunger for a perfect symbiosis between mother and daughter can be appeased at the painful price of having to lose one's individual self-identity. As the critical consensus agrees, Coraline does not struggle against a hostile antagonist but her own infantile desire for dependency and a fantasy of self-sufficiency that risks disintegration. (Gooding 398, Myers 247). The film adaptation's tagline echoing cautionary fairy tales' morale—"Be careful what you wish for."—also encapsulates this idea that could easily fit any of Coraline's psychonarrations. A self-reflective narrator she comments on her psychic processes, her unspoken wishes and fears, as she instructs the other Mother—her own fantasy construction!—about the nature of desires which by definition should not be fulfilled because the appeal they hold as imaginary possibility surely turns horrific upon their realization. "Coraline sighed. 'You really don't understand, do you?' she said. 'I don't *want* whatever I want. Nobody does. Not really. What kind of fun would it be if I just got everything I ever wanted? Just like that, and it didn't *mean* anything. What then?'" (139) A peculiar specificity of metafantasy here is that it reflects not only on the dangers of wish fulfillment by imaginative practices but also on the unreliability of one's own desires (which upon coming true might horrify us to death).

Coraline's major themes, uncanny's uncertainty, the ominous discontents of desires, and identity crises are emblematized by the motif of *mist* that takes the physical shape of ambiguity itself.[13] When Coraline is bored in consensus reality, her real mother gives her a sheet of paper urging her to draw something. But Coraline can only decorate the blank page by writing in one corner the single word "M$_I$ST." This is a trace of her failed but deviantly fulfilled authorship inspired by unimaginability. Instead of picturing a thing, Coraline verbalizes Nothing—that eventually comes real in the Other Mother's realm in a groundless "misty, milky whiteness" with "no temperature, no smell, no texture, and no taste" (87), a "nowhere" (111) of "formless, swirling mist with no shapes or shadows" (122). Perhaps Coraline is the author-in-the-making overwhelmed by the fictional universe she is inventing for herself, struggling with the Unimaginable she designates as the central governing theme of her narrative. As David Rudd points out, the I typographically dropped out in the word M$_I$ST via a subtle *mise-en-abyme* marks the overlooked, lonely I who is not *missed* and who hesitates between resisting or embracing the engulfment by the mist that belong to the Other Mother's realm (2–3).

The dilemma between independence and dependence can be translated into the anxiety of authorship too: to be alone of one's kind marked by the difference authored by oneself or to depend and merge in the tradition built by the predecessors? It is exciting to consider the Other Mother's figure as a literary foremother whose misty world is described –in metafictional terms, related to the anxiety of authorship—as "a pale nothingness, like *a blank sheet of paper* or an enormous, empty white room" (87, emphasis mine). Symbolically speaking, from the perspective of Gaiman's novel as a reimagining of Carroll's classic, it is up to Coraline to find her way in the mist, to revindicate her own place, to fill the whiteness with words of her own and to emphasize her singularity in a literary space haunted by the specter of her literary foremother, Alice. In Rudd's reading, M$_I$ST is a graphic representation that shows how we are all caught up in the symbolic system of language where we must constantly negotiate the positionality of the "I" as a fleeting and relative signifier that gains meaning only in connections to other signs, representing the individual in a non-individual "hazy" way available to all who try to speak. The hardship of the I "to signify anything meaningfully, to ward off the abject whiteness of the page" (Rudd 3), to win over meaninglessness and the dependence on other signifiers is a struggle that takes place in the arena of creative artistry and literary adaptation too.

Another instance when Coraline attempts at the pen is even more revealing: on her father's computer she types a story in all capital letters coupled with spelling mistakes about a little girl named Apple who "DANCED AND DANCED UNTIL HER FEET TURND INTO SOSSAJES." Here, the anxiety felt over the priority of the established original turns into carnivalesque parody. Alice's metamorphosis is reduced to a ridiculous transformation of Apple's feet. The typewritten words lack of individuality is compensated for by the drawing Coraline decorates her story with, and the horror of the blank page's signifying void is overcome by a humorous embracement of nonsensical meaningless ("sossajes") that becomes a unique differential feature of the young authoress' individuality standing in a sign system while subverting it. The confidence gained by creativity is also manifested upon Coraline's ultimate return to consensus reality, when in her psychonarration she registers the world as "interesting" (158) she must realize that she no longer needs her parents "to make the world interesting" (58) for her but will find her fun way on her own too.

Coraline is an exciting piece of preadolescent fiction because it starts out typically as a cautionary horror fantasy about actual childhood fears related to the loss of home, family, the "womb" representing the boundaries of children's whole world (left behind through a portal to play out psychological dramas in an alternate reality [Balay 8]), yet, unexpectedly, instead of reinforcing the confines set by parental discipline it finishes in a triumphant tone celebrating an autonomous agency wholeheartedly embraced by children and supported by adults. In fact, a common feature of children's Gothic fiction is the challenging of the nuclear heterosexual family romance plot and the overturning of the Father-headed household as a conventional, phallogocentric mode of cohabitation, normatively prescribed and idealized by the patriarchal ideology and canon. Characteristic of the genre, this narrative subversion, Rachel Blau Du Plessis calls "writing beyond the ending" (1985) and Judith Roof deems essential for an alternative, non-hegemonic reconstruction of narratively constituted identities (1996), is performed from the perspective of children, who constitute protagonists and target reading-audiences in one. As a result, children's rebellious revisionings tend to be interestingly invested with feminist ethical and political potentials. Coraline's fight with the evil double of her mother completely reevaluates her and our ideas of an ideal family and femininity alike.[14]

Parsons, Sawers, and McInally criticized Gaiman's novel for debilitating women's empowerment by allowing "material feminism slip seamlessly into [inefficient] postfeminism" (372). As they point out, Coraline's real mother, a fictional embodiment of material feminism, pursues a career unsubdued to childrearing, frantically works on a gardening catalogue, refuses to cook daily meals or to sacrifice all her attention to her needy daughter, and shares household duties with a rather maternal, mothering father-figure. Yet, it is also the real mother's relative empowerment that calls to life the fantasy of her dark double, the Other Mother whose strength is portrayed as tyrannical and sadistic. Female-to-female bonds are represented as either fatally dangerous, like the Other Mother-to-daughter bond

Daniel Daekazu Kordek, "Coraline and her two mothers." Digital fan art, 2014 (courtesy of the artist, http://daekazu.deviantart.com).

(Parsons et al. 373) or as horribly repulsive, regressive and mutant, like Misses Spink and Forcible, the crone-like siblings' cocooning into one single, horribly unformed creature during one of Coraline's night-time visits. Moreover, it is a memory of male heroism, of the real father bravely protecting Coraline against an attack of wild wasps that provides her a positive identificatory model that becomes a token of her coming of age and survival, and helps her fight the monstrous mother's female villainy. Thus, in Parsons, Sawers and McInally's reading, Coraline's maturation takes place at the cost of consolidating conventional gender hierarchies: conforming to the Oedipal scenario she must learn to identify with masculine bravery and fight feminine power (including her own desires for power) to succeed at her quest. However, Parsons et al.'s excellent paper is weakened by the classic psychoanalytical terms—phallic mother, castrated woman, penile imagery—it relies on to interpret Coraline's journey through a Lacanian landscape while disregarding the specificity of a *girl's* adventure story which cannot be so easily modeled conforming to the schemata of the masculinized subject's psychosexual maturation.

Unlike Parsons et al, I think that the annihilation of the Other Mother figure does not mean a rejection but a reevaluation of empowered maternity. There is a feminist critical potential lurking beneath the Gaimanian fantasy's inseparable conjoining of idealized and demonized motherhood via the Gothic doubling of Coraline's apparently-inefficient 'good enough' Real Mother and the seemingly-perfect monstrous Other Mother. This character-confusion seems to be an ironic, fictional recapitulation of Mary Russo's argumentation outlined in her *The Female Grotesque* (1995) describing the inevitably paradoxical social positioning of the female subject who must undergo a cultural "monstrification" as a side-effect of her engendering by patriarchal ideology. Accordingly, if a woman fully submits to the social requirements of her gender role (like sacrificial motherhood or feminine subservience), she is deprived of autonomy and her subjectivity becomes primarily identified as objectified, over-embodied and fundamentally grotesque; whereas if she rebels against the passive scenario prescribed for her, she is considered mad or monstrous. The real mother's grotesque negligence and the Other Mother's monstrous over-protectiveness as mirror-images to each other shed light on the difficulties feminized subjects have to face in a masculine hegemony where femininity (or motherhood) and subjectivity (or autonomous agency) are radically incompatible terms.

This ambiguity could be another tribute to the Carrollian universe permeated by a nonsense illogic. The unreasonably malevolent maternal figures Alice encounters—the Duchess, the Queen of Hearts, the Cook, the Red Queen and the White Queen—might be telling of the author's distaste for mature femininity (Pilinovsky 179). They might present a political satire about the dangers of unrestrained womanhood according to Victorian morals which engendered power positionalities as always already masculine and regarded women usurping them as monstrous (Knoepflemacher 172). And they might just as well enact fundamental contrastive plot devices to a travesty of the didactic Victorian *Bildungsroman* about a tomboyish girl child reluctant to achieve proper womanhood.

Gaiman's negative portrayal and Coraline's eventual rejection of the Other Mother's ideal caretaking as a false and flawed parental relation demythologizes the patriarchal fantasy of submissive mothering as a cornerstone of harmonious family relations. The animation adaptation's tagline "Be careful what you wish for" suggests that Coraline, in the end, recognizes that the kind of maternal care encapsulated in the other maternal promise "We're here to love you and feed you and play with you and make your life interesting" (58) "for ever and always" (42) "you and I shall understand each other perfectly and we shall love each other perfectly as well" (88) is not what she wants after all because it would debilitate and deform mother and daughter alike. The Other Mother caters for but also strictly delimits all Coraline's needs; she gives her miraculous toys, delicious nourishment, and abundant care but would like to trap her infantilized in a maternal space deprived of dreams and desires of the daughter's own making. As Gooding suggests, the novel illustrates that the prolongation of the psychoanalytical myth of the "infantile desire for a permanent (re)union with the mother" necessarily leads to "a parasitic substitute of love that destroys difference" (397).

Unlike in the first spooky tales invented by 18th century nursemaids to discipline and teach children to obey to adult guidance, Gaiman's contemporary children's gothic offers for children a lesson on the advantages of autonomy—for children and mothers alike. I fully agree with Gooding who argues that 'moral' of the text resides in Coraline's recognition that the increasing independence her real parents demand of her are not synonymous with rejection and abandonment, but signify a love that encourages the prosperation of her individual otherness and its engagement with the colorful outside world, a kind of love that does not wish to sew uniform buttons in place of her eyes, but lets her see and explore everything for herself, to shape a worldview of her own. In a wonderful passage on the last trial of Coraline's quest towards autonomous selfhood, it is the voice of her "real, wonderful, maddening, infuriating, glorious mother" simply saying "Well done, Coraline!" (155) that enables the little girl "to close the door on" the fake lure of the ideal-monstrous Other Mother's Other World. Gooding stresses that the Real Maternal praise comes before Coraline's actual accomplishment of her act (of triumphing over the Other Mother) (399). This indeed suggests that parental encouragement and advice are worth more than instruction and moralizing. Both Coraline and her real Mother seem to agree on that as neither makes any attempt at improving her imperfect mothering ways after the daughter's return. A new family dynamics for the 21st century is circumscribed here where affection may coexist with independence. Thus, Coraline's earlier claim, "I think I've become a single child family" (48) is perhaps more triumphant than fearful.

The very concept of childhood is reevaluated: neither idealized nor demonized, far from the innocent immaculacy Victorians or the polymorphous perversion Freudians identified it with, it is not meant to be a period of prolonged dependency or of precocious self-sufficiency but of street-smart exploration and wayward imagination, activities that truly contribute to infantile identity's development. The new underage gothic heroine instead of fleeing the despotic patriarch in a bridal gown fights it in her pajamas. As Balay opines, she is a tomboy who is at ease with traditionally masculine tasks of "saving souls, capturing talismans, and defeating demons" (Balay 10) but she also knows how to perform cleverly girly activities—like playing with dolls. She uses by means of "a protective coloration" (151) that help her trap the unsuspecting disembodied hand of the other mother willing to seize her. In Balay's words "gender [serves] as a system of camouflage here, used to hide from danger, from our own uncertainty, and self-doubt" (8). The alternate world's dis-eased lack of gender rigidity illustrated by the creepy transparency of ghost children is counterbalanced by Coraline's empowering skill to enact and manipulate gender roles in subversive ways, described above, pointing towards gender-trouble famously described by feminist philosopher Judith Butler (1990) as a performance with a parodic potential. According to this logic, even Coraline's miming of her father's masculine heroism, criticized by Parsons et al., may qualify as a type of gender-bending "female masculinity" (see Halberstam 1998). Through expanding gender roles the novel "gives girls an expanded sense of imaginary options": to manipulate girlishness to create complete and independent identities, occasionally "to choose masculinity instead of femininity, [and not only that] but also to persistently, deliberately choose both, and to refuse to choose entirely" (Balay 13).

Interestingly, in *Coraline* the expansion of gender roles coincides with an expansion of the protagonist's imaginative faculties—which belong to a specifically feminine fantasy in so far as they are maternally inspired and position the little girl as an implied author of her own story. Balay quotes an important passage—Coraline "could only think of two things to do. Either she could scream and try to run away, and chased around a badly lit cellar by a huge grub thing, be chased until it caught her. Or she could do something else. So she did something else. " (131)—to convincingly demonstrate that Coraline avoids binary logic and does not make a choice between two alternatives, but rather "between choosing and refusing," to opt for "that which exists outside the realm of meaning and the possible" (9). However, I think the emphasis here is neither on *not* enacting the expected feminine responses to a potential threat, nor on the *refusal* to make a choice at all, but rather on "*doing* something *else*," the capacity to imaginatively make-up new options, to reinvent *her* story. Balay's assertion that Coraline "chooses candles and pajamas over flashlight and jeans because she knows she is in a fantasy novel and wants to do it right" (11) should be complemented by the remark that, besides conjoining horror with humor, this gesture turns her into a highly self-reflexive author (and reader) of the events which not simply happen to her but are incited by her imaginative agency. Numerous details relate the horrific quest-narrative to instances of infantile creativity—the adventures are initiated as an antidote against boredom, the fight against the monstrous mother is regarded a game of hide-and-seek, the other house disintegrates flattened into a child-drawn sketch. Coraline seems to play it safe as she is toying with a pretended fear called to life and resolved by her own imagination happily embracing nonsense and impossibility too.

According to Coats, the Gothic theme focusing on the most common childhood fear of losing one's Home along with the caring family, static comfort and protection from responsibility it affords refers to a rationally based anxiety all children must face when growing up. Pretending this fear serves "to work out possible plans of response" to it (Coats 83). Significantly, the Freudian uncanny, the strangely familiar, familiarly strange Other Home that "ought to have remained secret and hidden" is called to life by Coraline's dark fantasies. It is comforting to know that the horror and the horrific are products of Coraline's imaginative, interpretive consciousness, since this means that, complicit in their creation, she can also control or terminate them.[15]

Coats stresses as a primal source of anxiety the suspicion about parental sexuality Coraline both is curious about and reluctant to witness as a would-be primal scene of her psychosexual maturation. Yet, I believe that the most telling bit about the empowering nature of Coraline's imaginative agency is the last phrase on "the room remaining empty until the exact moment that she opened the door" that guarantees mastery over the alternate universe by suggesting that its very existence depends on Coraline's perception of it or presence of perceiving it. Coraline is not a victim but a provocateur of weird circumstances. Her curiosity—conventionally a fault that needs to be corrected in the original scary tales with a disciplinary intent—becomes a primary token of her girl power. On exploring the Other House she is exploring her own imaginative capacities. Via an exciting *mise-en-abyme*, the reading experience of the child reading the children's Gothic novel mimes the safe play with fear enacted by the protagonist she is reading about.

It is also noteworthy that Coraline's imagination is paradoxically inspired by her "boring" Real mother who is unwilling to play with her but shows her the locked door and the hidden key, encourages her daughter to explore the house, and hints at the possibility of adventures lurking beyond the apparent boredom of the Real House. It is significant that the Real Mother does not entertain Coraline but rather stimulates her to find (out for herself) amusements of her own. In Coats's psychoanalytical terms, the Real Mother does not fulfill all Coraline's desires but shows her how desire may be pursued as a project, how boredom's sense of loneliness may be exploited as an imaginative space for dreaming and desiring, for testing who one is (86). Thus, the maternal lesson teaches imaginative agency, courage to discover one's own desires.

Coraline's quest ends with a happy return to an imperfect home where she can live, desire, and fantazise free beyond the frames of the conventional heterosexual nuclear family romance. From then on her ordinary *being* home will constitute the greatest adventure. This is nicely encapsulated in Coraline's words she utters on her return home, "the sky had never seemed so *sky*, the world had never seemed so *world*.... Nothing, she thought, had ever been so *interesting*" (158), and, at last, "as the first stars came out Coraline finally allowed herself to drift into sleep" (184).

Coraline was adapted to the screen as a stop-motion animated 3D fantasy film written and directed by Henry Selick (produced by Laika and distributed by Focus Features) released in the U.S. in 2009. Predestined to become a box-office hit with a highly favorable critical reception, it fused a traditionally popular literary trope (troubled child hero), an emerging genre (children's gothic fiction), a trendy new medial technology (3D cinema), Gaiman's cult following, and a provocative mixture of family- and dark fantasy film.

According to Lindsay Myers, although animated *Coraline* belongs to those 'honest' family movies which demystify sentimentalized family relations and innocent childhoods for the sake of depicting real life traumas and breakable or broken homes, still the film in its depth remains conservative and unprogressive due to the "adaptation trading off the novel's theme of child empowerment for adult fears about child safety" (247). By exchanging the novelistic celebration of the girl heroine's agency for the cinematic horror of the Other Mother's abduction, the family movie serves market needs governed by adults whose anxieties are reflected in the film functioning as a mirror to the dominant socio-cultural climate (Myers 246). Oddly enough, this piece of children's gothic does not so much aim to ease infantile phobias as it foregrounds grownups' "moral panic" about "stranger danger" (Myers 245) and casts the child protagonist within the stereotype of innocent victim endangered by mad adult desires and in need of reasonable adult protection. Following this logic, even the film's tagline "Be careful what you wish for." might be addressing adult spectators warning parents about the dangers of their repressed desires not to be disturbed by their irritating offspring, who one day might actually disappear like Coraline lured away by her monstrous abductor.

Myers provides a convincing overview of the changes from novel to film which shift the power relations in an unfavorable way for children whose original empowerment is replaced by entrapment throughout the adaptation process. While the Other Mother is granted more agency on being transformed from a passive aggressor (who can destroy but not create in Gaiman) into a serial predator, Coraline is deprived of her autonomy on multiple grounds. She seems to be just one in long lineage of kids kidnapped by the Beldam driven by the malicious intent to turn them into ghost children to feed on their souls, and she is given a male sidekick, Wybie who does most of the action in the fight against the evil in her place (instead of Coraline's elaborate trick of protective coloration it is Wybie's punch of fist that crashes the Other Mother's creeping hand). According to Myers, Selick's animation deprives children's gothic of its subversive powers by fusing shock horror tropes borrowed from Hollywood horror film (full moon, zoophobia, monstrous femininity) with the iconography of anti-child abuse campaigns (the child as a defenseless ragdoll) and a moralizing aimed to instruct adult viewers (stressing the need for an exemplary home and parenting).

In a way, Myers is right in the above, however the inclusion of Wybie's character was likely not so much a conscious choice to delimit Coraline's feminist agency but just a necessary outcome of the shift between media characterized by different specificities. As Gaiman claimed in an interview in *Coraline* DVD Extras, the introduction of the boy companion in the film was a dramaturgical decision "so that you wouldn't have a lonely little girl walking round and talking to herself all the time." Two other alternatives considered—

to have Coraline break the fourth wall and talk in a metaleptic way to the audience or to have her act as a narrator to the story—were surely rejected to have a more dynamic, action-packed than a dreamy atmospheric movie. What works as psychonarration in popular novelistic form accessible to preadolescents and young adults would move filmic narrative into an art cinematic register beyond the confines of mass culture. (According to Selick's more pragmatic explanation, a direct adaptation simply would have led to a much shorter movie therefore his screenplay needed expansions, like Wybie's character.)

Much of Myers' succeeding criticism disregards the inevitable consequences of media shift and hence verges on rather outdated fidelity criticism. The animation's two other taglines "An Adventure too Weird for Words." and "Oh. My. God." clearly locate the adventures in the realm of the transverbal unspeakable, moving away from the verbal towards the visual regime of representation. Although the filmic Other World ceases to function as a distorted mirror to its real world counterpart because of the great disparity between the two (Myers 249), but the loss of its original uncanny quality is compensated by an equally strange, more spectacular carnivalesque grotesque effect. Dave McKean's spooky, shadowy black and white ink sketches of deformations of homeliness illustrating Gaiman's novel are replaced by concept artist Tadaro Uesugi's stunning bright colors belonging to exaggerated, artificial joys of a phantasmagorical theme park. While the former visual artist's images are freeze-frame shots recording the two worlds' similarity, the latter's moving pictures highlight the difference. Both visualize the dangerous intrusion of the self by the other, McKean from the perspective of this world and Uesugi from the perspective of the other.

Myers opines that the film's too colorful and self-affirmative embodiment of Coraline's character distinguished by a bright yellow mackintosh and blue hair visually contradicts the novel's original thematization of the heroine's quest for self-knowledge. She strangely presumes that children's obsession with bright colors is a sign of psychological immaturity. Thus, she remains oblivious to the fact how color motion picture films can strategically shape the iconography of story worlds creating emblematic signifiers throughout distortions of novelistic originals (like in the case of Dorothy's ruby slippers donned on her only in the silver screen adaptation of *Wizard of Oz*). The filmic Coraline's blue hair eventually becomes her major personality marker that facilitates her impersonation and recognition in fan art and cosplay alike.

Moreover Uesugi's frenzy of colors has its deep textual origins too in the novel where Gaiman associates colors with dangerous desires: in waking reality Coraline yearns in vain for Day-Glo green gloves, she enjoys the green limeade Miss Spink and Forcible feed her and ponders about their silly advice not to wear green in her dressing room if she wants to avoid forthcoming danger, in the nightmare realm the Other Mother's door is painted green, the marbles holding the ghost children's soul shine with a green glow, and Coraline's other bedroom is an "green-and-pink parody of her own bedroom" (80) where the pink is more ominous than sugar sweet, reminiscent of an atavistic animality and an abject fleshliness, the pink of rats' tail, the cat's tongue, and the raw bacon the Other Mother is cooking. If the Other World's endlessly static desirelessness is represented by the gray and white colorless Nothingness, vivid colors mark the excitement of consensus reality granted by a pure joy of being alive that Coraline revels in after her ultimate return to a home she learns to find interesting on her own.

> The light that came through the picture window was daylight, real golden late-afternoon daylight, not a white mist light. The sky was a robin's-egg blue, and Coraline could see trees and, beyond the trees, green hills, which faded on the horizon into purples and grays. The sky had never seemed so *sky,* the world had never seemed so *world* [158].

As the above passage demonstrates, Gaiman's novel is a colorful text full of vibrant visual impressions Selick's animation adaptation adequately translates into the filmic medium. Many of these are related to the fantastic food Coraline is entertained with in the other world: the cotton candy in Mr. Bobinsky's mouse circus, the chocolate shared with dogs in Miss Spink and Miss Forcible's burlesque theatre, and especially at the Other Mother's dinner party including a pink birthday cake, mango milkshake tapped from the chandelier, and gravy carried around the table on a little train. The preeminence of sweets-turned-monstrous places the common children's literary tropes of food lure and oral transgression within the frame of horror fiction centered on cannibalistic devouring and nauseous disgorging. The Other Mother eats black beetles as if they were butterscotch balls, the other Miss Spink and Miss Forcible's cocoon is covered in chocolate wrapper and filled with jelly, and the old candy chunk with a hole in it turns out to be a mysterious, magical talisman that helps Coraline to find the souls of lost children. The terrible treats provide a criticism of the cultural identification of childishness with sugar sweet cuteness, too. (The undoing of childhood's saccharine idealization is supported by Wyeborn's gloomy naming (homonymous with "Why born?") and the closing of his mute double's mouth upon all oral delights sewn shut by the Beldam.)

A critically undervalued strength of Coraline's animation adaptation is the clever matching of visual and acoustic nonsense. The surrealistic beauty of the strange garden the Other Father makes for Coraline—a tribute to the garden of live flowers Alice encounters in Wonderland—abounds in a wild vegetal growth that is accompanied in the soundtrack by a jazz improvisation whereby the joy of acoustic unpredictability matches the visual craze of the unearthly plant hybrids. On numerous instances, the filmic sound effects manage to increase the Gaiman novel's nonsense implications which resonate the most with the Carrollian original. Mr. Bobinsky the ringmaster of a circus troupe of singing rats, represented as a gigantic ex-acrobat with blue skin—due to his time as a Liquidator at Chernobyl Nuclear Power Plant catastrophe (see Selick's DVD commentary)—speaks in an odd Russian accent until he disintegrates into a coat of squeaking rats incapable of human speech. The voice of Coraline's Mother and Other Mother is lent by Teri Hatcher famed for impersonating one of the *Desperate Housewives* in the eponymous TV series that has provided an equally satirical commentary on social expectations of femininity. The movie's end credits song composed by Bruno Coulais is sung in a mesmerizing gibberish reminiscent of nursery rhymes, a lullaby, or daydreaming children's play with meaninglessness pointing towards transverbal realms whereby one can cradle herself into an enchanted, ecstatic state of non-being.

The lyrics of the nonsense song verbalize the unspeakable as if to echo the numerous scenes toying with ambiguous interpretations of the unimaginable. The horrific message of Miss Spink and Miss Forcible's tasseography turns humorous when with the reversing of the tea cup the shape of the scary hand transforms into a giraffe and leads to the conclusion that "to avoid danger you might need a long ladder." In another episode, unfortunately cut from the final movie, Coraline collects a bunch of wild flowers from which an odd little bug drops into her mother's coffee cup and climbs out to leave on a blank sheet of paper its footprints that the little girl decodes as strange traces providing the basis of an abstract pattern of curvy lines she dreamily doodles to fill the page. The maternally inspired daughter's art (bouquet, coffee and paper belong to the mother) challenges the representational confines in so far as it is nonfigurative, transverbal, and unintentional—nonsense at its best.

Coraline: A Graphic Novel adapted and illustrated by Craig P. Russell (2008) is the reworking of an original story that already has had a few memorable visual interpretations. Treading in the footsteps of Dave McKean's illustrations decorating Gaiman's novel and Henry Selick's animation analyzed above, Coraline in sequential art form also maps the uncanny experience on the level media transition. There is something truly familiar about it, yet it is not exactly the same. Acclaimed graphic novelist, Russell, winner of the prestigious Harvey and Eisner Awards, and coined "the king of comic adaptation" has transplanted the words of Gaiman, Bradbury, Hoard, Moorcock, Wilde, and Kipling into images, constantly "fascinated by the challenge of taking a piece apart line-by-line and reassembling it into an entirely different art form" (Smith 2008). Already its cover acknowledges the work's inevitable entanglement in a complex intermedial web, defining itself as: "The graphic novel adaptation of the magical national bestseller. Now a major motion picture." Hence, chronologically speaking, Russell emerges from the beginning as a successor to Gaiman (and McKean) (illustrated novel) and to Selick (film). Besides Russell's, the name of the original author Gaiman features on the cover typeset in large capitals as if emphasizing the preeminence of the novelistic original. Accordingly, the graphic novel adaptation remains absolutely faithful to its source-text, it lacks the animation adaptation's licentious deviations and variations on the original theme. Russell does not add a single line to Gaiman's, if he must omit passages he does his best to transplant verbal passages into a condensed visual form that simultaneously makes meanings more explicit (fixing them within set pictures) yet also maintains the ambiguity contributing to the story's trademark uncanny feel. The most exciting picture panels are the ones visualizing unspeakability: either by representing horror's uncanny dread, the fear of being afraid or Coraline's psychonarrations, stream of consciousness with metaimaginative implications, I will analyze in the following.

The cover wholeheartedly embraces the children's gothic tradition in so far as it features an androgynous young adult character with an anxious but determined look on her face, holding a single candle, looking both vulnerable and valiant against a pitch-dark backdrop turbulent with flying bats. The contrast between dark and light is used consistently throughout the work to express the difference between consensus reality and the Other Mother's world. The detailed realistic backgrounds of the former are contrasted with the disturbingly empty backgrounds of the latter which create a nightmarish atmosphere by casting Coraline in blank spaces of Nothingness surrounded by unidentifiable shadows, thick fog, or receding abstract motifs of wallpaper patterns at most. All signify non-signification itself with an extreme shortage of stimuli, suggestive of static states of non-being, amnesia, claustrophobia, or sleep paralysis.

The uncanny effect provoked by the trespassing between the two worlds is realized in the graphic novel's change of perspective. While on one panel we see Coraline from the back opening the secret door, on the next, much larger panel she is already facing us peeping

at the unknown she is curious to discover, and in the three-panel tier below at the bottom of the page she is represented from the back again, disappearing into the darkness on a repetitive sequence of smaller images which are hauntingly identical replicas of each other except that she is slowly getting farther away from us to create a narrative tension and suspense with the slow pace of events as she is walking into danger step by step (29).

In the case of the large panel the spectator-reader's positioning is highly ambiguous: Coraline faces us with the comforting glow of our world shining behind her in the doorway that constitutes a smaller light-filled frame within the panel frame entirely black apart from a few rays of light coming from Coraline's direction and a few gray puffs of dust or fog or malicious thoughts emerging from the opposite direction, that is the locus of the other world and the interpreter too. Thus, by a simple play with perspective, much in line with the dilemma thematized by Coraline's story, Russell's graphic novel interactively destabilizes our sense of belonging. The lines accompanying the panel "THERE WAS A COLD AND MUSTY SMELL./ IT SMELLED LIKE SOMETHING/ VERY OLD AND/ VERY S L O W." are neither separated from the image as in the case of captions nor integrated into Coraline's thoughts as they would be in the case of thought balloons. Set in wavy, undulating lines, with gaps gradually emerging between letters, and flowing from the light towards darkness, the text(ual meaning) seems to disintegrate and hence recalls the picturing of onomatopoeic sound effects in comics, all the SMACK! and WHOOSH!, which bridge the gap between word and image, and paradoxically foreground the pictorial dimensions of verbality while expressing orality. (Moreover, to heighten the synesthesia an olfactory sensation is highlighted here.) If sound effects in comics point towards transverbal realms, the slow and old (No)Thing awaiting Coraline marks the familiarly strange and strangely familiar uncanny's unspeakability.

Like all graphic novels, *Coraline* can make a clear differentiation between the focalizer heroine's stream of consciousness represented in thought balloons, the audible monologue of her uttered words emerging in speech bubbles and the omniscient narrator's commentary figuring in captions or at the edge of the image panel. The adaptation's generic requirement to abbreviate the source text does not allow for all psychonarrative passages to figure in thought balloons in their full integrity, and most often Coraline's daydreamings are not action packed enough to make it into the graphic novelist's encapsulations, i.e., his capturing of the pivotal points of the story. Still Russell finds exciting means to convey into visual art form the passages of psychonarration so integral to Gaiman's original text. For example, when Coraline attempts to win back the soul of the ghost children from the evil doubles of Miss Spink and Miss Forcible, she thinks to herself—both in original and adaptation—"I'M NOT AFRAID. I'M *NOT*." but the graphic novel page (112) fails to add the ironic addendum complementing the line in the novel "She did not believe herself." Obviously, the physiological symptoms of Coraline's anxiety described in details throughout the novel's psychonarrative passage (her taking a deep breath, reassuring herself of her own courage and disbelieving herself, her hesitating, walking slowly afraid, not being able to think of anything scarier than that, her heart pounding in her chest [118]) are graphically rendered in the portrayal of her dilated pupils, trembling hands, screaming mouth, and face distorted by fear.

Opposite: P. Craig Russell, from *Coraline: A Graphic Novel* (New York: HarperCollins, 2008, p. 29) (courtesy of the artist).

However, Coraline's self-doubting hesitation is best reflected in more abstract panels such as the one—right after the line quoted above—reducing her to a tiny figure pausing lonely at the bottom of a vertically elongated panel, the upper half of which is filled with bat-like creatures and their shadows. The Coraline figurine's facial features are largely simplified, become barely recognizable, bordering on the abstract (112)—as if to represent her momentary loss of faith culminating in identity crisis but also turning her individual features into the mask of everyman extremely easy to identify with for all interpreters. This strategy is called by comic book scholar Scott McCloud "intensification through simplification" (44).

On the same double page (112–113) we find further instances of 'faceless' portrayals 'disfiguring' Coraline by means of visible corporeal indicators of her nascent disbelief in her own heroism she firmly believes in: after a close-up of her determined but frightened face she is first shown from the back,[16] then in a shadow outline, then as the forlorn disidentified figurine analyzed above, and finally by fragmented body parts divided between neighboring panels, her hand and the talisman stone on one and her elbow and the monstrous cocoon hiding the lost soul in the other panel. (This visual fragmentation has its verbal equivalent in the next two panels' caption broken into five separate chunks disconnected by ellipsis evoking the excitement caused by pauses in oral storytelling: "CORALINE TRIED TO MAKE AS LITTLE NOISE AS SHE COULD... ...AFRAID THAT IF SHE DISTURBED THE THING IN THE SAC... ...IT WOULD OPEN ITS EYES... ...AND SEE HER... ...AND THEN..." [113]).

The layout of the page (112) is highly challenging. Below a larger panel of a close-up of Coraline's defiant yet disturbed gaze we find in the same size a close-up of the creature she must witness, "Miss Spink and Miss Forcible, but twisted and squeezed together, like two lumps of wax that had melted and melded together into one ghastly thing" (Gaiman 120). The ambiguity of the image sequence results from the fact that the horrid creature constitutes a logical counterpoint to Coraline's daring look to undermine the credibility of her self-assuredness, but the disintegrating lump of faceless Misses also mirrors Coraline's emerging identity-crisis recorded on the three smaller panels, vertically positioned by these two larger ones, which literally represent the brave little girl's "losing face" as she slowly submits to fear. Moreover, the two close-up panels might easily depict one single moment from different angles, freeze-framing a critical temporal instance to urge a complex interpretive activity on behalf of readers interactively involved in the process of meaning formation by sharing Coraline's doubts.

Russell's graphic novel adopts further exciting solutions to emphasize Coraline's fantasizing agency. Besides the speech balloons and thought bubbles, light blue air-bubbles with marine lettering are used to record the ghost children's communication and the hypothetical words of the real mother ("Well done, Coraline!") encouraging her daughter to leave behind the realm of the Other Mother. This in-between solution suits the transitional being of border crossing spirits with an unstable existential status, balancing between opposites such as life and death, our world and the other world, and most prominently fact and fantasy. Since Coraline reunites with the ghost children in her dreams and gains relief from a maternal support she recalls mentally, these characters—depicted in blue—can be regarded as tutelary companions produced by her own imagination. Coraline's daydreaming is differentiated from her conscious thoughts and words with the help of the color blue

(blue bubbles, text, and figures) that suggests transparency, invisibility, and the likelihood that these experience might be inaccessible for others but herself fantasizing them into being. If the Other Mother stands for nightmares undermining self-confidence, the solidarious ghost children and the supportive specter of the real mother stand for daydreams reinforcing a stable sense of identity. The assumption that this struggle takes place in Coraline' mind is supported by Russell's strategic refusal to depict Coraline with her mouth opened when she speaks. The girl's shut lips suggest that all the words might belong to her imaginative inner monologue contemplated throughout sleep-talking at most.

The dream frame surfaces as a particularly vivid homage to Carroll's Alice when Coraline returns home. Relieved because of her flight from (her fantasies of) the wicked Other Mother, she allows herself to be engulfed by the pure joy of living; neatly encapsulated in Gaiman's memorable psychonarration: "the sky had never seemed so *sky*, the world had never seemed so *world*.... Nothing, she thought, had ever been so *interesting*" (158). She rests in an armchair drifting into sleep in a position similar to the cat napping in her lap. In neighboring panels a parallel is drawn between the feline and the human girl face dreaming. Via a possible intertextual wink at Carroll's original, Coraline's epiphanic revelation concerning the wonder of reality is induced by the company of her cat as the text by the twin panels of dozing girl and cat reads: "SHE LOOKED DOWN AT HER LAP AT THE WAY THE SUNLIGHT BRUSHED EVERY HAIR ON THE CAT'S HEAD. NOTHING, SHE THOUGHT, HAD EVER BEEN SO INTERESTING. // AND CAUGHT UP IN THE INTERESTINGNESS OF THE WORLD, CORALINE BARELY NOTICED WHEN SHE FELL INTO A DEEP AND DREAMLESS SLEEP" (154).

These passages clearly evoke how the initiation of Alice's journey beyond the looking-glass is believed to be "the black kitten's fault entirely" who was naughtily "having a grand game of romps with the ball of worsted" while "Alice was sitting curled up in a corner of the great arm-chair, half talking to herself and half asleep" until she is led to the mirror by the kitten (143). (Another feline similarity I already mentioned is the one between Wonderland's Cheshire Cat and the talking cat in the Other Mother' realm—both self-ironic helping figures with a predilection of nonsense and sarcasm who nevertheless assist the heroine on her impossible quest.)

Gaiman and Russell also follow the Carrollian game with the relativity of dream and awakening, confusing states of passive rest and active adventure, suggesting the ubiquity of marvels produced by fantasmatic agency constantly at work everywhere. While Coraline's sleep is dreamless, her waking life can be never fully void of thrills. Much in line with the predictable horror fiction scenario, on her awakening she must be prepared for the return of the evil, to defeat again the Other Mother (reduced to a metonymical fragment of a spider-like left hand). In the end she can finally allow herself to drift into a calm sleep unafraid of new adventures to come marked by the beginning of the school term next day (184–185). This ending reaffirms the psychologically beneficiary effects of children's gothic fiction that proves young readers that fear can be overcome with the help of fantasy.

Russell's graphic novel adaptation of Gaiman's novel inspired by Carroll's Alice, does not only encourage reluctant readers to familiarize themselves with the image-text dynamics of an emerging new genre but may also eventually enable them to embark on book experience about a brave little heroine, in original and adapted form alike, while discussing questions of belonging on a generic (meta)medial level, too.

The Meanings of Madness in Participatory Culture: From Psychological Thriller Computer Game to Televised Family Adventure Romance to Fanfiction and Cosplay

Popular game designer American McGee is best known for his twisted sequels to Carroll's Alice tales he planned from the beginnings to take the form of a trilogy meant for a (young) adult audience. The first two dark adventures, *American McGee's Alice* (2000, developed by Rogue Entertainment, published by Electronic Arts; for PCs) and *Alice: Madness Returns* (2014, developed by Spicy Horse Games Studios, published by Electronic Arts, for PC, Mac, PlayStation 3 and Xbox 360 consoles) are first person shooter horror action-adventure computer games in which traumatized teenage Alice's mission is to flee the madhouse where she was incarcerated shocked with self-blame after the tragic death of her parents. She must fight the Red Queen embodying her own inner demons, save herself and revindicate the powers of her imagination by becoming a violent action heroine able to survive and redeem a nightmarish Wonderland. The final installment *Alice: Otherlands* still in the making in 2015 is advertised on Kickstarter as a series of dark steampunkish animated short films where Alice relies on her superheroic powers of telepathic mind voyage to enter the most curious brains of Victorian London—including those of Darwin, Edison, Bram Stoker, Jack the Ripper, and Queen Victoria—so as to battle an organization threatening with an institutionalized manipulative thought-control.

I wish to argue here that if all Wonderland stories are inherently metaimaginative on accounts of being products of Alice's mind, at the core of McGee's reimaginings we find deranged mental disfunctioning and misbehavioral patterns exploring a large spectrum of madness ranging from Alice's irresponsible daydreaming to mournful catatonia, hallucinations, suicidal self-loathing and aggressive rage. Moreover, gamers' imaginative reluctance is activated in connection with the ultimately Unthinkable notions of one's own dementia and death, which logically defy and transcend rational thought, while they provide disturbing pleasures of a *funcanny*—funny and uncanny—experience based on a replayable loop of decease and resurrection, loss of reason ad infinitum alternating between a surging into daydreams and a (possibly false) awakening to a nightmarish reality.

As Cathlena Martin argues in her study on American McGee's *Alice*, classic children's stories and fairy tales prove to be easily adaptable to the medium of computer games for various reasons. 1. They fit the basic narrative criteria of games in so far as a hero fights a villain to save someone in need of rescue. 2. Their numerous versions make them part of cultural knowledge, hence immediately accessible for gamers. 3. They allow for an interactivity enhanced by uniquely executable game worlds whereby, through alternate ways of navigating the narrative, players can reinterpret the source text (134–5). Gaming itself is a structural framework of Carroll's *Alice* tales organized by the logic of cards and chess games. However, Alice's original nonsense fantasy stories are closer to anti-tales than traditional fairy stories in so far as, for example, they clearly lack precisely the hero versus villain antagonism or the quest theme Martin mentions as ideal material for PC game adaptations.

In fact, McGee's games foreground precisely those latent dark undercurrents of the *Wonderland* tales which turn them odd if not unsuitable readings for children (such as

Alice's death jokes, the Red Queen's hysteric commands of capital punishment, the Duchess' physical abuse of the pig baby or the frame poems' melancholic evocation of mortality in Carroll's original). They thematize death, violence, rage, madness, aggression and guilt for a more mature gaming audience. The M rating signals suitability for youth over 16 years old because of blood and gore, sexual themes, strong language and graphic violence involved in the games.

The protagonist is recognizable as an Alice figure but the game designer's dark differentiations strategically imprint his own brand name on the end product turned into American McGee's instead of Carroll's or Disney's Alice. We are reminded that adaptation always involves a violent power struggle over cultural appropriation and in particular over the privilege of authorship. Alice still wears a blue dress with a white pinafore but her clothing is decorated with astrological symbols and splattered with blood, her Baby Jane shoes are changed to black leather boots, her hair is fastened back with a skull instead of a bowtie, and she is fully armed with "deadly toys" like an axe called the Vorpal Blade, ice wind, fire imps, and in the sequel a lethal Pepper Grinder, a Teapot Cannon, and a Clockwork Bomb. Alice's carefully elaborated gloomy looks attract teenage gamers and expand the market for tie-in products ranging from cosplay costumes, make-up tutorials, and accessories inspired by the multicultural trends of the Gothic Lolita and the Japanese guro kawaii (grotesque cute) fashion style to music by Nine Inch Nails member Chris Vrenna responsible for acoustically elaborating McGee's Alice's menacing and melancholic persona with sounds of wind, whispers, and screeches. These spin-offs, and in particular *American McGee's Alice* products marketed online, are characteristic of the 21st century production and reception of fairy tales and fantasies conditioned by pressures of globalization and hypercommodification complicit in a gradual disenchantment process described by Bacchilega (2013, 14). But they also promise an augmentation of magic via a transmedia experience enhancing our intimacy with the spirit of Wonderland due to gadgets, applications, and reliquia facilitating the identification with Alice.

As the back cover blurb of *American McGee's Alice* warns "The fairy tale is over." Accordingly, Wonderland is no longer a ground of innocent play but an origin and endpoint of tragic traumatic events. Conforming to the background information we learn at the beginning of the game, Alice's house was set on fire by a gas lamp accidentally overturned by her cat Dinah—a mediating character between waking life and dream world and a plot-engine in the original novels, too. While Alice was woken up and saved by the Wonderland creatures whose voice came real from Carroll's book she had been reading before falling asleep, she blames her absent-minded daydreaming for not being able to rescue her parents. Thus, the rabbit hole she falls in, institutionally represented by the madhouse she is locked in, is the psychopathological state of catatonic numbness resulting from her incapacity to deal with the death of her beloved. Quite fittingly it is her old stuffed rabbit a nurse gives her that shows a way out of the pit of pain by urging her to revisit and liberate the wondrous lands of her dreams turned terrifying by the tyrannical rule of a monstrous Red Queen clearly symbolizing her rage, grief, and guilt. The role of the gamer is to help Alice win this freedom fight and resolve her ambiguous relation with Wonderland circumscribed both as a cause and cure of her madness. It is a psychogeographic realm simultaneously associated with trauma and remedy, a sight of dangerous self-risking and empowering revenge which provide therapeutic release from suicidous passivity and remorse while facing fatal annihilation.

Certainly players' pleasure mostly results from their interactive share in transforming Alice from passive good girl to aggressively assertive action heroine throughout her dreams constituting the gist of the game. One gamer offers a typical summary of the reasons why to love McGee's Alice (in Madness Returns):

> She has a triple jump. She wields a Vorbal Blade. Hysteria mode is terrifying. She says: 'Save myself? From death? Is that it? Is that why I'm here? I'm not afraid to die. At times I've welcomed death.' Being imprisoned in a Victorian asylum after being accused of being responsible for the death of her family does not stop her. Goth stylings. Lovely diction" [Maiquitol on Twitter 13 June 2014].

As this quote illustrates, 'playing Alice' implies activating a heroic agency thoroughly aware of mortality and apt to defy death. Yet, as Brooker stresses, it also involves the difficult experience of 'dying as Alice,' mingling the empathetic concern for the vulnerability of a familiar childhood icon with a morbid fascination with gory details and a frustration felt over a lost fight (240–1). The gamers' identification with the Alice character is further reinforced with the remorse felt over this remorseful character's death. However, the discrepancy emerging within the identification process as a result of the imaginative reluctance to accept one's own death is cleverly resolved by the game's plot structure whereby each time Alice (and the player identifying with her) dies at the end of an unsuccessful game, she just wakes up from a broken dream of nightmarish Wonderland fight to an alternate fictional reality of Alice closed up in a psychiatric ward.

Hence, McGee's uncanny universe features the dark Alice figure doubled: one is numb, catatonic, melancholic and suicidous in the Victorian asylum that is notorious for ill-treating madwomen, the other is an aggressive champion in chaotic Wonderland (reminiscent of Tenniel's illustration of the Jabberwock-slaying beamish boy whose striped stockings and long flowing hair already indicate a heroic Alice-double also manifest in Tim Burton's movie). The strange splitting of Alice's personality does not stop here. While the Red Queen embodies her violent self-loathing for having lost her reason and freedom, the Jabberwock—who represents the traumatic unspeakable in many adaptations—stands for her shameful guilt felt over the death of her parents. Moreover, a handwritten letter addressed to "Dear Mr. Dodgson" that appears as a prop in McGee's Alice's room also associates her character with Alice Liddell the real-life muse of Lewis Carroll's original Wonderland tale. Alice is an immortal fantasy fighter who dies and resurrects with each new game while struggling with the memory of her deceased parents, the murderous Magna Mater Queen, and the myth of a long dead muse. Her multiple trafficking with/as the living dead proves to be symptomatic of our time's difficult relation to death.

The maddening knowledge of the inevitability and unacceptability of mortality is soothed by the fictionalization/fantastification of vulnerability granted by the gamer's capacity to revive Alice doomed to meet her end in a Wonderland turned into a realm of "sheer chaotic terror and unmitigated bloodshed bent on destruction" (Brooker 234). The explicit visualization of extreme violence results in troubling yet familiar sensations. On the one hand, we recall the compassion fatigue we experience daily due to live media broadcasts of inhuman brutality, televised images of war, terror and abuse we grow accustomed to with a sad stoicism. On the other hand, we face the recreational mourning, a perverse fascination with the passing of celebrities, disaster movies, or a harmless yet oddly joyful, Freudian death-drive-driven contemplation of the idea of our own annihilation. The game invites players to experience death from a safe distance for entertainment ends. Online critics recommend it for "horror survival fans" and "disaster lovers," while the designers have introduced into the sequel Hysteria as Alice's ultimate superpower to enable a strategic victorious use of mad self-deconstruction.

The techniques of intermediality involved in the game serve to increase terrifying effects. As Brooker points out, a cinematic camera move shows things unseen by the avatar to evoke "an eerie feeling of helplessness" (238). Gamers placed into the spectator position are debilitated in their empowering participatory agency spanning from the genre's inherent interactivity. They helplessly lose control over the character they are meant to help, control, and identify with. The alteration of immersion into and alienation from Alice's world evokes the feeling of uncertainty permeating the Carrollian Wonderland. But the distancing achieved through the cinematic total plane might also serve to evade the avatar's/ gamer's responsibility over acts of violence, suggesting that madness belongs to the world and not its inhabitant whose following the logic of this world is a mere means of survival.

According to Brooker, the players witness medial change as "the picture becomes full motion color, so the process imaginatively represents a shift in technology from Carroll's form of photography through silent film to contemporary cinema, or CGI" (234). However, the process is more ominous than nostalgic. The game includes several nods to Carroll, such as a dark portrait of Dodgson hanging in the castle of Pale Realm, playing cards and croquet balls used as weapons, riddles to solve and a Shrink Sense to use to complete levels, a skeletal and tattooed Cheshire Cat acting as a helper figure to Alice, the monstrous Jabberwock as the tyrant Queen's key operative, the Gryphon and the Turtle as rebels against the system (Martin 139), or the initials of buttons playfully arranged Load, Save, Delete to acknowledge psychedelic readings of Wonderland (Brooker 234). Level themes based on iconic sites like the Pool of Tears, the Hatter's den, or the Caterpillar's Plot alternate with horror/adventure game themes (Fire and Brimstone, rollercoaster runaway mine cart) and turn into macabre parodies of Disney theme park attractions (the hedge labyrinth of Majestic Maze or the Hatter's Crazed Clockwork) (Brooker 247). The book that McGee's Alice is reading when her house catches fire is a fictitious sequel to Carroll's tales that sets up the gloomy game narrative: on an open page, decorated by a Tenniel pastiche, the calm title "A reunion tea party" transforms into the words "Smoke and fire" by means of a warning that wakes up Alice to save her from death and doom her to a madness caused by the remorse felt about her being the only survivor. Hence, the adaptation process builds on the shock tactics of defamiliarization: the game exploits the recognizability of the original story just for the sake of shattering the familiar apart with those obscenely dark twists which undermine the assumed child-friendly meanings of the source text (foregrounded by numerous other adaptations, like Disney's).

New York Times critic Charles Herold relates the violence of the game to the aggression implied in the adaptation process that he mockingly interprets as an intercultural, intermedial revenge of the New World/ Media upon the Old. In his witty wording,

> [Carroll] disliked American children, considering them ill-mannered. He would probably think this child [McGee's Alice] needed some discipline. "Now Alice," he would say, "I won't tell you any more stories of Wonderland until you put down that knife." And this very American Alice would carve Lewis Carroll to ribbons [2000, G9].

McGee's Alice pursues her determined freedom fight against external forces driving her mad. Within the waking life of the frame narrative she strives to escape madhouse doctors' normative attempts at her controlling her mind. (In the 2000 game she is incarcerated in the Victorian Rutledge Asylum, while in the 2014 game, ten years after her release, she is still under the strict supervision of a private psychiatrist, hypnotic Dr. Angus Bumby.) Within her fantasies she struggles to free Wonderland from the despotic rule of the Red Queen. And within a hypertextual reference frame all her acts are moves in a battle over the ownership of Wonderland as a cultural product equally claimed by Carroll, Disney, and McGee. As the designer American McGee claims on the future film's Kickstarter page, Alice's madness represents a teenager's rebellion against a hypocrite world of the adult villains, while it also provides a commentary on the soul-crushing birth of industrial society, and a critique of the Disney enterprise's mindless and sugarcoated commodification of fantasy.[17]

However, considering that Wonderland is both a product and a mental site of Alice's deranged fantasies, the real struggle takes place on the meta-imaginative plane of her changing attitude to her own imagination. Her initial naïve daydreaming is first seen as a disability because of her incapability of saving her parents from the destructive fire subconsciously associated with her fancies she blames herself about. The resulting submersion into mad hallucinations is symptomatic of her revengeful rage. Lastly she is overwhelmed by a triumphant pride taken in her hyperactive imaginative agency that allows her to save Wonderland, to save herself, to save and reclaim the empowering potential of her creative mental games. The reinterpretation of madness on a new media platform peaks in acknowledging the regenerative powers of foolish behavior and deeds via old media, too. At end of the game, a tableau of peace restored, friends resurrected and Alice calmed fades into a pastiche of a Tenniel drawing. Then we witness Alice reading "the final chapter to her third Carroll adventure" titled "Happily Ever After," and the book text blurs into a line celebrating the reader-player actively participating in the shaping of her story: "'YEA ALICE! You saved us!' And she had done more than that, she knew ... she had saved herself as well." (Brooker 249)

The family adventure fantasy romance TV series *Once Upon a Time in Wonderland* created by Edward Kitsis, Adam Horowitz, Zack Estrin, and Jane Espenson, aired on ABC from October 2013 to April 2014 shares a starting point with American McGee's *Alice* PC games. Because of her realistic accounts of impossible adventures in Wonderland, Alice (Sophie Lowe) is labeled mad and incarcerated in one of Victorian England's infamous madhouses where doctors aim to cure her with a lobotomy-like surgical intervention meant to terminally erase her presumably false memories. Like in McGee's adaptation, Alice is in her late teens or early twenties, and is deeply traumatized. Here, she is tormented both by her failure to convince her beloved father about the veracity of the enchanted land so dear to her heart she keeps on revisiting in search of proofs of its existence and by her departure from her true love, the genie Cyrus she met in Wonderland and fears to have lost forever due to the evil plots of the Red Queen and Jafar who apparently kill him. The Knave of Hearts and the White Rabbit rescue Alice in the very last moment from the mental hospital's operating room and inform her that Cyrus is still alive. She follows them determined to find her fiancé and fight the wrongdoers of Wonderland who want to take hold of the genie's bottle and the three wishes it granted to Alice in order to manipulate the rules of magic to their own malicious ends.

A spin off to ABC's highly popular fantasy series *Once Upon a Time* tracing a web of intertwined reimagined fairy tales, like the mother franchise *Once Upon a Time in Wonderland*, belongs to the crossover fantasy genre in which the story's characters originate from different fictional universes and travel between a magic-less consensus reality and a more homely magical realm they long to get back to. The adaptation of the Western classic *Wonderland* (clearly recognizable by iconic figures such as the vanishing Cheshire Cat, the hookah smoking Caterpillar, mushroom that make you big, the grotesque Tweedles, the tyrannical Red Queen or the monstrous Jabberwock besides the protagonist Alice) is grafted with characters from the Oriental tale *Arabian Nights* (turning the Genie in Aladdin's magic lantern into Alice's love interest and the flying carpet riding sorcerer Jafar, the chief antagonist in Disney's 1992 animated feature film *Aladdin,* into the couple's arch enemy). Furthermore, the show is coupled with allusions to other Disney productions, popular supernatural TV series *Lost* and a number of other well-known tales including Cinderella, Peter Pan and Robin Hood. In fact, Alice's sidekick the Knave of Hearts is Will Scarlet of Sherwood Forest himself. However, the greatest myth the series wholeheartedly relies on is that of True Love popularized by the family romance genre that celebrates sincere emotional bonding socially sanctioned by the idealization of trust, fidelity, caring as well as the institution of marriage and the sociocultural value attributed to the procreation of children.

Apparently, this Alice is no damsel in distress. With the traditional gender roles reversed she is the one who embarks to the rescue of her beloved. A chivalric figure, she faces dangers with courage and wit, fights monsters, and solves riddles to save the weak. However, the feminist potentials of the adaptation remain questionable despite the producers' intention to create a show starring empowered heroines. As Viviane Golasowski (2014) points out, Alice's quest is driven and directed by her affection for two men: her daughterly love for her father for whom she wants to prove the existence of Wonderland and her romantic passion for her fiancé she wants to rescue from Jafar and the Red Queen (and she later assists in finding his beloved's brothers). Her determination comes from her being madly in (filial/erotic) love and her autonomy is undermined by her sentimental relationality, her subservient emotional dependence on men who not only influence her actions but on the whole gain more screen time than she actually does on trying to please them.

Initially, Alice seems to insist on the importance of cunning feminine strategies of survival when she provocatively and flirtatiously tells during their courting to Cyrus that she has never been that comfortable with sword fighting but managed to survive since there are lots of ways to fight in Wonderland; you just have to be creative and beware of trusting anyone. Alice surely proves to be inventive in the first episodes, like in the scene when she saves herself and her companion the Knave of Hearts from drowning in a marshmallow pond by using fire exhaled by dragonflies to make smore, harden the top of the lake and gain a solid surface upon which they can climb out and escape.

Yet, later she gives credit for her victories to Cyrus who taught her how to swordfight or how to trap and turn to dust a dangerous bandersnatch. Not only does she adopt violent masculine means of warfare but she also renounces of the glory and attributes the triumph to her fiancé instead of herself. Even the rare moments of ironic pragmatism in Alice's acts are mirrored by Cyrus' deeds as if to reflect their romantic belonging instead of the heroine's clever agency. For example, both lovers rely on the literalization of figurative meanings to outwit opponents when Alice uses her wish received from the genie materialized in the form of three red rubies to cut with their sharp edges the rope holding her captive in a beast's house and when Cyrus uses a wishbone to open the lock of his cage where Jafar imprisoned him. Hence, Alice ends up exchanging her female autonomy for a mimicry of and dependence on men. She replaces her original mental feats with imitated physical ones. And she renounces of her rational skepticism for the sake of embracing a sentimental trust in a happily ever after with a beloved to whom she devotes herself unconditionally.

The heterosexual family romance story eventually peaks in a finale celebrating reproductivity besides creativity. In the series' epilogue Alice is telling a tale to her daughter about her Wonderland journey. The restoration of status quo implies that she must settle down ending her thrilling adventures to embrace the satiety of marriage, motherhood, and a tranquil domestic life, giving up her rebellious autonomy to fully submit to her True Love. Embracing the conventionally prescribed happy ending of family romance is a sacrificial gesture on Alice's part in so far as her movement toward the patriarchal realm signifies a distancing from her comrades she befriended in Wonderland. Alice's maturation from adventurer girl into storyteller mother can function as an homage to Carroll's original novels framed by poems nostalgically commemorating the adventures surviving in stories to tell to future generations. In an even more positive reading, it can be a subtle feminist gesture meant to guarantee the continuity of her adventurous spirit transmitted as the part of a matrilineal heritage.

If American McGee's Alice's madness resulted from her traumatizing familiarity with mortality, the major motivation of *Once Upon a Time*'s Alice's actions are her being madly in love. Her amorous persona fits the fictional universe of Wonderland where power relations and moral values are equally organized by the characters' emotional ties and affective capabilities. As Golosowski (2014) opines, the virtuous and the evil are distinguished by their capacity or incapacity to love. "Fake love" used for manipulative ends to gain power over others with the illegitimate help of black magic and amoral seduction is contrasted with the "True Love" of pure hearts whose ultimate aim is to unite equally in the sacred bond of marriage while altruistically aiding others' well-being. This contrast is personified by the two couples: Jafar and the Red Queen representing fake love troubled by betrayals and Alice and Cyrus standing for true love, sincere emotions based on mutual trust. In the end the good win over the bad—but even for them there is hope. Simple Anastasia turned into an increasingly ravenous Queen when she renounced of her love for Will the Knave of Hearts but once she reembraces her romantic passion for Will she can defeat the evil magician Jafar and contribute to saving the inhabitants of Wonderland.

The progress of Alice's quest is influenced by the presence or absence of love. While the Knave's broken heart and cynical repression of emotions hinders Alice on her way to Cyrus, her own pure heart allows her to make the leap that seems impossible at first sight. This message ("A pure heart shall make the leap.") is spelt out quite explicitly—even didactically—in the series. It is carved in a stone plate at the edge of a deadly chasm Alice is supposed to cross by relying on her faith in the powers of love. After taking a few steps levitating over the abyss, Alice falls down to meet in the depth—easily associated with her subconscious—her past childhood self. Little Alice is recognizable clad in her trademark hair band and white-and-blue pinafore, but her tangled hair, tired eyes, and an overall miserable outlook suggest that something is wrong with her. She proves to be an embodiment of despair and mad rage as she throws a tantrum trying to force her own older self to exterminate the evil Red Queen who stands as an obstacle to her happiness. Present day Alice—a transitory figure negotiating between monstrous child and bad mother—passes the test and proves the purity of her heart on refusing to hurt her enemy. With her mature pacifism, possibly a feminist solidarity, and the rejection of madness identified as an infantile weakness she redeems her younger self who immediately transforms into a Tenniel-illustration-lookalike visually attesting her innocence regained. The fairy dust Alice receives as a reward helps her to find her way to beloved Cyrus and allows the Red Queen to secretly revive her ex-love-interest the Knave previously turned into a stone statue under a magic spell. Madness—deranged acts driven by obsessive thoughts disregarding the rational consideration of consequences—is put in the service of romance instead of revenge.

In *Once upon a Time in Wonderland,* the trademark Carrollian nonsense—in a fairy-tale fashion matching the series' title—comes from the intimate vows of lovers blinded by a passion that defies rationality with endearments taken to an extreme illogic. Just to mention some instances of nonsensical paradoxes parading in the guise of the great myth of True Love: Alice does not make a wish to the genie Cyrus because the only thing she wishes for is his love; throughout their tumultuous adventures the lovers promise never to move on and stick with each other forgetful that the stasis involved in the promise contradicts the turbulence of e-motions; the lovers submit to a voluntary bondage in each other's arms because it is only love that can truly free them…

American McGee's and *Once upon a Time*'s Alices are exciting because of the emotional responses they inspire beside the intellectual ones. The affective reactions thematized in these (young) adult adaptations include despair, anger, hope and overall madness that takes the forms of hate and love both destabilizing the self, risking who one is. These are feelings all have encountered and hence make the struggling heroine easy to identify with. It is even more tempting when instead of just watching Alice behave independently one can gain unique pleasures and cope with repressed anxieties by interactively controlling her. This is the reason of the immense popularity of contemporary participatory cultural performances of Alice revived to one's own liking in fan fiction and cos(tume)play alike.

Texts chosen as objects of fandom are called by John Fiske "producerly" (42): open, filled with gaps, contradictions, and irresolutions they elicit fan productivity. The story of *Alice in Wonderland* meets these criteria in so far as ambiguity—that calls for the consideration of a variety of possible interpretations of impossible events and a continuation of fantasies—is a par excellence feature of the tale. (No wonder that on *Fanfiction.net* in March 2015 we find over 3000 story sequences inspired by Alice's tale. The influence of visual adaptations is attested by the 2675 takes recycling Burton's 2010 film, while the 177 texts devoted to *Once Upon a Time in Wonderland* proves that a TV show running for a single season and terminating with a happy ending closure of the storyline offers limited imaginative freedom to fans, limiting their participation in textual production.) Alice's primary characteristic feature, curiosity is shared by fans, a subcultural elite from a larger audience of mass consumers, who dive passionately into the story world wondering what else could have happened, what led to the actual events, and what will happen next. Their quest for meanings is motivated by an "affective sensibility" involved in fan fictional writing and role-playing performance alike.

Fan fiction, by definition, is created by devoted nonprofessional authors, enthusiastic admirers of a fictional universe who imagine sequels, prequels or alternative storylines, and fill in syntagmatic gaps of the narrative to elaborate on characters, motifs and settings established by an original artwork referred to as the canon. The question of originality is particularly intriguing in the case of fandom focusing on adaptations where already a novelistic source-text lies beneath a visual remake—like a televised series teasing with the continuability of the story with each new episode—that allows for fans' interactive involvement in the fantasy world they are thoroughly familiar with and can reimagine on their turn as radically strange. Moreover, fans' participation and voluntary feedback may occasionally influence the flow of the original production. Fan fictional products and performances, freely circulated among members through an extensive distribution network, also enter into dialogue with each other coexisting in an immense fairy tale web called to life by new media platforms like the popular internet site *Fanfiction.net* or international fan convention *Comic-Con*.

On *Fanfiction.net* there are over a hundred fan fiction pieces inspired by *Once Upon a Time in Wonderland*. Labeled by telling topic categorizations including "Family/ Romance," "Hurt/ Comfort/ Friendship," "Angst/ Romance/ Drama" and occasionally "Romance/ Humor" or "Supernatural/ Horror/ Romance," practically all the writings focus on emotional conflicts of characters introduced by the TV show. With the love lines creatively tangled, fans explore a surprising variety of amorous sensations and inventive pairings called shippings (derived from the word relationship). They trace the happily ever after of desires left troubled or unfulfilled in original series (Knave/Red Queen), the passion rising between adversaries (Jafar/Alice), friends (Knave/Alice), master and slave (Tweedledum/Queen), same-sex desire and queer affections beyond the heterosexual matrix (Cyrus/Will, Queen of Hearts/Red Queen), crossover shippings (Peter Pan/Alice), the romancing of family ties (little Millie wishing for a big sister Alice who turns out to be magic), and even the fate of the unbeloved Jabberwock, once a girl who metamorphosed into a monster due to a broken heart. In OUATIW fandom Alice tends to lose her autonomous identity as stories are often referred to by the fused names of lovers shipped in the given alternate universe: Knalice and Jalice denote love stories happening between Alice and the Knave of Hearts or Jafar, respectively. Plots driven by pure romantic emotions are easily reducible to lovers' conflicts and teary departures or reunions and revel in a sentimental rhetoric perfectly illustrated by the teaser tagline to DreamWing231's story sequence *Happy Never After*: "Deep down all you want is love. The pure kind we all dream of. But we cannot escape the past. So you and I will never last." Practically all of the OUATIW texts on Fanfiction.com depository safely belong to the family romance genre: rated K+ or T they are intended for a general audience including children over the age of five, their content is supposedly free of any coarse language, violence, profanity, or adult content. The authors' nicknames attest the same pure-heartedness while paying a tribute either to the series (LittleGenie, BrokenStatue) or to Carroll's original and the Alice in Wonderland myth in general (Hattersglasschild, MissBrokenTeacup, followsrabbit) or to the fantasy genre tradition at large (wolfenqueenyuri, DreamWings). Mad passion is sublimated into the very act of relentless writing (fanfiction is most often serialized into a long sequence of episodes going on for weeks, months or even years) the headline featuring on Fanfiction.net pays a tribute to in the single line of encouragement: "Unleash your imagination."

According to Janice Radway (1984) a leading theoretician of romance fiction, fans of the genre are mostly women whose readings and re/writings allow them to boost their self-confidence debilitated in a patriarchal world, to assert better their own rights within the structure of marriage founded on their economical exploitation and psychological suppression, and to legitimate feminine values (vulnerability, sentimentality) against masculine ones (violence, rationality). However, female romance fans' empowerment remains dubious in so far as often they fail to radically undermine stereotypes or to bring about real change on the level of collective social action, and rather remain in the stage of compensatory fantasies. Still, the most attractive quality of fandom John Fiske calls "emotional productivity" (Fiske in Lewis 37) surfaces emphatically in romance, like in *Once Upon a Time in Wonderland* and the fanfiction inspired by it: the adoring audience develop emotional ties with a cultural product that turns into a major plot-engine emotions—which co-productive fans increasingly acclaim as their own.

Fans' affectively charged game targeting the fictional reconstruction of identity to rebel against oppressive ideologies, unsatisfactory circumstances of everyday lives, patriarchally prescribed scripts dictating the law of the genre/gender emerges

"American McGee's Alice Madness Returns Cosplay." Model, styling, costume: Enji Night. Photo, edit: Balázs Sármai. Original character: Spicy Horse EA. 2013 (courtesy Balázs Sármai, www.sarmai.com).

in a different way in another field of Wonderland fandom: Alice cosplay. Cosplay inspired by American McGee's Alice is particularly interesting because it turns a computer game's digitally simulated reality into real life three-dimensional active play. Cosplay—originating from a portmanteau of the words costume and play—means a mode of masquerade, a performance art in which participants create and wear elaborate costumes, make-up and fashion accessories to impersonate their favorite fictional character—mostly from popular cultural sources such as comics, cartoons, manga, anime, video games or live action films.

Cosplayers' imaginative self-stylization through role-playing performances reworking an original character to their own fashion serves multiple purposes. It aims to reach an immediate, intimate relationship with the admired artwork while superseding the passive pleasure of consumption by an active investment in a difference of one's own making (Grossberg in Lewis 50); and to live to the fullest moods, sensations and politics projected on a particular persona. It also attempts to construct more empowered identities than those available in real social life and put these subversive meanings into circulation in line with a communal identity asserted by one's membership to a given fandom.

As Lisa H Kaplan highlights in her 2014 ethnographic analysis of ComicCon as a decisive pop cultural phenomenon of today, the post-feminist identity performances of "cute, tough, geek girls" have gained an increasing popularity at cosplayer conventions. "Killer girl characters" like McGee's Alice—easily impersonated by a few iconic props like the bloody kitchen knife, the blood-splattered apron decorated by esoteric symbols, the reversed horse-shoe necklace that brings bad luck, and the gothic black boots—have turned into a palatable trend rather than isolated occurrence. In the guise of American McGee's Alice cosplayers reclaim girls' right for anger, violent action, and the powerful assertion of one's will traditionally regarded as masculine privileges, socially urged to be internalized repressed in women hence causing depression, anxiety, passive aggression and eating disorders (Kaplan 54). Fans celebrate McGee's PC game for its mainstreaming the visibility of empowered aggressive girls, an identity position rarely available without penalty for female adolescents. As Fiske suggests, "normal adults'" disapproval called forth is an unadmitted but integral part of fan pleasure (38). (Like any carnivalesque act the cosplay performance' pleasures are strictly limited in time and place, yet its memories can be preserved in photos and camera recordings.) Moreover, in Kaplan's view, impersonating killer girls like McGee's Alice offers a cool identity position for defiant geek girls who celebrate girl power by challenging the original gendering of male geekdom, too. The persona they embrace is just as much aesthetically pleasing, flirtatiously feminine as it is physically potent, strong-willed, and behind the mask, overtly intellectual with an expertise in genres, gaming, comics, and fantasy (54).

According to Fiske, the objective of fandom is "to turn the text into an event, not an art object" while minimizing the difference between original artist and co-productive audience (40). The struggle over cultural appropriation is not over: Alice is no longer Carroll's, nor Disney's and not even McGee's but becomes the common cultural capital of fans who contribute to the unlimited multiplication of the fictional character, each designing Alices of their own making, in cosplay and fanfiction alike, giving them revolutionary new significance. Although Lewis highlights the difference between "official culture [that] relies on aesthetic evaluations of texts and elevation of individual artistry" and "popular cultural proponents [who] tend to formulate personal (social) connections with texts and to participate in textual production" (Lewis 2), I believe serious academic scholarly analyses and fans' reinterpretations are quite alike because of the passionate attention they devote to the text they work with.

3

Picturing the Erotic Girl

"we are but older children, dear, who fret to find our bedtime near."

Harassing Wonderland: The Sexualization of the Author, the Muse and Their Titillating Fictional Incarnations

The Alice tales undergo a curious (yet nearly canonized) eroticization, as popular (mis)interpretations of the original oeuvre tend to over-sexualize Lewis Carroll's authorial persona and, as a result, identify his literary nonsense with discursive perversion. A considerable number of (post)modern adaptations from the 1960s onward 'reload' Alice's adventures with erotic (dis)contents by projecting upon the title-character, situated in an intensely intimate connection with storytelling, collective cultural fantasies of liberation from sexual, linguistic, representational restraints.

The sexualization of Carroll's authorial figure is ironically the outcome of a posthumous mythologization that was initially crafted by his first official biographer, his nephew Stuart Dodgson Collingwood with the intention to protect the purity of the famous artist relative as a token of the untarnished reputation he established as a children's writer amongst Victorian audiences. But the same myth—centered on the modest and devout eccentric, Carroll's "safe" intimacy with the angelic infantile as a major source of inspiration—eventually came to be regarded as suspicious to modern critical eyes troubled by the restrospectively constructed image of the shy, stuttering, socially maladroit, unmarried clergyman and scholar with an exquisite "fondness" of what he called "child friends," mostly little girls[1] (Collingwood 416), and especially one particular Alice Liddell, daughter of the dean of Christ Church where the Reverend Dodgson taught mathematics. The famous tale he improvised for her on a bright summer boating trip came to be commonly regarded as a document of the author's secret amorous infatuation with his underage muse.

The speculations about Lewis Carroll's guilty passions arise out of 'biographical evidence' filtered through various media, transformed in the service of iconization. Verbal evidence includes subjective personal remembrances (by relatives, colleagues, and numerous child friends who all, paradoxically, confirm the innocent and mutually devoted nature of the artist's creative partnership with his underage muses). Tell-tale signs are presumably revealed in his verbose correspondence with little girls (full of romantic lines like the ones he wrote for a ten-year-old: "Extra thanks and kisses for the lock of hair. I have kissed it several times—for want of having you to kiss, you know, even hair is better than nothing"

[Cohen 186]), or further odd manifestations of his graphomania such as his meticulously composed, alphabetically arranged, obsessive listing of dozens of names of "girls photographed or to be photographed" (Mavor 7, Nickel 19).[2] Yet, the strongest argument relies on the 'visual evidence' of his artistic photographic work of prepubescent girl nudes, which posterity cannot regard but as pedophiliac, pornographic and perverted.

Oddly, even the 'gaps of the unsaid or the silenced' within the biography came to be considered to be proofs of his hideous desires. Firstly, Charles Dodgson's adamant willingness to "remain, personally, unknown to the world" (Carroll in Cohen 296) as a children's writer and to stay hidden behind his fictional identity covered by the penname Lewis Carroll. Secondly, his discretion about his photographic portraits he regarded as private 'labors of love,' never meant for public exhibition, and only shared with a narrow circle of trustworthy friends, family members, or potential future models. (Carroll's lack of ambition to exhibit his photographs even came to be regarded as a sign of his deviantly "feminine lightheartedness" [Gernsheim 29].) Thirdly, his missing diary pages (either expurgated by his family anxious to "circulate an orthodox appraisal of his life and work" (Frigerio 140) or perhaps torn out by himself), his extremely vague allusions to the "inclinations of his sinful heart," "unholy thoughts" (Collingwood 322)—oddly confessed by Carroll the Anglican deacon and unordained priest in his introduction to his *Curiosa Mathematica* II—and his unexplained sudden break with the Liddell family.

However, we must note that this paranoid, (post)modernist, post–Freudian compulsion to seek a subtext of sexual deviation[3] beneath the complex meanings of nonsense fantasies is misleading in so far as it relies on an utter historical decontextualization of Carroll's work and life. Hugues Lebailly reminds us that the photos should not be detached from the Victorian frame of mind where the child was considered to be an embodiment of angelic innocence, of beauty in its pure, ideal form, and as such, a mediator towards aesthetic cultivation and spiritual elevation, so that child-loving earned respect instead of moral panic (see Lebailly 1998). Practically, pedophilia was a meaningless, non-existent concept at the time of the publication of the Alice stories, as Krafft Ebbing introduced it as a psychopathological category only decades later in the 1880s. In fact, his contemporary biographers insisted on Carroll's child-loving because the prepubescent girl before age twelve was regarded as safely asexual, angelically disembodied being, whereas the consorting of older girls might have risked suspicions of improper desires. Surely the Victorians' romanticization of childhood innocence does not automatically mean that children of the era were actually asexual, sexless beings. Yet if we consider Carroll's child-loving as a perversion, we must be aware of the fact that in the Victorian era it is a perversion of epidemic proportions, a "mass perversion of a mass culture" as Leach ironically notes (in Gubar 103).

Still, suspicions surrounding Carroll's posthumously crafted fantasy figure could not help becoming gradually fossilized as vague assumptions and hazy anecdotes gained canonical status. Karoline Leach primarily blames biographers such as Langford Reed who likely conferred his own virtuous Victorian child-worship, misogyny, and "unhappy difference" onto his contemporary Carroll, and Anthony Goldschmidt whose psychoanalytical reading of textual indices of "subconscious abnormal emotions of a considerable strength" (70) beget in the 1930s the modern idea of Carroll as repressed sexual deviant. Unfortunately, "the grotesque carnival mask of [t]his incredible superficial mythology" (Leach 78) came to fully define Carroll, and was further reinforced by the indeterminacies and allusive rhetoric of even the most prominent Carroll-authorities, as Morton L. Cohen writing about Carroll's "hidden sexual force […] effectively suppressed" (530) channeled into creative fiction, Hugh Haughton coining him "a Casanova of the Victorian nursery" whose diaries were a "roll-call of conquests" (xxvi), or Jackie Wullschlager portraying the artist by a supposedly telling anecdote about him regularly carrying to his seaside visits "a black bag full of toys and gifts to woo little girls, plus a supply of safety pins to hitch up the skirts of those who agreed to paddle in the surf" (36). Small wonder, Carroll's speculative public image turned into common sense.

More surprisingly, the sexualization of the author prevails even in radical challenges to the child-loving Carroll myth. Michael Fitzgerald uses a pseudo-objective medical scientific tone but becomes tangled up in a paradoxical logic when he diagnoses Carroll with high functioning autism cum Asperger's syndrome to circumscribe his asexuality,[4] his impairment in reciprocal social intimate interaction—compensated for by an excellence in creative, mathematical and spatio-visual abilities—in terms of a sexual(izing) pathology. For Fitzgerald, the "undeniably" childish author obsessively cultivating children is "undoubtedly" a case of arrested development, with "possible scopophilia," "echoes of the behavior of a pedophile," and "clearly a [case of] perversion" (174). Self-contradiction and misdiagnosis peak elsewhere too, when critics cite Carroll's would-be repressed homosexuality as a reason for his pedophilia (Marsh 134). Karoline Leach's controversial argument in her book-length study *In the Shadow of the Dreamchild* (1999) debunking the child-loving myth by disclosing Carroll's vivid private affairs with mature, often married women—including artist Gertrude Thomson, writer Anna Thackeray, and Alice's mother, Mrs. Liddell—centers her revisionary biographical insights around Carroll's resexualization. She relocates the desires of "the artist as a serial sexual adulterer" conforming to the standards of a heteronormative sexual economy that deems promiscuous sexual (hyper)activity to be a natural manly feature. Her evidence include adult nudes revealed in Carroll's private collection (164) which are meant to support the author's "robustly normal erotic urges," as one her reviewers claims (Langley in Brooker 57). Eroticization even permeates the language of literary criticism, as Kali Israel's sensual wording suggests in connection with the profusion of *Alice* adaptations and reinterpretations: "But if no one can keep their hands off Alice, few can not wonder what it means to touch her." (279)

Besides biographers' preoccupation with the presumably suspicious biographical circumstances of Carroll's artistic productions, psychoanalytically inspired 'literary pathologists' embarked on a programmatic uncovering of the text's repressed perversions and latent sexual contents. Ironically, the classic Freudian interpretive methodology mostly (mis)fits Alice, a solitary figure who fails to make friends or any real contacts with the creatures of Wonderland or behind the looking-glass, only in so far as it produces lonesome masturbatory fantasies, relying on biographical forgeries, legends, and half-truths parading as facts, instead of genuine critical dialogue. Freudian psychoanalytical interpretations sexualizing Alice abound in farfetched arguments regarding the fall down the rabbit hole as symbolizing sexual penetration, the doors surrounding the hallway representing female genitalia, and the selection of the small door standing for copulation with a female child instead of an adult woman; while Alice's growings and shrinking hold a phallic significance and even the sneezing baby implies an autoerotic event (Goldschmith 280–281). Although Goldschmidt's first psychoanalytical take on Alice in 1933 was possibly intended as a hoax to spoof Freudian terminology (Nickel 69), it became an influential piece with many similar studies to follow.

The affective charge characterizing readings which regard Carroll's authorial persona and Alice the muse and fictional character as inseparably united by emotional ties—be it Platonic adulation, pedophiliac perversion, or savant-autistic love-lack—is complemented here by the explicit sexualization of the female figure for the sake of her male author's (and critics') erotic excitement. In William Empson's complicated analysis, Wonderland is a battlefield between uncontrollable carnal passions (embodied by the Red Queen) and the conscious intellectual detachment from sexuality (impersonated by the disappearing Cheshire Cat), yet it also stages an allegory of reproductive development, whereby Alice personifies a father who descends the rabbit hole to become a fetus at the bottom and to be reborn amidst her own pool of tears, by becoming a mother producing amniotic fluid (358). Clinical psychiatrist Phyllis Greenacre diagnosed Carroll's "intense, unconsummated love" for Alice as "a reversal of the unresolved Oedipal attachment" caused by his mother's premature death. In John Skinner's view the adventurous little girl is a shapeshifted, compensatory version of "adult masculinity," while Paul Schilder regarding Alice as a "substitute penis," goes as far as to ponder explicitly over the following dilemma: "What was his [Carroll's] relation to his sex organ anyhow?" (291).[5]

Carol Mavor's witty Freudian wording calls Dodgson/Carroll's *sans habille* photos of little girls, like Alice, "keepsakes of sexual indifference, a "pocket phallus" (34) that both records and wards of fears of sexuality, as a charm to fight impotence, castration, vulnerability, forgetfulness, along with the painful awareness of mortality. His photographic *tableau vivant* of Alice Liddell as "The Beggar Maid" (1858) remains today his most frequently problematized visual artwork that is alternately regarded as a visual proof of his condemnable desires and as a feat of a Victorian aesthete's attempt to "recharm" fleeting moments of a nostalgically idealized past on a girl's body held still in ink and emulsion—a challenging image that is relentlessly paid homage to in practically all contemporary adaptations thematizing Dodgson's pioneering photographic agency as a 'dark art' complementing Carroll's bright and lighthearted tales. On that staged photo, Alice appears barefoot, in rags, her arms outstretched as if asking for alms, her chest half-uncovered allusive of a child prostitute. She enacts the Victorian archetype of the poor orphan girl, an innocent sacrificial victim of her social circumstances, like a Little Matchgirl or an underage female Christ figure. In her middle-class contemporaries she likely aroused sentimental, religious reactions of pious compassion reminding of "obligations toward the less fortunate" (Susina 2010, 102). But her strangely fusing the Enlightenment idea of child as born innocent of sin with the more traditional religious idea of child born into sin also staged a troubling epistemological crisis of her era. Today's politically correct viewers criticize the inadequacy of her subversive intents on account of the ludic filter to the social sentiment, regretting how the safeness of the unendangered, cherished, bourgeois girl's pose reduces the beggar child's very being to a mere stereotype.

However, Alice's clenched fist on her hip apparently ready to punch and her defiant gaze—challenging the original, eponymous Tennyson poem's focus on male voyeuristic pleasures—convincingly hint at the rebellious resistance accompanying the vulnerability of the Victorian street urchin. These bodily indices of empowerment mark the lurking animalistic aggressivity of untamed Street Arab (as street children were called with this racist

Charles Dodgson/Lewis Carroll, "Alice Pleasance Liddell as 'The Beggar Maid,'" 1858. Albumen silver print from glass negative. 16.3 × 10.9 cm (Gilman Collection, The Metropolitan Museum of Art, New York).

term of the time). They also signal the inventiveness of the *orphan ingénue* surviving and seeking happiness against all odds—a character later on emerging in the tragicomic corpus of Chaplin's burlesque movies, more specifically *The Kid*. There is a social-critical, political intent to the childish pretense play's blurring of class distinctions. The bourgeois girl posing as a beggar repeats and reverses the rags-to-riches scenario of classic fairy tales, like Cinderella, but here Alice goes from riches to rags and then back to riches again from rags, as she moves on and off the photograph, dressing up and down in her fancy-dress. The performativity of class (gender/racial) identity are exposed along with the disruptive powers of social mobility. Especially so, since the image initially belonged to a diptych photographed on the same day at the Deanery: on one Alice poses as a proper girl in her finest dress, on the other she is a ragged pauper in a "kind of before-and-after reversal of social roles romanticized by the Victorians" (Nickel 62). Moreover, Alice's fancy-dressed theatrical pose on the *tableau vivant* vindicates ludic joys as universal rights for all children regardless of class belonging. However, it also sheds light on play as work for some, hence offering a visual record of Carroll's "campaign on behalf of performing child(actors) to prevent their financial and sexual exploitation" (Warner 214).

"The Beggar Maid's" class-subversion is coupled with gender bender, as Alice's undressing has no feminine secrets to reveal, she confronts spectators with bodily markers of an overall tomboyishness—flat chest, short bob-cut hair, defiant gaze—which resist her subjection to conventional eroticization. Feminist analyses highlight the potential of a female spectatorship, and related narcissistic, lesbian desires. Mavor and Auerbach call attention to the Carrollian girl child model's self-awareness of her own "sexuality without parameters" (Mavor 42), while Hacking regards the child nude as a means to address or acknowledge the sexuality of respectable adult women who could have imaginatively substituted themselves for the eroticized child, suggesting that the disturbing complicity the viewer got involved in might have had to do with this more mature sexual dynamics (102).[6]

Nevertheless, the most real, authentic bodily momentum on the artificially staged photo—in my sense its Barthesian *punctum* (1981)—is Alice's balancing on her bent toes, as if she was about to turn around and run away, change her clothes and dress back to her real self, or flee away to play undocumented, hiding in disguise as another. Already a shadow of her absence falls on her presence, she is there while almost not there, daydreaming herself into fictional elsewheres, on a photo attesting the elusiveness of the child as a fundamentally mobile, metamorphic being who cannot be freeze-framed as an idealized icon of innocence. It is my contention that if the portrait is fetishizable it is not because of the disheveled costume's erotic implications, but the spectators' yearning is rather evoked by Alice's ungraspably distant closeness induced by make-believing as an intermedial, intergenerational creative collaboration between the visual storyteller and the child in focus.

Contemporary Fictionalizations of Carroll's and Alice's Desires

Today's most popular adaptations are perhaps the ones which 'reload' Wonderland adventures with erotic (dis)contents, move beyond the paranoia of male critical discourse, and let a mature Alice have her share of the fun. Quite tellingly, in an overview of "Victorian and Other Alices in Contemporary Culture" published in a 2000 collection *Victorian After-*

life scrutinizing postmodern cultural rewritings of the nineteenth century, Kali Israeli's focus falls uniquely on stories about desire related to the sexual agency or victimization of the Alice character to arrive to the conclusion that most contemporary fictional adaptations and criticism alike "are haunted by the 'problem' of those pictures [Carroll's child-nudes], and possible stories about Charles Dodgson, Alice Liddell, and other little girls" (255). Hence, dubious speculations about past historical possibility become circumscribed along the lines of suspicion and an erotic excitement rendered more comfortable through associating Alice with Lolita, a sexually aggressive child-woman instead of endangered, vulnerable infant. Helen Pilinovsky convincingly argues that Alice is retrospectively aged in order to excuse the contemporary readers' excited interest in her puerile figure and to resolve the tension caused by our "uneasy fascination" with her strange mythified relationship with Carroll. Alice's entry into the public domain gradually gives rise to a whole "Alice Industry" and a proliferation of more nubile versions of the originally seven year-old heroine whose "trade goods [nowadays] consist of more broadly salable lingerie than commemorative tea sets" (Pilinovsky 175). Paradoxically, posterity's project to avoid pedophiliac perversion is largely paranoid in so far as it builds on the assumption of an erotic charge (of children) that might not have been there in the first place.

The corpus of eroticized Alice revisions is truly heterogeneous ranging from softporn musical, adult fairy tale, and graphic art novel to feminist manifesto and fictional court trial record. In the 1976 soft-porn musical comedy movie *Alice in Wonderland*, subtitled *An X-Rated Musical Fantasy*, the journey to the other side of the looking-glass serves by means of a sexual initiation for the virginal, prudish, young librarian Alice. She is introduced to her imagination's pleasurable powers in a wondrously idyllic realm of licentious carnal delights and eternal orgasms, and on her return finds herself at ease integrating into an ordinary grown-up life enriched by sex, even if in its safe, monogamous form. We find the same theme of sexual liberation complemented by a fictional, "moral pornographer" problematization of the cultural construction of desire and the unequal social distribution of pleasures in Angela Carter's weird, magical-mannerist love story of two social outlaws, feral Mowgli-like Alice and beastly vampire Duke. "Wolf Alice" published in her 1979 collection of rewritten fairy tales entitled *The Bloody Chamber* is, in fact, a companion piece to her pro-porn feminist culture-critical analysis on *The Sadeian Woman*.

Numerous postmodern (meta)texts are explicitly sex-centered and ironically deprived of any idyll or illusion. The 2006 collection *Alice Redux* edited by Richard Peabody contains paradigmatic short-fiction such as Bruce Bauman's "Lilith in Wunderland" on adult Lorina undergoing psychoanalytical therapy with Freud because of her childhood experience with that "fucking mad rabbit" and the "crazy old wanker" "Dodo" (109), or Beth Bachmann's piece with the telling title "Dodgson mumbles (After reviewing the supreme court ruling on virtual child pornography)." Jeph Loeb and Tim Sale's Batman comic book *Haunted Knight* (1996) attests "a nudge-nudge awareness of the Carroll-as-pedophile rumor" (Brooker 155) by introducing as Batman's nemesis the schizophrenic Hatter who merges features of Tenniel's iconic illustration with those of Carroll and is renowned for kidnapping runaway kids to shut them in his hideout where he forces them to drink drugged tea dressed in Wonderland costumes. As for cinema, although its production was discontinued, *Phantasmagoria: The Visions of Lewis Carroll* a fantasy-horror film was planned to be the directorial debut of controversial Gothic rock metal singer Marilyn Manson who also heartily embraced the sexual deviance myth. The 2006 trailer introduced Carroll (Manson in the leading role) as "a divided soul," an insomniac pervert fantasizing about bizarre, sadomasochistic sexual preoccupations with Alice, Alice's alter ego, and a dream wife in the dark Wonderland of his isolated castle where "all nightmares know [his] name," and Tweedle Dum and Dee are nymphomaniac lesbian twin sisters. The ghastly erotic vision culminates in a Roxy Music song about the impossible infatuation for "a disposable darling," an inflatable sex doll, tellingly entitled "In every dream home a heartache."

Other fictional pieces intertextually abuse Carroll's work to provoke readers with the juxtaposition of the innocent Wonderland of infantile fantasy implied in Alice's name and the traumatizing reality of graphic violence such as the one depicted in A. M. Homes' *The End of Alice* (1996) in which a young girl Alice is sexually harassed to be mutilated and killed by a unrepentant pedophile. (Similarly grim "pubescent variations" on the same theme include *Go Ask Alice* [1971], "an anonymous morality tale of a teenage girl's drug induced demise," Stephanie Grant's *Passion of Alice* [1996] that turns Wonderland into an eating disorder clinic, and Lisa Dierbeck's *One Pill Makes You Smaller* [2004] with a too rapidly growing eleven-year-old heroine who "gets hit on by dirty old men" [Peabody xiii].) In an even much harsher vein, abusive countercultural products such as international child pornography networks called *Wonderland Club* or *Alice Club* brutally distorted Carrollian fantasies to their own ends (Brooker 51, 53). It is certainly under the influence of such offensive defamations of the Alice-myth that some campaign-posters fighting the violence against children make underage models mime postures familiar from Carroll's child-photography as if to suggest to visually literate spectators that the ragged cloths and bare feet of "The Beggar Maid" are indubitably tell-tale signs of child-abuse. As Will Brooker notes, the maintenance of Carroll's two-faced status as child-lover genius, "both a national treasure and a vaguely suspect enigma" consistently serves to enhance his marketability as a cultural icon regardless of defacing the authentic authorial image (64).

Mutable collective desires intertwined with changing cultural anxieties and aspirations have been projected in fictionalized form upon Alice's imaginary erotic personas. Accordingly, the eroticized Alice figures embody counter-cultural icons of the 1970s' sexual and political libera(liza)tion, initial "new leftist" ideas of Marxism, psychoanalysis, and feminism, 'revamped' by/in increasingly self-reflective (self-ironic or self-destabilizing) post-modernist metanarratives. Moreover, many of these various adaptations associate female sexual pleasures with a specific female creativity, an imaginary apt to reach an intimacy both with the "otherness" and the corporeality patriarchally excluded from the subject, and with the polysemic, ambiguous, nonsensical wordplay banished by the symbolic, phallogocentric order's solidification of meaning. (On the plane of theoretical writing, we find poetically erotic yet politically charged manifestos by feminist psychoanalyst philosophers: Luce Irigaray's "The Looking-Glass, from the Other Side" a preface to her *This Sex Which is Not One* (1977), Hélène Cixous's 1982 "Introduction to Lewis Carroll's *Through the Looking-Glass* and *The Hunting of the Snark*," and Teresa De Lauretis's *Alice Doesn't. Feminism, Semiotics, Cinema* (1984) all gain inspiration from Alice to outline subversive "libidinal" writing/reading strategies motivated by feminine bodily energies.) They portray sexual and discursive initiation as coincidental, traumatic, ecstatic experiences which trouble the very logic of representation, but can be soothed by the therapeutic act of storytelling, of sharing nonsensical, sensual tales of love and desire. Alice's falling down the rabbit hole equals her falling in love and into the story. A fall that inevitably results in the blurring of the dividing line between reality and imagination, presence/surplus and absence/loss of sense, and a succeeding free, uncorrupted eroticization of the indeterminacy of meaning.

In the following I venture to analyze just a few of the fascinatingly (re)imaginative postmodern adaptations which have indulged in sophisticated fictionalizations of the author's alleged affections for his child muse. The heterogeneity of my selection—including lyrical biografiction, photographic simulation, sentimental film, artistic-pornographic graphic novel, and feminist ideology-critical manifesto—is meant to represent the multi-faceted interpretive possibilities of this amorous creative partnership.

Long(ing) Exposures: Lyrical Biografiction of Alice and her Photographer in Prose, Poem and Dance

Some of the most exciting recent literary revisitings of Lewis Carroll and Alice Liddell's intimate relationship and creative partnership refuse the futile attempt to collect enough historical evidence so as to produce an objectively balanced, truthful account of the authentic selves of author and muse. Instead they embrace the ambiguous genre of *biografiction* that is both based on and deviates from those real-life events which are assumed to remain largely unknowable because of forgetful misremembering, nostalgic idealization, or mythologizing demonization constituting inherent parts of any memorial practice. They disclose how posterity's reconstruction of an iconic artist figure is primarily driven by the fantasmatic urge of making(up) a legend. Biografiction renounces of truth-claims to pay homage to the spirit of the artist, a fictitiously summoned phantasm. In a way, this approach is much in line with postmodern theories of subjectivity, language, and memory. If identity is a cultural script's individually improvised carnal act and discursive performance (see Bollobás 2012), narratives of the self are inherently insufficient because any verbal *representation* is an unreliable means of mediating our psychic *experiences* which already constitute subjective filters to a physical *reality* that must remain ungraspable, inaccessible. Since these misrepresentations can only generate misinterpretations, the real self, the authentic ego is only accessible in a mediated form: always already an other, an image, an imaginary construct (see Kérchy 2008, 78–95).

Contemporary fictional takes on the Alice-Carroll intimate relationship take hold of an elusive, illusory glimpse at the true face of their biografictional subject, rendered mysteriously mutable and multi-faceted because of the secret desire constituting the kernel of his personality. The titles of Katie Roiphe's 2001 novel and Stephanie Bolster's 1998 volume of poetry imply the biografictional strategy the artists take to trace the double portrait of author and muse. *Still She Haunts Me* is a line from Carroll's frame-verse to *Looking-Glass* nostalgically commemorating the passing of time and in particular childhood joys ("Still she haunts me, phantomwise,/ Alice moving under skies/ Never seen by waking eyes" [287]), while *White Stones* refers to the phrase "I mark this day with a white stone"—originating from Catullus[7] and widely quoted in Victorian times—Dodgson used in his diary to indicate particularly pleasurable life events he meant to cherish in his memory for ever, like his encounter with the four years old Alice Liddell on 25 April 1856, a day he marked with this expression. The titles emphasize how Carroll/Dodgson himself seems to have been aware of the elusive nature of memories. In his mental imagery Alice figures either as a ghostly apparition or as a souvenir object, a tiny tombstone for what she has been—both very far from the real girl's actual fleshly presence. These two women writers' emphasis on unreliability, ambiguity, and affectivity instead of rationality as grounds of reminiscence might point towards a specifically feminine mode of life-writing that allows itself to function in a more embodied, emotional, and impressionistic manner than the male authored biography driven by the intent to record exemplary facts of a Great Man's teleological life-line (see Séllei 2002). Paradoxically, both Roiphe's and Bolster's themes are governed by photographical metaphors and the metaphor of photography, a medium conventionally regarded as apt to produce images of truth, unquestionable visual proofs of reality, used to highlight how 'his Alice,' 'the Alice he loves' can be captured only in the dark room of Carroll/Dodgson's cabinet processing photographic film and of his turbulent mind troubled by a passion difficult to make sense of.

Katie Roiphe's *Still She Haunts Me* (2001) includes in its subtitle a generic designation that emphasizes fictionality: *A Novel of Lewis Carroll and Alice Liddell.* However, Roiphe's self-designation as a non-fiction writer, critic and journalist, as well as her biografiction's paratexts, seem to play with the destabilization of the factuality/fictionality divide. The initial mottos are biographical fragments—sketches of life-writing from Langford Reed, Mark Twain, and Virginia Woolf—which all reflect a certain uncertainty or unknowingness about Carroll's real character. The first double-page includes by means of documentary evidence a slightly blurred replica of an actual black and white photograph, an intimate snapshot of the three Liddell sisters lazily reclining unashamed in front of the photographer Dodgson/Carroll's gaze that remains invisible for us. The blurb and the review extracts featuring on the front and back cover celebrate creative imagination's capacity to create a verisimilitude, in this case the palpable semblance of a reality ("a strange relationship," "a man's personal disintegration") that might have never actually been but is still brought real in "a disturbing story handled with great subtlety and penetrating insight" where "you can almost feel the sweat dripping between the crinolines, the stultifying torpor of tea parties and college dinners" (*Independent*). Roiphe allegedly produces biofiction inspired by the real life of Charles Dodgson and his relationship with Alice Liddell, mixing his actual writing—some letters, *Wonderland* passages and quotes from unpublished manuscripts, like his ballad opera—with invented diary entries and speculations about significant life events, such as the rift with the Liddells.

The book starts with the ultimate mystery preoccupying all Carroll biographers: the potential reasons of his break with the Liddell family—which could also explain the nature of his relation with his girl muse—Roiphe vaguely relates to the mother's discontent with Dodgson's improper photographies of Alice, a central theme of this ekphrastic novel. On the first pages, instead of the writing Carroll's joy we get an intimate glimpse of the reading Dodgson's pain he feels upon receiving a letter from Mrs. Liddell asking him not to visit any more. His confusion surfaces in his first reactions; he reaches for his photo album with Alice's pictures and puts it back on his shelf without opening it, then mutilates his diary—formerly, a sympathetic companion and a reassuring proof of his ordinariness—to embrace "Unsaid passages, unspoken frames of mind. Missing bits of bones and cartilage" (2) as part and parcel of his life story. The memory of Alice is henceforward connected to Dodgson's self-mutilation, a forced entry into the realm of the unspeakable (torn diary pages) and unimaginable (unopened photo album).

A veritable artist, he self-reflectively ponders about his experience of that traumatic freeze-frame "moment of recognition of loss" by identifying himself with a classic Shakespearean heroine, the Fairy Queen Titania from *Midsummer Night's Dream*, who, after the lifting of the spell sees the donkey just before falling out of love with it, "still enspelled, but suddenly aware," "observing, as if from a balcony, with a binocular, her own desire." A sudden shift of pronoun invites spectators to "see that impossible love laid out in front of you and still be caught in it, that lonely time, not released but trapped. All the beauty and ugliness you are capable of converging in this one love […] The heart's rough quite. Donkeys running wild." (5) The "heart's rough quiet" emblematizes *affective nonsense* at its ultimately intensive peak when the sudden lifting of the spell, the realization of the impossibility of one's desires brings about a self-reflective moment of disenchantment that curiously results in a conscious retrospective realization of one's past enchantment.

Dodgson's infatuation with Alice is systematically described in terms of photographic metaphors. Other little girls seem to be "blurred, overexposed versions of their more radiant sister" (12) who is the "unruly daughter" (13) with a "fierceness of imagination" (15) ever so challenging to be captured on a photograph since she is in a "constant progression of disorder," "perpetually in disarray" with her bruised knees, tangled hair, wrinkled or stained clothes, shedding buttons, trailing sashes, losing hems producing an "unraveling appearance" (14). She is Dodgson's favorite photographic subject as the very embodiment of ambiguity. She is "oblivious of her body" but there is a playful theatricality to all her actions; her elusiveness is hard to keep track of but even despite her disappearings she seems to be "more *there* than the others"; she stays in and runs out of focus; and her dynamism enacts an "energetic liveliness" that contrasts the stillness (the still life!) of the photographic medium.

Roiphe provides various reasons for Dodgson's obsession with child nude photography so often problematized by posterity. One of the (invented) diary entries reveals his understanding of the body in terms of geometric abstraction, aesthetic idealism and transcendental mysticism, an entity charged with scientific, philosophical, aesthetical, and esoteric significations predominating personal meanings. He confesses that "the camera allows [him] to consider all angles & possibilities—to contemplate beauty—as in perfection of form—the size of ankle—the width of a waist—the narrowness of hips," and contemplates how "[i]t is a truly difficult aesthetic problem—how to take the flesh out of a woman, & leave the beauty of soul" that is present in the angelic body of the girl child, "the perfect reflection of God's intentions" (31).

Of course, the photo shooting sessions are also interpreted as games belonging to the private mythology of the artist and the muse who hide in the darkroom as "two beings changing and fluttering above the earth" (36) bonded by the unbearable lightness of "a friendship structured like a private joke: everybody could hear it but only they understood what it meant" (39). In the developing room, the precious silence or intimate whispers, the strange smelling liquids and the heat of the chemicals, and even the topsey-turveydom of the processed images are associated with the erotic frisson of the unsaid, that oddly neither Alice nor Dodgson seem to be fully aware of, as they merely sense and do not entirely comprehend, not to mention verbalize or act upon it. In Roiphe's reimagining of the relationship, "the underground remains underground" (105). Only his gaze touches her, desires are suspended, diffused, forever in a state of anticipation, emotions are purified and refined by the pain of a longing observed but not inhabited. Photography offers a compensatory means for this strange couple to "try to find ways to talk about things there are no ways of talking about." (76)

Picturing Alice also opens up a path towards self-knowledge for the photographer himself. Dodgson takes photos of her to keep something of himself he had never seen before. For instance, he is stupefied by his own feelings—described again with a photographic metaphor as "the quick chemical conversion of mood" (35)—when he empathizes with the little girls' sentiments all too intensively, as his heart goes out for her upon the breaking of her beloved china doll. It is his compassionate identification with her in place of a passionate (sexual) objectification of her that he freeze-frames on a photo he makes of Alice, while dipping his head underneath the calico curtain of his camera.

In another fictitious diary entry, Dodgson describes his camera as a fantastic apparatus that enhances his vision and allows him to see the invisible, and image the unimaginable. The agency attributed to the camera permits a peaceful reunion of the two: he is relieved of the culpability felt over the forbidden sight and she is saved from objectification by having her image cradled in the lens. The denuded little Alice emerges for Dodgson as an epiphanic vision, a divine revelation, her beauty a proof of God's existence. Yet the real enchantment results from the recognition that her perfect, heavenly ethereality exists side by side with a flawed, vulnerable corporeality. She is like an oxymoron, a portmanteau, a pun, *nonsense eroticized*. Dodgson's amorous gaze borders on anatomical scrutiny and a devout ravishment originating from a mutual eyeing, a rare experience in a repressive era of furtive glances. Moreover, this stream-of-consciousness passage reflects the artist's struggle to find the appropriate words to speak the unspeakable, his desire "to say for once what [he] really sees," to find the adequate verbal equivalent for a visceral visual stimulus. This yearning is neatly represented in a powerful lyricism characterized by a "sensual slowness dripping with a sense of the forbidden" (Childers 2001).

And then I turn & look—through the camera—eye through lens—It is the crushed glass that sees her—cradling her image in its crystal depths. The room shakes in my hands & then falls into place. The camera can see what I cannot—enacts my vision and releases me.

And then I see her, a pearly perfect stretch of Alice, heavenlike and.... No, let me say for once what I truly see: delicate olive-tinted skin, purplish bruise rimmed with green on her thigh, to tiny swells, a stomach slightly protruding, a red crease where her undergarments pressed into her stomach, ribs outlined, black eyes staring defiantly at the camera. As God designed her. Mirabile dictu [176].

One of Roiphe's feats is her introduction of a variety of perspectives reflecting on Dodgson's photos of Alice, which attest a multiplicity of potential interpretive takes, and suggest that the meaning of any image resides in the eye of the beholder. *Wonderland*'s illustrator, Tenniel never sees the real Alice, and transforms Carroll's dreams into "pastel fantasy inhabited by harmless creatures and blond girls" (163). Alice's sister Edith, upon seeing the photo of "Alice sans habillement" feels *Schadenfreude* and relief, lifted out of the jealousy she felt so long, for she "*sees* that there is something wrong with Alice" and not herself, and thinks that "if this what Mr. Dodgson's friendship meant, then it was not worth having" (187). The mother Mrs. Liddell regards Dodgson's art along the lines of an ominous oddity causing a nervous suspense, an imminent danger she must protect her daughter from. Previously, via a case of visual *mise-en-abyme*, readers already watched her watching over Dodgson watching her daughters, as she noticed Dodgson's curious gaze "contemplating children's game like it was the ceiling of the Sistine Chapel" (13). She acknowledges the magnificence of his "The Beggar Maid" photograph of Alice, but associates it with a "heaviness in her chest," "the invisible potential" of an unspoken threat experienced as a "remote possibility, a book that might fall, a table's sharp edge that might cut" (42). When she finds out about the nudes, she fears making a scandal because she realizes that "Dodgson achieved a subterranean marriage of their destinies" (218) and whatever happens to him, inflicts Alice, too. Her only option is to break the bond all together as if it has never existed. Carroll's speech therapist Hunt also would banish the image into the realm of the invisibility: "he wished the picture did not exist, he wished he had never seen this little girl standing naked, knee bent, foot pressed against the wall" "childlike and knowing" (203) making spectators play hide and seek with the ambiguous meanings generated. His objective description of the photo in medical terms is troubled by his recoiling from its tyrannically imposing upon onlookers one way of looking, a dangerous fantasy that draws into a sensual sway, "creating new avenues that you had not known existed in yourself," making his discourse deviate towards poeticity, as in the line: "The slit looked bare and so exposed there. Velvety, peach-like" (203). Alice's sex constitutes a vertiginous aporia for Hunt, but the portraits "bleed into the world around them" and "force the imagination into strange positions" because one feels the story unfolding behind the picture, "how he got her to stand like that, how she pulled off her dress with the single careless gesture of a child … how Dodgson took it off the floor and folded it," how he put his "love in the photographs, in the story of *Alice's Adventures*, in the confusing fall down the rabbit hole" (202) one finds difficulties in making sense of.

For Alice, unlike for the others, the photo shooting session and not the artistic end product proves to be a formative experience. While undressing for the ominous nude photograph, she spots herself in the oval looking-glass of Dodgson's room and then reflected in his eyes, and suddenly grows conscious of her own nakedness, her beauty, and perhaps even the piquanterie the situation holds because of its future implications. The scene reminds of the Freudian primal scene denoting a child's first encounter with sexuality, usually witnessed when peeping at the lovemaking of one's parents, but here Alice feels the budding potential of desire within herself. The "longing for the I know not what," CS Lewis believes fairy tales arouse in young readers, is charged with erotic contents that the little girl struggles and eventually fails to fully comprehend. She is much like Alice on meeting the textual monstrosity of the Jabberwocky nonsense poem contending, "Somehow it seems to fill my head with ideas—only I don't exactly know what they are!'" (156)

An awkward passage describes the child's wrestle for/with meanings upon her experiencing desire as nonsensical, while the third person singular personal pronoun denoting Alice turns readers complicit onlookers by Dodgson's side. In a quick succession of reinterpretations, Alice first seeks refuge in the Wonderland tale Carroll crafted for her, but reciting a few lines to herself does not help since she is overwhelmed by physical sensations sprung from the intense cognition of her denuded bodily presence and antagonistic affective reactions fusing fear and pleasure of to-be-looked-at-ness. Roiphe's play with perspectives contributes to the destabilization of meanings. While in her own mind's eyes she sees herself as the virgin seduced by goblin men in Cristina Rossetti's famous poem, for outward spectators, with a more sublime metaphor indicating an immaterial contact, she is Athena sprung from Zeus's head, a muse and heroine called into life by her artist maker. Alice's tears constitute a form of body-writing, for the lack of words, a compensatory corporeal reaction to her encounter with the unnamable. The passage is worth to be quoted at length.

> She had seen her naked self in the oval mirror of Dodgson's room. A partial sideways sliver of her nakedness flew at her and startled her: Alice undressing for a man.[...]
>
> She thinks of crawling into his lap, safely there, on his knees again, her head against his chest. *But wait a bit, the oyster cried, before we have our chat. For some of us are out of breath and all of us are fat.*
>
> The air is cool on her skin. [...] Her arm is folded across her chest, and then down by her side. His eyes on her. Eyes across skin. The damp look she has seen before. She is peeled open. [...] Her stomach feels funny. The whole room is drawn into her, wood floors, fireplace, white ceiling. The fear, clarifying and electric, in front of the camera. The look in the strange familiar eyes, suddenly terrifying; like goblins chewing mangoes, pears, plums, melons. She is stuck there like a pit inside plump fruit. [...]
>
> Through it all she felt an emerging loveliness. A new being sprouting fully formed like Athena from the head of Zeus. Her skin satin. The light caught in her hair. A crown of flowers. The beauty she had not known was there. Running through her the pleasure of his looking; not his attraction to her, her attraction to herself.
>
> She stood differently, aware of his watching her. The tears were an unloosing of something in herself she had never felt. An overflowing of feeling she could not put in words. [...] She stood in front of him, feeling the excitement rising through her body, the luxury of being appreciated, the fear, and then—there was something else. She was waiting without knowing precisely for what, an she felt it—the waiting—in every muscle. The tightness coiled up in her; the newness of standing there naked and goose-pimpled, feet in rough rug, back of calves rubbing against worn satin sofa, feeling every brush against every surface differently than she has before, his gray eyes on her; it was desire, more than anything else, that was making her cry [178–9].

Roiphe excels in maintaining readerly excitement by hesitation. The italicized quotation of a cannibalistic passage from the *Wonderland* episode about the Walrus and Carpenter luring ignorant baby oysters into their dinner plates might equally refer to Carroll's storytelling skills exploited as a means of pacification to make the model stand still during the long photographic exposure time and can also refer to desire 'devouring' its unknowing victim, desired and desirer alike. Even if the book revolves around Dodgson's photography of Alice, it remains unclear whether the various spectators are reflecting upon the same image or not, and if this child portrait is a fictitious, fully denuded version of an actual photo by Dodgson of Alice as "The Beggar Maid." The toying with kaleidoscopic perspectives supports the basic generic assumption of biofiction: "truth is whatever you want it to be."

Stephanie Bolster's collection of poems *White Stone: The Alice Poems* (1998) is dedicated to exploring the life of the real Alice who sat for Dodgson's camera and inspired the fairy-tale fantasy books which prompted his rise to fame as Lewis Carroll. By means of paratexts, the poems are complemented by a biographical note on Alice Liddell along with a list of "sources" including the most seminal works of Carrollian life writing, from Morton L. Cohen to Karoline Leach, which provided information and inspiration for Bolster, who did not want to limit herself to facts, and allegedly relied on biofictional and fictional pieces too—namely Dennis Potter's documentary-fiction *DreamChild* (1985) and Jan Svankmajer's surreal animated *Alice* (1988)—while composing her poems. The fusion of factuality and fictionality is reflected by the cover design's merging a blurred photo of Alice by Dodgson, a photo-negative replica of Tenniel's illustration of the White Rabbit, and a receding landscape one might associate with the mental image of Wonderland in the making.

As the volume's subtitles suggest, practically, all the poems focus, on a thematic or a metaphorical level, on the themes of visibility, spectacularization, and the unseen, photographic art and dream imagery as the grounds of an unbreakable bond between Dodgson/Carroll and Alice. The first part, "Whose Eyes," concentrates on Alice's childhood.

The initial poem turns the "Dark Room" into a locus of unrealized desires and imaginative pretense play where the girl's denuded body is distanced on the photographic portrait emerging as a communal creative output, the result of a closeted complicity, a game interrupting the tediousness of a teatime representing Victorian morals and allowing Alice to temporarily toy with becoming someone else.

The following poem, "Aperture, 1856" starts out from technical difficulties of 19th century photography to emphasize the challenge represented by capturing Alice's likeness, and continues with an open-ended poetic question that encapsulates the enchanting essence of the creative partnership between artist and muse, while the closure offers a tentative answer, allowing the emerging photographic image to take the place of the transverbal unspeakable.

"The Beggar Maid" photograph holds a plethora of embodied significations. The picture is the record of a ludic tie, a play of hide and seek, of a pretense game and a bittersweet memento of the last moment before Alice's first menstruation separating her from Carroll ("The Curse"). It is also the "twin picture" of a portrait of Dodgson as an abused child begging for the mercy of his tormentors ("Portrait of Dodgson as the Beggar Maid," 18).

The final poem of the section, "Thames" builds the duo into a *ménage à trois*, as the poetess Bolster seeks her place amidst her two protagonists, Carroll and Alice, asking where does she fit in their story, which myth version, which character can she identify with while preserving her own artistic autonomy. Her feat is choosing the in-between positionality of an insider-outsider who can switch perspectives, embrace uncertainty, and alternately empathize with both author and muse, considering the devastating and rewarding effects of their desires alike.

The second chapter, "Close Your Eyes and Think of England," considers Alice's adulthood. The poetic ponderings inspired by actual photos of Alice taken by Dodgson's contemporary, photographer Julia Margaret Cameron, great aunt of Virginia Woolf (Alice posing as Cordelia, Pomona, or St. Agnes) are followed by snapshots of Alice Liddell's most important life events. Her romantic involvement with Queen Victoria's youngest son interrupted because of class discrepancy, the compromises of her married life with wealthy cricket player Reginald Hargreaves, the birth of her first son, the death of her beloved sister, her delight in woodcarving art and a door she made for the church of St. Frideswide in the East End of London in 1890 depicting the image of the Saint arriving in Oxford by boat (reminiscent of another boating trip that led to the birth of *Wonderland*), her receiving a honorary doctorate from Columbia University in 1932, her growing old, and eventually her death. All the way through her life, the make-believe dreamchild in Wonderland stays the hard kernel of Alice Liddell Hargreaves' reality. To avoid a pathetic tone, Bolster adds black humor to an ultimate photographic metaphor meant to reveal how the advent of death and a madness turned senility defies representational confines to open up the absolute blackness of the vertiginous rabbit hole.

The third part, "Portraits of Alice, Annotated," undertakes to silencing her words with the critics' commentaries, attempting to make sense of nonsense, annotations which are counterbalanced by an absurd poetic piece on a "Portrait of Alice as her own foot" (a nod to how she addressed her elongated feet in a (foot)note in Carroll's original novel). Alice is taken on a picaresque journey out of Wonderland, to curious encounters with iconic figures associated with legendary elsewheres. She meets Elvis in Memphis, Persephone Underground, Christopher Robin in the Hundred Acre Wood—turned King of Hearts, Queen of Hearts, and an incestuous twin brother, respectively. On further poetic portraits, Alice moves in and out of the guise of *Wonderland* creatures. In homage of the smoking caterpillar, she transforms into a chrysalis who wonders about metamorphosis. She is pictured as the epitome of undecidability, first a white rabbit, then a dormouse written with a gaping "o," and a Cheshire cat. Despite critics overwriting her, her identity remains enigmatic.

In the fourth part, "Hide and Seek," "Alice discovers the New World and eludes the poet." The verbal accounts of her photographic portraits describe Alice as a missing person, Alice born 100 years later as a hippie, fifteen in 1967 in San Francisco, with flowers in her hair, listening to Grace Slick's psychedelic musical tribute to Wonderland, and Alice as spirit, as English landscape, as a lake, and eventually, as her own universe, blurred and decipherable only by guesswork. Bolster's poetry is a feat of intermedial transition that turns the legendary texts into visual impressions, imaginary photographic snapshots, often meta-photos of a photography in the making, described verbally to trace the most authentic portrait: a kaleidoscopic vision of an intricate interplay of endless defacements and self-maskings, Alice as she really is.

Falling Through the Aperture: Scottish Ballet's Alice

Scottish Ballet's *Alice* performance premiered at Theatre Royal Glasgow on 12 April 2011, conceived by choreographer Ashley Page and stage designer Antony McDonald, featuring the musical score of composer Robert Moran, video design by Annemarie Woods, and lightning by Peter Mumford. The director realized an intermedial challenge in bringing together different art forms in invigorating ways throughout the creation of a "wordless piece of theatre [in dance form] about a book in which words and wordplay are almost the subject." He felt that a fresh appeal could be given to the well-known tale by placing in center stage the fascinating figure of the author, his real-life relationships, obsessions, and polymath artistic activities (Page in Scottish 5).

As dance critic Mary Brennan writes in the souvenir program, the makers of the ballet performance "pored over illustrations and biographies [until] something just clicked—like the shutter of a camera.... Dodgson's own camera. [So they figured that] the key they would use to unlock Wonderland was photography" (12). Not only do Carroll's original photographs of Alice Liddell take part of the surrealistic stage design with magic lantern show like projections in the background, but Alice's journey into Wonderland actually starts with a photographic session where she is lulled to sleep by the story Carroll tells to keep her amused and eventually finds herself tumbling through the aperture of his camera into a strange elsewhere. The inside of the camera represents the inside of Carroll's mind, so throughout her wanderings when Alice encounters the whole cast of oddball characters from Wonderland and Looking-Glass Realm, she experiences what he sees through the lens of his camera, the third eye of his imagination.

However, Alice, blurring the real girl from the photos and the fictional character from the novels, is more than just a vehicle of Carroll's thoughts. The libretto puts them on equal plane by consistently referring to them by their first names, as Alice and Charles. Moreover, Charles appears in Alice's dreams as a fantasy figure who is nevertheless endowed with a heroic metafictional might. He repeatedly modifies the plot to rescue Alice from dangerous situations (the Court Executioner Jabberwock in Act 1 Scene 2 and Act 2 Scene 4, deadly hypnotic flowers in Act 1 Scene 3, a dizzying Lobster Quadrille in Act 1 Scene 6, biting mutant insects in Act 2 Scene 3). He knowingly consoles and comforts Alice that "she's actually not doing too badly in this new world which doesn't always seem to make perfect sense" (Scene 3 in Scottish 6). And he finally fully breaks the confines of the story frame when he frees Alice from the trial by "affectionately poking fun at his own inventions as, after all, this is his story and these are fragments of his own imagination" (Act 2 Scene 7 in Scottish 8). Via a complex *mise-en-abyme*, Alice is a figure in Carroll's mind, but in Alice's dream Charles embodies the voice of her subconscious urging her to discover more about herself, to dare to disrespect elders, to accept the nonsensical nature of the world, and to learn to rebelliously "say enough is enough." The didactic lessons of subversion encapsulate the essence of the story explicitly spelt out by the libretto of Scene 5 tellingly entitled "Alice and Charles." The final scene "Epilogue/ Awakening" reinforces this ambiguity: as we witness Charles fallen asleep in the same armchair in which Alice had been previously posing for the photographs before the advent of the adventures, we likely revision the classic Carrollian question "Who dreamt whom?"

Photography serves as a frame to the story but our vision remains blurred as Alice and Charles "float in a dreamlike limbo as familiar figures from the adventures drift in and out of focus" in the paradigmatic Act 2, Scene1 called "The Wandering." The ambiguity is maintained by the juxtaposition of two radically different visual regimes. The ocular orgasm of surrealist eccentricity and the melancholic restraint of sepia-toned Victorian portraits combine in the montage-projections of the stage design to convey the bizarre spirit of the adventures.

The makers' decision to include surrealistically revamped photographical and biographical mementos in a very postmodern ballet staging of the original novel was allegedly driven by the intent to avoid the three major pitfalls of any Carroll adaptation: a slavish rendering of the classic book, or a misreading affected by sugary sweet nostalgia, or a demonization of the author's fixation on pre-pubescent girls. Although Charles primarily emerges in Alice's dream as a fantasist, writer, photographer, pedagogue, and even a chivalric savior or a faerial guide but still there is plenty of space for the ghost of the child lover to hover over the story. According to the libretto, their dance duo enacts how "his desire for her happiness is complicated by the contradictions of his own yearning," while the epilogue stages Alice climbing back out of the camera lens to "gaze at Carroll with a confusing mixture of fondness and regret before quietly leaving him to rest alone" (Scottish 8). Complicated emotions subtly charged with eroticism characterize a relationship that is seen idyllic only because it is doomed to end. The performance abounds in dark humor but a certain dark romanticism weaves the plot leading from the duo's "alone together" to separation and solitude. In the final scene, representing the loss of childish ties, Alice triumphantly reclaims the gaze, ready to hold a camera of her own. While the spectators are offered visions of wild imaginings to identify with, "the bigger picture deals through the eye of the camera with transience, memory, creativity" (Scottish).

Much like in Burton's 3D CGI cinematic adaptation, a stunning visuality substitutes the puns and riddles of the original Carrollian language games but the Scottish Ballet's retelling of Alice, besides the stage design, also relies on the intermedial fusion of choreography and music on trying to capture the spirit of Wonderland. Composer Robert Moran claims to have gained real inspiration for his theatrical score from John Cage's minimalistic compositions as well as a 1966 black-and-white BBC production *Alice* directed by Jonathan Millar featuring a brave little girl standing up against a hostile environment. Moran's experimental orchestration matched with Page's clever choreography reflects a violent imagination peopled by eccentric figures with surprising moves and tunes. The caterpillar is an impatient dance instructor eager to teach Alice a Turkish tango, the Mock Turtle lowing a muted trumpet and the Gryphon "hoofing to the mournful strains" are a pair of vaudeville artists past their prime, the mutant insects rush in a swarm of swanee whistles, the Queen's croquet game is introduced by a grand waltz from the Royal Orchestra, while the leitmotif of Charles and Alice's wanderings within the camera is a dreamily slow, serene music.

The ballet adaptation was complemented by other Alice themed initiatives spanning across a wide variety of media, offering a truly multisensorially stimulating transmedia experience. These included a performance project combining dance and parkour called the Hatter's Garden, a photography competition inspired by Wonderland, a mad tea party, a museal exhibition in the National Library of Scotland in Edinburgh displaying early editions of Carroll's novels, along with costumes, set visuals, and behind-the-scene videos from the Scottish Ballet production (Scottish 4), and even special label editions of burgundy white and Bordeaux red wine.

A most interesting addition to the classic ballet dance is parkour or free running, a holistic body training discipline and a non-competitive sport, based on human movement, developed from military obstacle course training, in which practitioners move through a mostly urban environment regardless of its built or natural obstacles by making use of athletic-acrobatic skills: running, jumping, vaulting, climbing techniques, relying only on their bodies and their surroundings to propel themselves forward. Scottish Ballet's Mad Hatter's Garden project targeted youngsters between twelve and eighteen with the aim to make them explore the brute physicality of the seemingly fragile bodies used in dance, the trained muscle work in the background of choreographed harmony, and fill sports movements with artistic meanings. The changing of positions implies the changing of point of views. To "turn the perception of what is movement is on its head" is a fundamentally Carrollian project. The creative eccentricity necessary to find one's way in topsy-turvy Wonderland, parkour's reinterpretation of environment in term of potentialities for movement, and ballet's transformation of mundane motion into graceful poise all focus on challenging perspectives, on "turning things upside down," as Catherine Cassidy associate director of education of Scottish Ballet puts it (25). This alternative view coupled with the illusion of lightness approaches ballet to photography.

Puerile Passions and Forgetful Senile Desires in Contemporary Art Photography and Film

Maternal Erotica? Polixeni Papapetrou's Wonderland-Series

Contemporary Australian photographer Polixeni Papapetrou pays a long-term transmedial homage to the Carrollian (representation of the) girl child in three succeeding photo-series which portray her daughter Olympia impersonating Alice in many forms. The first, 2002 project tellingly entitled *Phantomwise*, with reference to one of Carroll's poems, uses Victorian masks to transform four-year-old Olympia's persona to reveal her hauntingly uncanny alternate selves ranging from gypsy-queen to clown, sailor and grandmother. The third, 2004 series simply called *Wonderland*, posits Olympia (age six) within the well-known John Tenniel illustrations reproduced as life-size canvases (by Robert Nelson, Olympia's father and Papapetrou's partner) she can interact with on reenacting Alice's adventures. In-between the cultural-historical and paratextual contextualization of Alice as a Victorian subject and a picturebook figure, the second, 2003 photo-series *Dreamchild* provides the most fascinating, face-to-face encounter with the girl child friend. Throughout restagings of the most memorable specimen of Carroll's original photography, Olympia mimes the postures of his favorite models, Alexandra Kitchin, Julia Arnold, Irene Mac-

Papapetrou, Polixeni, "Pepper Soup." *Wonderland Series.* **Type C photograph. 105 × 105 cm, 2004 (courtesy of the artist, Stills Gallery, Sydney, and Jarvis Dooney, Berlin).**

Donald, and of course Alice Liddell, fancy-dressed-up for *tableaux vivants* or dressed-down for the much debated *sans habilles*.

Papapetrou's three photo-series form the base of her doctoral dissertation entitled "A studio investigation into the theatricality and performative subject of the child subject in photography" defended at Monash University in 2007 in which her main intention was to "explore the transformative power of fancy dress and scenography in its ability to disrupt the traditional and romantic representation of the child as an innocent" (McCaw 71). For Papapetrou repeatedly emphasizes Olympia's volunteering herself for the role of the photographic subject.[8] The disruption of innocence signifies the refusal of the girl child's objectification and the celebration of her autonomous agency, her empowering ludic capacity to engage into conversation with stories and children of past eras, to reflect on youth both represented and lived, and to take her active share in the creation of the contemporary revisionary artwork.

While critics praise the images for "celebrating and testing the field of play between adults and children" (Stanhope 2013), the artist herself stresses her role as neutral channel and caring facilitator allowing for the satisfaction of infantile narcissistic desires. What saves Papapetrou from charges of becoming a voyeur to masturbatory delights, is simply her being a woman(photographer) and the mother of her model. Her photos attest a "maternal erotics" familiar from Victorian female-photographer Julia Margaret Cameron's portraits of her little girls, suggestive of a safe, protective and proud maternal pleasure in looking at the natural physical form of the offspring she gave life to, a scopophilia fully deprived of the dangerous sexual implications of the male gaze. The images provide an extended role-play for the mother keen on keeping her baby's body under her care in an innocent, infantile realm preserved and prolonged by her photographic means. Her maternal gaze functions as a kind of filter between her daughter and the viewer, while purifying and taming emerging meanings. According to Hacking, this very aim must have driven Victorian mothers to giving their consent for Carroll's photo sessions with their children (101).

Through an exciting play of (rather Carrollian) mirrorings, the child model's narcissistic delight also reflects the mother photographer's "furtive and labyrinthine way" of self-introspection, looking at/for herself under the "most profound disguise" of her own daughter('s portrait) she contemplates to see if it is herself or another staring back (Butler 2001). Papapetrou's work systematically explores *disguise* as a means of "both revealing and concealing, functioning as a kind of trap for the gaze" (Butler 2001). One wonders whether amidst the multi-layered implications of role-playing—challenging boundaries and connections between fiction and reality, self and other, past and present, child and adult, art and play—there remains at all any place for Olympia as an individual herself? Especially because of the mother-daughter working relationship's being infiltrated by such a complex network of desires here, I feel particularly pertinent the questions formulated by the curator of Papapetrou's *Dreamchild*-exhibition Zara Stanford: "How is Olympia's subjectivity acknowledged within the character that two adults have predetermined for her? Is her determination of self influenced by seeing herself as other? Does her desire to be seen differ from that of Dodgson's subjects, whose imaginative play she is knowingly replicating?" (2003).

On the one hand, Olympia's artificial poses clearly strive to identify the abstract ideal of the mythified Dreamchild convincingly enacted by her predecessors in the original *tableaux vivants* which provided the rare privilege of limelight to the severely disciplined

Victorian children whose joyful "to-be-looked-at-ness" Olympia so cleverly replicates. Yet, on the other hand, her portraits display a singularly postmodernist self-awareness that renders her unique personality unmistakable visible by virtue of a variety of subtle representational strategies and considerations. Olympia consciously toys with spectators by playing hide and seek behind masks, amidst the labyrinth of gigantic Tenniel-tableaux, or rudimentary, faux-Victorian stage-props. Her role-playing of role-playings invests her modeling with a "knowing" metafictional intelligence. Throughout her inventive mimicry she generates a complex interplay of past/present, child/adult, male/female gazes, as she never simply inhabits a role, but highlights its performativity and reiterability with a difference. On her reenacting for her mother Alice enacting Beggar Girl for Carroll she couples identification with alienation, staging a showy rope-dance between self and other, as if mockingly suggesting just the opposite of the photographic message, in the Magritte-ian subtextual claim, "This is not (just) a Beggar Girl."[9] Olympia offers a reasonable celebration of imaginative faith as little girls' communal gift. But the anachronistically fake-looking props, painted backgrounds, and ill-fitting masks framing her body do not only represent the enchanting fictitiousness of fantasy worlds where infantile consciousness may escape but also ironically demonstrate that "alternative reality, envisioned and enacted by photography, remains always within the sight of adult love, desire" (Stanhope 2003) and symbolic surveillance.[10]

Despite these sophisticated meanings and Papapetrou's careful attempts to avoid the iconography of child-abuse she thoroughly researched prior to the making of the photographs, the publication of five-year-old Olympia's nude (posing as Lewis Carroll's Beatrice Hatch before White Cliffs) on the cover of the July 2008 issue of *Art Monthly Australia* caused a veritable scandal. Prime Minister Rudd declared his hatred of any artwork displaying naked children while sensation-seeking media camped outside the artist's home for days until Olympia (by then 11) decided to publicly express her own opinion on a Lateline TV report. Supported by her art-critic father she rejected offensive and simplistic interpretations of her mother's photography and thus implicitly voiced the "art subject's" right for the freedom of self-expression. "Absolute love" as the maturing model's affective response to her past portrayal seems to stand as ultimate guarantee of the benign aesthetic pleasure the photo holds.

Apparently, Olympia has kept her critical sensibilities and the pride in her child-nudes, as recently she gained media attention for taking an intelligent, feminist stand against the increasingly competitive trend towards sexualized selfies teen girls post on social media, like Facebook or Instagram. She criticized these online self-portraits' sexually-suggestive imagery, self-harming exhibitionism, and neurotic drive at popularity which "transform relations into a sexual rat race" where "the aesthetic yardstick is whatever is seen in pornography" and contrasted their immoral "visual promiscuity" (Nelson 2013) with the pure artistic value and comforting emotional bonding expressed by her past child-nudes (The Drum, 7 November 2013).

Kissing Carroll.
David O'Kane's Digital-Collage Simulacra

One single photographic record of Carroll's alleged pedophiliac perversion has been circulating on the World Wide Web for a while provoking similarly shocked responses as

Papapetrou's nude homages did. The image is used by a number of websites to illustrate that "Charles Dodgson, or Lewis Carroll as he was more famously known, was in fact a raging kiddy tickler" as *Don't Panic Online Film Magazine* put it in a 2010 article undertaking to reveal the rarely known, "secret truth" about the author of *Alice in Wonderland* à propos the release of Tim Burton's film adaptation. The image captures that magic moment associated with the missing diary pages and subtextual suspicions fascinating myth-making posterity's imagination the most: the kiss of Lewis Carroll and Alice Liddell, author and muse. She, in virginal white frills, but with her lips half-parted, spine curved, her hands firmly clutching his shoulders as if about to strangle, feline, vampiric, and bold, voracious voluptuousness in miniature. He, clad in a somber, monkish raven-black, with his eyes closed, as if dreaming, not daring to believe, his fingers hesitantly fingering her waist for fear of her fragility, for fear of her flying way. The picture provides a powerful statement about how the intimate intercourse of two different kinds of innocence stimulates cultural fantasies accompanied by the compulsive construction of culpabilities.

Certainly, the documentary quality of the image is just a hoax or rather a misconception based on a myth turned online urban legend. The photograph entitled "Lewis Carroll and Alice" is Irish artist David O'Kane's 2005 digital collage made up of Carroll's most famous self-portraits combined with the artist's own features (including his lips and hands) and of a fragmentary detail from Carroll's 1860 photograph of the three Liddell sisters eating cherry. O'Kane clearly highlights the sensual contents of the seemingly saccharine original scene where one sister appears to gently feed the other yet, at a closer look, Alice impersonates a baby bird who hungrily steals the fruit from her sister's hold, grabbing on her reluctant hand, gaping bestially to shed light on the violence involved in children's games. The picture's subtitle also holds disturbing implications if we interpret the simple command "Open your mouth and shut your eyes!" as an instruction the middle aged male photographer gives to his young girl models instead of a teasing line between the sisters at play.

O'Kane claims to be fascinated by how Carroll takes photos of infants (sic!) in photography's infancy (O'Kane in Clancy 2007). His artwork inspired by Carroll's person and/in pictures adopts a similar identification of photographic subject theme and applied technology, interfacing (de)myth(ologization) and montage, while drawing a parallel between the Victorian anxiety over origins and the postmodern concern with originality. The artistic role-playing in O'Kane's *tableau vivant* brings postmodernism's major philosophical project to perfection on problematizing simulacra and simulation's spectacular play with making up the real through a plethora of referentless signifiers and semblances (see Baudrillard 1981). O'Kane's camera focuses on kaleidoscopic identities. He enacts a hyperrealistic double of Carroll calculably mistaken for the real life person but the girl he is kissing is not even a flesh-and-blood human just a duly manipulated inanimate image—a virtual Photoshop or a cardboard replica—a recycled artwork, a ghost of/from the past facilitating male bonding between two artist generations. Throughout O'Kane's revisionary project the Victorian expression for photography "taking one's likeness" gains brand new significations. The photographic image dupes spectators as an ultimate guarantee of presence that nevertheless proves to hide absence in itself. Instead of exact identity we only gain impressions of similarity, with O'Kane standing in for Carroll and an artwork (constructed/fetishized by Carroll and deconstructed/fragmented by O'Kane) substitutes the real girl. O'Kane never intended his photo to be read along the lines of truthfulness either as hoax or real, but rather meant to make a comment on perception, the retrospective subjectivities and meanings applied to past pictures and persons by the contemporary gaze, as well as the nature of images in the internet age that allows them to be redeployed at will for any number of motive. The dilemma his picture speaks to was brought real by the audience reactions it received (O'Kane 2015).

Marina Warner's stresses the (pseudo)memorial function of art made of a "stuff of shadows" (159) (a metaphor fitting for photography that literally records lights and shadows by means of chemical, electronical technologies).[11] Warner's *Phantasmagoria* traces the cultural history of spirit visions analyzing the intricate interconnections and overlappings between fantasy and deception, and suggests that photographs may foster the generation of false memories. Most of the photographic material we come across has no direct connection to our own lived experiences, yet our mind integrates them among our memories of actual, personally witnessed events as through "the ordinary activity of our imagination [these images] become alive, acquire warmth, scale, animation, and other qualities of reality" despite the fact that their subjects have never been accessible for actual sensory perception (Warner 2006, 209). Via a self-deceptive simulation, representation is perceived as presence—in the past perfect. Along the same lines, O'Kane's digital collage of Carroll and Alice is a catalyst that recalls mental images based on narratives that form a part of a shared cultural background including fantasies, myths, urban legends, speculations (like the ones surrounding the authorial persona) which create fabricated recollections that pose as memories.

The uncontrollable flow and self-stimulating proliferation of these memory-morsels is illustrated by O'Kane's large format digital photo-collage strip called "Walled Garden" (2005) that presents a multitude of little girls, cut out from Carroll's photographs, all wandering in a labyrinthine maze evocative of the artist's (and the interpreter's) mind. More than fifty girls, several Alices, Xies, and Beatrices (Dodgson's original models) coexist side-by-side, playing, reading, napping or chatting with each other; their individual personalities seem to come to life by virtue of their interactions, animating their *tableaux vivants* with ludic energies. The walled garden, besides recalling a gigantic playground and the convolutions of the artist's brain, also evokes a secret plantation endowed with a special microclimate sheltering a collection of rare flowers. We might discover a daring allusion to a haunting Biblical story of temptation, about Susanna and the Elders, where the walled garden is the scene of both an alleged tryst and an attempted rape—both contradictory relations speculatively associated with the Carroll-Alice couple. The multiplication of the same or similar girl-figure(s) several times, hiding and revealing herself under a bush, on the top of a tree, or beneath the wall, renders the picture a dreamlike quality enhancing the destabilization of the photo's credibility and truth-value.

O'Kane also pays tribute to the anxiety over in/visibility as a specific characteristic of the Victorian era that was fascinated by subjects appearing only to the inner eye of imagination in extreme states of inwardness, reverie, or dream but remaining inaccessible for regular physical sensory perception. Mesmerism, hypnotism, somnambulism, clairvoyance, spirit photography inspired scientific, philosophical, and religious inquiry, as well as entertainers and artists (Carroll among them) who all pondered about the status of illusion as "supernatural sign, inspired creation, mad delusion" (Warner 2010) or shameless hoax. Their incertitude provided the major ground of their fascination.

Invisibility associated with the secretiveness surrounding the unseen and the unsaid gains multimedial problematization elsewhere in O'Kane's Carroll-inspired work. In a 2004 digital photograph entitled "Self Portrait (as Lewis Carroll)" viewers are offered an oddly clandestine peep at Carroll enclosed in the darkroom of his desires, embracing his camera (the tripod's legs recalling those of a venomous black widow spider he addictedly clings on to), surrounded by his child-photos scattered all over the floor as evidence of his voyeuristic pleasures strangely stimulating and suffocating him in the claustrophobic space of the tiny developing room with walls made up of huge, larger-than-life painterly reproductions of his child-friends (of his photos of them) looming over his forlorn figure. The spectators' aim at an all-knowing, transcendental metaperspectivism is mocked via the unusual camera stance. Our eyes meet O'Kane-Carroll's looking up at us, as if taken by surprise, since the top-most part, the ceiling of his photo-studio is removed like the lid of a box, so that we contemplate him and his photographic collection as cherished items of our own collection. Via a cunning *mise-en-abyme*, the collector becomes collected. This is also a critical commentary on how mythologization within the communal cultural imaginary transforms the artist into a fictional character and eventually a commodity product: the pose of O'Kane-Dodgson/Carroll echoes illustrations depicting Alice stuck in the White Rabbit's tiny cottage, grown too large to be contained by the world, changing too dynamically "to fit, physically and figuratively, the stories enacted *in medias res* by each of the Wonderland characters" (Sigler 139), expanding towards fantasmatic realms, as a reluctant icon unwilling to be framed within delimiting interpretations.

O'Kane's more recent work—after videos made of children in Dodgson's images opening their eyes to confront the viewers' gaze—the 2009 *Doppelganger Series* contains a thought-provoking animation based on a pair of identical paintings made of Lewis Carroll's standing self-portrait. While the painting in the right stands still, its animated left-hand double sits down, picks up the open book from the table-top, leafs through it, and starts tearing out its pages, until the sudden swirl of the white sheets of paper brings about the blurring of the self-portrait and a general black-out of the background. This multi/intermedial art piece—an animation film of a painting of a photograph—revitalizes the shadow-self of the (auto)biographical subject, the turbulent unconscious beneath the quiescent consciousness, the frustration within fascinating creation, and the illegible meaninglessness beyond set significations.

Forgetful Senile Desires.
Gavin Millar's Film *Dreamchild*

Gavin Millar's 1985 film *Dreamchild* invests the titular Carrollian key-concept with ambiguously melancholic and ironic overtones, as it is an octogenarian Alice Liddell, now widowed Mrs. Hargreaves who tries to remember and come to terms with her complicated childhood relationship that led to the writing of the legendary fairy-tale fantasy stories dedicated to her. The aged muse's flashbacks of Wonderland and her memories of its author, far from being idealistic, seem ghostly, nightmarish apparitions sprung from haunting repressed traumas gradually unearthed by the knowing adult perspective now able to retrospectively decode meanings too troubling to have been graspable for the past-child-self. The elderly Alice's reminiscences threaten with disorientation and identity-crisis. Her anxious questioning of one "real" self is due to her having to face her present senile dementia and her past fictionalization for immortality in a children's classic by the admiring author's passive aggressive attempts at engulfing her in a fantasy of his making, as well as in the lovers' collective "we" replacing the neatly distinguished "I" vs. "you." Ironic incongruity arouses from the sentimentalization of a "legendary friendship" by Alice fans (on and off the canvas) contrasted with Alice Liddell's actual lived experience of her conflicted liaison with Carroll that equally left traces of anger, remorse, and hesitation[12] in her. A tint of nostalgia resonates in the film's conclusion celebrating storytelling and imagination as ultimate means of reconciliation.

Millar's biofiction provides an exciting view of the Carroll-Alice relationship. It retells a familiar story from the point of view of the traditionally silenced, objectified muse, and thus grants visibility, voice, and agency to the marginalized. The doubled perspective of the little girl and old lady Alice Liddell (plus Wonderland Alice) reflects on the simultaneous maturation, continuity, and potential splitting of one's identity. Carroll is presented as an eternal *voyeur* constantly supervising Alice with his gaze, but this onlooker is shown to us, spectators, as he is seen through the eyes of Alice who is looking at him looking at her. Through a complex interplay between the gazer and the gaze, as the retina of the other becomes a mirror allowing self-reflective introspection, the positions of spectatorship and to-be-looked-at-ness become relativized.

At the movie's outset old Alice embodies a reluctant spectacle. Mrs. Hargreaves (Coral Browne) was invited to Depression-era New York for the celebration of centenary of the birth of Carroll to receive an honorary degree from Columbia University awarded to the major inspiring figure beneath the author's text. Yet, much to the regret of the journalists frenziedly greeting her in the port upon her sensational arrival from England, she is clearly no longer the glorious dreamchild from fabulous Wonderland, but just a disenchanted blurry shadow, a pedantic and irritable has-been Alice who has grown so boring and bored with her own myth and old age, that her only message to children is a rational advice to "read sensible books in good light that does not damage their eyes." While a crowd of inapt tabloid reporters fail to capture and entirely give up on "the real Alice," Jack Dolan (Peter Gallagher) New York Herald Tribune's handsome young correspondent with a thick New World accent, unappeasable ambition, fanboyishly gleaming eyes, and a natural gift for flirtation courts Mrs. Hargreaves with the most cliché compliments ("You look terrific, precious lady!" he exclaims holding her hand, kneeling in front of her.) Hence, somehow he manages to convince her "to be again Lewis Carroll's Alice" to "remind America how much more there is to the world than economics and politics, there is fun, even in the middle of depression, troubles can be cured, we just need to dream a little." Old Alice first refuses "to play the part," snapping at the journalist, stressing her non-identification with the dreamchild: "it is difficult to be at my age to be what I once was, but it is utterly impossible to be what I never was." But eventually she becomes spellbound by his ravishment, and is dizzily reminded in a flash-back of another mesmerizing gaze, that of Lewis Carroll (Ian Holm) photographing her childhood-self (Amelia Shankley) fancy-dressed as Chinese in his mysterious studio sessions where his oddly prolonged hungry stares and ceremonious vows— "I like you exactly the way you are, I wouldn't change one hair of your head." implying that "he likes her just as he has made her and he wants her to keep" (Kali 263)—constituted odd counterpoints to her fidgeting, chattering, careless, infantile innocence. The child Alice's "becoming picture" evokes a troubling, eerie feel (heightened by the ominous, melancholic musical score to the scene) because of the latent erotic implications left unsaid throughout her fossilization as fetishized object of the gaze.

In the filmic diegetic present the boyish journalist's flirtatious flattering of the postmenopausal pensioner Alice possibly re-enacts her past traumatic experience of the aging photographer's drooling over the prepubescent girl Alice. According to our conventional, normative standards, in both cases, misplaced desires (suspiciously close to gerontophilia and pedophilia) target the presumably asexual(ized), forgetful or unknowing, inappropriate sexual partners, and hence disable, denigrate (the very thought of) erotic pleasures, which are nevertheless suggested by the film to lurk in these relations repressed. However, traumatic repetition leads to therapeutic self-recognition. Mrs. Hargreaves understands that Alice's mythified persona identified with her, young or aged, is always born out of a desire for her just as much as from a desire for an enchanting story. Although the film is far from being an explicitly erotic oeuvre, it wonderfully challenges the ideology of ageism, by offering a subtle view of elderly female sexuality. In her retrospective recollections, fantasies, and hallucinations Alice the advanced age muse keeps seeing herself as the projection of amorous stares dreaming her into (being in) image and text: in Carroll's Victorian-era photography, journalist Jack's Depression-era tabloid article, and her own unchanging introspective gaze in the mirror alike. She tries to find her balance amidst the chaotic emotional reactions of her anger at harassment, frustration by objectification, coexisting with her narcissistic delights and masturbatory fantasies. Eventually she comes to the conclusion that it is the story's pleasing its audience that matters the most. (The erotic frisson of the stories results from Carroll's "unspoken feelings being made manifest," albeit in a metaphorical manner, in the imaginary and is channeled into his Wonderland created to seduce her [see Francke 2009].)

The pleasure of Millar's biopic mainly comes from its clever use of the unsaid, of unresolved narrative gaps, telling silences, odd stares, and ambiguous innuendos. He allows an immense imaginative freedom to spectators invited to make their own sense of the curious intimate relationship between two persons who should not be judged but understood in their complexities. Alice oscillates between vulnerability and brutality, whereas Carroll is alternatively shown secretly spying, shamelessly staring, or shyly diverting his gaze from his "child friend." In the first filmic flashback, Carroll is awkwardly hiding in the bushes below the rectory window eavesdropping on young Alice and her sisters' childish chat and listens to their lightheartedly mocking his stutter and to Alice's self-assured answer to parental interrogations about his confidentiality to her. "He confesses to me because he loves me, of course," she says, to be immediately corrected by an elder sister "he loves us all, each and every one of us." The scene ends with close-ups of the mother's gloomy, knowing squint inside and Carroll's timid blush outside the room—both corporeal reactions avoiding verbalization but suggestive of secret significations to be sought.

Further clandestine correspondences lurk in another flashback of the famous boating trip that holds a special importance since elderly Alice recalls it in association with the very word "dreamchild." Throughout the rowing expedition Carroll acts as a most troublesome voyeur at his worst. His gaze—overwhelmed with a tormented, unrequited love incomprehensible for the child—is transfixed upon the object of his infatuation. Alice apparently absentmindedly caresses playfully the waves flowing by their boat and all of a sudden splashes the cold spring water in his staring eyes. When scorned by her mother for her un-lady-like misbehavior she retorts sassily: "But he was looking at me so!," and then, at a spur-of-the-moment decision, half-pretending to be ashamed, she dries with her pretty little lace handkerchief Carroll's "pathetic" face "soaked with incredulous tears of the Mock Turtle" (Mavor 42), and gives him an innocent little kiss by way of consolation. As Carol Mavor convincingly argues, the scene provides a perfect illustration of the Victorians' complex phantasm of "the girl," that desirable, inapproachable, unpredictable *femme-enfant*, an immaculate but mischievous underage muse artists could never be certain about, could never fully capture (save in a work of art). Alice appearing as an elusive water nymph indeed makes one wonder whether Carroll's unanswered love was truly that unasked for, too? Especially so because her own memories, maybe misrememberings, recreate her past self, eroticized by and for Carroll's eyes, so one wonders if a touch of provocative performativity might have contributed to creating her charm? (Old Mrs. Hargreaves' wording might be telling: she refuses to "be Alice" on grounds of not willing to "play the role.")

For sure, in both flashbacks Alice realizes something the others in the narrative diegesis fail to perceive even if it stands 'stark naked' in front of their eyes: the uniqueness of her relation with Carroll, the special attention he devotes to her (his love, his stare) that serves fertile ground for stories to come, and her active part in making up the timelessly immortal Wonderland. The outsiders' blindness to the obvious fabulousness of their friendship is represented in a ruthlessly ironic manner. When Alice's mother chaperoning her offspring on the boating trip overhears her daughter's daydreamy conversation with Carroll—"I wish it would go on and on forever," says Alice "Perhaps it will." Carroll replies comforting her— she is frustrated by these strange soul mates' understanding each other's wishes from half-words and her inability to make sense of what she decodes as their 'miscommunication.' Her disagreement with their enigmatic intimacy makes her rudely exclaim "Nonsense!" and hence she involuntarily names the very literary genre the communal fantasies sprung from this unsupported, unrecognized friendship belong to. Director Millar's decision to include Alice's mother in the boating trip scene—contradicting biographical evidence that make nowhere any mention of her participation in the event—serves to turn spectators into accomplices to Alice and Carroll. Posterity is familiar with the seminal significance this trivial episode holds for the textual genesis and the enduring nature of this creative partnership—now literary historical facts the hostile mother stays ignorant of, unlike us, today's readers who are invited to retrospectively cherish this odd liaison.

Eventually, in the film, it is Carroll's inventing the personalized Wonderland tale for Alice that succeeds in provoking a genuine heartfelt smile of the little girl previously shown to cast rather indignant, irritated, impish, or uncomprehending eyes over him. Even if they intellectually do 'touch' and 'share a moment,' this does not last long because of the different meaning the story holds for them, a central philosophical dilemma of Millar's work. While Carroll sees the story as a fragile, furtive fetish-object he shyly offers to his muse, she appreciates it, on her turn, as a source of communal pleasures to be freely shared and disseminated throughout endless re-tellings. The child Alice, naturally closer to orality's delights, fails to grasp the symbolical, material significance the handwritten gift-book holds for its author. She greets his ceremoniously presenting her the single dedicated copy of Wonderland with an outburst of enthusiasm ("It's the most exciting, and charming book ever, and I shall read it again and again!") but she downright refuses Carroll's begging to stay inside a little longer with him tête-à-tête to ponder in mutual make-believing and rather rushes away with child-companions calling her to join them on some roguish outdoor activity. The farewell she suddenly cries out to Carroll is meant as a consolation but borders on an insult: "But it's only a book!" Her words resonate in the room, as her author sadly contemplates her through the window, as she disappears in the mist.

Further instances of such misunderstanding emerge elsewhere in the filmic flashbacks. When Carroll asks with an amorous gaze in the semi-darkness of the developing room if child Alice has thought about whom she would like to marry, she automatically replies that the one thing she is sure about that he can certainly come over and amuse her and her future husband with funny stories. Later, when Carroll recites the song of the Mock Turtle to amuse the company on an outing, Alice, already on the verge of her teens, willingly shares a laughter on his impotent stutter with the eligible gentleman companions present on the trip she aims to impress. The ashamed silence to follow is compensated for by an elderly sister reading out from "Wonderland" the famous poetic postface iconically idealizing the Dreamchild. Fantasy is sharply contrasted with reality, yet both constitute two facets of the very same person: Alice, once a desired object (in Carroll's fantasy) and once a desiring subject (in an actual reality of her own making). Likewise, the girl's careless, playful mischief and the man's contemplative, philosophical melancholy constitute apparently contradictory readerly, interpretive attitudes which nevertheless function hand-in-hand throughout our attempts to make sense of nonsense fairy-tale fantasies' multi-layered meanings.

Old Mrs. Hargreaves retrospectively invests the above-mentioned episodes with a heartbreaking quality because of these two desires' inability to positively interact and respond to one other. In her reminiscences, Carroll's innocent admiration and Alice's innocent incomprehension of it constitute mirror-images reflecting one another, parallel realities which prevail pointing towards infinity but can never meet. In her inauguration speech at Columbia University, Alice regrets having been "too young at the time to appreciate the gift and acknowledge the love that has given it birth" and reaches even more general epiphanic insights about herself. "Perhaps love has always frightened me" she confesses, feeling sorry both for her unloved (inadequately loved?) admirer and her child-self who could not handle his infatuation. She tries to make amends by means of a hallucinatory mis-re-membering of an imaginary reconciliation. She recalls the stuttering Carroll's humiliation at a poetry-recital and pictures her childhood-self hugging instead of deriding him. Critics agree on the importance of this daydreamy snapshot. Alice "understands at last the nature of the succinctly repressed adoration that her personal fabulist had for her 10-year-old self" (Francke 2009), so that "the teenager's [phantasmagorically replaced] kiss becomes not a parting regret for the end of childhood but a symbol for the psychological recapturing of a lost Wonderland" (Cook 113). Mutual forgiveness and the (auto)biographer-Alice's inner peace may be reached with the help of an adequate memorial agency willing to reframe one's past in terms of open-ended, ambiguous, polysemic stories.

Carroll's memorially reconstructed self is emblematized by a Wonderland creature, the crying Gryphon. On the previously mentioned boating trip the drops of water on his wet face recall the Gryphon's tears; in the Columbia ceremony a choir of handsome young men sing his arch-companion the Mock Turtle's song; and in the film's very final scene (that also appears at the beginning and hence serves as a cinematic frame) we witness the pair of the Gryphon and the Mock Turtle—animated by Jim Henson's puppet workshop to be "genuinely unnerving" (Israel 263)—accompanied by young Alice and Carroll on the seaside. She looks at his seemingly broken figure hiding his face in his palms, and asks "What is his sorrow?" (a question originally referring in the Wonderland tale to the weeping Gryphon). After the Gryphon's enigmatic answer "Ah! It's all his fancy. He ain't got no sorrow." Carroll shyly smiling, playfully peeps at Alice from between his fingers still half-covering his face, and they all burst out laughing together in a frenzy of contagious merriment. The film ends with sounds of their joy and splashes of sea waves breaking on the surrounding cliffs, as the camera slowly moves away from the girl and the man holding each other's hands and the fictional guardian figures sprung from their creative imaginative partnership surrounding them. The ironic association does not so much question the necessity of the tribute but the tragic quality of it. The co-authorial pleasures and the story born out of this uneasy relation is celebrated mystified as a divine, immortal, supernatural reward for earthly sufferings and a compensation for human flaws, whereas the author's inspiration by a desire that never loses its charm on accounts of its insatiability is mockingly demythologized as a mere mannerism of his times.

The refusal to idealize is particularly strongly present in the elderly Mrs. Hargreaves' (re)visions of Wonderland immediately intertwined with anxieties of senile dementia, a phobic experience of solitude and death-angst of a gradually declining, weakening, terminally ill, old lady who is now haunted by the characters she was once so amused by, repulsed by their grotesquerie now more akin to Wasteland than Wonderland. When during an afternoon nap the telephone rings, and in a sort of a sleep-paralytic state, she is unable to pick up the receiver the horrifically aged, worn and weary figures of the wrinkled Mad Hatter and the yellow teethed, matted White Rabbit suddenly seem to materialize in her room. They scream at her threats and insults, enraged by her not knowing the time anymore: "There is no room! [...] you stupid, half-wit, ugly, old hag! You should be dead, dead, dead!" The past invading the present, be it in the forms of odd shadows of Wonderland creatures, ghostly apparitions of Carroll in mirror surfaces, or a double of her younger self—embodied by her companion, the inexperienced orphan Lucy—as well as the depressing experience of passing time, of wasting one's time that used to denote such sweet idleness in childhood now marks the inevitable approaching of death. Old age, when more recent memories diminish and ancient ones come back haunting unwanted, introduces a sense of vulnerability comparable only to the chaotic cognitive, emotional, psychic turmoil of being in love or being loved against one will.

With an inventive narrative twist—and perhaps a tribute to Nabokov, Russian translator of Alice, whose novel *Lolita* also played on contrasting the Old and New Continents' different attitudes to eroticism—the strangeness of America, too, is associated with a hostile Wonderland that provokes a real cultural shock for British Alice. She is stupefied by the Americans' incomprehensible accent, aggressive tabloid journalists, swing music, attempts at the commodification of her memories and odd expectations for a star persona she feels she cannot live up to. The pushy U.S. entertainment industry encroaches on her intimacy and violently urges her to verbalize feelings she never spelt out, never even confessed to herself (formerly disencouraged to do so by her prudish environment). Paramount Studios, making a cinematic adaptation of the famous Alice stories, paradoxically, want to commission her to verify the documentary truth-value of their (bio)fictional filmic opus, a film within a film. Hence, with rationalization overwhelming fictitiousness, they drive towards a disenchanting authentication of fantasy instead of an enchanting fantastification of reality. On hearing from the producers that Bing Crosby is to play the caterpillar, old Alice is suddenly intimidated by the questions she asks herself: "Who will be playing me?" Whose face or voice is supposed to be 'put on' when requested to seem and sound Alice-like in a TV advertisement? Has 'being the beloved Alice' possibly involved playing a role all along? In a sudden flashback of the fictional Alice's dialogue with the Wonderland Caterpillar monomaniacally inquiring "Who are you?" she realizes that magical metamorphosis, growing up, inherently implies turning old and advancing towards decay and death. With this sudden flash of recognition she recalls a repressed traumatic childhood memory of her mother tearing up all of Mr. Dodgson's letters, the paper vanishing in the flames, becoming a funeral pyre of emotions and memories, without her understanding why it has to be so. For adult Alice resurrecting their story is a Scheherazade-like strategy of self-preservation, a delightful and disturbing memorial and imaginative practice consummating desires in sublime artistic co-productivity.

Stripping Kiddie-Lit in Melinda Gebbie and Alan Moore's Art-Porn Graphic Novel Lost Girls

Succeeding adaptations trace darker sides of Alice's erotic adventures, like Melinda Gebbie and Alan Moore's 2006 mixed-genre art-porn graphic novel *Lost Girls*. Melinda Gebbie is an American pro-pornography feminist comics artist who became infamous with her *Fresca Zizis* (1977) designed without any titillating intent as an autobiographically inspired cautionary tale documenting the adventurous experience of a woman artist in the male-dominated underground comix scene, "a warning and a comfort to all those women who venture out too deep" (Gebbie in Gravett 9). Yet the book charged with obscenity provoked a court trial, got banned in Britain, and existing copies were ordered to be burned. This did not prevent Gebbie from devoting sixteen years to illustrate an even more controversial book, the erotic *Lost Girls* trilogy, a mixed-genre graphic novel saga she co-created with legendary graphic novel writer Alan Moore, who became her husband throughout the making of the book published in 2006 by the American publishing company Top Shelf Books. This three volume comics eludes conventional categorizations on grounds of strategically transgressing medial, generic, gender, and ideological boundaries; and as a result remains banned or restricted by some bookshops and libraries even in today's first world democratic societies that take pride in respecting the freedom of thought.

Lost Girls transforms Wonderland into "a place of nightmare, corruption, and debauchery, holding as little of lessoning as its inspiration, but considerably less in the way of wonder" (Pilinovsky 189), while exploring childhood sexual traumas and therapeutically compensatory erotic fantasies of the most memorable heroines of children's literature. The fabulously illustrated, lecherous web of entangled stories is fueled by the chance encounter of three women who meet in 1913 at the Swiss Hotel Himmelgarten near the Austrian border. The world-wise Lady Alice Fairchild a British, aristocratic, lesbian libertine in her late 50s, the plain Mrs. Gwendolyn Potter a middle-aged, middle-class, unhappily married English woman, and the rebellious Miss Dorothy Gale a 19-year-old farm girl from the

American Midwest turn out to be Alice from *Wonderland*, Wendy from *Peter Pan*, and Dorothy from the *Wizard of Oz*, respectively. Hotel Himmelgarten, literally meaning Celestial Garden, becomes a liminal space. The main idea is much in the classic tradition of Boccaccio's 14th century *Decameron* in which a group of youngsters flee from the plague-ridden Florence to a deserted countryside villa to entertain each other with erotic tales of love ranging from the wittily comic to the mystical, moralistic and tragic. Similarly, in the Boccaccio-inspired Marguerite of Navarre's 16th century *Heptameron* stories of love, lust, and infidelity are told to amuse stranded guest kept prisoners in an abbey due to natural calamities and criminal acts. Hotel Himmelgarten is a ritualistic threshold where one's identity can be restructured beyond the confines of cultural restrictions and taboos. It is a refuge where one can be temporarily sheltered both from the haunting ghosts of past traumas and the threat of the unrestrainedly upcoming first World War; a nearly phantasmagorical, magical locus where Eros is meant to rule over Thanatos by means of erotic storytelling. The carnal delights of self-fictionalization serve to keep the ruthlessly rationalistic, ideologically biased, fatally annihilating History (the transnational catastrophe of war and inhumane violence) at bay.

Via an exciting eroticization of the narrative structure, multiple verbal and pictorial narrative threads embrace besides the graphic novel's generic given, i.e., the hybrid, multimedial intercourse of image and text. The accounts of a carnivalesque plethora of sexual acts performed in the diegetic present in the Edenic, ecstatic space of Hotel Himmelgarten between the sexually over-heated guests and staff are coupled by orgasmic flashbacks from the "sexual autobiographies" of the "three queens of desire" ruling over this "decadent sensual paradise" (Hatfield 4). The heroines simultaneously stimulate and soothe one another by sharing their retrospectively recalled, self-reflective, confessional tales about their erotic awakenings, sexual formation, and carnal adventures. Memories surge in a fleshly, embodied manner, provoking the calculable corporeal reactions of the pornographic genre, and allow for the communal reexperiencing of past delights.

A further titillation of the erotic imagination, and a certain mirroring of the girls' past and the hotel's present joys, is guaranteed by the so-called White Book placed in each of the hotel room's nightstand drawers. It is basically a high-artsy forerunner of Tijuana Bibles, illegal, anonymous, underground, little pornographic comic booklets popular in the interwar U.S., which often depicted popular cartoon characters, like Popeye or Mickey Mouse, engaging in a variety of sexual adventures (Tribunella 638). But it is also a mocking allusion to Huysmans's *A rebours,* a novel of lascivious and philosophical, amoral, Parisian decadence that Oscar Wilde referred to as the major corruptive influence on his fictional character Dorian Gray, coined the "Yellow Book" in an enigmatic wording that subsequently gave the title of a major late 19th century journal of aestheticism edited by Aubrey Beardsley. The book pays an inter(image)textual homage to masterpieces of Western erotic art from Beardsley, Wilde, and De Sade through Pierre Louÿs, Colette, Apollinaire to Mucha and Schiele; and as a book-within-a-book it also holds a metafictional significance. It was designed by the erotomaniac hotel manager Mr. Rougeur an ex-counterfeiter of original art who emerges as a self-ironic fictional alter-ego of *Lost Girls*' illustrator Melinda Gebbie whose wonderful drawings clearly gain inspiration from the abovementioned erotic-pornographic canon, albeit combining expert pastiche with stunning original ideas and style. Still, the genuine nature of artistic creativity and of erotic desire are questioned hand in hand, hinting at the significance of cultural influence and former fantasies. Moreover, Mr. Rougeur's concept of Hotel Himmelgarten as an erotic retreat continually satisfying all sexual fantasies, a place where "everyone [can] act how people do in fictions. In *romances*" (Chapter 23, page 5) tells it all about the eroticization of fantasy and the artful fantastification of erotica, as guiding principles behind *Lost Girls*' making.

Lost Girls' straightforward celebration of sexual liberation takes place through a dizzying array of rather explicit representations of bold erotic gambits, daring sexual positions, nonconventional forms of pleasuring (way beyond the heterosexual, reproductive, penetrative sexual economy), as well as experimental, perverted carnal practices ranging from transvestism to gruppensex, incest, and bestiality. The effect of this erotic excess borders on the vertiginous, if not the risibly bizarre or hauntingly grotesque so poignantly grasped by Sandifer's summary of the graphic novel. "This is a story where Dorothy is fucked up the ass while masturbating a horse, Captain Hook jacks off on Wendy while she's deflowering Peter Pan, and Alice is kept in an opium-induced haze while the Red Queen orders her to rape the servant girls into submission" (2006, 4).

The sexual saturation of the Alice homage is equally hardcore. Moore and Gebbie's Carroll image "'aggressively courts the pedophilia thesis" (Brooker xv, Kidd 2). They depict the author as a child molester, an aged, balding, spectacled, White Rabbitish, family friend called Bunny who seduces the girl Alice in front of a mirror. Her first underage orgasm is witnessed reflected in a looking-glass, and her immature mind, by means of a psychological distancing, projects all pleasures taken onto her mirror-image. She identifies with her double as she enters an inside-out, upside-down world of debaucheries, in guise of the lesbian "invert" (a late 19th-early 20th century word for homosexual and a pun on the symbolical significance of mirroring), who duly takes after Carroll to become a seductress and storyteller on her turn, a veritable Sadeian "mistress of ceremonies" (Hatfield 7). At one point in her autobiographical reminiscences Alice blames Carroll/Bunny that "pink, flustered man [for having] shoved [her] down a moral rabbit-hole" towards the "drug-addicted lesbian prostitute" she will have become (3.26.7). Alice's adult debaucheries are emblematized by an explicitly eroticized Wonderland imagery pointing back to "her own youthful peccadilloes" ranging from the garden of live flowers turned garden of earthly delights (Pilinovsky), an orgiastic mad tea-party, and a hookah-smoking caterpillar amidst the folds of her female partner's labia.

The strangest strategy of the graphic novel—that made some bookstores to actually ban the book from its shelves—is the troubling association of this unleashed sexual licentiousness with infantile innocence. The sexually explicit narratives about Alice, Wendy, and Dorothy are framed within the confines of children's literature they intertextually revisit to burst its "safe" generic boundaries with taboo-breaking themes taken from the "adult genre" of pornography radically mismatched with the presumed purity of children's literature. Already, the epigraph to Book 1, "We are but older children, dear, who fret to find their bedtime near," a line taken from *Looking-Glass* invests the notion of the bedtime-story with twisted, tongue-in-cheek meanings. While problematizing the idea of defining target audience on the basis of age group belonging, and questioning the possibility to neatly distinguish children's versus adult books from each other, *Lost Girls* debunks the "'I know it when I see it' approach too often taken with childlit as well as porn, [...] and forces us to look twice" (Kidd 10). Practically, all the critics partaking in the *Lost Girls* roundtable of *ImageSexT*, in a special 2007 issue of *ImageTexT, an Interdisciplinary Journal of Comics Studies* agreed that Moore and Gebbie's "perverse brainchild" undertook to expose children's classics as "always already adult" (Kidd 2) by activating the latent sexual contents of these innocent readings (Hatfield 7, Alaniz 276). Their fictional heroines "have the greatest hold on Anglo-American imagination" because their "erotic aims remain, in some fashion, ungoverned by social and gender rules" approaching them to "poster-children of queer theory" (Quimby 13 in Kidd 8). "Stripping the fantastic out of children's stories" (Sandifer 7)—turning the Scarecrow, the Lion, and the Tin Man into farmhands Dorothy sleeps with, the Red Queen into a nymphomaniac schoolteacher, and Peter Pan into a young male prostitute—does not automatically result in disenchantment but the (re)generation of further weird wonders disorganized by desire. Eventually, *Lost Girls* is not only "perversely faithful" (Kidd 2) to its sources, but "much less creepy" (Eklund 7) than its originals, too, because it "replaces putative innocence with a forthcoming knowingness" (Hatfield 4). *Lost Girls* combines in "luxurious, exclusive, difficult fine art" (Wolk in Tribunella 630) marginalized, hybrid genres, children's literature, pornography, and graphic novel, which all deal with the rhetoric of maturation and the liberation of repressed (sexual) fantasies through artistic imagination (Tribunella 629).

These interpretations are heavily indebted to feminist psychoanalyst Jacquelin Rose's seminal book *The Case of Peter Pan or the Impossibility of Children's Fiction* (1984) where she argues that children's books—as well as cultural-, critical responses to the genre—are fuelled by adult desires they are meant to fulfill. They perpetuate adult fantasies about an idealized, immaculate, innocent childhood which underage readers are urged to identify with and emulate even if this essentialist, universalizing self-definition along the lines of their pure and primitive simplicity deeply disregards actual children's individual differences (race, class, gender, etc), heterogeneous selves, and real-life desires or interests. According to Rose, this child ideal also satisfies the adult dreams of linguistic transparency, of a representation apt to simply and truthfully reflect reality as it is, of an accessible archaic past, and of a stable and secure experience of selfhood and sexual identity. Rose's wording about children's fiction which "colonize," "solicit," "chase," or "even *seduce*" (2, emphasis mine) children into adult ideals is certainly evocative of the Freudian theoretization of human psychosexual development.

However, *The Case of Peter Pan* and *Lost Girls* seem to provocatively invite us to reconsider our scientific knowledge and stereotypical social preconceptions about relations of seduction, especially between adults and children. Both texts subtly remind us that what we are familiar with today as the cornerstone of psychoanalytical theory, the Freudian Oedipus complex, was originated in and came to replace a forgotten hypothesis referred to as the Freudian Seduction Theory[13] that initially provided a significantly different understanding of intergenerational erotic bonding. Whereas the original Seduction Theory (1896) explained the patients' hysterical and obsessional neurotical symptoms with early childhood sexual abuse and molestation, Freud's succeeding modifications to the theory reinterpreted the repressed memories of actual harassment as imaginary fantasies of make-believe erotic encounters. Thus, he shifted the emphasis (and the blame) from the desiring adult as a sexual agent objectifying the child to the eroticized child burdened by unreliable libidinal fancies about the adult. His insistence on primordial infantile desires culminate in the Oedipal scenario (gaining an emblematic significance as of 1910) whereby the child's yearning to sexually possess the parent of the opposite sex is coupled with aggressive impulses turned against the rival parent of the same sex. These emotions and drives must be repressed into unconscious realms throughout the socialization process as the boychild (Freud's archetypal subject) learns to identify with the Father and find erotic substitutes for the Mother. This chronology of the evolution of Freudian theory shows how desires belonging to adults are projected on children in one of the great master narratives of Western scientific thought willing to compensate for the shame felt over child-loving, for violating, albeit mentally, speculatively, the incest/pedophilia taboo.

Lost Girls tackles a major related dilemma: Whose desires emerge in the narrative throughout adult fictionalizations of children's sexuality? Moore and Gebbie's graphic novel, published by the tellingly named *Top Shelf Books* (i.e., X-rated material beyond the reach of children), clearly fits in a genre targeting the sexual arousal of grown-up audiences and follows patterns familiar from typical pornography. (E.g., the heroine's transformation from inhibited repression to liberal sexual openness, the characters' sexual ever-readiness, and their utter neglect of post-coital worries related to sexually transmitted disease or pregnancy [see Hatfield 7]). But it also adopts a theme fully incompatible with the porn genre's utopian, eternally orgasmic and omni-potent fictional universe by incorporating episodes of traumatizing childhood sexual abuse within each of the lost girls' sexual autobiographies. In that sense "it parts company from pure porn in precisely that place: it's all about consequences" of repressed and reemerging past memories (Gaiman in Pilinovsky 186). The nauseating rhetoric of rape ("Don't tell anyone!" "I know what's good for you." "You can't resist me.") resurface on each instance of victimization—be it enacted by Mr. Carroll, Captain Hook, or a disembodied tornado respectively. Sexuality is posited under the suffocating control of oppressive power regimes to show that the lost girls' fictionalization of carnality is not a sign of false-memory but a natural reaction attempting to deal with the frustrating, transverbal experience of unwanted initiation into adulthood. On a more abstract, metafictional plane this abusive victimization might also refer to the author seducing his heroine into the story where she will stay eternally trapped, silenced, with his (her maker's) voice speaking up in her place. In Alice's case this means ensnaring the real-life girl muse within the fictionalized figure. Paradoxically, both sexuality and fantasy are regarded to be violent acts which are nevertheless instrumental in fighting against psychic and social repression, the most dangerous forms violence can take. This is a deeply Foucauldian double bind: while *Lost Girls*' pornographic representation subversively challenges the child body's disciplinary asexualization, its taboo-breaking verbosity satisfies the more cunning—non-repressive, but productive—ideological technology of the "incitement to discourse" (1978, 17), and hence purports the power network it aims to undermine by making transgression visible, audible, and controllable.

Ambiguously, both the (unspeakable) traumatic and (ververbalizing) therapeutic kernel of stories are rooted in childhood sexual experience. It is an impetus for the "fall from innocence," responsible for inflicting wounds in psychosexual prehistories to produce "damaged adults" (Tribunella 631) (a drug-addict Alice, a nymphomaniac Dorothy, and an apathetic Wendy). Yet, simultaneously, it also serves as a starting point for relieving, elevating, curative storytelling sessions (that can remedy Wendy's bourgeois prudishness, Alice's man-hating, and Dorothy's shame over the incest with her father) apt to enhance the grown-up women's sexual healing and empowerment through reconnecting them with their long-forgotten girlhood selves. As female/feminist versions of Peter Pan's followers the Lost Boys—who were accidentally abandoned by their parents and whisked off to Neverland doomed to eternal(ly pure and primitive) youth—here, the Lost Girls must find and rescue their own childhood selves through/in open-ended life-narratives of their own making. They surpass clichés of asexual innocence and unrestrained jouissance alike, come to terms with their reawakened past memories, and seek community with fellow female storytellers. Hence, the first person plural pronoun in Wendy's explanation to Dorothy why her confessing her desires and dreads will benefit her: "There's different *possibilities* now… We can't disown the girls we were. We can't … let them remain *lost* to us." [emphasis Moore's and Gebbie's] (78). Paradoxically, innocence is recuperated via the unashamed, sincere discourse about absurdly filthy sexual acts and decadently refined erotic practices. If lostness is identified with the Unsaid and the aggressive silencing of culpable carnality, to be found implies daringly speaking up to reunite in "companiable lust" (Hatfield 4)[14] spread in verbose, confessional, self-reflective tales of desire evocative of the Freudian psychoanalysis' talking-cure (explicitly referred to in the text[15]) yet lacking the normativizing self-correction thereof. Lesbian Alice's being healed of misandry does not entail her heteronormativization, just an expansion of scales of pleasures towards unabashed bisexual delights matching the straight Dorothy's experimental introduction to Sapphic sex. The celebration of the multiplication of erotic possibilities challenges the Freudian understanding of desire as a compensatory, insatiable yearning fundamentally based on an irredeemable loss and a frustrating sense of persistent lack, absence. In *Lost Girls* desire overabundantly flows everywhere, you only have to find the adequate words to get hold of it.

For Moore, "intelligent pornography" equally aims at sexual gratification, moral education, and spiritual healing, appealing to audiences of all sexual orientations (Moore 2006). It is much in line with Angela Carter's notion of "moral pornography" outlined in her *The Sadeian Woman* (1979) as an argument stated in a fictional form, a critique of the unequal relation between the sexes, and a "demythologizing business" for "pouring new wine in old bottles to make old bottles explode" (Carter 1983, 69) destined to burst generic frames, gender confines, and social hypocrisy alike. Sexuality is not a biological given but a cultural construct, subject to ideological influences responsible for shaping as distinct sexual economies as the ones distinguished by Michel Foucault in the first volume of his seminal *The History of Sexuality* (1978). Foucault contrasts the Western *scientia sexualis* (governed by repressive, corrective, punitive, reproduction-fixated, medical and religious and criminal discourses about sexuality) versus the Eastern *ars erotica* (characterized by a mystical, philosophical, poetical attitude to sensual pleasures passed on to the initiates to liberate them) (51–75). Naturally, Moore and Gebbie take side with *ars erotica*'s joy and verbosity instead of *scientia sexualis*' silence and shame. In an essay tellingly entitled "Bog Venus versus Nazi Cock-ring" (2006) Moore argues for a beneficial influence artistic pornography could have on society by "venting sexual pressures harmlessly before they can explode in sex crime or abuse." He encourages all to forge a more enriched and relaxed cultural atmosphere by acknowledging the crucial role that sexual imagination has always played in our lives. *Lost Girls* even attributes to sexual liberation a certain magical ritualistic potential, exaggerating its healing efficacy, occasionally forgetful of the fact that the traumas to be cured have been caused by sexual initiation in the first place.[16] Conforming to the original etymological sense of the word *pharmacon*, poison and cure are identical, in *Lost Girls*' paradoxical understanding of sexuality.

Eklund opines, that the "ethic and aesthetic [of *Lost Girls*] can be described as a magical realism of the fuck" (6). And indeed the vivid sexual phantasmagorias that the girls' *ménage-à-trois* entertain each other with in the shadow of boring marriages, ephemeral affairs, and disinterested political maneuvers leading to the world war, create a clandestine, alternate reality where they can find comfort and joy to reach another, fuller "dimension of existence." This is the case in the theatre where they are pleasuring each other to the rhythm of Stravinsky's and Nijinsky's *Rite of Spring* without any other spectator noticing their trespassing. (Alice later wonders about the fantasmatic nature of this specific sex-act—that took place amidst an actual historical event of the audience breaking out in a riot during the play—asking in her diary: "Did that really happen?"[10:6].) Their cathartic world-making relies on a blurring of history and fantasy, a combination of libidinal and creative artistic energies. The emblematic fantasy-lands belonging to each heroine—Neverland, Wonderland, and the Land of Oz over the rainbow, respectively—come to indicate the unspeakable orgasmic subtext they can share through physical and narrative intercourse alike. The Lost Girls' erotic storytelling sessions as shamanistic rituals imply metafictional significations. Through conjoined erotic and imaginative agency, altered states of consciousness may be reached to interact with a spirit world denoting both the original authors (Carroll, Barrie, Baum) whose fictional realities are evoked to be revised, and the current readers whose belief in the new versions brings the heroines to life and renders possible their sexual healing, along with the readers' own. Eklund attributes shamanistic gifts to Moore and Gebbie who grant injured characters with sexual empowerment and spread the curative powers of their stories to reading audiences, too (13).

As the preface to the special 2007 *ImageSexT* issue argues, *Lost Girls*' superfluously overabundant artistic project revolves around a "lack that demands more." It offers excessive verbal and visual narrativizations of sexuality, a theme or experience identified with fundamental unspeakability. As if being verbose about silence, or explicit about the ambiguous, it points towards a certain representational "beyondness" reaching over the endpoints and intersections of image-, text-, sex- practices. The imagetext is naturally embodied here in an eroticized way. The storytelling sessions (words) about sexual adventures are mostly interrupted by further carnal acts inspired by past passionate memories (mental images) which in turn help shaping future sexual self-identities. The intermedial imbroglio is coupled with temporal and spatial confusion. Past, present, and future delights mingle in the remembered, reenacted, forecasted ex-stasis (ecstasy's etymological elsewhere) of the erotic subject. Sexuality and the representational attempts thereof demonstrate a certain insatiable continuity: in Sandifer's witty wording, "The arresting power of the pornographic image demands more looking. The fumbling inadequacy of talking about sex demands more discourse. As for sex itself..." (9).

Yet, there are sudden momentary outbursts of erotic and creative energies, discharges of accumulated tension, orgasmic peaks which disrupt the flow of the imagetext (both the sequential visual panels and the linear verbal narrative). These full-page size illustrations, rather visionary illuminations, of the unspeakable and un-image-inable sexual climax allow for the emergence of the fantastic into the realm of sexuality that has been conventionally coded as the adult world of reality deprived of innocence and imaginativeness (Sandifer 8). These splash-pages of climactic money shots spell out the correspondences between the source texts (Carroll, Barrie, Baum) and Moore and Gebbie's re-envisioning (Hatfield

7). We witness fantasticated versions of sexual initiations and the first orgasms: Dorothy masturbating upside-down in a twister in the surrealist company of cupboards, bed sheets, a horse, a wheelbarrow, an automobile and a cat swirling around her (Ch. 7, p. 6), Wendy flying (and masturbating) with Peter Pan rubbing fairy dust on her clitoris under in moonlit sky (Ch. 8, p. 7), and Alice dreamily plunging into the mirror to perform cunnilungus with her own reflection (Ch. 9, p. 6). Further full-page sex scenes are equally unrealistic. Captain Hook and Peter Pan are sword-fighting with their erect penises (Ch. 19, p. 7), Wendy suckles five feral and furry Lost Boys (Ch. 15, p. 7) and gets gang-banged by a troop of pirates (Ch. 26, p. 6), Hook grabs on Wendy's panties as he is being swallowed by a monstrous vagina-(dentata)-crocodile (Ch. 27, p. 6). Dorothy is penetrated in a variety of inventive ways by practically all the characters of the Wizard of Oz: by a ragged Scarecrow (Ch. 14, p. 6), a cowardly Lion (Ch. 18, p. 6), and a robotic Tin Man suspending her upside-down in manacles (Ch. 24, p. 4). Alice has her share of pleasures in a Bacchanalian school dormitory turned into a garden of live flowers (Ch. 16, p. 6), in an opium den where tiny copulating couples creep upon her (Ch. 26 p. 6), as well as at an orgiac mad tea party organized by a former teacher Mrs. Redman where "women [are] pinned down with croquet hoops, then stroked with hedgehogs and flamingo feathers, the hostess never takes off her Ascot hat even when in flagrante, and one mousey little girl comatose with hemp tea [gets] penetrated with a carrot by a girl masked as a rabbit," while Alice "dissolves in tea and luscious nonsense" as a cat licks her privates (Ch. 17 pp. 4–5–6).

Even her insane, erotic nightmares have an enchanting quality. Alice imagines the Jabberwock as a "dream-horror" rampaging closer and closer in the form of a giant penis chasing her (Ch. 29, p. 6). "I pictured veined neck, its swollen head and slitted eyes. It crashed through the turged, bulgey ... *tulgey* undergrowth making a slurred bubbling ... a burble ... as it ejaculated. It was a monstrous, a quivering cock, and it wanted to *jab* me" (Ch. 29, p. 5). It is significant that Alice has the vision of the giant phallic Jabberwock when she is temporarily institutionalized in an insane asylum, after she runs out of words due to her erotic excess, and can barely communicate except for nonsense. The Jabberwock that stands in the original for a monstrous "name without a thing" here becomes a sexualized embodiment of the Unspeakable that threatens and tempts Alice with taking her to the nonsensical discursive register, beyond all words and sensations. The single splash panel of the Jabberwock-cock perfectly attests in itself how *Lost Girls* conjoins the challenging of the limits of representation with the breaking of sexual taboos and the fight against unimaginative repression or rationalization. However, this gambit is just as dangerous as it is delightful. The full-page orgasmic flashbacks constitute "ruptures of fantasy" which intrude into mundane reality by offering "transitional gateways" (Sandifer 9) into "an inverted world where nothing made sense in the way it once did," as Alice says (Ch. 9, p. 8). Hence, the simultaneous coexistence in multiple presumably incompatible—but now radically confused—realms (reality and fantasy, fairy tale and pornography, childhood innocence and knowing adulthood, original and revision, even the crossover of different fictional universes) will normally risk schizophrenia, incomprehensibility, and misinterpretation. These are the risks *Lost Girls* willingly embraces upon relocating children's classics within an adults-only[17] world that is traditionally "marked by the abandonment of the exact sort of fantasy world it is being equated with here" (Sandifer 9).

Its genre is primarily distinguished by a graphic, visual explicitness yet *Lost Girls* also

Alice at an orgiac Mad Tea Party organized by her tutor, Mrs. Redman. From Alan Moore and Melinda Gebbie's graphic novel *Lost Girls* (2006) (© Alan Moore and Melinda Gebbie, courtesy Top Shelf Comics/IDW and Knockabout Ltd.).

excels in a singular linguistic dexterity throughout its attempts to "repeatedly gasp, grunt, and moan the unspeakable" (Sandifer 11) in an uninhibitedly verbose imagetext. Moore's erotic writing pleasures readers with metaphorically dense, movingly poetic, and shamelessly sensual passages. He performs a nearly impossible discursive endeavor on verbalizing the orgasmic peak's momentary loss of words (of rational denomination and conventional meaning) that does not leave any lovers in the dark, though, but brings a bright illumination by an intimate encounter with the unnameable. The description of Alice's first sexual experience is so illustrative of the above and so paradigmatic of the language of *Lost Girls* in general that it is worth to be quoted at length. On the same page (Ch. 9, p. 6) we see three large image-panels below each other. The first shows a mirror reflection of young Alice being courted by the paternal friend Carroll Bunny. The second offers a closer look at the girl Alice falling or flying in the mirror, with arms outstretched for embrace, undone hair and bare breasts, moving towards her older-self (metonymically indicated by her wrinkled hands holding the mirror). And on the third we see a close-up of Alice's wide-eyed, parted-lipped, cathartic face and her nude torso and trembling hands reaching beyond the confines of the looking-glass that melts and liquefies like water, ready to meet mature Alice, who is immersing her hands within the fluid mirror-image, in the moment just prior to their touch. She is bursting the boundaries of representation as the image steps out of the frame, and allows the spectator to enter within, at an ex-static limes. (The next page contains the full-page splash I have already analyzed above.) The images are accompanied by the following text:

> It seemed like a dream. The wine that made sweet vinegar of my saliva now began to make the room revolve, negating gravity. I fell or floated down a hole inside myself, and at its far end all that I could see was mother's mirror, there across the room. Inside me fingers fluttered, strange birds in a deep salt pool, their movements making ripples I could neither name nor own [Image 1].
>
> The bird moved faster caught up in a race with rules beyond my comprehension, purposeful and frantic. I imagined that I heard their cries, then knew them from my own. I fell and from the hole's far end she fell towards me, half bare, hair like wild rape, white lace petals opening about her skinny legs. His hand was hot between my thighs. I made pretence that it was her [Ch. 9, p. 6, Image 2].
>
> The mirror-glass was melting into silver, boiling into mist, and I reached out and felt young muscle in her shoulder, in her neck, the child-silk at her nape. We slid together, wet with mirror, slick as mercury, smeared kisses down each other's hips and rolled each other's wine upon our tongues. Legs twined into a warm caduceus we clung, pressed shivering against reflected heat; lost, tumbling in brightness [Ch. 9, p. 6, Image 3].

The struggle with unspeakability is thematized most amusingly on metafictional planes when serious language-philosophical, socio-psychological, and ideology-critical theoretizations, verbose eulogies about sexuality's and literary erotica's subversive transverbal powers are interrupted, fragmented, and rendered nonsensical or silenced by the actual carnal praxis. The loquacious idealization of porno-graphy's utopian discursive elsewhere—reminiscent of Moore's own *ars poetica*—is mocked in a highly self-ironic manner. The manifesto-like monologue turns into a dialogically embodied body-text by means of meaningless moanings incited by the actual sex-acts' shared delights pointing physically beyond the realms of representability. The following passage illustrates this tendency.

> Pornographies are the enchanted parklands where the most secret and vulnerable of our many selves can play. They ... oh, your cunt. So warm.... They are the palaces of luxury that all the polices and armies of the outer world can never spoil, can never bring to rubble. They are ... oh. Mademoiselle Gale? Is that your finger inside Madame Potter next to me? No ... no, don't stop. They are our secret gardens where seductive

paths of words and imagery lead us to the wet, blinding gateway of our pleasure ... beyond which, things may only be expressed in language that is beyond literature ... beyond all words... [Ch. 3, p. 22, image 8].

However, the most authentic narrative about unspeakable sexuality is offered in the above passage by the ellipsis' recurring row of the three full stops suggestive of the silent sighs marking mutual orgasm. These triple-dot punctuation marks denote a suspension of speech, a trailing off into silence towards intimately meaningless moanings and mutterings, a transverbality that is both insignificantly inaudible yet tells more than any words ever could. Moreover, through a highly sophisticated typographical titillation, the triple-dots also provide a tongue-in-cheek iconic representation of the libidinally invested bodily orifices which play a crucial role in the pornographic genre that is cunningly summoned and surpassed here.

Besides its playful connotations, unspeakability also bears traumatic implications. The advent of the First World War haunting the storytelling Lost Girls' diegetic present introduces a national historical contextualization of the retrospectively recalled, narratively healed personal childhood sexual traumas. Individual psychic turmoil is matched with the collective cultural trauma of historical cataclysm. For Moore and Gebbie, War signifies the triumph of Thanatos over Eros, a failure of fantasy with inhumane and dark results, destroying "'all the art and architecture, the fields of flowers and young people's dreams'—in short, as Alice says, 'All the *imagination*'" (Ch30, p3) (Hatfield 13). At the end of graphic novel's final, third volume the German troops arrive to burn down the hotel, annihilating its emblematic objects. They destroy the White Book (the collection of curative pornographic tales located in each room, that is also an intratextual *mise-en-abyme* double of *Lost Girls* itself) as well as Alice's looking-glass (a gateway to sexual pleasures released from repression and a portal opening intertextual paths towards recyclable classics).

On the final page's six-panel image-sequence we see in passionate black-and-crimson colors a young soldier's corpse left behind by the army's raid. His horizontal body-position, parted lips and legs, and the finger-muscle contractions of his hands eerily recall the Christian mystics' notion of *petit mort*, or "small death" euphemistically denoting the fatally self-shattering, mystical-mortal orgasmic experience accompanied by sacred visions, hallucinations, and sense-impressions meticulously recorded in their writings. Yet the body outstretched in a pit torn in the earth's flesh by a mine-explosion shamelessly displays its insides, guts uncontrollably bursting out of a wound inflicted by war violence, so that this anatomized, disemboweled body deprived of the eroticism that has been previously a major marker of human flesh in this work sheds light on the limits of corporeal intimacy and representation. While the skin-surface is a locus of erotic excitement, whatever is beneath it, the bodily-inside provokes fear, disgust, and guilt.

However, even if the young soldier's share is just pain instead of pleasure, *Lost Girls* still seems to end in an ambiguously open-ended, yet potentially optimistic note. After the initial close-up zoom at the corpse we move out and away from the pit to get a more distanced view of the same scene from a low-angle shot that also reveals a single red poppy blooming by the barbwire fence of the battlefield. The poppy stands for a national symbol of remembrance of soldiers who died during the First World War in the trenches of Flanders, but it also has a significant function in the personal mythology constituted by the Lost Girls' sexual autobiographies. It is the very flower that blossoms after Dorothy and Alice's first making love and Wendy overhearing them. Hence public and private spheres and stories become radically indistinguishable from each other, pain and pleasure coexist side-by-side, like the threat of eternal sleep and the promise of resurrection after death, like the poppy-field in children's fantasy (in the *Wizard of Oz*) and adult reality (Trenches of Flanders). The poppy, with its fragile petals and fuzzy center including opiatic seeds of a pain-relieving quality, is a symbol of the vulva and feminine tenderness contrasted with masculine violence. This binary logic is recalled to be troubled with the opposition of naturally pleasurable sexuality (poppy) vs. self-destructive civilization (trenches)—which are nevertheless organically connected, motivating and manipulating each other.

Along the same lines, even nonsensical meaninglessness gains gendered implications. In the heroines' reminiscences "Desire's a strange land one discovers as a child [...] where nothing makes the slightest sense" (Ch. 6, p. 3) and most of the fantastic sexual debaucheries—punctuated by orgasmic instances of unspeakability discussed above—seem to be deprived of rational sense. Yet these feminine autofictional phrasings of transverbal beyondness constitute clear counter-points to the aggressive linguistic invasion enacted at their stories' end by the hostile German troops burning down the hotel. The all male army's linguistic exchanges violate conventional communication, consisting of military instructions, swearwords, and animalistic grunts which are left untranslated and hence become highlighted as traumatically meaningless, malignant tumor-like, for English-speaking audiences.

However, the end of this story certainly does not mean the end of storytelling per se. The final image of the poppy blooming by the corpse against all odds is a sign of regeneration, of new stories to come and old stories to be retold. *Lost Girls*' initial project is brought to full realization by reminding readers that the Scheherazade-like figures are meant in the first place to tell their teasing tales in order to ward off death and the fear of mortality. Hence, the pleasure of the fantastic erotic imagetext brings collective cure by promising survival in cultural memory.

The conclusion of Moore and Gebbie's graphic novel precedes the final incomprehensible war-images and soldiers' rant: it is spelt out by Alice who claims that "beautiful and imaginative things can be destroyed. Beauty and imagination cannot. They blossom, even in wartime" (3.30.3). Political violence, dictatorship, and censorship are contrasted with imaginativeness that increases empathy and tenderness towards fellow beings and prevents all from hurting others or oneself (see Gebbie in Sneddon 51). This gigantic work of graphic erotica ultimately offers a "humane and seductive defense of the inviolable right to dream" (Faber 10). Thus, Alice willingly abandons "the mirror that held her trauma" and is ready to start with her Lost Girl companions a new life driven by the passion of storytelling, even after "the end of Europe's innocence." In a true Carrollian vein, Wonderland invigorated by imaginative agency appears as "a journey, and not a destination" (Pilinovsky 194).

4

Embodied Language, Multisensorial Nonsense

*"somehow it seems to fill my head with ideas
—only i don't exactly know what they are!"*

This chapter explores contemporary revisitings of Wonderland focusing on embodied language and multisensorially stimulating nonsense as the decisive experience of the journeys. I begin with the analysis of three texts which date to the late 20th century but provide perfect illustrations for the creative repurposing of the Alice theme throughout a sequence of interrelated medial transitions which eventually outline how transmedia storytelling may take place (even in the case of artworks relatively distant from each other in space and time): Carroll's *Alice* tales were adapted into a Czech puppet animation turned into a film that inspired a philosophically charged, English short-story that called forth an American poetic novelistic tribute, on its turn. Each repurposing reflected upon the postmillennial epistemological crises, the corporeal turn and the speculative turn, by problematizing our embodied experience of the enchanting, the curious, and the inexplicable and mapping out onto the surface of the gradually disintegrating body the stakes of our encounter with the Unimaginable. Via various manifestations of body-genres, grotesque corporeal metamorphosis becomes identified as the major leitmotif of Wonderland and a clue to the unstable core of our selves.

Surrealist puppetry and the uncanny magic of toy objects govern Czech animators Jan Švankmajer and Eva Švankmajerová's film *Something from Alice* (1987). Rejected found object composites are revitalized by energies gained from little girls' imaginativeness, surrealist anti-aesthetics, hermeticist esoterism, Eastern European politics, and the philosophy of object-oriented ontology leading to 21st century epistemological shift called the "speculative turn" (Bryant, Srnicek, Harman, 2011). Švankmajer's cinema of sensations invites audiences' calculated corporeal responses surpassing simple visual delights by toying with haptic aurality, interpellating what Vivian Sobchack (2004) calls *cinesthetic spectators* who simultaneously experience *synaesthesia* (the stimulation of one sense causes a perception in another) and *coenaesthesia* (the perception of one's whole sensorial being). This body-genre functions by means of *anatomo-(in)animation* that brings to screen the abjectification of the subject via incomplete or infinite variants of grotesque bodily metamorphosis, identified as Wonderland's leitmotif.

Angela Carter's "Alice in Prague or the Curious Room" (1990) dedicated to Jan Švankmajer's Alice film, as a literary homage that performs an intermedially twisted recycling of a visual adaptation of a novelistic original, while highlighting the inevitable palimpsestic overlappings of source-text and rewrite, imagination and reality, and the embodied voices in image and text. Carter re-reads Alice along the lines of revolutionary "isms," major intellectual movements such as mannerism, surrealism, postmodernism, even magical realism, fused stylistically and thematically to challenge the ideological-cultural technologies of truth-production, the warranty of paradigmatic thought patterns, the preconditions of epistemological transformations, possibilities of radical cognitive revolutions, the limits of knowability and imaginability. Wonderland transformed into a Curiosity Cabinet becomes a microcosmic site of epistemological crisis destabilizing the reliability of language and the reality models circumscribed by it while anatomizing the speaking subject's corporeal de/constitutions.

Rikki Ducornet's *Jade Cabinet* (1994) inspired by Carter's Alice story and the Lewis Carroll myth investigates processes of fabulating, creating, remembering and misremembering. The quest for a perfect primal language powerful enough to conjure the world of Things is intertwined with the longing for Etheria, a transient, acorporeal yet sublimely erotic and enigmatic being, the mute elder sister of narrator Memory and the muse of Carroll, featuring as a family friend who can truly capture her delicate, elusive, transverbal beauty in his art. This Alice alter ego ends up as a magician who eventually finds just the opposite of "lingua adamica" and invents the word that can make everything disappear.

The poetic discourse of Carter and Ducornet resonate with the numerous musical homages to Alice, such as the linguistic grotesqueries musicalized in Tom Waits' 2002 album *Alice* co-written with partner Kathleen Brennan for an "art musical" theatrical play directed and designed by Robert Wilson. Carroll's Alice tales are marked by a musicality bursting representational frames in so far as literary nonsense language's sensorially stimulating stress on vocality subverts conventional verbalization by privileging the pleasure of sounds (resulting from rhyme, rhythm, and repetition) over rigidly rationalized common sense. This revolutionary intent is self-ironically foregrounded by the numerous poems, songs, and dances embedded in the narrative throughout the Wonderland creatures' oddly embodied attempts to get in touch with Alice who is alternatively surprised, amused, and bored by their lack of habitual communicational strategies. While Waits and Brennan's lyrics refer to self-destructive dark obsession and the gloomy heartbroken melodies trace a biofiction that revisits the myth about Carroll's sinful intergenerational passion, Wonderland characters turn into stage performers of Victorian low countercultural entertainment forms like freak shows and funfairs to shed light on the inherent theatricalization of intimacy and to stress the tension between the surface innocence and the underlying troublesome anxieties of the Alice tales.

I complete my analysis of postmodern embodiments of the *Alice in Wonderland* theme through studying how the semioticization of a fundamentally heterogeneous and vulnerable corporeality constitutes such an unmasterable challenge for representational strategies that it inevitably ends up in a subversive "somatization" of meaning formation (Brooks 1993). Conventional, commonsensical signifying practices become engulfed by the uncanny return of the formerly repressed, 'unspeakable,' 'unimaginable' carnality, invading the signification process with the use of embodied kinetic nonsense, incarnated voice, and materialized metaphors in 21st century repurposings: the embodied storytelling of Samantha Sweeting's immediately contemporary carnal performances and taxidermy art, the Royal Ballet's 2011 gracefully grotesque *Alice* choreography, and curious culinary adventures conceived by the cookbook *Alice Eats Wonderland* and star chef Heston Blumenthal.

Surrealist Puppetry and Uncanny Magical Toys in Jan Švankmajer's Something from Alice

The difficult categorization of Czech intermedia-artist[1] filmmaker Jan Švankmajer is reflected by the oddly 'in-between' labels associated with his name. He has been coined "puppetry's dark poet" (Clarke 54), "an alchemist of the surreal" (O'Pray 254), a "prodigious visual poet" (Cardinal 82), a surreptitious "giant of contemporary cinema [producing] philosophically profound, visually rich and stylistically innovative work" (Uhde 94). Fellow countryman director Milos Forman even described him with an unlikely mathematical formula: "Disney plus Buñuel equals Švankmajer" (Jackson). Švankmajer's growing cult-following enjoys being perplexed by his bizarre, dreamlike, cacophonic harmonies fusing incompatibles such as fantastic fairy tale and gut-churning horror, stop-motion animation and inanimately photographed live action, surrealistic vision and infantile nightmare, a complex critique of totalitarian ideological and representational regimes. He offers a plethora of sensorially stimulating synaesthetic effects sprung from a spectacularized stream of deranged consciousness, experiments with tactile dissonance, sound montages, grotesque found-objects, living-dead puppet-composites, or collages of disassembling drawings—all revolving round the idea of unlimitable metamorphosis from one (physical, psychic, medial) state to another.

Švankmajer's fictional-world-making strategy makes seemingly unconnected threads converge in a Gordian knot. He pays tribute to the surrealist artists' "paranoiac-critical method" summarized by Salvador Dalì as an aim to achieve irrational knowledge based on the systematic objectivity of associative interpretations of delirious phenomena. He also intermedially transplants onto the silver screen visual equivalents of Lewis Carroll's portmanteau language games which originally fuse different sound and sense into new neologisms to provide verbal formulas of the fantastic bodily transformations permeating the text. Thus, he spectacularly reveals the immediate kinship children's imagination holds with surrealist dreamscapes and literary nonsense. Via multiple media transitions, visual, vocal, tactile, and even olfactory and gustatory ambivalence collide in Švankmajer's best artwork. His first feature film is *Alice*, a 1988 fantasy written and directed by him, undoubtedly as a homage to his two major sources of inspiration: in a daring surrealist adaptation of Alice's adventures it explores the wonderfully sinister and absurdly surprising dark undercurrents of the children's classic. His version of the well-known tale came to be celebrated by critics as an anti-dote to Disney's 'antiseptic' sugar-sweet musical Wondertale and proved to exercise major influence on a number of decadent independent filmmakers, including the Brothers Quay, Terry Gilliam, Tim Burton, Henry Selick—who eventually all came up with their own radical reinterpretations of *Alice*.

The film's plotline tells it all about the trademark hauntingly grotesque quality of Švankmajer's art. Alice's (Kristýna Kohoutová) solitary play in a run-down hiding place is disrupted by the sudden animation of one of her odd toy companions. A taxidermically stuffed rabbit bites the wire fixing it in place, breaks out of its glass case, and puts on a fancy dress to act as her bizarre, sawdust-leaking guide. The Wonderland they explore together remains within the home's confines, restricted to the marginal realms of the house (the lumber room, the larder, the cellar, the shed, the henhouse cage, or the junkyard) rendered mysterious by infantile imagination. Alice is led to a deserted writing desk where she pricks her finger with a rusty compass in the fashion of fairy-tale initiation, gets sucked in by a ravenous desk-drawer, and experiences a series of falls punctuating the plot, montage-like, as a stream of false-awakenings from a dream, all relativizing truth. She plummets into a cavern, stumbles slap-stick-style over a bucket, tumbles down an elevator-shaft-like hole, drops deep into a heap of dry leaves, splashes in a pool of tears, then a jar of milk, and crashes through a number of *trompe l'oeil* cardboard landscapes. She encounters resisting passageways, drawers she cannot open, doors she cannot get through, windows she cannot un/lock. She chases and flees oddly hybrid monstrous creatures composed of skeletal remains, household detritus, and her own cheap little bric-a-brac she treasured at the beginning of the film (buttons, drawing pins, playing cards, paper boats, dead insects, chipped china toys, dog-eared storybooks and the like). She undergoes a series of metamorphoses transforming from live girl to tiny china doll or huge plaster effigy and then back, and sometimes she makes her environment change in size as a result of her consuming inedible objects, drinking ink, eating pebble-cakes, sawdust, or chips from a darning mushroom.

The Wonderland creatures whom Alice meets balance on the thin dividing line between menacing nightmarish horror and grotesque black humor.[2] The Mad Hatter is a woodworm-damaged old marionette puppet with hollow innards and punctured holes

AliceWanders, "Homage to Jan Švankmajer and Eva Švankmajerova's *Alice*." Mixed media fan art work. Pencil, collage, digital art, 2016 (courtesy of the artist).

leaking all the tea he selfishly gulps. The March Hare is a worn wind-up plush bunny toy awkwardly rolling around in a mini wheelchair that constantly needs wounding up and must have its eye pulled back into place. The White Rabbit keeps snapping its rusty scissors at Alice always just about to carry out the Queen's execution sentences but never actually harms her and in the end it is eventually the awakened Alice who ponders whether or not she will cut *his* head off. The bizarre Švankmajerian bestiary seems more farcical than frightening; nevertheless the audience's laughter is filled with discomfort, and just as much embarrassed or alarmed confusion as amusement.

As Dirk De Bruyn (2002) puts it, "*Alice* is an 86-minute film, a 125,000-frame puzzle, and a meticulously constructed infantile dream." Švankmajer repeatedly refers to Alice as his "alter-ego," a manifestation of his "mental morphology" (1987, 52) and an emblematic icon of childhood he associates with disturbing anxieties and ambiguities sprung from overvivid imagination, wild curiosity, unsocialized cruelty, and a daringness to face and transform the darkest depths of reality. These depths include the frustrations caused by parental control which suspends minors, puppet-like, "between a static innocence and a stalking dread" (De Bruyn 2002). The "spiritual affinity" Švankmajer's Alenka holds with Carroll's Alice (Hames 122) has nothing to do with the adult's nostalgic, sentimental yearning for a distant, long lost Eden but rather implies a shocking realization of the imminently present dangers of existence mediated through the infantile realm full of secret wishes, anxieties and unrestricted, instinctive phantasmagorical play. As Michael Richardson puts it, for Švankmajer as for surrealists in general, 'innocence' does not exist or if it does, it is never an inherent quality, only a counterpoint to the corruption of the world, and the terrors of childhood remain with us and must be revisited in order to understand their effect on adult life (121–2).

Švankmajer's fundamentally ambiguous view of childhood as a space where dreams and demons coexist admittedly stems from autobiographical roots, his own traumatic encounter with LSD in 1972 he experienced as a volunteer for research in a military hospital in Prague. Under the influence of drugs he felt a "regression to *infancy* and a feeling of utter helplessness" that was followed by paranoid flashbacks afterwards. He developed a phobia of riding trams at night because of the static reflection of the tram's interior meshing with the moving exterior, and the resulting "crossover of dual realities" that triggered the same "disintegrating feeling" he had felt at the onset of taking the drug (De Bruyn). Accordingly, infancy in Švankmajer's mythology is identified with a haunting and hallucinogenic revelation of one's insignificant smallness amidst the incommensurable infinity of being. This epiphany of vulnerability is accompanied by an unsettling multiplication of the real into confusing parallel-universes and convergent (unrealized, hence impossible) possibilities which takes multiple, protean forms—ranging from hazy adult remembrances of childhood to lucid dreams recalled in waking life or paranoid impressions about the depersonalization of subject reduced to waste. These add up to that neurotic, traumatic kernel that emerges as a vital engine of Švankmajer's cinematic oeuvre. His Wonderland hosts an amazing plethora of anxieties: Alice is buried under ground, hurts and soils herself, gets disoriented in time and place, is harassed by objects and occasionally gets objectified herself. A further potential source of inspiration for Alice's unnerving metamorphoses—rhyming with the director's personal drug experience—relate to the 1960s's psychedelic readings of Carroll's oeuvre which labeled the Victorian author "the first acidhead" (Fensch

1968) and interpreted the voyage to Wonderland as a hallucinogenic vision induced by mind-altering substances as the "eat me!" cookies, the magic mushroom and the Caterpillar's hookah—an approach most memorably recorded in Jefferson Airplane's 1967 LSD anthem "White Rabbit."

Paul Wells labels Švankmajer's "animation of anxiety" a par-excellence specimen of the "agit-scare" genre. It primarily aims at thematizing our 'fear of fear' through appealing to the horrific recognition that "humankind is fundamentally driven by obsessive and compulsive needs and desires, often rooted in childhood anxieties, and played out in dreamstates" which revolve around the archaic fear and necrophiliac lure of the animated inanimate. Lifeless objects come to life to agitate by reminding us of the cultural constructedness and ideological objectification of every human subject in any disciplinary socio-political regime (especially the totalitarianism Švankmajer has had to painstakingly submit to for several decades) and to evoke the shared burden of our mortality, the human destiny that makes us all end up, dust to dust, as dead matter. The very medium of stop-motion animation encapsulates these moral-philosophical dilemmas Švankmajer summons us to perform an impossible rebellion against, minding the insupportable yet inevitable human condition: the all too ephemeral nature of our animatedness. According to the adult perspective Švankmajer's authorial cinema adopts, the child's mindscape merges bestiality and intellect in so far as it wildly fantasizes about its environment in terms of potential menaces. Bodily integrity is endangered and enchanted by the possible blurring of clear-cut distinctions between inanimate and animate, by the curious, vertiginous lure of the Freudian death-instinct tempting all organic beings with a return to the quiescence of the inorganic state (of non-being), a pleasurably self-destructive dissolution into the non-differentiating totality of being. In the director's view, it is only the transgressive gesture of animating the inanimate objects that can truly uphold the truth of childhood, while bringing back its authentic imagery, physicalizing its alternative perspectives and giving back its credibility (Švankmajer 1987, 52).

It is small wonder that the original title of the film is *Něco z Alenky* meaning "Something from Alice" given that the film seems to be (dis)organized by the little girl protagonist's object-oriented imagination. Her cherished collection of worthless items, she arranges during her initial pretense play, becomes increasingly life-like as the objects become animated and turn into fundamental story-motivators and plot-organizers throughout her fictitious adventures. A worn sock with a pair of false teeth and eyes come to personify the Caterpillar, a toy babycot sprouts wings and claws to fly about as a miniature mythical monster, a burbling bottle of ink turns into a magic potion for shape-shifting, an ever-snapping pair of scissors appears as iconic marker of the ruthless, reckless White Rabbit, a rusty mousetrap can capture a rodent foe (and pay a tribute to the Carrollian Wonderland-character Dormouse's original tale about the three little sisters who lived in a treacle-well and learned to draw everything "that begins with an M, such as mousetraps, and the moon, and memory, and muchness"), jam jars get filled with vigorous pins to disturb culinary delights. Clearly, Alice embodies, yet again, a metafictional self-portrait of the artist: this time a stop-motion-animator who remodels the monotonous, mundane environment in the shape of vivid dreams (see O'Pray, Zipes 300).

In fact, this metafictional theme is elaborated in the integrity of Švankmajer's cinematic oeuvre that keeps on systematically exploring the development of little girls' imaginative faculties. Throughout the filmography the autobiographical double progresses from a victim to an agent of her fantasies. From a paralyzing terror of her paranoid imagination she passively subordinates herself to (in *Down the Cellar*) she moves towards an increasing awareness of her ability to interact with the other dream-world (in *Alice*) and ultimately becomes a self-conscious manipulator of her surrounding reality rendered malleable by the playful gift of her creative imagination (in *Little Otik*).

Moreover, the feminine gender of the implied author focalizer, the underage heroine Alice attests the inherently heterogeneous multiplicity of artistic agency that results from Jan Švankmajer's life-long creative partnership with his wife Eva Švankmajerová, an internationally known surrealist painter, ceramicist, who collaborated on most of her husband's movies, including *Alice*, up until her death in October 2005. Jan's meticulous attempts to find for *Little Otik*'s protagonist a child actor resembling Eva's past girlhood self perfectly illustrate how the same metafictional self-portrait may provide a symbolical, metaphorical embodiment of Ian's infantile fears, while simultaneously acknowledging the creative contribution of Eva by holding an indexical, mimetic visual relation with her child-body. Via a marvelously grotesque androgynous fusion, Ian's adult angst takes the physical form of Eva's girl self. We find another tribute to the artist couple's cooperation and interconnected self-fictionalization in *Alice*. Eva did not simply paint the evil cardboard queen in her own image but was also in charge of making the March Hare puppet, whereas Jan created the Mad Hatter figure in his own likeness. The scene where they change heads symbolizes the significance attributed to the mutually enriching dimension of a dialogue, a recurrent theme of their cinema (see Hames 101).

Švankmajer's Alice also seems to revive the surrealist artists' favorite authorial alterego, the *femme enfant* (child-woman). This "rebellious debutante" "figure sends fissures through the best organized systems because nothing has been able to subdue or encompass her" as she is "an agent of critique and disruption" marked by her non-compromising, daring fantasy's subversive powers (Breton 45 in McAra). Catriona McAra describes how this enchanting, liminal, guerrilla girl icon has often been dismissed by critics of surrealism as a conservative, sexist, idealized, metaphoricized non-entity despite the fact that the self-fictionalizing identification with her has also allowed artists to "transgress the confines of their bourgeois nursery." She enabled them to interrogate their class origins, family backgrounds, art-historical heritage dominated by male masters, and perceived notions of reality while celebrating little girls' imaginative agency and empowering epistemophilia (a desire to know). McAra reads Carroll's Alice as the par excellence embodiment of the creatively curious *femme enfant* who shows up in several seminal surrealist paintings.[3] Švankmajer's Alenka animates things by interconnecting them in new relationships imperceptible to flawed adult eyes. Her child-like freedom of imagination and behavior make her akin with *femme enfants* who act as surrealist doubles by "reconciliating distant realities on new and unexpected planes to produce sustained bewilderment" (Stern 137).

The objects Švankmajer animates stress his position as a rebellious outsider to today's trendy, overelaborate, computer animated digital industry that reaches perfect cinematic verisimilitude via a sterile simulation of the real it never gets in actual contact with. His hybrid imaginary creatures are composed of ordinary household goods shattered, broken, discarded from everyday use, unwanted remains of the once-usable, now forgotten waste, all in the plainest common and visibly decaying materials (confusing the organic with the inorganic, in flesh, bones, feathers, wood, clay, shell, stone, paper, fabric, and metal). The resulting "rudimentary automata manufactured from elementary components" as "products of a pre-industrial era" parade as "tokens of the authentic craftsmanship of an individual imagination" (Uhde 62) but also "mountebank with their straightforward naiveté" (Uhde 1994). The lifeless rejected objects are animated by virtue of the creative imagination turning them into curious art object composites. Yet, as they come to a life of their own, they rapidly reach self-awareness and "refuse to stay rooted in their machine-object reality" (Warner 07). This "unholy zoo" (Strick) of all the hybrid imaginary beasts sprung from Švankmajer's and Alice's individual mythology quite self-ironically seems to realize the polysemic implications of the phrase "art objects" by acquiring agency, rebelling against their maker, mismatching ready-made narrative frames, and crafting new stories of their own—in their own noise predominating Alice's human voice throughout the entire film. These curious composites are mobilized with the old-fashioned, time-consuming technology of stop-motion-animation, manually manipulating objects shot-by-shot to create the illusion of their movement when the series of frames is played as a continuous sequence.

This anachronistic method suits brilliantly the adaptation of a Victorian fairy-tale fantasy. It pays tribute to the visual imagination of late 19th century heavily influenced by attempts to stop time and freeze-frame the moment in a still image that might be saved and scrutinized via the emerging photographic technology. It also realizes a more contemporary gambit to record temporal flow, the passing of time, that is conceived in a singularly 21st century fashion as a continuum made up of isolated fragments, all charged with a multiplicity of possibilities concerning inner, outer, and intermediary time experiences (private memories, collective histories, fantasmatic dream-states) alike. This temporal regime is equally irreversible and always-already-happened too, as the half-rotting apple cores scattered all over this bizarre Wonderland suggest, by mockingly reminding us of the sinister consequences of having eaten from the tree of knowledge, and as a result, having brought about the Biblical fall. Švankmajer's Alice is perplexing because her free-playing imagination's *innocence* feeds on her dark inner Odyssey rendering her fundamentally *experienced*.

Obviously, Švankmajer's *Alice* can be easily related to the popular fairy-tale theme focusing on inanimate found objects, particularly toys, coming to life. Nevertheless, the film evokes this tradition only to shockingly violate its sentimental conventions. It corrupts the cuteness-coziness-combo of Winnie the Pooh, and disrespects the celebration of friendship's emotional bonds of the Velveteen Rabbit, the tragic heroism of the Steadfast Tin Soldier, as well as the magical wish-fulfillment of Pinocchio. The comparison Dirk De Bruyn draws between stop-motion-animation *Alice* and a digitally animated tale of the same theme, John Lasseter's 1995 *Toy Story* is particularly telling of the uniqueness of Švankmajer's dark art. Whereas in the computer-animated buddy-comedy adventure film by Pixar Studios the toy objects are all plastic dolls lovingly stored in a neat plastic toy-box at the foot of the child protagonist's bed, the materials of the Švankmajerian Alice's object-composites "are more likely to be found discarded and forgotten on the nature-strip for a council refuse collection"—hence the difference between the two tales is metaphorically represented by the "difference between sanitized plastic sheen and rotting sawdust" (De Bruyn 2002).[4] As Jack Zipes puts it, Švankmajer's is "a trip into Wonderland that resembles a horror-house ride in a motley amusement park that is falling apart" (2011, 299).

Moreover, the (toy)objects in Švankmajer are called to life not by the love but the fear of their owner. The identification with them risks the abjectification and disidentification of the subjectivity that the spectators are summoned to inhabit. As the live-actor heroine transforms into a puppet with immobile glass eyes, chipped china skin, tangled flaxen hair, and broken movements "we are expected to maintain a continuity of physical identification [with a grotesque body] thrown into crisis" (Hames 88). Alice-turned-doll embodies the Freudian *uncanny* invested with the paradoxical feel of the self, surfacing as uncomfortably strange and the alien other occurring as uncomfortably familiar. This odd combination of antagonistic gut reactions (repulsion, attraction, intimidation), emotional dissonance, and intellectual uncertainty (aesthetic fascination, anxiety, debilitated rationalization) emerges even more predominantly in the case of further incongruous object-assemblies which foreground identity in terms of difference in ways much more gloomier than the doll does. Dirt stains, saw dust, rust scales, chunks of rotting meat, or disintegrating skeletons all metonymically indicate the constant threats which might violate the self's safe boundaries with a corruption that might render the internalized 'innocent' subjectivity radically undifferentiable from external objects and their contaminating capacity. As De Bruyn points out, such wasting of the self, "the creation of piles of 'rubbish' can be considered as a cathartic project in itself, as can its gleaning by others" (2002). The cause of the Švankmajerian cinema's fascinating ambiguity is that the horrific, nightmarish appearance of the curious composite creatures is undermined by the ridiculous grotesqueness of their animated movements, while their decompositions alternate with a series of random recompositions throughout a relentless metamorphosis. Conforming to the (il)logic of the carnivalesque grotesque, antagonisms amalgamate in a chaotic cyclicality. Life gives birth to death (that is pregnant with mortal life on its turn) and vice versa: a blinking bird skull hatches out of an egg, a bagel sprouts nails, the opening of a tin can calls forth a cockroach-invasion, a raw steak crawls on the kitchen floor, and the White Rabbit cannibalistically devours his own sawdust stuffing leaking from his belly while he rushes around menacing with mutilation by his castrating scissors but also mending the ones inflicted by him by simply securing gaping chests with safety-pins. All creatures are left half-open, half-undone, in a transitory state, malleable to transformation and reinterpretation.

Obviously the most significant inspiration for these curious object animations comes from the surrealist (anti)art movement's program to discredit conventional reality via an attack on its basic irreducible components, i.e., everyday objects which are wrenched from their usual normal context and alienated from the banal significance of their regular use value with the intent to invest them with surprising new meanings as sources of radiating energy (Ray 1971 in Stern 122). The surrealist recycling of "found objects" (in the French original *l'objet trouvé*) takes mundane objects to slightly modify them by a mere recontextualization or interconnection that leaves them undisguised and largely recognizable in their original ordinary form yet also adds to them defamiliarizing new artistic connotations, in the fashion of Marcel Duchamp's scandalous, 1917 museal exhibit, a porcelain urinal titled *The Fountain*. The resulting avant-garde concept artworks called to life by surrealistic gambits go way beyond simple eye-pleasing entertainment and would rather put back art in the service of the mind. Their anti-aesthetics multimedially provokes—shocks, scares, and teases—spectators to creatively get in contact with the external world and attempt to decipher both the authentic inner qualities and the clandestine potential given of objects.

Švankmajer's art is indebted to the international surrealist movement. He treads in the footsteps of the interwar avant-garde gambits of Breton, Aragon, Ernst, Dalí, Míro, and Buñuel who sought to resolve the contradictory conditions of reality and dream; developed techniques based on psychic automatisms allowing for the expression of the unconscious functioning of mind and the pure play of thought absent of all rational, moral, aesthetic control; and revealed the strangeness of the everyday and the mundanity of the miraculous via realistic representations of the irreal, and irrealistic reformulations of the real.[5]

The (calculated) random coincidences, incompatible fusions, and magical causalities embraced by surrealist art claim to be equally indebted to children's unrestrained imaginative free play and adult mental dysfunctioning surrendering to the irrational and the subconscious. The leader of the Czech Surrealist Group, the poet Vratislav Effenberger, associates Švankmajer's cinema with "a variety show from a child's imagination with its individual 'turns' divided by a wall of bricks repeatedly knocked down by a black cat"—an emblematic scene repeatedly reappearing in his 1971 animated short *Jabberwocky* (Hames 2011). Accordingly, the energies drawn from the infantile, the animalistic, and the inanimate are major organizing principles of the oeuvre.

With a telling simile Švankmajer compares himself to an "old alchemist continually distilling the water of [his] experiences, from childhood, obsessions, idiosyncrasies, anxieties" until "the heavy water of knowledge essential for the transmutation of life begins to flow" (Hames 113). The esoteric language is not employed by chance, but marks another special local flavor, a cultural specificity of Švankmajer's art. His native city Prague he so lovingly commemorates in numerous interviews and reminiscences as a major formative influence is a "cultural landscape that has been home to the mannerists, Archimboldo, the alchemists, the Inquisition, Czech folktales and puppetry, Kafka's bleak visions, and forty years of totalitarian regime, all of which have blended" in his trademark surrealist perspective (Uhde 68). Indeed, the main inspirational loci belong to a Prague of his childhood, more specifically 'non-sights' as "chipped walls, the dirty staircases of blocks of flats, mysterious cellars, hidden courtyards, the suburbs" (Švankmajer in Stafford 2011), buildings which have undergone magical transformations because of their historicity, their traumatic affective memorial charge, and the fantastification-defamiliarization of their usage as invented playgrounds. Throughout an alchemical transmutation all built objects appear as rebuildable: susceptible to be liberated of their utilitarian functions and given back their primeval, ritualistic, magical meanings and powers (Švankmajer in Wells).

Conforming to the religious, philosophical tenets of the ancient Hermeticists, who set the cornerstones of Western esoteric tradition, Švankmajer believes that objects have a secret inner life of their own. They absorbed the aura of the public and private historical events they witnessed along with the mental, emotional states of the people who held them and with adequate handling the alchemist-artist can make them "emanate the ambiguous mixture of menaces and pleasures" (Warner 2007) they concealed within themselves. He considers animation a sort of magical ritual, an aid to coerce the inner life and the intense memories out of objects which he regards to be "more alive, more permanent, and more expressive" than people (Švankmajer in Cherry).[6] He claims to "lovingly give the starring roles in his films to objects" (Hames 116) but the overall goal of this fetishistic project is humanitarian, since it commemorates past people's memory structures nested in the collective unconscious (De Bruyn) and stages infantile narcissistic, masturbatory pleasures sublimated into the passion for collecting objects. The alchemical transmutation connecting un-connectable things emerges in intermedial art's inventive combination of different media's various material vehicles, representational technologies, multiple sensory stimuli, and modalities of experience.

As for the local flavor, Prague was once ruled by a hermeticist collector, the eccentric Habsburg emperor Rudolf II (1552–1612) renowned as a major patron of Mannerist masterworks and a devotee of occult sciences as well as a collector of all things curious from exotic animals to mechanical moving devices—a mythical historical persona highly influential of Švankmajer's art. Rudolf embarked on a lifelong quest to find the Philosopher's Stone with the help of Europe's most famous alchemists such as Queen Elizabeth's court magician John Dee, he came to be regarded as high-priest Hermes Trismegistos by the initiated of his time, got represented in folklore legends as a cause for the making of the Golem, and eventually gave the city a mystical reputation that prevails up to this day. Rudolf's Prague Castle housed his precious Cabinet of Curiosities (*Kunstkammer, Wunderkammer*) a proto-museum-like, encyclopedic collection of uncategorizable 'wonders of the world' the Renaissance nobility was fond of amassing during the sixteenth to the eighteenth centuries in Europe. The collections of these Wonder-Rooms consisted of a wide range of rarities of all kinds including freakish biological specimens, medical oddities, religious relics, exotic, historical, super refined artifacts, and bizarre artworks or machines. Found and made wonders –a chip from the cross of Christ, a taxidermied crocodile, a tribal mask, a miniature clockwork doll, a painting of a deformed dwarf, a mermaid skeleton or a unicorn horn—took place side by side, often mixing fact and fiction, many of them retrospectively reevaluated as hoaxes.[7]

This historical tradition is revitalized by Švankmajer's identification of the Wonder Room with Wonderland where the weird wondrousness of the hybrid inhabitants stems from their belonging to a bizarre inventory of mixed mundane objects, ranging from minerals to machines, all animated by the odd juxtapositions dreamt up by Alice's fantasy. Curiousness is not an inherent quality of the objects but a result of the beholder's curiosity and creative imagination manifested in her peculiar organization of the collection. Alice is a collector, a storyteller, a heroine, and an implied author, autobiographer in one, responsible for making intricate interconnections which shed light on her subconscious psychic functionings, on how her soul opens up, in esoteric fashion, to enter into a dynamic play with the soul of objects.

This intimate, affectively charged relationship contradicts contemporary commercial culture's devaluation of objects as mindlessly masterable entities which are either reduced to their use-value and are dispassionately discarded and replaced by mass produced replicas or are aggressively accumulated, temporarily fetishized for their shallow symbolic worth dictated by ephemeral fashion trends' tyrannic cult of the New. This attitude, best exemplified by "Disneyland's soulless consumerism" (Hames 116), matches any hegemonic political regime's exploitative objectification of homogenized subjects deprived of their difference.

The ideological stakes of such object-relations are also recognized by today's emerging school of philosophical thought called object-oriented ontology (OOO) that paves the way for perhaps the most significant epistemological shift of the 21st century called the "speculative turn" while it surprisingly seems to reprocess, in my view, the tenets of ancient hermeticist esoterism, too. OOO a metaphysical movement of speculative realism rejects the privileging of human existence over the existence of nonhuman objects, and argues that objects are not uniquely products of human perception and cognition but rather have a proactive existence of their own (see Bryant et al. 2011). Much in line with this, Švankmajer (and his Alice) neither aim to possess objects nor allow themselves to be possessed by them, but rather claim equal status to human subjects and nonhuman objects, arguing for an inextricable enmeshment of all things, sentient and non-sentient, animate and inanimate alike. A person's adequate arrangement animates the objects which in turn will interact, "do things back" to him/her. An enriching relationship between humans and things is founded on a dialogue that liberates from utilitarian subservience and reveals primeval, magical interconnections of ancient times when "the first things man created were indeed alive and it was possible to converse with them" (Švankmajer interview with Effenberger in Richardson 128). Eventually the dynamics of our very world results from these correspondences, and the resulting "disintegration that is livelier than preservation that stifles the life out of things" (Richardson 126). Švankmajer's wording illuminates how collection is not so much about ownership as philosophy: "I collect impressions of my scattered feelings which I find in certain objects, whether that object is without value or whether it is a work of art, a product of nature or a chance find. The objects are not dead artifacts. I lovingly give them starring roles in my films." (Hames 116)

Objects act as prime agents of anamnesis in Švankmajer's memory-theatre in so far as the autobiographical subject's singular encounter with them allows for artistic self-expression and self-fictionalization alike. The metamorphic objects turning against themselves stage the identity crisis involved in the immersion in the imaginary realm (encapsulated by the collection) that provides a bizarre but masterable alternative to reality. If the locus of Wonderland adventures is the darker side of collective unconscious and "the uncanny inside of a child's mind" (Cherry), Švankmajer's *Kunstkammer* is a "laboratory of the self" (Kiss 1995, 15–23) where the recollection of things past of "what has been lost, forgotten, or effaced" signifies a remembrance of "what has made us who we are." But this alchemical "anamnesis" by animation is also "a work that transforms its subject, always producing something new" reminding us of what we could have, the potential to become (see Bryant, ii).

Alice's decaying cellars, winding stairs, and drawers within drawers are subtle references to the Wonder Room[8] in Gothic style where the ultimate maze is the imaginative human mind. Cabinets, drawers, and doors provide passageways between reality and dreamworlds, conscious and unconscious realms and lead way to delusional, visionary phantasmagorias as antidotes to blindness and tokens of political clear-sightedness through a deliberate disorganization of senses. (In Švankmajer's words, "Unless we begin to tell fairy tales and ghost stories at night before going to sleep and recounting our dreams upon waking, nothing more is to be expected of our Western civilization" [1987].)

The sense of disorientation, of being out of place, of losing track of metamorphosing matter, memories and one's mind are experience of the dream voyage which increase the Gothic horrific effects of the film that explicitly aims at the pausing of life (stop-motion) and the revivification of the dead (object animations) in a self-appointed "necrophiliac" way (Švankmajer in Vasseleu). Brigid Cherry sees Alice as a Gothic heroine who goes on a quest for buried secrets, and must face throughout her nocturnal, underground wanderings the Undead: zombie-like monstrous creatures like the constantly disintegrating, resurrecting White Rabbit or by disgusting daily detritus radiating a scary sublime splendor attributing the *couleur locale* to this labyrinthine Wonder Room turned sepulchral Gothic castle. Underground is a "doppelganger tomb" literally "trapp[ing her] inside her own effigy" (a china doll or a plaster figure), a locus of her culturally repressed (buried) but reemerging (undead!) fears, anxieties, and desires (sadistic, masochistic, sexual urges). As Cherry concludes, the cultural neurosis, moral ambiguity, and metaphysical complexity characteristic of Gothic fiction become translated into the cinematic genre of body horror.

Besides its cultural hyperliteracy (numerous scientific, cultural, artistic allusions from esotericism to surrealism to ideology-criticism) the lure of Švankmajer's art resides in its multisensorially stimulating, embodied visualization of the "shared language of our subconscious" (Johnston 2001). In *Alice's* case, the corporeal relationship between bodies on and off screen is governed by the (il)"logic of an infantile dream full of secret wishes and anxieties" about bodily metamorphosis (a theme, the director identifies as the Carrollian source-text's leitmotif) (Hames 114).

Alice's trademark distinguishing feature is her transitional body. In Carroll she undergoes curious corporeal deformations, shrinkings, growings, disappearings, body-dysmorphic self alienations and misrecognitions, all matching the twists and turns of nonsensical language defamiliarized from its common sense use. For the surrealists, she is the child-woman embodying coming-of-age, swaying in-between infantility and maturity, dream and death, libidinous totality and sexual difference. In Švankmajer, the journey into Wonderland stages the fascinating and fearful risking of the bodily integrity that normally serves as the ground of subjective consciousness. Natural, fleshly, biological bodies prove to be just as malleable as inanimate object bodies both in their socio-cultural, aesthetical, political meanings and material realities. Throughout, what Paul Wells calls in a Foucauldian vein the "animation of the anatomo-politics of the human body" (178), bodies in Švankmajer undergo change, consumption, colonization. They are subject to mechanical manipulation, organic decomposition and brute physical violence, yet—precisely because of their mutability—they might also somatically revolt against their ideological control, utilitarian habits, codes of politeness and burst their conventional cultural and representational confines with their subversive corporeal energies, and the dynamic succession of their decay and reanimation.

The excessive absurdities of Alice's abuses oddly provoke amusement: her grotesque shape-shiftings into miniature and gigantic puppets, her being menaced by abjectified tasty meals as biting buns or jam filled with drawing pins, or her harsh physical contacts with creatures like the mole who believes her to be an island in the Sea of Tears and hammers a stake into her skull, puts a cauldron on it, and sets her hair on fire to prepare his outdoor feast while Alice contemplates stupefied his involuntary wrongdoings. As the scene of the mole's campfire suggests, all the bizarre events compromising the heroine's bodily integrity take place on, or rather *in* her head; everything belongs to a safe, fantasy play with testing one's physical and psychic limits to awaken numbed imagination by s(t)imulating culturally tamed corporeal sensations which upon returning from repression produce ambiguously uncanny, titillating effects. When Švankmajer identifies his *Alice* with "a realized dream" he primarily refers to the pleasure derived from this embodied imaginativeness:

> While a fairy tale has got an educational aspect—it works with the moral of the lifted forefinger (good overcomes evil)—dream, as an expression of our unconscious, uncompromisingly pursues the realization of our

most secret wishes without considering rational and moral inhibitions, because it is driven by the principle of pleasure. My *Alice* is a realized dream [Švankmajer in Stafford 2011].

Švankmajer's is a cinema of sensations that invites carnal responses overwhelming conventional visual spectatorial delights. Feminist film critic Linda Williams' term "body genres" (1991) denotes "low," popular filmic genres which manipulate viewers by urging their sensorial, emotional, physical over-involvement, eliciting calculable corporeal reactions predominating the cinematic experience. Direct spectacles of the human flesh or its bodily fluids call forth a primary, somatic identification on the part of audiences who spontaneously "mimic" the thematized physical, psychic experiences. Horror provokes the chills and terror with images of bloody violence making spectators shiver and scream. Melodramas, tellingly called weepies, elicit sympathy and boost handkerchief sales with the sight of heartbreak and tears. Pornography creates sexual arousal with the explicit representation of the libidinal, orgasmic body culminating in the mandatory "money-shot" (see Williams 1999).

Švankmajer's *Alice* seems to complement Williams' body-genres with a fourth category: what I chose to call his *anatomo-(in)animation* brings to screen incomplete or infinite variants of grotesque bodily metamorphosis. Surrealist stop-motion sequences about fleshly, anthropomorphic incarnations of inanimate matter and alienating objectifications of animate, organic subjectivities, all bizarre blurrings of boundaries of physicalities and ir/realities, provoke a curious spectrum of sensorial excitement, flashes of pleasure, horror, anxiety, experienced as fleeting possibilities, mixing, transforming into each other to surprise audiences and create an overall tickling effect that elicits just as much a complex corporeal feel of impending self-decomposition as it offers a teasing-troubling mind game, an intellectual challenge to make sense of the embodied filmic riddle. Unlike in Williams' other body genres, sensual over-involvement fuses with aesthetic appreciation and mental exercise. This uneasy relationship between the spectator's lived bodily presence and filmic representation fits Lesley Stern's notion of the cinematic "sense of the uncanny" generated by the tension of discontinuities between the bodily knowing that the cinema encourages while "opening up the recognition of a peculiar kind of non-knowing, a sort of bodily aphasia, a gap which sometimes may register as a sense of dread in the pit of the stomach, or in a soaring, euphoric sensation" (in Sobchack 74)—all affects akin with Švankmajer's work.

Marina Warner quite poignantly attributes the fleshly sensations caused by Švankmajer's embodied cinema to the tricky transitions between different representational techniques, genres, and media which summon different interpretive attitudes and carnal reactions from spectators who become enchanted by his fantastic, anti-documentary *Gesamkunstwerk* reminiscent of the magician's sleight of hand performing illusions untraceable for the unknowing, naked eye. The bodily responses are alternatingly delightful and disturbing ("He wants to make the viewer shiver and tingle and gulp and gasp and gag" [Warner 2007]) but the most overwhelming experience is that of enchanted surprise.[9]

When Švankmajer undertakes the project "to expand reality beyond our perception" (Richardson 127) by relying on sensorial s(t)imulation expanding the moving image beyond its medial confines, he draws inspiration, yet again, from surrealist dreams, alchemical transmutations, and children's corporeal explorations. These connect presumably unconnectable things to forge unprecedented subject/object formations and open up new perspectives, surprising (non)senses and (non)sensations alike. As Cardinal highlights, the idea that "intensely savored physical sensations lead to insights of metaphysical order" is a claim common to poetry and religious mysticism (74). However, I believe, there is a certain ironic and infantile ring to how Švankmajer squeezes the "superior quintessence" of illuminations out of "ritually collected worthless objects," discarded waste and disgusting matter reprocessed in odd combinations causing revelation by "accelerated confusion" (Cardinal 74).

Švankmajer keeps stressing how his art is fueled by the ancient esoteric alchemical belief in the secret soul of material objects. Among others, he explains in a 1987 *Afterimage* interview with Vladislav Effenberger that "objects conceal within themselves the events they have witnessed" because people "deposited their feelings and emotions in them through their *touch. The more an object has been touched, the richer its content.*" The objects can only be made to speak out to reveal their hidden experiences once they are *touched* by human gazes and hands. We can see that the essence of a meaningful relationship between humans and things is principally founded on a *tactile* dialogue that nevertheless arouses further sensations and engenders a complex synaesthesiac effect via a multi-transmedial gambit. As Švankmajer aims to "touch objects, to listen to them, and then illustrate their story" tactile, aural, and visual realms interact to replace rational, utilitarian, pragmatic isolation with "primeval, magical meanings" infusing lifelessness with life, intricately interconnecting senses and sensations (in Richardson 128, emphasis mine). The "united vessels" (Hames 114) of different sensorial stimuli (touch turned into sound into image), different artistic media (live action turned puppetry turned claymation turned graphic art turned sound montage) and different states of consciousness (reality turned dream and vice versa) provide somatic, technological, and phantasmatic equivalents to the magical, ritualistic alchemical transmutation.

The intensive corporeal connection with a malleable reality primarily sensed and shaped by tactility belongs to childhood in surrealist Švankmajer's view. Children blur distinctions between the animate and inanimate world, attribute special memorial function to objects personified by their affections, and experience the vitality of being through touching and being touched. Childhood is the terrifying and pleasurable realm of spankings and caresses marked by a bodily immediacy and interconnectivity lost or rather numbed with maturation. With the initiation into adulthood, an anthropomorphized, animated teddy-bear (a doll or a white rabbit) will no longer be cherished as a comfort object turned imaginary friend but will represent the Freudian uncanny threatening with the return of the repressed and the destabilization of the safe boundaries between self and other, living and dead. For Richardson, Švankmajer's engagement with the tactile defies the prohibition 'do not touch' to take "part of a spirit of demoralization of the adult world, one which most specifically links his work with alchemy, the tradition of which has remained alive in Prague as nowhere else" (132).

His sensorial subversivity feeds from international artistic inspiration (surrealism), national cultural heritage (Czech alchemy), individual psychic traumas, subconscious contents, and most preeminently, primary pleasures of infantile embodied experience. Vasseleu seconds that view by naming as major sources of Švankmajer's "tactile creativity" (92) childhood, erotica, and dreams which he strategically revisits to use their transgressive creative energies apt to violate taboos, awaken repressed memories, arouse sensorial sensibilities, and eventually liberate imagination with unexpected connections eliciting magical metamorphosis and embodied epiphany. The aim of Švankmajer's "tactile art"—to become "communicative," to touch the world, to make ties between people and things—is reached by relying on what he calls a "tactile memory that stretches back to the most remote corners of our childhood, from which it bursts out in the form of analogies evoked by the slightest tactile stimulus or by stirred tactile fantasy" (Švankmajer 1994, 234, Vasseleu 97, Hames 100).

Švankmajer's cinema puts us in touch with objects which prove to be storehouses and engines of infantile tactile memory. *Alice*'s grotesquely mismatched object-composites—thorned sweets, a skull in a crimson velvet cap with a tiny golden bell, a rotting beefsteak crawling in the dust—abuse their users by their tactile responsiveness, intensifying and transforming "sensations that we barely perceive in our everyday lives into fragments of transgressive poetry" (Vasseleu 97). They abduct us on a time travel back to childhood's extreme sensorial, emotional agitation that has been repressed by socialization but can be revived by Švankmajer's touch. Although Švankmajer gains inspiration from his recollections of childhood's material vitality, he shuns from making 'art for children' that he identifies, in a severe criticism of Disney animations, with "the birch (discipline) or lucre (profit)," and a "dangerous taming of the child's soul or the bringing up of consumers of mass culture" (Švankmajer 2002, 5). (Vasseleu makes an exciting point by vehemently opposing the "Švankmajer touch" with the "Disney touch," contrasting the former's frightening, ludicrous, tactile analogies with the latter's giving an illusory life to objects via a banal realism that dampens children's ability to imagine [99].)

Švankmajer's fixation with touch as an instrument against the totalitarian, utilitarian anesthesia of senses dates back to the transmedial tactile experiments of a whole series of group explorations and collective games he devised and performed in the 1970s with the Czech surrealist group "investigating such areas as touch, fear, eroticism, analogy, interpretation, creativity and, of course, dream, humor, and game itself" (Hames 2011). His findings were first published in a samizdat book edition with a tactile cover in 1983 under the title *Touch and Imagination* (*Hmat a Imaginace*) offering a philosophical tribute to his fascination with psycho-sensory dynamics in a collection of his artistic-theoretical writings co-authored with Eva Švankmajerova between 1974 and 1983. Way before decisively turning to the alchemical aid of film animation Švankmajer created hand-made found object composites, gestural sculptures, kinetic collages, tactile drawings into which he manually squeezed his emotional turmoil without seeking aesthetic analogies with any particular feelings or thoughts, simply aiming at fluid fossilizations of kaleidoscopic impressions instead of passive, representational artwork. Vasseleu neatly summarizes the essence of his tactile art: it all "dwells on the textures, temperatures, densities, surfaces and malleability of objects" (97) which absorb and stimulate psychic-sensorial states of creators and beholders, so touching them allows for poetic self-expression for all parties involved in this embodied, object-oriented communicative interaction.[10]

Throughout his subsequent attempts to surpass cinema's predominantly (audio)visual medium, Švankmajer continues to explore how touch merges with sight in 'normal,' in psychotic, and in aesthetic perception, and how the tangible feel of an object can be visualized in moving image. His animations focus on how appropriate touch summons the immanent secret vitality of physical objects which "abandon their handy function[al purposes] in life to become tactile metaphors for denied memories, emotions, sexual fantasies and alternate ideologies" apt "to touch and move spectators in unexpected ways" (Vasseleu 98). His heroine, Alice embodies a reanimator whose look and touch bring to life dead matter. She attunes us to the curious "cross-over of sensory experience at play in [the] touch-vision" of tactile cinema (Švankmajer in Vasseleu). In her eyes and hands the stuff of Wonderland is pictured in a way that invites the viewer's touch: extreme close-ups emphasize the textures of objects and body parts which display their perishable materiality with a gut-churning realism that is nevertheless rendered dream-like by the merging of pleasurable stimuli within the feel of horrific revulsion. Snow-white, soft rabbit fur punctured by sharp, rusty nails, the slimy flesh of a tongue licking dead insects from a broken glass plate, a piece of putrefying meat chasing a delicate china doll, the chirping of birds disturbed by the sight and sound of a slap on a hand, all explore contrasts to awaken deadened senses. As Noheden puts it, tactile memories are activated from the audience's real sense impressions united in odd new combinations to make them experience things they have never encountered in real life (2013). These illicit tactile conjunctions turned multisensory introduce to the feel of the *jamais vu*.

Švankmajer's tactile animations bring to perfection the possibility of embodied spectatorship film theoretician Laura U. Marks calls in her book tellingly entitled *The Skin of Film* a "haptic mode of visuality." This multisensorial kind of seeing uses the eye as an organ of touch. The camera "grazes" over surfaces, textures and spaces rather than gazing into illusionistic depths. Spectators are brought closer to things which provoke sensuous memories of touch or movement. Touching the object with our eyes might produce painful images "calling up raw, bruised eyeballs scraping against the brute stuff of the world" but the immediate contact between perceived object and perceiving subject can also be "as gentle as a caress," too (22).

Haptic visuality predominates from the very first shots of *Alice*. Bored little Alice is throwing pebbles into a stream on a bright summer's day, we feel the sun's gentles caress, the wild forest aroma, the weight and warmth of the small stones in her sticky hands, we remark the stains the earth clogs leave on the soft fabric of her skirt, hear the trickling and splashes of water as the solid gravel sinks into the ice-cold fluid of the rivulet, we sense Alice's fingers flipping through the paper pages of the book her sister is reading and the elder girl's irritated slap on Alice's prying hand, a sudden sound of physical violence breaking the idyllic chirping of birds. Moreover the same sensorially stimulating scene is immediately reenacted in the next few shots of Alice's miniature memory theatre, a make-believe play directed by a self-pleasuring repetition mesmerizing spectators. Back from her outing, in her wonder room hiding place Alice arranges two dolls in the exact same position she occupied with her sibling by the riverbank, we see her throwing from the smaller doll's lap pebbles she pretends to be sugar cubes into a chipped china cup filled with tea, and hear her starting to tell a story to herself by imaginarily animating the odd toy collection keeping her company. Her succeeding adventures are all duly filled with corporeal stimuli ranging from pricking her finger with a rusty compass, to thumping in a heap of dry leaves, and sinking into a jar of milk-like fluid—all addressing the audience in complex physiological and sensorial ways. Alice's discovery of Wonderland is largely based on a tactile epistemology we are invited to embrace imagining the feel of getting in touch with curiouser and curiouser things. Elena del Rio explains the phenomenological structure of the somatic cinematic experience with a tactile metaphor, in terms of the touch between bodies and images as mutually malleable surfaces. "As the image becomes translated into a bodily response, body and image no longer function as discrete units, but as *surface in contact*, engaged in a constant activity of reciprocal re-alignment and inflection" (in Sobchack 65).

However, the somatic effects of Švankmajer's art inherently seem to enhance our total synaesthesiac involvement whereby the stimulation of one sensory pathway brings about the excitement of numerous others. According to Vivian Sobchack's radical reinterpretation of cinematic spectatorship the meanings made in/of movies belong to a "common-sensuous experience" fundamentally determined by the totality of bodily responses of viewers interpellated as "corporeal-material beings" (65). Throughout any film experience "vision is always already 'fleshed out'" informed by "other modes of sensory access to the world: our capacity not only to see and to hear but also to touch, to smell, to taste, and always to proprioceptively feel our weight, dimension, gravity, and movement in the world" (60). Movies provoke "carnal thoughts" grounding conscious analysis, and engage the "sense-making capacities of our bodies" (they bruise, move, touch carnally, emotionally, and consciously) so the "cultural hegemony of vision is overthrown."[11]

For a perfect definition of the subversive body in the film experience Sobchack introduces the neologism *cinesthetic subject* as a coinage of three words: *cinema* plus two conditions of the human sensorium, *synaesthesia* (an experience in which the stimulation of one sense causes a perception in another) and *coenaesthesia* (the potential and perception of one's whole sensorial being) (67–69). While coenaesthesia denotes how our bodily awareness is formed by impressions arising from organic sensations which become variously heightened and diminished as "the power of history and culture regulates their boundaries and arranges them into a normative hierarchy," synaesthesia refers to the vivid, involuntary cross-modal exchange and translation between and among the senses (e.g., perception of sound as color or shape as taste). Synaesthesia is an automatism characteristic of the open, pre-logical sensual condition of infants and young children that normally remains the carnal foundation for the later hierarchical ordering of senses in adulthood. It might prevail as a primary mode of pan-perception in the neuroatypical cases of synesthete persons and might become foregrounded in conscious experience through perception-altering narcotic, hallucinogenic substances (Sobchack 69). In Sobchack's view, somatic cinema, on its turn, strategically enhances our coenaesthesiac bodily awareness that we are all synaesthetes— and thus 'seeing' a movie equally stimulates all other senses as an experience of touching, hearing, tasting, and smelling images, too. "The cinesthetic subject feels his or her literal body as only one side of *an irreducible and dynamic relational structure of reversibility and reciprocity* that has as its other side the figural objects of bodily provocation on the screen" (78).[12]

Just how energetically Švankmajer's movies embark on a general project of cinesthetic sensitivization is illustrated among others by his exciting combination of tactility and aurality via a "haptic aurality" (Marks xvi). Sounds play a significant role in creating an embodied experience of his Wonderland, but the real-life noises, strangely oppressive silences and uncategorizable sound-montages of a Švankmajerian animation could not be any farther from the catchy sentimental melodies of the traditional Disney-type cartoon. There is no room for any emotionally manipulative, culturally charged, earworming music. We only hear a wide range of creakings, squeakings, groanings, chirpings, warblings, knockings, pitter-patterings, splatterings and clattering which are disturbing (and delighting) because of their unidentifiable origins and our assumption that they originate from the inanimate objects, the household detritus brought to life by Alice's contact with them. The touch of sound is nowhere more obvious than in the already mentioned first filmic shots where the comforting feel of the idyllic birdsong is suddenly interrupted by the slap of the sister's palm on Alice's soft hands mindlessly poking at the pages of the book her elder reads. In this metafictional, metamedial scene the sister's visual pleasure is disturbed by Alice's prying touch just like somatic cinema meddles in spectators' conventional ways of seeing. We also witness the foregrounding of sound from background track to plot device. Already the initial birdsong is more complex than it seems as it evokes Švankmajer's trademark "aural (acousmatic) objects" which never actually appear on screen and exist only by virtue of their sounds, hence implying the existence of uncanny, hidden meanings (see Sorfa 2006) overabounding in Alice's house, a home turned unhomely on accounts of its unusual sonorization.

The curiosity of combining the sounds of birds' chirping and of a hit on the bare human flesh comes from the sound montage that provokes immediate psychic, physical reactions by combining incompatibles. This is an acoustic equivalent to the surrealists' favorite found-object composites, literary nonsense fantasies' metamorphic, grotesque, hybrid bodies-in-becoming, and the Carrollian portmanteau's verbal coinages, as well as the haptic dissonance of tactile cinema. Švankmajer's multimedia art peaks in a multisensorial confusion of senses.

To this synaesthesiac synergy of the visible, the audioverbal and the tangible one should add gustatory sensation as another physical stimulus that preoccupies Carroll's, Alice's and Švankmajer's imagination. In the original *Alice* tales, food often appears in guise of animated objects that speak up to spoil polite discourse with aggressive physical urges: a piece of cake gains a voice anthropomorphizing it only to urge its own abjectification and self-destruction by inviting Alice to cannibalism ("Eat me!"), while the mutton chop Alice must introduce herself before the royal feast evokes the interchangeability of eater and eaten, and mocks the hypocrisy of table-manners and the brutality of the powerful devouring the objectified. Švankmajer is keen on emphasizing these unsettling aspects of the infantile oral pleasures permeating Alice's story where shapeshifting is consistently brought about by consumption. Menacing meals mirror the "decay at the heart of Wonderland" (Cherry) and provoke viewers' gut reactions of food loathing as the White Rabbit munches on sawdust spilling from its own belly, an animated tongue wags on dead insects, and Alice alternatively slurps jam filled with pins, nails, and needles, licks a rusty, oily key fished out of a sardine can, or sucks on her own bleeding finger. These gobblings stage "the primacy of matter over speech" (for one cannot talk with a full mouth) (Cardinal 71) and point towards unspeakable carnality.

Curiously, taste is always tactile in Wonderland. Paul C Ray's seminal *The Surrealist Movement in England* describes how surrealists discredit conventional reality through the decontextualization of objects as "irreducible, elementary particles of reality put into an unbecoming use to become a source of radiating energy" (Ray 30). The example he provides is a passage from one of Carroll's letters to a child friend in which a decontextualization of sensations also takes place via a systematic confusion of culinary and tactile shocks and delights. "I like very much a little mustard, with a bit of beef spread evenly under it, and I like brown sugar—only it should have some apple pudding mixed with it to keep it from being too sweet. Also I like pins, only they should have always a cushion put around to keep them warm" (29). The somatic strategy of causing surprise by troubling and transmuting taste, texture, and thermal stimuli clearly feels to be a precursor to surrealism in general, and the Czech animator's art in particular. This synaesthesiac intent constitutes the kernel of Švankmajer's *ars poetica* he tellingly formulates in a 1999 self-portrait as follows: "I am a hand with six fingers with webs in between. Instead of fingernails I have petite, sharp, sweet-toothed little tongues with which I lick the world." (in Vasseleu 91)

This surrealist confessional fragment highlights the most vital organ inspiring Švankmajer's art as a privileged locus and instrument of the synaeshtesiac boom of tactile, aural, gustatory, oral sensations: the human tongue. Although the tongue does not normally form a part of our conscious body image decisive of identity-formation, it functions as a primordial site of somato-sensory receptivity and belongs, in Švankmajer's view, to those "passive parts of our bodies" which act as links to our most intensive sensory experience because of their "connections to the entire surface, cavities, internal organs and mucous membranes" (1974, 43).

The opening shots of Švankmajer's *Alice* show a close-up of the little girl's lips muttering the lines "Alice thought to herself.... Alice thought to herself.... Now you will see a film ... made for children ... perhaps.... But, I nearly forgot ... you must ... close your eyes ... otherwise ... you won't see anything." This beginning foregrounds intermedial confusion as an embodied experience. We get an extreme focus on the movement of Alice's lips, the glitter of saliva on her front teeth, the soft resonation of her pink tongue as she is uttering the words of her opening monologue. The overture communicates a sense of the fleshliness of meaning formation, of the embodiment of voice throughout phonetic articulation. The somatic close-up on her speech is punctuated in the beginning by textual shots of the film's cast list appearing during her momentary silences. Lacking any response, Alice's story-telling voice remains solitary during the entire film, accompanied only by the recurring, magnified close-ups of her flesh-and-blood mouth which get juxtaposed with action shots of puppet objects animated as her doubles to produce a rhythmical "kinetic collage" (Uhde 1994) troubling spectatorial identification with the in/animate and the un/said.

The visual-vocal proximity of the fleshy orifice of the open mouth with a wiggling tongue inside defamiliarizes the organ's familiarity, by rendering its cuteness grotesque, oddly obscene, both emphatically vulnerable and voracious, a rabbit-hole-like dark passageway for stories to come.[13] While the image of Alice's doll/girl mouth 'in-between dry outside and wet inside' simultaneously stages contradictory cultural assumptions about the disembodiment and over-physicality of children, its voice pondering about the appropriate age of the film's audience ("Now you will see a film ... made for children ... perhaps...") tackles potential risks of endangering and domesticating children's art.

Since no one seems to listen, nor respond to Alice, her talk targets a primary oral self-pleasing rather than conventional verbal communication. The little girl's lending her ventriloquized, playfully pretending voice to virtually all the imaginary creatures of her Wonderland illustrates the embodied voice's capacity to animate alternative realities. However, the nearly microscopic close-up of her moving mouth visually emblematizing the flow of her voice besides strangely reinforcing her narratorial presence as "a kind of uncertain anchorage" (Hames 91) also seems to serve by means of a Brechtian device of alienation producing an acoustic uncanny effect; especially with the English dubbed film version's lack of lip-synchronization! The mismatch of her voice's sound and her lips' sight foregrounds the transmutation of perspectives, personas, and realities—all shaped by the words we use and the stories we chose to partake in. Alice realizes one's inherent transformation into a character from the very first entry into representation and tackles a whole row of succeeding dilemmas: Whose words am I saying? Which are the right words to describe who I am? If I choose different words to denote me will I be someone different?

This intermedial opening of the film mocks our culture's prioritization of verbality based on the assumption that articulate speech is a guarantee and prerequisite of personhood gifted with a capacity to master narratives via metacognition. As Richardson contends, Švankmajer's cinema profoundly distrusts verbality and allows understanding to emerge only from most primary, corporeal means of communication like touching or eating which are curiously considered as akin with recognitions contained within the power of images. Images are superior to words because of their mutability: "it is precisely because images can lie that they can also tell the truth. [...] It is necessary to engage with them; to question them and draw out their meaning. In contrast, the word, due to its immutability, is always false because it ties meaning down" (Richardson 125). Švankmajer's tactile images spontaneously enhance viewers' sensual presence allowing for the emergence of an embodied knowledge "that goes way beyond the sense of rational understanding." (Richardson 126)[14]

Paradoxically, this preeminence of visuality is stressed only to be questioned as we witness in the first shots the object of ocular obsession. Alice's open mouth pronounces an imperative call to spectators: "Now you must close your eyes otherwise you won't see anything!" This playful command might be a clandestine intertextual allusion to one of Carroll's photographs entitled "Open your mouth and shut your eyes!" (1860) featuring the trio of the Liddell sisters, Edith, Lorina, and Alice immersed in a game of feeding each other fruit attempting to find out flavors without looking. Alice pictured with her eyes closed, her mouth gaping hungry for tasty sensations, fingering the hem of her sister's blouse appears to be a clear precursor to Švankmajer's (non)sensual Alenka. Her words also transplant into moving image the instructions from one of the early tactile experiments of the Czech Surrealist Group inviting participants to "First have a careful look at the drawing. Select a place from which to begin and start touching. Gently place fingers on the starting point, close your eyes and set off on a journey from memory. The whole way keep repeating in your mind: 'I will never see this again'" (Švankmajer 1994, 168 in Vasseleu). Another obvious intertextual, metafictional reference is to the initial scene of Buñuel and Dalí's famous surrealist movie *An Andalusian Dog* (1929) that opens with the cutting of an eyeball, a violent challenge to ocular-centrism, physically and psychically abusing spectators to break their habits of visual sensation and stimulate their multisensorial imagination. The imaginary montage of the mental image of the blinking eyelid and the actual close-up of the moving mouth shed light on the fundamental connection between seeing and speaking as corporeal experiences affecting the constitution of knowledges based on subjective experiences of reality. They hint at how Švankmajer's world of telling silences and alternative viewpoints from blind spots are meant to explore "surrealism's celebrated wonder, the capacity for seeing the world as if for the first time" transformed by imagination and desire, to see the world as madmen, children and dreamers do by endowing the banal objects of everyday with new metaphorical meanings standing for transverbal emotions and abstract ideas, turning poetry governed by irrational, magical correspondences and artistic nonsense into the primary mode of being. This is the message implied in Alice's lullaby-like call inviting spectators to enter Wonderland's dreamworld domain of extravisual multisensoriality.

With the simultaneous challenging of verbality and visuality as privileged means of communication, Švankmajer pokes fun of our collective fears of muteness and blindness based on naturalized presuppositions about the mastery of the voyeuristic gaze and articulate speech constituting the grounds of autonomous personhood.[15] Silence and voice, blindness and sight are inherently intertwined complementaries transmuting into each other as well as further sensations throughout a gradual process of tactilization. They provoke polysemic, ambiguous meanings which slip under the control of waking life, adult reason, and "State censorship primarily concerned with policing audiovisual mass media" (Vasseleu 2009). Like in Carroll's time, the framework of the revisited children's fairy-tale fantasy genre guarantees "an authorized license" for the plethora of disturbing messages which all "interrogate the validity of reality through probing language, space, and time" (Stern 123) in a postmodernly revamped, subversively uncategorizable mash-up of multiple media and sensation stimuli. Švankmajer's film eventually brings us to the realization that Alice's unanswered monologue-fragments, preverbal noises, and silent daydreamings constitute empowering elements of her own story-telling. Absence proves to be formative of presence, as the missing White Rabbit attests at the end of the film when his not being there in his usual place serves as the only evidence of Alice's adventures. His non-existence validates in a way the existence of Wonderland. The empty spot marks the spot. The unseen tells it all.

Literary Nonsense in the Curiosity Cabinet

ANGELA CARTER'S *ALICE IN PRAGUE* OR *THE CURIOUS ROOM*, DEDICATED TO ŠVANKMAJER

The dedication preceding Angela Carter's short-story, "Alice in Prague or the Curious Room" (1989) spells out that "this piece was written in the praise of Jan Švankmajer, the animator of Prague, and his film of Alice." The analytical essay Carter wrote as a paratextual addendum to her speculative fictional sketch (published by some editions as introduction, by others as afterword, and fully omitted elsewhere) elaborates further the parallels involved throughout the intermedially twisted recycling performed by this literary homage to a visual adaptation of a novelistic original, toying with "a spiral of intertextual layering in search of the Alice hypotext" (Ryan-Sautour 68). Not only does the Carterian Alice's look take after the "frail teeth, flaxen hair, stern expression, and pink frocks" of Švankmajer's doll girl heroine ("although she might change," as the authoress hastily adds), but what she calls her "sequel" also undertakes to follow the master's "furious disruption of rationality" embracing "the aesthetic of surrealism and its exploration of the unconscious via the adventures of the image" retransplanted, with a difference, into the world of literary nonsense (Carter 1990, 216). Moreover, Carter even borrows from the Czech animator the enigmatic initial line—Švankmajer's "Alice thought to herself.... Now you will see a film" modified to "Alice said: now you're going to read a story"—that defines those formal parameters of the story readers will be made to systematically subvert throughout the complex somatization of the text.

In the short story Alice breaks through the looking-glass to find herself in late 16th century Prague, in Emperor Rudolph II's Renaissance Curiosity Cabinet, where she comes into being as an alchemical homunculus sprung from the crystal ball of English expatriate esoteric scientist and court magician Doctor Dee. Alice's miraculousness seems mundane in so far as she perfectly fits the eccentric Archduke's collection of curiosities compiled of mandrakes dressed in nightgowns, bottled mermaids, crystallized angels, and the like. However, after her metamorphic growth and shrink elicited by a tasty strawberry and an *elixir vitae* the Doctor feeds her, Alice comes up with logical conundrums and mathematical riddles which do not only make a mechanical clockwork doll disintegrate into its organic constituents but also puzzle and leave entirely speechless the learned men of the Renaissance who cannot follow her nonsensical reasoning. The ambiguous ending abandons Alice's questions unanswered, resonating in the air, only replied by a raven's senseless crow and an enduring silence (the last word of the story) that both empowers her as an enigmatically unknowable *femme-enfant* and thwart her way back home, "back through the mirror to 'time will be,' or, even better, to the book from which she had sprung" (408), preserving her in a freeze-framed here-and-now that always already belongs to a fictionalized version of our past.

The story thematizes the challenge of/by rationality on various levels. The Carterian Wonderland imaginatively reinvents a historical late 16th century Prague as an era characterized by a simultaneous "longing for knowledge and belief in wonders" (Frankova 129), marked by an interest in interconnected incongruous means of understanding reality surfacing in the enthusiasm for the nascent natural sciences blended with supernatural occult esoterism (Dr. Dee is both an astronomer and an astrologist), organic beings' enhancement by corruptive technological artificiality (Arcimboldo builds an automaton from exotic fruit), and imaginative high-flights intertwined with hyperrational down-to-earthness (Rudolph's belief in the knowability of wonders). Moreover, Carter's *Alice* tale blurs the *Zeitgeist* of the transitional historical period of mannerist Prague with the imaginary dreamscapes of Švankmajer's surrealist aesthetics, focusing on their common denominator, the confrontation of rationality by curiosity. The result is a postmodern patchwork that foregrounds the epistemological crisis shared by late-16th century mannerism, post–World War I surrealism, and late-20th century postmodernism alike. All three cultural movements record and react to their given epoch's general loss of faith in the prevailing representational/interpretive strategies' efficiency to make sense of their surrounding reality, a collective dilemma that opens the way for a series of fearfully troubling yet playfully liberating self-questionings and destabilizations of meaning- and identity-formations. Carter's introduction to the text explicitly explains that the Curious Room epitomizes the place of birth of mannerism, "born out of the inability of the rational, critical methods pioneered by the humanists to embrace the expanding universe of the sixteenth century and bridge the gap between the new versions of reality that the scientific discoveries of the Renaissance offered and traditional assumptions" (216). In Carter's multifocal view, mannerist "aesthetic dominated by irony, eccentricity, wit, strangeness" (Carter 216) rhymes with surrealism's quest for new forms of knowledge which can overturn bourgeois rationalism and banal common sense with the innovatively illogical yet strategically organized powers of dreams, desires, madness, and the childlike—all apt to liberate transgressive, imaginative, new thoughts, in the fashion of Švankmajer's art. As a tribute to Dalí's paranoid critical method, Prague is referred to as "the capital of paranoia" allowing subconscious images to predominate its sphere (398). Certainly both the mannerist and the surrealist projects of self-destabilization remind of the cognitive dissonance experienced throughout our own "postmodern condition" described by theoreticians like Baudrillard (1994) and Lyotard (1984) as the recognition of the plurality, ambiguity, malleability, insufficiency of the available interpretive strategies, representational apparati and narrative frames meant to decode and depict our world. The self-reflexivity involved in mannerism, surrealism, and postmodernism alike nearly necessarily elicits a "serious play" (Ahmed 1998, 17) with the culturally approved yet increasingly defamiliarized, decomposed means of knowledge-production and discursive conventions brilliantly activated throughout Carter's trademark "demythologizing business" (1983, 69). The performative, political agenda of Carter's literary writing dives deep down the rabbit hole in so far as it attributes to curiosity a moral function to explore the world by explicating inexplicable phenomena by (meta)fictional means (Ryan-Sautour 67).

Tellingly, the contents of Rudolph's Curiosity Cabinet each manifest the ambiguous, impossible meanings nascent from the epistemological crises stimulating the revolutionary cultural movements at the root of the short story. But the chaotic collection also represents how the bundle of hypotexts (Carroll's *Alice* tales, Švankmajer's film, *The Surrealist Manifesto*, Dr. Dee's and Rudolph II's biographies, etc.) bear witness to Carter's perception of "artistic creation as a true pleasure of confluence rather than a [Bloomian] anxiety of influence" (Thomas 35). Accordingly, the *Kunstkammer* stores a stuffed dodo, a fallen star, and a mechanically anthropomorphized automaton-woman made of fruit: each an embodied intertextual homage, to Lewis Carroll nicknamed for his stutter Dodo-dodgson, to mannerist John Donne's paradoxical love song about infidelity "Catch a Falling Star," and to Rudolph's court painter Arcimboldo's fruit composition portraits, respectively; not to mention the numerous allusions to surrealism's emblematic items including a realization of Lautrémont's beauty ideal of "the chance encounter of a sewing machine and an umbrella on the dissecting table." The intertextual play with former artistic works and historical epistemes elicits an experience of *déjà lu* whereby the multitude of source texts are all regarded (*déjà vu*) as the surrealists' found object composites defamiliarized from their banal use and reprocessed into artistic carriers of metaphorical meanings. Carter performs a stylistic bravado in her pastiche of mannerism's intellectual sophistication, ornate artificiality, compositional instability inoculated with the surrealists' experimental representational technique of an automatic writing beyond calculation, logic, politeness or plotting. Thus, the story's passion for carnivalesque self-disintegration (resonating with the lavish decadence of the Renaissance masques and surrealist dreamscapes) highlights postmodern's indebtedness to the modern and proto-modern. In Carter's hybrid narrative, the found objects are recycled word composites, verbal equivalents to Svankmajer's bonepuppets and Arcimboldo's fruit automata. Their metamorphosis performs an authentic "alchemy of the word" reflecting "quotation [as] the strategy of a sensibility that sees reality slipping away along obscure and tortuous paths" (Carter 1990, 217) exploring "shimmering vistas of perhaps yet undiscovered worlds" and words (Frankova 131).

With its palimpsestic re-reading of revolutionary "–isms," Carter's *Alice* tale problematizes ideological-cultural technologies of truth-production, the warranty of paradigmatic thought patterns, the preconditions of epistemological transformations, possibilities of radical cognitive revolutions, the limits of knowability, and the inevitable overlappings of reason and imagination. All these dilemmas are crystallized in the ultimate question of origins she finds at the kernel of any quest for knowledge and formulates in a pair of enquiries intertwining objective existence with personal experience: "In the beginning was ... what?" "Where was I before I was born?" The curious room emerges as the locus of the tentative answer to these answerable questions and a utopian place of blissful omniscience forever lost, hence attributing a psychoanalytical significance to the epistemological anxiety permeating the text.

> Perhaps, in the beginning, there was a curious room, a room like this one, crammed with wonders; and now the room and all it contains are forbidden you, although it was made just for you, had been prepared for you since time began, and you will spend all your life trying to remember it [401].

The Curious Room might just as well stand for the maternal womb as the creative unconscious. The question of origins "Where do babies come from?" a topic of kindergarten mischief and existential philosophy alike is intimately connected to an erotic interest in the textual body constituting a literary theoretical dilemma condensed in the metafictional question about the origins of a story "Where do books come from?" and a general enquiry about how social meanings and discursively constituted subjects come into being?

According to a Lacanian psychoanalytical reading (1992), Alice's journey through the looking-glass can both reenact and reverse the traumatic socialization process whereby the maturing child must move from the Imaginary to the Symbolic realm, exchanging the immediacy of bodily interaction within the primary Maternal realm of non-difference for the universal sign system of substitutive, compensatory language of the Paternal Law; accepting that instant preverbal gratification must be traded for the disciplinary discourse of 'thou shalt not' if she wants to find an adequate means of communicating with the outside world. The Carterian Wonderland summons this primary renunciation and prohibition only to immediately provoke its transgression: "Outside the curious room, there is a sign on the door which says 'Forbidden.' Inside, inside, oh come and see! The celebrated DR. DEE" (397).

In Sarah Gamble's view, the curious room "invites to trespass of the most voyeuristic kind, those who dare to come and see are rewarded with spectacle, marvels, incident, and adventures—since for Carter, a lifelong atheist and a stringent opponent of Judeo-Christian apparatus of belief, there is no such thing as inappropriate knowledge" (Gamble in Benson 42). Karima Thomas calls the story a parody of Plato's allegory of cave (44) and emphasizes (mock)epiphany by visual presence. However, besides promising the *spe(cta)cular* satisfaction of epistemophiliac curiosity identified as a taboo-breaking carnal desire, the Wonder room also sheds light on the significance of *language* and *verbal embodiments* in reformulating our realities in search of all-knowingness. Carter's introduction to the short story defines her fictionalized Cabinet of Curiosities as an "ur-museum [of memories], a manifestation of an *omnivorous* curiosity, a *gluttony* for the world, but also a potent image of the unconscious [...] the underworld in which language develops a life of its own" (217).

In my view, the real concern of this Alice adaptation is precisely how the creative consciousness can revivify the subversive powers of language by embracing repressed, irrational, corporeally-motivated subconscious urges, a physical hunger for words (stressed by Carter's above italicization) which cease to be omnipotent markers of reality or divine guarantees of truthfulness, and surpass transcendental, essential denotations to become limitless, playful, ambiguous, and imaginative, as the word becomes flesh to dwell in(between) us devouring and disgorging it. The rebellious invitation to the Curious Room reads as a fictional reformulation of French semanalitician Julia Kristeva's theory on the self-subversive potential of signification, the embodied sense's revolutionary capacities activated in/by poeticity's unconventional language use (Kristeva 1984). Rhyming ("see"/"DEE"), repetition ("inside, inside"), and musicality (serpentine sibilants, orgasmic oh) foreground transverbal qualities of meaning-production which make (non)sense on the level of corporeal experience. Thus, they have the capacity to uncannily plug back the speaking subject into a semiotic good vibration, immediate (unmediated) satisfactions of the primary blissful symbiosis of fetal/infantile and maternal body, preceding the paternal, phallogocentric symbolization, differentiation and repression which will be brought along with the advent of signs. The Curious Room stands for a microcosmic Wonderland, a soft spot of immediate corporeal presence, a flash of innovative nonsense located always already at the heart of the conventionally governed common sense produced by any representational system.

In the following, I wish to explore how the various recycled "-isms"'s epistemological endeavors to challenge quasi-objective truth-claims, justificatory methods, belief systems, along with linguistic transparency and the reliability of reality-models coincide with an "anatomical scrutiny" of the speaking subject's corporeal de/constitutions Attila Kiss describes in his comparative studies which interface the problematic of paradigm change throughout Renaissance proto-modern and contemporary postmodern epistemological crises (see Kiss 2006, XX). In Carter's *Alice* tale a plethora of metamorphic grotesque bodies act out collective cultural anxieties about knowability through staging the "abjectification" of individual subjects (Kristeva 1982, 4), a disintegration affecting the discursive constitution of selves. This semioticization of bodily instability (heterogeneity, vulnerability) allows for a subversive somatization of meaning formation. Conventional, clichéd representational practices get reanimated ('reincarnated'!) by the uncanny return of the formerly repressed, 'unspeakable' carnality, invading the signification process with the use of embodied nonsense, incarnated voice, and materialized metaphors.

One of the most memorable instances of embodied nonsense in Carter's story is the automated fruit woman, an organic-mechanical hybrid constructed by Arcimboldo as "a loving metaphor" materializing all possible pleasures and wonders (402). The creature is alternatively referred to as "Summer" and "It" implying an uncategorizable monstrous-marvelous thing without a proper name whose designation purely indicates its symbolical qualities. Rudolph trusts the logic of contagious similarity implied in the metaphor when he has intercourse with It in hope of fructifying his barren cold winter kingdom and eventually becoming a harvest festival himself. Yet, much like a fundamentally unreliable sign-system, the disseminating ambiguous meanings, the vegetal clockwork doll decomposes through each act of love (a subtle substitute of the interpretative act) into its delicious, sensorially stimulating constituents: a strawberry nipple landing in front of Alice's feet, a dark, viscous, "sticky puddle of freshly squeezed grape juice, and apple juice, and peach juice, juice of plum, pear, or raspberry, strawberry, cherry ripe, blackberry, black currant, white currant, red…" (403). The eroticism of this delirious list of words undoing common sensual coherence with melodic repetitions and play with sounds—reminiscent of the wild gustatory and verbal delights of Christina Rossetti's poem "Goblin Market" (1862)—is further enhanced by the narrative voice's inviting readers to interact with the carnal joys vibrating the text, to "dip your finger in the puddle and lick it. Delicious!" The teasing of taste buds is complemented by the olfactory aphrodisiac of the sentence "the room brims with the delicious ripe scent of summer pudding" (403). A primal physicality seems to overwhelm articulate language. Only the "Ting-a-ling!" of a bell resonates the air agitated due to the jolting and rhythmic lurching of the bed where the Archduke and the Automaton copulate. Later, Summer is "wobbling, clicking, whirring … and utters a gross mechanical sigh" before her collapse, that is never final or ultimate since Arcimboldo rebuilds her whenever Rudolph's yearning arouses again.

However, Carter's point here concerns precisely the viability of transhuman self-expression, of a transverbal language she relates to the undefinable species where alchemical homunculus Alice and automated fruit doll belong, "something, God knows what" (401) clearly embodying the Unspeakable. Similarly to Svankmajer's toying with the idea of the secret lives and thoughts of things, Carter ponders in her introduction whether these artificially animated fetish "objects that jerk and shudder into a semblance of life, do they believe themselves to be human? And might they become so by the sheer intensity of their belief?" (She quotes Chasseguet-Smirgel's book *Creativity and Perversion* to argue that our fetish objects born out of the hubris of animating the inanimate console us because they give us the feeling that a marvellous and uncanny world not ruled by our common laws may eventually exist.) Certainly these dilemmas evoke the famous philosophical thought experiment asking "If a tree falls in a forest and no one is around to hear it, does it make a sound?" that raises questions relating to the significance of sensorial observation and interpretive consciousness in creating any knowledge of reality.

Carter persistently pursues her project to challenge rational discourse as a fetishistic token of truth grounding common sense regarded as the only culturally sanctioned, valid mode of self-expression. On the one hand, the automaton's clicking and drippings as well as Alice's mute gaping and autotelic riddles are tentatively decoded as readable traces of conscient existence. On the other hand, an apparently articulate cry repeatedly piercing the text "Poor Tom's a-cold!" proves to be a referentless, nonsensical, fake significatory act performed by the ravens' mindless miming human language's sounds without any intent of meaning formation. Language turns out to be just as easily de/recomposable into its minimal units of sounds as the clockwork girl falls apart into fruits and juices undone by the Archduke's carnal desire and Alice's logical conundrums.

The Automaton's disintegration is accelerated in/by language as the Carterian narrative adopts the associative logic of surrealist automatic writing, allowing for a free stream of consciousness that sheds light on the inherent poeticity of a language whereby words necessarily mean more than intended. Restrictive common sense is inevitably transformed into ludic nonsense in which speakers can re/invent meanings as they like. I have already discussed how the mechanicalized fruit composition makes a cultural historical allusion to Arcimboldo's artistic oeuvre—including a painting of Rudolph as Vertumnus, the Roman God of seasons—characterized by a cumulative method and a metaphorical worldview paradigmatic of his times, and how the Automaton becomes a sensually embodied metaphor, a carnivalesque metaphor of Summer.

However, we witness a hypermetaphorization in the passage when the Archduke is effecting intercourse with Summer who is identified in a quick succession of images with a fruit salad, Carmen Miranda's hat, a hand of bananas, enthusiasm for the newly discovered Americas, a street in Prague called Novy Svet (New World), weird plants like warty mandrake roots that originate in the sperm and water spilled by hanged men, and magnificent specimens from of the "coco-de-mer, or double coconut, which grows in the shape of the pelvic area of a woman," as well as vegetable marriages of the two planned in his greenhouses to raise the curious progeny *man-de-mer* or *coco-drake* (402). Both the esoteric and exotic penchant of the Archduke's erotic fantasies are excited by an innovativeness, a hunger for the new deemed impossible, that is satisfied on the level of language by subtle rhetorical interconnections. The Americas and a Prague street can touch because of sharing a geographical proper name; the vegetable marriages of the *man-de-mer* and the *coco-drake* constitute embodied portmanteau words; the formal similarity enabling the mandrake's identification with the phallus and of the banana bunch with the hand is the same that grounds the nonsensical language-games turning homophones or homonyms into synonyms (in Carroll's *Alice* "we called him Tortoise because he taught us" and trees bark "Boughwough!" so their branches are called boughs). Moreover, the fruit salad on Carmen Miranda's hat is an allusion to the favorite actress of language philosopher Ludwig Wittgenstein renown for tracing the limits of representation through studying the unspeakable kept silenced and the associative interactions of language games.

The same Wittgensteinian homage[16] lurks in the grunts of the Archduke's pet lion interrupting the intercourse. The lion's being called a watch dog instead of a guard cat supports "language as a means of expression rather than denotation" (Thomas), while the pondering about "opening up his brain this moment, [to] find nothing there but the image of a beefsteak" (401) evokes the elliptical comment from *Philosophical Investigations* "If a lion could speak, we could not understand him." This stresses the significance of "social forms of life," embodied experience shared by an interpretive community in understanding linguistic utterances. This certitude about the miscomprehension arising from the radically incompatible lived experiences of lionness and humanness doomed to prevent the convergence of linguistic denotations actually rhymes with the Carrollian Alice's inability to comply with Wonderlands' expectations of Alice-hood, implied in Humpty Dumpty's insistence on her name necessarily meaning something, "like the shape I am." (219)[17]

The failure of denotation or just the opposite proliferation of connotations are instances of literary nonsense which reflect the epistemological crisis thematized by Carter. The numerous tributes to Carroll include "the random juxtaposition of a raven and a writing desk" in the Archduke's collection of curiosities by means a tongue-in-cheek reference to the Mad Hatter's unanswerable question—hence turning the language-game into visual pun physically incorporating the subversion of meaning. Further examples of embodied nonsense include the hyperlogic—familiar from the *Looking Glass* King's response to Alice's "I see nobody on the road" "I only wish I had such eyes to be able to see Nobody!" (234)— when Doctor Dee's round ball of solid glass is reflected in his assistant Kelley's fleeting thoughts considering whether the ball is solid enough to crash the master's skull and reaching the conclusion that its transparency implies an optical lightness that can be equated with a physical lightness: one can see through it so it must weight nothing. Polysemy emerges as magical metamorphoses elsewhere too in a montage merging vital bodily experiences of sexuality, metabolism and mortality: Kelly is reluctant to observe his male member for fear the phrase "well hung recalls the noose which he narrowly escaped in his native England for fraud" (400).

We even find verbal/visual embodiments of the *exquisite cadaver (cadaver exquis)*, surrealists' wordplay and montage game of surprising coincidences and consequences, whereby a random succession of collectively gathered images perfectly match shifting into each other, in the fashion of the English tradition of nonsense it drew an inspiration from (see Carroll's portmanteau or the Victorian parlor game Consequences).[18] The grotesque found object composites inspired by Svankmajer and the compositional style of Carter's postmodern, self-decomposing pastiche toying with elusive significations both seem to be compiled in this ludic fashion. Our starting point is, yet again, the crystal ball in Dee's curious room that is compared to a huge eye-ball to unchain a complex ocular metaphor elaborated by a *cadaver exquis* game's associations which enhance the weakening of visual mastery. As the organ of seeing loses its elementary constituents it gradually disintegrates but will never cease to mean things, no matter how nonsensical. It never becomes meaningless, it "remains on the side of sense" (Thomas 38) to stimulate the proliferation of significations. Hence, the blurred vision of the crystal eyeball—an organic-artificial instrument of science and magic—becomes an embodied metaphor of epistemological crisis predominating Carter's Wonderland. The crystal ball resembles "aqueous humor, frozen," "a glass eye, although without any iris or pupil," "a tear, round, as it forms within the eye" but its apparently blinded sight is "apt to see the invisible" since this "fearful sphere contains everything that is, or was, or ever shall be" (397). Its faulty panopticism hints at the very unspeakable whose naming must be unsatisfactory. The ball also evokes the onomatopoeic sound sequence "drop" charged with differing meanings and mental images kaleidoscopically sliding into each other via a montage-verbiage technique: a round teardrop formed in the corner of an eye, a drop of semen on the tip of the doctor's morning erection, a drop of dew about to fall from the unfolded petals of a rose, and even Do Drop Inn inviting visitors with a jovial pun showing a dewdrop in the act of falling on its sign. The falling dew is more tear shaped than spherical and hence differs from the original signifier of the crystal eyeball it was meant to stand in for. As Karima Thomas suggests, this stages a language philosophical dilemma preoccupying Carroll too, related to sense preceding denotation (37): a tear is thought of pear shaped even before its fall. In other words, if you take care of the sense, the sounds will take care of themselves, as the Duchess puts it. The polysemic "drop" turning from falling liquid (noun) to the act of fall (verb) engenders the transition of visual nonsense into verbal nonsense, as the analogy by physical material form (transparent, fluid, spherical mass) is substituted by homonymic linguistic analogy by spelling and sound.

Moreover, the sign's visual pun also illustrates the open-ended nature of the signification process. Neither discursive representation dryly substituting for the presence of corporeal immediacy, nor the overflow of associative connotations can succeed in grasping the real as it is: like the drop endlessly about to fall, truth always remains at the tip of our tongues. Ironically the ultimate drops of a more base material nature seem to take the same course: the faeces flies out of sight, the piss freezes in the act of falling down the hole in the privy at the top of Rudolph's tower, cadavers fall into graves only to be ditched for sakes of necromancy, and texts are revisited to become always already *déjà lu* on their turn. The drops' common denominator (movement) seems to encapsulate the essence of the adaptation process which innovatively recycles literary originals while keeping a certain degree of fidelity to the original that must remain recognizable. It refuses the closure of ending, metamorphoses while remaining the antithesis of metamorphosis, and "retains the perfection of its circumference only by refusing to sustain free fall, remaining what it is because of refusing to become what it might be" (398). And we are certainly reminded of Alice's long-lasting fall down the rabbit hole that initiates her adventures and the cognitive dissonance accompanying them as affective experience of an epistemological crisis.

When Carter's Alice drops out of the crystal ball, it is not by chance that it is Doctor Dee who awaits her in the Curious Room beyond the looking-glass. This polymath consultant to Queen Elizabeth I and later a prestigious guest of Rudolph II's court, an outstanding scientist and occultist of his times, divided his attention between the devoted study of alchemy, divination, Hermetic philosophy, and most importantly the quest for the *lingua adamica*. The Adamic language, God used to address the first humans before the fall, was believed to be a perfect, prelapsarian, unmediated means of truly naming reality via an archaic, direct communication lost with the Babelian confusion of tongues. Throughout spiritual conferences conducted with an air of Christian piety Dee allegedly contacted archangels with the help of a crystal-gazer and his assistant medium Edward Kelley who helped him to transcribe the perfect language he then meticulously studied to find out how it could express unequivocally even the unspeakable. Dee's dissatisfaction with the limited nature of human discourse reflects the era's epistemological crisis.

In the short story Dee bids a graceful welcome to Alice in "the language of the tawny pipit" a passerine bird. He believes that the angels' "piercing voices" speaking the lost Adamic language are the closest to "bird creole" (400), and perhaps hopes that the short repetitions of a loud disyllabic *chir-ree chir-ree* in the pipit's song could perform a transverbal poeticity, a non-referential nonsense, a melodic immediacy surely apt to touch the voiceless alchemical homunculus sprung from his crystal ball. Once Alice manages to find her voice she comes up with logical conundrums borrowed from Carroll's mathematical riddles— he called "pillow problems" and embedded in his *A Tangled Tale* (1885)[19]—in a "voice as clear as a looking-glass" (405). It is truly puzzling why her questions leave utterly speechless Dee who was just as much a logician mathematician and a language philosopher as Carroll himself. Carter's introduction to the text explains that "Alice was invented by a logician and therefore she comes from the world of nonsense, that is, from the world of non-sense— the opposite of common sense; this world is constricted by logical deduction and is created by language, although language shivers into abstractions in it" (1990, 215). The aim of Dee's quest for the *lingua adamica*, the narrowing down of sense to ultimate meanings, is much in line with the straightforwardness of mathematical abstraction and the logical, linguistic constrictions of literary nonsense's world building. He might be stupefied by the earthly, non-transcendental origins of Alice's obvious yet ambiguous speech acts which, far from angelic songs, can be decoded as meaningful communication performed in human language that nevertheless still turns its intelligibility dubious, defamiliarized, along with the conventional representational and interpretive strategies meant to make sense of it.

Accordingly, Alice's final riddle "If 70 percent have lost an eye, 75 percent an ear, 80 percent an arm, 85 percent a leg: what percentage, at least, must have lost all four?" (407) is rightly assumed to have just one single non-negotiable answer (the solution, number 10 is provided by Carter's endnote) but implies much more. In fact, the question might shock Dee because it confronts him with the exciting Janus-faced duplicity of nonsense discourse. One side is the meta-textual rhetorical facet of nonsense praised by Jean-Jacques Lecercle for eliciting a self-reflective awareness concerning the ambiguity of common sense and the (mal)functioning of our sense-making methods through revealing the inherent poetic-metaphorical, associative-imaginative surplus, as well as the authoritative ideological charge, socio-historical residue and cultural framing of 'ordinary' language and representation at large (Lecercle 1994, 2–3). The other side is the transverbal corporeal facet calling into life the physicality of the represented and representing bodies and revivifying the materiality of signifying activity's lived experience, as surplus meanings (nonsense!) are generated by the incarnated rhythms and sounds stressing the sensorial stimulation of and by the human voice. In Alice's nonsense, a literal somatization of the text takes place through the overnarrativization of a bodyliness endowed with a radical unspeakability that eventually decomposes itself in the text. The riddle's undoing of common sense rhymes with the disintegration of a strangely undefined, multiplied, collective corpus losing some of its organs throughout the dissemination of pluralized meanings.

Alice's literary nonsense language equally belongs to *abstract art* as a self-decomposing composition that may exist with a certain degree of independence from visual and linguistic references in the world, but it also functions as an inherently *embodied art* form rooted in the fleshly lived reality that keeps vibrating its representational practices with a physical presence. This titillation fuels the non-sense of "language *shivering* into abstraction" (Carter 1990, 215) along with readers' quest for its meanings (Lecercle).

Ryan-Sautour refers to Vincent Jouve's three levels of readerly engagement with the fictional narrative conceived in terms of game-playing to argue for the multi-layered functioning of Carterian fiction that allows for a coexistence of the intellectually self-conscious reader (the *lectant*), the reader willingly suspending disbelief, interacting with the illusion, playing the fictional game of the text (the *lisant*), and the instinctive 'read reader' drawn into a corporeal experience on a visceral level of interpretation (the *lu*). Accordingly, "Alice in Prague" addresses readers on multiple levels: it operates with a complex web of intertextual and intermedial references; it invites to imagine eccentric characters, places, and events; and it affects on primordial, preverbal, physically-stimulating levels of fascination, agitation, repulsion, and curiosity alike. Carter manages to capture the fundamental ambiguity of the Alice figure, demonstrating how opposing modes of reading—such as the ones described by Hugh Haughton as "reading for adventures and enjoyment" like the Gryphon and "reading for explanations and education" like the Red Queen (Haughton xi)[20]—are not mutually exclusive, but necessarily complementary attitudes throughout attempting to make sense of nonsense in Wonderland.

Rikki Ducornet's Jade Cabinet as an Intertext of Angela Carter's The Curious Room

Rikki Ducornet's *Jade Cabinet* (1994) inspired by Carter's *Alice* story and the Lewis Carroll myth reflects on the interconnections of memory and desire, language and power, embodiment and meaning/lessness. The book starts out with an ambiguous *bon mot* "*Memory presents us with thoughts of what is past accompanied with a persuasion that they were once real.*" (9) and, with a matching pun, presents the memoirs of a girl named Memory who tells a twisted love story of passionate quests. Memory recalls how her father, an eccentric Victorian amateur scientist, obsessed with finding the perfect, primal language, traded for a collection of precious jade her mute elder daughter, the beautiful and brilliantly imaginative, golden dreamchild Etheria Sphery—an Alice alter ego because of her embodying an "insatiable desire for knowledge, both worldly and divine." Etheria is married off to Radulph Tubbs, a caricature of stubborn, short-sighted pragmatism and ruthless colonizing intent associated with virility, prosaicity, and industrialization. (He processes Egyptian ibis mummies into soup powder, abuses his wife as an erotic object, and quickly exchanges her for the Hungerkünstler of Prague—a nod to Carter—he steals from his father in law's curiosity cabinet.) Etheria first suffers, then flees, and uses magic to vanish and find just the opposite of pre-lapsarian "lingua adamica" that makes Things truly present, as she invents the word 'after the fall' that can make everything disappear, turn ethereal, like herself. The real meaning of life, that is beyond all words, comes neither from the father's perfectionism nor the husband's pragmatism, but a dumb girl's illusionism, demonstrated by "Etheria metamorphos[ing] from victim—a creature in jar—to magician, an animating air, a vital breath" (157).

This is also a metafictional story about storytelling, the unreliability of memory, the inevitability of confabulation, the elusiveness of words and the heterogeneous range of sensations they stimulate. All this, epitomized by the titular jade cabinet, as Memory explains: "Let's suppose memory is like a jade cabinet, but a cabinet belonging to an infinitely irresolute collector. Each time we look inside, the jade appears to be the same, yet the mind is forever replacing one chimera for another that resembles it. Let's suppose the memory is a cabinet of chameleons and the mind as unstable as the moon" (92). Since Memory's memoirs rely on Stubbs' journals "misinformed by a certain callousness of heart" (9) and Etheria's torn, nearly illegible diaries, she stays aware of the dubiousness of their credibility. The only thing that remains certain is the enchanting, magical power of language that can conjure ghosts of the past in fleshly form and "transform dead snakes into animate nature" and when it fails, "as when memory fails, all we can hope for is an airless cabinet reeking of badly preserved specimens!" (157)

The novel's afterword, subtitled *Waking to Eden*, attempts to provide a factual clue to the fictional text. In an autobiographical flash-back, Ducornet comments on the sensual experience of her advent into language, recalling a decisive childhood memory of her first reading adventure. The passage is dense with the lyrical musicality, transverbal vibration, and corporeal excitement Kristeva associates with the revolutionary powers of poetic language. Besides acoustic delights of word and sound, letters become sources of visual pleasure, provoking an intense erotic experience of imagetext that is embraced spontaneously, immersively by the child and subsequently rationally reflected upon by the adult self.

> I was infected with the venom of language in early childhood when, sitting in a room flooded with sunlight, I opened an alphabet book. **B** was a Brobdingnagian tiger-striped bumble-bee, hovering over a crimson blossom, its stinger distinct. This image was of such potency that my entire face—eyes, nose and lips—was seized by a phantom stinging, and my ears by a hallucinatory buzzing. In this way, and in an instant, I was simultaneously initiated into the alphabet and awakened to Eden [155].[21]

Like for the child Rikki, the materiality of writing as textual trace holds a special significance for mute Etheria who communicates with handwritten notes disrupting the conventional typographic print of the book in which they are embedded. The spectacularized visuality of her girlish handwriting, with a crown drawn on the word "glory," a skull in place of an "o," spikes growing out of the initial of "disagreeable" tease and trouble the verbal flow of the narrative. On one instance, she enters into written conversation with no other than Mr. Dodgson (whose actual rebus letters to child friends possibly inspired her illustrated notes).

The amorous relation between letters provides a model for the interpersonal dynamics of a creative partnership. Just like A is in need of B to create a desirable, legible text, Etheria's silent charm is brought to full realization by a knowing reader capable of inventively deciphering, answering and stimulating her enigmatically embodied personality. Although Charles Dodgson apparently emerges as a minor fictive character of the novel, a casual acquaintance from the neighborhood befriending the sisters, the numerous passing allusions to him, gradually disclose him as Etheria's only real soul mate who manages to understand her being. He writes her funny letters (one "figures a bottle of *anti-matter* oil bearing a luminous crown and a pair of angelic wings, the Holy Grail stands besides it and indeed one cannot tell the one from the other" [12]), photographs her naked [with angel wings, silk kimonos, and a cat's tail], makes her toys [miniature kites, whistling paper birds, and a magical fish Ask! Ask! Ask me wish! penned on to its sides], entertains her with games of whimsy, witticisms and nonsensical mockeries [such as "flies and mosquitoes are the materialization of vowels and consonants uttered by fools, and this explains why there are so many of them"] [15] or "When God thinks, it looks like a spiral staircase" [51]), and, as Tubbs suspects, writes her a tale recording "the invisible knots which tied" (101) them together as friends.

This tale is, of course, *Alice's Adventures Underground* that is described in Ducornet through the interpretive filter of the jealous husband who steals the manuscript to obsessively re-read it, looking for clues for Etheria's reasons of abandoning him. The unimaginative Tubbs is not an ideal reader of Carrollian nonsense to say the least. He calls the tale's meanings persistently elusive, the story devoid of sense, and yet a profoundly subversive text on accounts of giving reason to a senseless child. Infantile irrationality is justified as a viable worldview in a tale where "away went Alice like the wind" like Etheria who "had run after magic," (101) emblematized by the white rabbit playing hide and seek in and out of the magician's top hat. Moreover, the little book is a storehouse of "potent witchery" that cleanses Dodgson's reputation possibly compromised by his child photography (130).

Etheria reappears for a final conjuring act as a female magician to succeed in her vanishing act by finding the silent Word that makes her disappear forever, while fading all things into Nothing. Thus, she commits a rebellion against her treacherous father and his dream of a Divine Tongue capable of bringing all things into Being (154). The paternal dream of "a language of pure, unadulterated light in which even ugly words such as *hassock* and *antimacassar* oil 'palpitate as medusa in the sea and scintillate as a comet in the sky'" (12) is travestied by Dodgson's rebus letter entertaining his child friends with the nonsensical notion of anti-matter oil, motivated by the assumption that language should be treated as an instrument of play instead of an object of adulation. No wonder that Etheria's ultimate nonsensically ethereal embodiment finds a kinship with the trickster Dodgson who is there in the audience with two little girls, each to an arm, and watches her vanishing with "his shocked face expanding, leaving its body behind, to float up into the air" (135). If Dodgson becomes a real-life double to his fictional Cheshire Cat, evaporating Etheria, too, embodies the Carrollian grin without a cat, present in its absence, a phrase emptied of meanings, the unsaid unspeakable defeating rational verbalization. She is described with a phrase attributed to Dodgson: "all that remained of her was her smile and the illusion of a miracle" (75).

Etheria's evanescence signifies a passing out of sight, memory, existence, and meaning. In her narrator sister's words, "memory is an act of magic, we transform the outer world of facts: rabbits, hats, silk scarves, and painted trunks into those things we wish to keep, for whatever reason" (126). Beyond *Alice*, another intertextual allusion made to Dodgson's "doctrine of mist," captures the essence of Memory's carnal memory of Etheria and raises a phenomenological philosophical conundrum: "things exist only because we perceive them, and we exist because we are capable of perception," but "if all is idea, then nowhere is the inherent contradiction of corporeality more evident than during the act of remembering." (126)

Carroll's novel is full of curious rooms challenging Alice's sense of orientation and increasing her disidentification through physical changes she must undergo, as she becomes too large, too big, or too irritated to be herself or to be able to properly remember who she is or has been. The corridor where she lands after her fall with the many minuscule doors offering a peep at magical gardens impossible to reach, the White Rabbit's cottage trapping her enlarged body, the Duchess' kitchen guarded by frog and fish footmen and suffocating with a peppery atmosphere, the courtroom as a twisted locus of un/justice serve as sensorially shocking, transitory stations to her picaresque journey in Wonderland. In Carter, the curiosity cabinet condensates the essence of Wonderland within the alchemist's microcosmic fusing incompatibles like the Carrollian portmanteau and providing a fictional reformulation of "Carter's own idea of the room as the space that contains all the secrets of a person's life before they are born, and which they spend their lifetime trying to remember" (De la Rochere 2015, 17). In Ducornet, Father's study equals Wonderland, a site of freedom and fantastication in Etheria and Memory's early childhood: they play 'Hunt the Thimble' among bottled snakes and tree frogs and 'My Lady' Slipper' beside a fully assembled skeleton and a stuffed orangutan named after Dr. Johnson, they firmly believe a library of lepidoptera, a butterfly collection pinned in rosewood boxes to be books with stories written over their bodies, and they pen their little treatises on natural history there, including a treatise *On Insect Eyes* and a fashion book for fairies Etheria prepares especially for Mr. Dodgson. (The sisters call Dodgson's room where he makes nude photos of them, Nicobar Rooms with reference to their father's tales about natives of Nicobar Island, a human race with tails like cats, who run naked as the night and converse with shrill, persistent cries of bats.) If the Father's hybris is to exchange all this lively imaginativeness for an inanimate collection of jade stones, his daughters manage to rebel against his Faustian deal: Etheria flees from his claustrophobic cabinet towards a magician's grand theatre stage and then evaporates into thin air as if enacting the elusiveness of meanings, while Memory matures into a storyteller enchanting with the world-creating power of words.

Linguistic Grotesqueries Musicalized in Tom Waits' Alice Album

Carroll's *Alice* tales are marked by a musicality bursting representational frames in so far as literary nonsense language's sensorially stimulating stress on vocality subverts conventional verbalization by privileging the pleasure of sounds (resulting from rhyme, rhythm, and repetition) over rigidly rationalized common sense. This revolutionary intent is self-ironically foregrounded by the numerous poems, songs, and dances embedded in the narrative—parodies of Victorian didactic literature's emptying language with tired-old moralizing clichés. These are the Wonderland creatures' oddly embodied attempts to get in touch with Alice who is alternatively surprised, amused, and bored by their lack of habitual communicational strategies. These strange vibes are reactivated in the poetic language of Carter's "Alice in Prague" story and even more explicitly in the numerous musical compositions inspired by Carroll's children's classic. Just to mention a few: the 1951 Disney animation's cute little ditties ranging from silly ("Unbirthday Song" composed by Al Hoffman) to saccharine ("In a World of My Own" performed by Kathryn Beaumont), the Beatles's hippy, trippy revampings of nursery rhymes and Carrollian wit ("I Am the Walrus" [1967], Jefferson Airplane's psychedelic rock coupled with hallucinatory mishearings ("Feed your head!" the Dormouse says instead of the Queen's "Off with her head!" in the song "White Rabbit" [1967]), David Del Tradici's neoromantic *An Alice Symphony* (1969), his succeeding *Adventures Underground* (1971), *Vintage Alice* (1972) and *Final Alice* a contemporary opera for soprano, folk ensemble and orchestra (1976), Marilyn Manson's nightmarish, cannibalistic, gothic "passion play" ("Eat Me! Drink Me!" [2007]), and Avril Lavigne's girl power affirming lead single and end credit to Burton's 2010 film. This random sample illustrates the diversity of the tunes.

In the following I wish to concentrate on a peculiar musical adaptation of the Wonderland theme that generates embodied nonsense defying all generic categories in a subversive spirit worthy of Carroll. American singer-songwriter Tom Waits's album *Alice*, released in 2002 on Epitaph Records, contains the majority of the songs co-written with partner Kathleen Brennan for an "art musical" theatrical play directed and designed by Robert Wilson (with Carroll's text adapted to stage by Paul Schmidt), originally set up in Thalia Theatre in Hamburg, Germany, in 1992, premiered in the U.S. as the opening event of the 1995 Next Wave Festival at the Brooklyn Academy of Music, and performed in various theatrical venues around the world ever since. Instead of faithfully following the storyline of the novels, Waits' record and Wilson's original play—two acts based on the two Alice books with seven scenes and seven knee plays (intermezzos) each—contain dreamy sketches of breathtaking ballads tied together by the leitmotif of impossible love. The variations on the same theme of insatiable yearning include illustrative examples such as Alice's naïve laments (in "No One Knows I'm Gone") and the White Knight (aka Carroll)'s ballad on the impossible love of a little bird and a whale who must part but will always pretend to be each other's in their hearts (in "Fish & Bird").

The song cycle definitely verges on sentimentality. This melodic commemoration of the artist's infatuation with the dreamgirl holds piquantly personal implications. Waits has been consistently crediting his co-writer, collaborator wife Kathleen Brennan, a catalyst of all works conceived since their marriage, in terms reminiscent of (the canonized mythical speculations about) Carroll's appraisal of Alice Liddell: "She's an incandescent presence on all songs we work on together" "I think we sharpen each other like knives. She has a fearless imagination…. And she puts the heart into all my things. She's my true love…. Somebody who finishes your sentences for you" (Waits 1999). In fact, this creative partnership is also comparable with Jan and Eva Svankmajer's legendary cooperation. Just like in the case of the Alice-Carroll relation, the meeting with the muse marks a paradigm shift in the artistic development. Throughout Waits' lyrical fictionalizations of this inspirational passion, many memorable lines can be coincidentally put in parallel with Carroll's clandestine confessions. This autobiographical similarity is more consciously exploited than only fortuitous on the *Alice* album.

However, in Waits and Wilson's biofictional take on Alice and Carroll's relationship the recurring references to secret kisses, insatiable yearnings, and self-destructive dark obsession go way beyond Romantic tropes of impossible love and transient happiness to clearly revisit the biographical myth about Carroll's sinful intergenerational passions. The art musical's plot is quite straightforward in this theme. Alice falls into Wonderland while fleeing from Dodgson who attempts to photograph her. Dodgson alias Carroll alias the White Rabbit alias the White Knight/Black Knight guides Alice through the various stages of her adventure where she grows gradually uncertain about her identity as Dreamchild conceived by the artist or him being an invention of her own imagination. All the curious creatures of Wonderland duly show up like the Cheshire Cat making sly innuendos. Flashes of the future display Alice Liddell grown up, forgotten by his love, alone, drinking and Charles Dodgson lonely and sleepless, tormented by visions of the past. Still, the finale of each act is based on a trial scene in which both are found "guilty of their relationship," of having dreamt each other up in an elsewhere (Wilson).

Tenderness turns twisted throughout Waits' trademark, self-ironically overplayed theatricality, too. This love story can be interpreted as just another act of the tongue-in-cheek tragedy relentlessly chronicled by his oeuvre, marked by the pathetic pathos of a rundown travelling circus sideshow that refuses to take itself seriously, being aware of the transitoriness of carnival. Each heartbroken lover is a clown; each melody is bizarre and bittersweet. In fact, the artist admitted that for *Alice* he strategically used iconic figures from the dark underside of Victorian life, lowly popular countercultural entertainment forms like freak shows and funfairs—often called Wonderland or Dreamland like the one operating on Coney Island, New York from 1904 to 1911—which served to stress the tension between the surface innocence and the underlying troublesome anxieties of the *Alice* tales often interpreted as emblematic texts of their own era (Waits.com).

The White Knight's song called "Poor Edward aka Chained Together for Life" revisits "the true story" of Edward Mordrake (more likely a turn-of-the-century urban legend) about a handsome young man, a talented musician of noble origins, who had a woman's face on the back of his head, a sort of a hideous evil twin whispering awful things to him in his sleep which eventually drove him to suicide. This is just as much a metaphor for any obsessive compulsive attachment to another person and the fantasy about the fatal consequences of a feared separation, as well as an embodied representation of how the subtextual gibbering of another voice speaking in tongues resonates beneath any meaningful artwork, hence, doomed to an inevitable decomposition. Along the same lines, "Table Top Joe" sung by the Caterpillar, revives the real-life entertainment-historical figure of Johnny Eck, a sideshow celebrity with a congenital disorder, born with the lower half of his torso missing, who became Ringling Brothers Circus' renown bodiless pianist stage named Half-Boy, excelled on the keyboards and conducted his own orchestra, was a human exhibit in several Ripley's Believe it or Not Odditoriums, and starred Tod Browning's 1932 cult classic film *Freaks*. Waits' tribute to the Half-Boy celebrates in a jolly swing-like tune the unusual, unexpected artistic talents of a disabled man. His song stages a revolt against social majority's consensual, ableist definition of normality that discredits and discriminates disability as an insignificant, meaningless, lesser mode of being. This is yet again an embodied representation of literary nonsense's revolt from the margins against commonsensically delimited mainstream meanings. The freak show performer's anatomical alterity constituted a perfectly functional, livable (ir)reality: Johnny Eck lived and prospered until age 80, like many other stars—Bearded Ladies, Lilliputians, Siamese Twins, etc.—who made a career out of the self-stylization of their atypical embodiments which never inhibited their agency.

I see a strange parallel between literary nonsense's defamiliarizing reenactment of language and the freak's *l'art-pour-l'art* exhibition of mundane skills, such as playing the piano, drinking tea, or embroidering, that gained a special, sensationally grotesque quality simply because of the performer's unusual physical form and the act's simultaneous staging of similarity and difference, turning the spotlight on the self-identicality of the other and the otherness within ourselves.[22] We can spot the same repetition with a difference in the original Carrollian Jabberwocky's gibberish or the Caterpillar's silly questions which resemble language and hence must signify *something*, only we cannot make up our minds exactly what they mean since they refuse to fit conventional narrative, interpretative frames, by making their point precisely their pointlessness. Accordingly, the fragmentary, fluid (de)formations of Table Top Joe's bodiless piano-playing hands associated with the Caterpillar's limbless larval form in this mock documentary-style balladistic rendering of the Wonderland menagerie represent a challenge to the social disciplining of body and discourse alike—on accounts of turning (corporeal and linguistic) lack into the surplus of surprised enchantment.

The theme of low countercultural entertainment resurfaces elsewhere on Waits' *Alice* album. The song "Reeperbahn" is set in a raunchy bar in Hamburg's red light district where elderly transvestite Hans and broken-down movie star Rosie have a final drunken dance with all the fools. "We're All Mad Here, aka Hang Me in a Bottle," rattled by the Mad Hatter, the March Hare and the Dormouse in Wilson's play, offers a crazy and creepy rendering of the classic dance macabre.

The transverbal cacophony in the lyrics meet the spooky noises of the musical composition verging on the experimental by mixing industrial, instrumental sounds with organic ones. The vibratos of musical saw, Stroh violin (a violinophone, a violin outfitted with a metal horn for amplification purposes), the rattling of bones, the whispering of ghosts, and Waits' trademark "scarred baritone" remind of the transience of life and the dark forces underlying everyday quiescence, all the tragicomic meaninglessness (death, madness, despair) underneath the common sense. Indeed critics agree that the strange soundscapes of Waits' orchestration embrace the sounds of heterotopiac elsewheres eluding social control, the sphere of the circus, the carnival, the vaudeville cabaret, or the fairground. A 2002 BBC review by Dan Hill captures this feel on describing the White Knight's song tellingly entitled "Everything You Can Think Of" as music distinguished by "Mexican border town edginess, a demented waltz careening around the fairground looking for a fight, Waits' aural Hall of Mirrors hemmed in by blowing smokestacks and puffing, wheezing steam trains, his voice suddenly transmogrified from reassuring whisper into scabrous, growling barks."

Besides the above-mentioned dubious biographical references to the fantast fathering Alice and fellow freaks, Waits and Wilson's *Alice* is deeply Carrollian in spirit because of the countless ingenious language games ranging from word puzzles Dodgson poses to Alice to Humpty Dumpty's verbal witticism and the classic Jabberwocky nonsense poem's repeatedly reenacted by eight Victorian Vicars, first in dance and song, then in a mute pantomime meant to reveal with bodily gestures that you can only understand if you pay close attention. Wordplay is the basis of the album's most intriguingly incomprehensible song, too. "Kommienezuspädt" is a musical monologue shouted in a crepitating megaphone to a crazy polka tune in a language that sounds like German but proves to be pure gibberish, reminiscent of the White Rabbit's monomaniac muttering and nonsensical exclamations in pretend German evoke (mock)echoes of Nazi military orders familiar from war movie soundtracks, just as much as stage instructions from the absurd musical theatre of Kurt Weill and Bertold Brecht, or a circus ringmaster's curtain calls distinguished by a fake foreign accent. The aim of this language game may be to reveal how the relentless repetition of a perfectly meaningful word can make it sound senseless through the defamiliarization of the sound sequence marking a given material referent (signified and its mental image), and how the obsessive repetition of a meaningless word can invest any nonsensical gibberish with a simulated ultimate meaning. Hence, the ludic anti-rhetoric of self-deconstructive children's games (nursery rhymes' repetitions targeting the loosening or loss of meanings) meet the ideological technology of verbal truth production (political propaganda's or consumer cultural advertisements' repetitions targeting the manipulated, manipulative construction of meanings and realities).

In Wilson's *Alice* play, this constitutive ambiguity of communication and meaning formation—the inevitability of misinterpretation coupled with the impossibility of meaninglessness—becomes charged with a marvelous monstrousness associated with the inherent relativization of fundamentally unstable significations. Accordingly, any possessive love holds the possibility of perversion. ("Duchess: A mother is like the letter M. Neither bad, nor good. It all depends on the circumstances. If a mother says "You're mine," that's good. If a strange man says it, that's bad. CAT: True enough, if you're a little girl. For grown up girls, it's just the opposite."). All intimacy is overshadowed by the impending doom of warfare, the collision of views between the proximate parties. (Humpty Dumpty: "I am the all-inclusive dialectic between here and there. If you want to know what's on the other side, you have to ask me. ... East Berlin and West Berlin, Palestin and Israel, Northern Ireland, enemies are kind of neighbors as well, the harbor is meeting point, it's all about conflict resolution.") This Wonderland is a world of disagreement: any meaning might turn out to convey a message different from the one the receiver first inferred or the sender intended, denotations are troubled by connotations, common sense is prone to become nonsensical.

The elusiveness of meanings is poignantly captured in Waits' song "Watch Her Disappear" a haunting banjo tango Charles Dodgson sings in the play about the gradual fading of his vision of the beloved. In Wilson's theatrical staging, Waits' lyrics belong to Dodgson/Carroll's love letter to Alice that remains unfinished and undelivered yet reaches its addressee in a strangely deviated path characteristic of verbal communications' sliding signifiers (note the polysemy of the word 'letter'!) which undergo multiple displacements as immediate *presence* is experienced in an individual *perceptual* manner to be *represented* in the consensual sign system of words meant to be *misinterpreted* because of their ambiguous (reductive yet metaphorically associative) nature. Dodgson/Carroll cramples up his amorous note and throws it to the cat to play with, but the cat takes his paper toy outdoors and forgetfully drops it, so the royal gardeners find it and offer it to the Queen who uses the document as an evidence of guilty desires, wanting to behead Alice because her name figures in the letter. In the play's highly metafictional finale bordering at once on the burlesque and the bizarre, the White Knight volunteers as the real author of the letter who should be decapitated in place of Alice, he is beheaded only to reappear as the White Rabbit who admits having composed the compromising message. After its execution the Rabbit takes the form of Dodgson who takes again the blame for his authorship and accepts death sentence on his turn, but when his head falls he reappears as Carroll who boldly affirms having truly written the letters, then he burns all his writings, making all the Wonderland characters vanish. In the light of this plotline, the song's title "Watch Her Disappear" is enriched with further new meanings. Besides the obvious melancholic lament about the gradual loosening of the bonds with the muse and the obsession with the unnameable unmentionable, it marks the twisted journey of disappearing and reappearing meanings shapeshifting in and out of an infinite variety of connotations throughout the representation/interpretation process. It also comments on the fictionalization of identity showing how the addressee Alice cannot help being fatally framed in the text risking the disappearance of her real self, and it problematizes authorship as an elusive concept by staging the deaths and resurrections of a multitude of co-authorial figures, and by asking who does a text belong to, who is to blame or praise for the meanings it generates.

Even if the letter fails to fulfill its purpose in so far as it is never read by its addressee, beloved Alice, as a private message of intimate confession, it certainly undergoes a curious metamorphosis. First, reduced to a paper ball cat-toy, its functionality as a communicational utensil is questioned, then elevated to the status of a judicial evidence it is ideologically overcharged with extra-meanings. In this textual game, as words of endearment are misused 'out of order' for juggling or judgment respectively, both the loss and the surplus of meanings result in nonsense destabilizing commonsensical reality. The epistolary relativization of truth recycles the Carrollian 'dream-within-a-dream' theme: the first line of the song invokes the Dreamchild while the last lines' self-repetitive echo stages her hallucinogenic fading away throughout the awakening from the dream. Words embody physical absences, transient touches, and displaced e-motions. In the play the letter almost ends up affecting its addressee more fatally than intended, pushing her towards execution instead of emotionally moving her, while in the song her final dance act dissolves into shadows in and out of his dreams.

Despite the overall sliding of significations, meanings never ever get fully lost on their labyrinthine way, and allow the ambiguity of nonsense to triumph over the closure of meaninglessness. A good example for that is the Waits album's titular song "Alice," a smoky jazz ballad sung by the White Rabbit in Scene 1 during Alice's fall down the rabbit hole where she sees objects plummeting past her into the abyss, including a mirror with her name written on it. The breaking of this looking-glass elicits the disintegration of the verbal marker of her identity and a symbolical loss of herself. However, upon Alice's entry into the realm of namelessness a multitude of transparent glass-like surfaces still reflect her name in a strangely mirrored, distorted manner that defamiliarizes linguistic signification and verbal meaning construction. Through the example of an emotionally charged proper noun, beloved Alice's name, emphasis is added to written signifiers' image-like transtextual look, the fleeting appearance and disappearance of connotations, a word's assumed touch-and-feel effect, as well as the anxious affective- and tremulous corporeal investment in the letters A-L-I-C-E.

In Waits' lyrics, Alice's name directs the elaborate choreography of the White Rabbit/Dodgson's figure skating, a dance on ice that provides an easily decodable metaphor for a dangerous relationship risking the self's integrity. Instead of abstract denotations, it is the physical materiality of letters (written signifiers) that is foregrounded, as graphemes become scarifications the skating singer narrator inflicts in the skin-like surface of ice to contemplate them from beneath the pond surface, as he is sinking down into the depths of textual meaning. The skate-scars on the frozen pond spelling out Alice's name constitute an embodied writing that is doomed to fade, melt, and evaporate leaving only emotional trauma behind. According to the lyrics, similar are the tears on Dodgson's face and the night sounds of the bushes which equally "spell Alice" via synaesthesiac, sensorially stimulating, non-verbal means, all melancholic because of their transitoriness, reminding us of the human physical frame's vulnerability and perishability—a mood musically expressed by "a lovely, candle-flickering tune, drums brushed around a breathy sax and gently chiming vibes" (Hill).

Faithful to the Carrollian dream-within-a-dream leitmotif, the ice-skating, amorous body-writing analogy crops up in another song "Barcarolle" performed by Alice and the White Sheep. Their song locates the female ice-skater figure as a prisoner in the snowball of his imagination, the pocket folds of his memory and make-believe, whereas the lyrics stand for the relativization of the dreamer-dreamt, artist-muse, writer-reader-character relational positionalities.

The album's last composition, "Fawn," an instrumental piece written for the "The Wood Without Names" scene of the Wilson play (adapted from "The Woods where things have no names" episode from chapter 3 of *Through the Looking-Glass*) is a terrifyingly beautiful, heartbreaking melody for a solitary violin played with false harmonics (by Carla Kihlstedt) that create glissando sounds and a hauntingly ethereal tone absurdly reminiscent of a magical singing saw, an odd musical instrument made of a simple handsaw. The idea of reinterpreting a noisy mundane object as a source of sublime euphony is a tribute to the metamorphosis permeating Alice's worlds. The tune resonates both as lament and mockery on offering a unique musical representation of namelessness, unspeakability, and silence thematized in this enigmatic episode of the story.

The enchanted woods constitute one of the dead ends of Alice's quest for meanings. All who enter forget how to name themselves, how to call each other, and how to verbally master their surroundings. Yet, surprisingly the crisis of language brings about a more direct form of communication. A loving embrace establishes an immediate intimate relationship between the wanderers, Alice and the Fawn, who are never really lost because they never feel the need to be found, and who never really feel at a loss for words because a tender touch can tell all one needs to know.[23] Silence serves the ground of understanding throughout their long walk in the forest until they come out of the woods and suddenly regain language as a system of differentiations meant to radically separate them. The narrative self-recognition is just as alarming as delightful, and makes the wild creature flee full speed away from Alice and her human realm of set significations and truth claims. Certainly, in a magic realm of talking animals there is no escape, all is kept in bondage by the insufficiency and inevitability of verbalization. Language philosophical considerations tackled by the wordless, dreamy outro of the *Alice* album leaves the tale open-ended and the listeners in a contemplative mood.

Waits's love songs never turn saccharine because of his unique, nearly uncategorizable, eclectic musical style boldly combining pre-rock music styles, primal blues, jazz ballads, vaudeville and cabaret theatrical approaches, Tin Pan Alley-era tunes, old waltzes, European folk songs, tango, rumba, country with experimental tendencies verging on industrial music and his trademark growl-like singing. Musicological critical appreciations of Waits' distinctive voice primarily praise the "vivid atmospherical" quality of "3-D cough" (Fricke 2002). The immediacy of a brute yet fallible corporeal presence resonate his music with a transverbal, transmedial sensation that eventually proves to contaminate the very language of the critiques commenting on it, hence turning the professional aesthete discourse into subversive body-text. Daniel Durchholz from *Musichound Rock* (1998) opines that Waits' voice sounds "like it was soaked in a vat of bourbon, left hanging in the smokehouse for a few months, and then taken outside and run over with a car." *Pitchfork* reviewer William Bowers calls the confidently expressive music's "spook-ass vibe flat-out cinematic [whereby] the instrumentals serve as aural Rorsharchs (the gorgeous violin of "Fawn" made me see bugs mating— now you try!) and Waits' voice is warmly recorded on each of the pump-organ-and-stand-up-bass dirges, some of which seem to channel the balcony-leaping spirit of a heroin-shriveled Chet Baker" (2002). *Rolling Stone's* David Fricke is downright reminded by Waits' "malignant growl" of a "burned-out coroner showing you the dead body with a tired sweep of his arm," arguing that this "ravaged voice surrendered all pretensions to melody ages ago; his throat is now pure theater, a weapon of pictorial emphasis and raw honesty." Accordingly, Waits' voice on the *Alice* album does not only enact a quite moving musicalized reinterpretation of a literary text and its theatrical performance adaptation (Carroll's tales and Wilson's play) but, with an intermedial twist, it also offers a visionary embodiment of multi-sensorially stimulating gustatory and olfactory hallucinations as well as of delusional images of passion, death, decay, and a resurrection involved in the infinite metamorphosis of imaginative associations.

Postmodern Embodiments in Carnal Art: Reanimated Rabbits, Gracefully Grotesque Ballerinas and Cookbook Adventures

This final chapter focuses on postmillennial embodied adaptations of the "Alice in Wonderland" theme which foreground how the interdisciplinary staging of a body in a permanent dynamic movement on account of its inherent heterogeneity, vulnerability, and metamorphic corporeality—experienced particularly vividly in Wonderland—constitutes such an unmasterable challenge for representational strategies that it inevitably ends up in a subversive "somatization" of "semioticization" (Brooks 1993), that is the understanding of meaning formation in terms of a fundamentally fleshly experience. I explore how conventional, clichéd signifying practices get reanimated (reincarnated!) by the uncanny return of the formerly repressed, unspeakable carnality, invading the signification process with the use of embodied kinetic nonsense, materialized metaphors, incarnated voice, tactile feats, and sensorial delights. I offer case studies of two 21st century repurposings, focusing on Samantha Sweeting's embodied storytelling via carnal performances or mobile taxidermy art and the body language of the Royal Ballet's 2011 gracefully grotesque Alice choreography.

Samantha Sweeting is a London-based interdisciplinary artist whose work performs what she calls an "embodied storytelling" that draws upon memory, myth, psychoanalysis, and erotic undercurrents of fairy tales and nursery rhymes, to explore the ideological containment, creative powers, and physical material stakes of femininity along with interconnections of the curious and the domestic, as well as "human and animal behavior, boundaries and desire" (samanthasweeting.com). As Catriona McAra points out, in 2007 Sweeting "went feral" during her residency in a menagerie in the French Pyrénées where her cohabitation with abandoned animals introduced major leitmotifs into her art: her "animal encounters" and her "lactation animations" (McAra 2014, 1).

The latter constitute the most controversial body of her work in the form of photographic, if not corpographic, records of how she invites various animals to suckle from her bare breasts—like on "In Came the Lamb" (2009) where she appears as a girl-woman nursing a lamb. The image certainly offers an erotic reappropriation of the popular nursery rhyme "Mary had a little lamb," but the grotesque disruption of the religious iconography of the Madonna and the Child with the incongruous element of the animal replacing the human infant allude to well-known nonsensical registers of children's fantasy literature, too. Carroll enthusiasts are reminded of Tenniel's image of Alice cradling the baby turned piglet during a memorable Wonderland metamorphosis. But the black and white tableau vivant photo staging "virginal sexuality" (Sweeting 2015) also echoes Dodgson's early photographs of Alice Liddell—especially because artist Sweeting shares the same hairstyle with the real life muse!—even if the Victorian child-woman titillating posterity's imagination is played out here by a self-directed adult body determined to play a trick on calculable, prejudiced or prudish readerly and spectatorial reactions. Transcending its frames, the image reflects on contemporary debates about the female body as a political site and women's rights to its ownership, as well as environmentalist moral lessons on interspecies intimacy, and the aesthetic challenge of contemplating innocence with a gaze untarnished by preconceptions dictated by social taboos. The image is also indebted to feminist performance artist Carolee Schneemann's *Infinity Kisses* (1990–1999) photo series sensually portraying the morning kisses she received from her cats, both vulnerable companions and powerful symbols of her work, embodying a feline ambiguity Alice faced in her pet Dinah doubled by the potential predator Cheshire Cat.

Sweeting's embodied imagetextual homages to *Alice* do not stop here. Her video entitled *Run rabbit, run rabbit, run, run, run* (2007)—originally shown as part of *Bestilalia (I never imagined life without you)* performance installation (2008)—is a silent, two-minute looped, stop-motion video film displayed on a television monitor on the floor, featuring a dead rabbit reanimated by the artist's hands which move the lifeless limbs to simulate running. The installation's presentation on view for Tate Liverpool's *Alice in Wonderland* exhibition (2011) suggests that, indeed, it is not too far-fetched to interpret this running rabbit "as a loose avatar for Lewis Carroll's eponymous White Rabbit character, driving this micronarrative while Sweeting's human intervention could be read [along the lines of the imaginative world-(re)making of] our curious Alice protagonist" (McAra 2014, 2). In a 2015 interview with *Filler* Magazine, Sweeting attributes the enduring popularity of the Alice books to the features she aims to thematize in her own artwork: the questioning of our perceived notions of reality and the resulting embracement of a child-like freedom of

Samantha Sweeting, "In Came the Lamb." Archival digital print, 241mm × 363mm, edition of 6 + 2 A/P, 2009 (courtesy of the artist).

imagination and behavior, as well as the exploration of philosophically challenging, nearly unthinkable notions of Time and Death in playful and accessible ways.

The Carrollian White Rabbit's pocket watch and the recurring line he monomaniacally mutters to himself "I shall be late!" indicates his hopeless struggle with time and mortality. This rodent psychopomp leading Alice underground (to escort her soul to an odd afterlife?) clearly belongs to a grotesque version of the *memento mori* tradition. On the contrary, Sweeting's rabbit flees towards timelessness, "caught in a perpetual loop of motion; his time has run out yet he must keep running in denial of his death" (Sweeting 2015). The artist's hands reanimate a road kill facilitating a fantastic metamorphosis that enacts just the reverse of taxidermy and preserves for eternity by endless mobilization. Simulating perpetual motion mimes an agency that resists the passive objectification by corporeal decay.

A privileged moment of a chance encounter—cherished in the name of 'luck' in fairy tales—gains a hypnotizing rhythm in the looped video display. The mesmerizing repetition of images offers a visual equivalent to the title's rhythmical ritual incantation ("*Run rabbit, run rabbit, run, run, run*") which evoke mysteries of a magic spell or the comforting 'good vibration' of a well-known nursery rhyme. It also invites us to consider serious philosophical dilemmas such as: does a rabbit lose its "rabbitness" once it can no longer run and hence becomes deprived of its most fundamental feature constituting the grounds of its very rabbithood? Moreover, the sight of the healing touch offers an intense tactile sensation: a manipulative puppeteer, a careless child playing with a fluffy toy, or an altruistic healer whose caress reanimates, all fuse to revivify the rabbit and to invite audiences to imagine carrying out the same action.

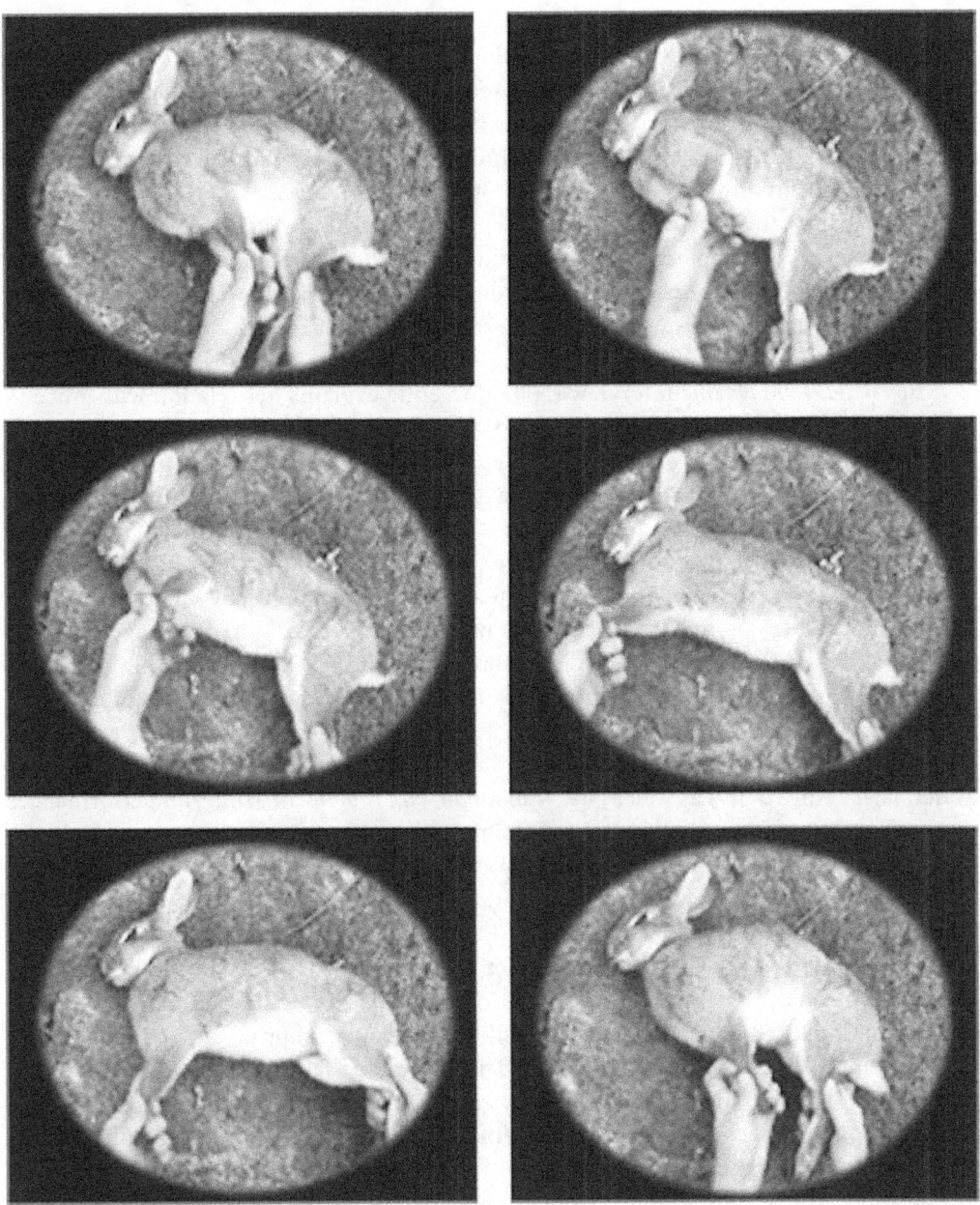

Samantha Sweeting, "Run rabbit, run rabbit, run, run, run." Film still from looped video, 2007 (courtesy of the artist).

The focus on the physical contact with the body holds exciting biographical implications. For her body art performance, Sweeting admittedly draws inspiration from formative experience of her life, such as volunteering at a home for sexually abused girls in the Philippines, training as a massage therapist, working with children at the Little Angel Marionette Theatre, and rescuing abandoned animals. She also pays tribute to—and therapeutically treats through sublimatory reenactment—her first traumatic childhood experience of passing, when she "cradled the skeletal body of her cat before it slipped into death." Retrospectively, she contends that the animation of the inanimate by means of "infantile pretense play, naïve puppetry and imagination" allowed her player self to understand death in its physical reality and hence come to terms with the impossibility of comprehending the incomprehensible. With this anecdote in mind, Sweeting's troubling micro-narrative documents the journey from childhood to adulthood, and integrates her own maturation within her reinterpretation of Carroll's *Alice* as a coming-of-age story. The animal corpse is used as a transitional object to revive a memory and share a touching story on touching. In Sweeting's words, "I am playing with it [death]; I am feeling its weight and stiffness; I am stuck in its unblinking stare. I make the rabbit run and I record it doing so because I don't want it to leave me." (2015)

In *The Filler Magazine* interview (2005) Sweeting explains her relation with Alice in terms of intimacy, a life time companionship, and an encounter with a lasting artistic alter ego. She tracks back the *Wonderland* inspiration beneath her art to the proliferation of Alice imagery "firmly embedded in popular culture and language" that nearly subconsciously shaped her fantasmatic agency since the childhood delight she took in adaptations overshadowing the original book experience. "A child, I grew up eating off Alice in Wonderland plates; I had a Queen of Hearts birthday party; I watched Disney. These secondary representations became my first encounters with the text" (2005). As a teenager, she was struck by the use of use of sounds, objects and animals in Jan Svankmajer's filmic take on *Alice*. This considerable influence on her aesthetic agenda shows in the interior design of her art studio home ("I am sitting in a room full of glass bottles, metal scissors, rusty keys, a taxidermy hare, my childhood doll's house, a wild boar skull and a porcelain facsimile of Svankmajer's Alice doll.") as well as her *Run rabbit, run rabbit, run, run, run* performance's creative use of taxidermy called to life by simple stop-motion puppetry. Even the interspecies dialogues and the animal anthropomorphism, which are of a significant interest in her work, are traced back to Wonderland, and more specifically emblematic visual adaptations of Carroll's classic: a postcard of Kiki Smith's "Pool of Tears" (Alice swimming by the side of birds and rodents) decorating her wall and Arthur Rackham's "Alice Holding Pig" featuring on her desktop. For Sweeting, Alice and the White Rabbit are more than just fictional literary characters; they are endlessly recycled cultural products which thematize the familiar adventure into the unknown. The suspended fall down the rabbit hole is a metaphor for falling in love, into sleep, away from Grace, towards an emotional turbulence resulting from the recognition of one's vulnerability, towards a hypnagogic, hallucinogenic state where dreams take over the wakefulness of reality.

Beyond Wonderland, the dead rabbit's manipulation into movement is indebted to Victorian inventor Eadweard Muybridge's pioneering photography experimenting on the borderline of still and moving image, as well as German Fluxus, happening, and performance artist Joseph Beuys' avant-garde performance piece *How to Explain Pictures to a Dead Hare* (1965), a performance re-created by Marina Abramović in 2005 at the Solomon R. Guggenheim Museum in New York as part of her series *Seven Easy Pieces*. Throughout Beuys' performance, the audience locked out of the gallery, could contemplate through the windows, for the duration of three hours, how the artist, his head entirely coated in honey and gold leaf, explained the artworks of an exhibition in mock-dialogic whispers to a dead rabbit, he carried around from one picture to another, before he stepped over a dead fir tree that lay on the floor, and sat upon a stool with the hare in his arms and his back to the onlookers. The performance piece offered an artistic meta-commentary on the prestige and abuse of imaginative powers. The honey on Beuys' head represented creative ideas, while the absurdity of his art lectures, remaining inaudible, silent to human spectators, was meant to reveal how mindless intellectualizing in politics or academia may become deadly to thought. The action provocatively tackled the interchangeability of human and animal consciousnesses throughout the process of meaning formation, arguing for an understanding based on interspecies solidarity. The Hare, as a symbol of incarnation (burrowing itself a home in the earth), enacted "something humans can only do in imagination" (Adriani, Konnertz, Thomas, 155), hence pointed in the direction of unimaginability.

Sweeting's rabbit shares some ambiguous similarities with Beuys' hare: challenging the confines of representation, both point towards nonsensical realms so comfortably inhabited by Carroll, and epitomized by Wonderland. The intellectual challenge inviting spectators to interpret the very act of interpretation is counterbalanced by the sensory experience, the gut reaction provoked by the confrontation with the corpse on the brink of abject corporeal decay. Speculations about mediation and submersion into immediacy meet. Beuys' vanguardist transmediality integrates verbal explication of visual works into carnal art, while Sweeting uses medial transition (from text to photo to film, and then all merged in the transmedia collage she creates on the basis of the original looped video) for a postmodern recontextualization of the original story to charge the source text with new—visual, kinetic, tactile, synaesthetic—meanings. In both cases the artist emerges as a self-reflective puppeteer whose touch revives the inanimate organic to create an artwork and bring a curious story into being. The minimalism of the action refutes the conventional plot line's narrative conventions and opens up an endless playground of unlimited meanings.

The artist's body holds a special significance. Beuys deciphers in details the symbolism he adopts in a commentary to his performance, but Sweeting sustains her ambiguity. Her hands moving the rabbit transform Beuys' initial acoustic contact with the animal (whispering in the hare's ears) into a more intensive tactile contact (making the rabbit run). They serve as metonymic indicators of the artist, half vanishing yet still present in the picture. And, most excitingly, her hands pay an intermedial homage to the Tenniel illustrations to *Wonderland* depicting scenes where Alice's hand intervenes in the course of events, as if to signal that she is more of an active director participator than a passive subject to her adventures. On one picture, Alice, having overgrown the White Rabbit's house, reaches out a gigantic hand ("An arm, you goose! Who ever saw one that size? Why it fills the whole window!" [Carroll 42]) to snatch in the air towards the Rabbit desperately fleeing from her, breaking the glass of the cucumber-frames on his awkward flight. Sweeting's performance reinterprets this scene focusing on the interspecies interrelationship. The disembodied female hands enact an empathic caress instead of a violent intrusion, as if to celebrate the kinship of all mortal beings, while self-ironically mocking her own melancholic attitude toward the inevitable impossible, and admiring death's disrupting the limits of representation.

The Royal Ballet's *Alice's Adventures in Wonderland* ballet in two acts (choreography by Christopher Wheeldon, music by Joby Talbot, orchestrated by Christopher Austin and Joby Talbot, dramaturgy by Nicholas Wright, design by Bob Crowley, co-produced with the National Ballet of Canada) arrived on stage for a world premiere at the Royal Opera House of London on 28 February 2011 as the company's first new full-length work since 1995, and was greeted with an immediate favorable response by audiences.

As the production's website and the booklet accompanying the DVD edition of the performance stated, composer Talbot managed to distil the original spirit of Wonderland into music by combining contemporary sound worlds with sweeping melodies that nostalgically gestured to 19th century ballet scores; while designer Crowley created authentic theatrical magic with wildly imaginative sets and costumes which drew on a variety of old and new media, including puppetry, masks, video projections and animations "to make Wonderland wonderfully real." But the real challenge was adapting to dance a literary classic so densely charged with cultural meanings and so easily confused with its numerous reimaginative adaptations. (If everyone believes to know Alice without having actually read the original, the question remains which is their Alice, and can a new adaptation satisfy at once so many different expectations?)

Although choreographer Talbot was aware that "up to now, on stage, historically Alice hasn't been very successful," he figured the beautifully drawn characters lend themselves very well to dance, and the episodic structure of the book matches ballet acts' fragmentation into individual, separate dance numbers. Moreover, in critic David Nice's words, the dance adaptation "never went pear shaped," because this Royal Ballet spectacular integrated four features within their take on the familiar theme: "a respect for the original tale's essential ingredients, a deliberate decision not to Freudianize Carroll's relationship with Alice, a contemporary stagecraft nod in the direction of old-fashioned theatrical magic, and the discovery of a frame that functions, and above all ends well" (Nice 2011). The makers likely figured that throughout their theatricalization of a literary classic, the pregiven verbal code (Carroll's novel) and the added visual and acoustic codes (stage design, costume, lights, music) could facilitate the comprehension of a multimedially enhanced nonsense extravaganza act by structuring the corporeally performed narrative. Choreography as a written annotation of stylized movement in space, a recording of a "topography of elusiveness" (Brandstetter in Czirák 7) has offered an adequate mean to describe the fabulous dream-voyage to Wonderland.

The frame with a happy ending turns the ballet into the love story of Alice (Lauren Cuthbertson) and Jack (Sergei Polunin), two youngsters first separated by a prudish Victorian matriarch's misjudgment influenced by 19th century class divide and reunited in the end, by their own will, as sweethearts on a date in the contemporary setting of a city park, flirting by the side of a coffee house mockingly decorated by Tenniel's drawing of the Mad Hatter, perhaps hinting at the craziness of their vows. The opening scene shows preparations for a garden party organized in the Liddells' Oxford home, where family-friend Lewis Carroll (Edward Watson) entertains his host's daughters by reading a story, performing magic tricks (folding origami hearts), and donning them fancy dresses (costumes of a butterfly, a pirate, and a Chinese, recognizable from his actual photographs); while curious guests keep on arriving to the event; and Alice's mother dismisses the gardener's boy for misplacing a red rose among the white ones and then offering the inappropriate flower to Alice. As the party begins, the girl is devastated by the loss of her fired friend, so Carroll attempts to console her by offering to take her photograph. As he disappears beneath the camera cloth, the lights go out, and after a sudden flash Carroll reappears turned into a White

Rabbit to lure Alice down the rabbit hole (represented here by his camera bag they both dive into). The extraordinary creatures she encounters in Wonderland are all strange but recognizable replicas of the party guests: an Indian Rajah becomes the caterpillar, an ugly lady acquaintance the Duchess, a vicar the March Hare, a magician the Mad Hatter, a verger the Dormouse, a butler the Executioner, some footmen Fish and Frog. Alice is charmed by the Knave of Hearts, a double of Jack, who is accused of stealing the royal tarts and is persecuted by the King of Hearts, an alter ego of Alice's mother. After she defends him in the final trial in vein, she passionately knocks over the accusers, and they flee hand in hand this alternately surprising, hostile, and unfathomable dream-realm to wake up together in a present day reality cleared of the obstacles to their relationship.

This plotline is saved from saccharine sentimentality on account of the inventive choreography that can be interpreted, in my view, in terms of the realization of *kinetic nonsense*. Each character's personality traits are expressed by their individual motion style. Alice's innocent lightheartedness is reflected by her pirouettes, jetés, and pliés as she gracefully leaps, whirls, and tiptoes through her Wonderland adventures, performs tenderly amorous, lithe *pas de deux* with Lewis Carroll/White Rabbit and Jack/Knave of Hearts alike, and from time to time embraces the madness of Wonderland by allowing her moves to border on the grotesque. For instance, at the mad tea party she freezes in the midst of a sprint run so that the tap-dancing Hatter and the hopping, somersaulting March Hare carry her around like a statue, and then becomes a full-right member of the gang by imitating the Hatter-Hare-Dormouse trio's wind-up clockwork doll automaton movements.[24]

Ballet dance is all about the stylized abstraction of ordinary motion, the speculative toying with (ideas of) 'unnatural' movements which do not necessarily have real-life referents with a physical or concrete existence. Its aim is not the authentic representation of an external reality, but rather a theatricalized enactment of gestures, shapes, colors, and textures, a play with irreal possibilities of physical maneuvers performed by a body light enough to defy gravity. Common ballet techniques, also adopted by the Royal Ballet's *Wonderland* choreography, include the *pointe* technique (dancing on the tips of fully extended feet), the turnout (completing movements with legs rotated outwards), the *port de bras* (a carriage of the lifted arms with the elbows held out and the middle finger slightly in and the index finger slightly out), or the *ballon* (the lightfooted jump), belong to kinetic nonsense in so far as they are simultaneously graceful and grotesque, they disintegrate our daily moves (like literary nonsense undoes commonsensical discourse), and hence make us self-reflectively aware of the mal/functioning of our bodies, and the illusions we cherish concerning the 'natural' course of movements and the inevitable distortions thereof. In modern ballet, a step is never simply a step: it is charged with metaphorical meanings due to the principle of expressivity (motion style becoming personality marker) and it strikes with its graceful-grotesque corporeal immediacy. If gracefulness results from the insistence on verticality (denying the dancer's physical weight) and on organization (arranging individual body parts and the dance troupe's collective body as parts of a unified, organic whole), the grotesqueness is a side-effect of the awkward vulnerability of human bodiliness reaching an all too ephemerally delicate balance in the ballet act meant to compensate for the ungainly clumsiness permeating our flawed everyday moves. Alice's aerial leaps symbolize a childish purity, a lightness of the soul simulated at the cost of a trying physical effort accompanied by all too material sweat and tears which should remain invisible to spectators. Even if the trademark Carrollian language games remain untranslatable to dance, modern ballet (with an emphasis on the shape of movements instead of progress) seems to be just the right medium to express the ambiguities involved in the literary nonsense genre. The emphasis on sound instead of sense finds its kinetic equivalent in the ballet moves' emphasis on physical free-play instead of functionality, and the general liberatory project to vehemently overwrite and subvert the conventional meanings pre-inscribed in our cultured embodiments (circumscribed along the lines of social expectations regarding our gender, race, age, class or other markers of our strictly disciplined identities). Classical ballet's codified movies and strict representational registers are unsettled by the corporeal presence of dancing Alice's body as "a dynamic archive of kinetic and narrative memory" (Maar in Czirák 21)—fusing embodied stories of the Carrollian heroine's metamorphic figure, ballerina Cuthbertson's stage performance, and their audience's carnal reactions.

Royal Ballet's choreography also succeeds in evoking the real feel of Wonderland by provoking an odd combination of horror and hilarity. The Queen of Hearts' (Zenaida Yanowsky) solo dance stages a parody of *The Sleeping Beauty* ballet's famous Rose Adagio, revisiting both Tchaikovsky's classic romantic music and Petipa's notoriously difficult choreography. Sleeping Beauty's suitors are funnily enough replaced here by the impersonated playing cards, intimidated young courtiers who are commanded to partner to dance their despotic Queen who threatens to behead everyone should they dissatisfy her. The humor originates from an angry woman's aggressive, histrionic reenactment of the cliché figure of the fragile ballerina—marked by her oddly fixed smile and an all-too-rigid graceful pose rather reminiscent of rigor mortis—and her partners' reluctance to participate in the dance for fear it would be their last one. Hence, as an exquisite dancer embraces the skills of a physical comedienne, what has been intended as a sublime performance ends up as an utter, ridiculous failure. Elegance turns burlesque on other instances, too, like at the queenly croquet game where the Queen desperately attempts to master flamingos used as mallets and hedgehog kids running around as balls.

The satirical re-enactment of classical ballet also points in the direction of kinetic nonsense in so far as the negation of traditional "grammatic structures of choreography" constitutes a paradox since—as José Gil (2005, 217) suggests—dance moves cannot perform an active denial, movement is always already purely affirmative, organized along the lines of statements, taking sides with presence and a surplus of meanings, instead of absence and a void of signification. The dancing body represents the surrounding world, the thoughts, emotions and fantasies it generates; consequently it represents itself as a perceptive and expressive agent endowed with a "tremulous private corporeality" (Barker 1984), a carnal residue eluding all representation.

Along the lines of ambiguity, all nightmarish episodes have a comic edge, a hint of black humor to them: the Duchess (Simon Russell Beale)—danced by a man, as a particularly ugly female impersonator—inhabits a house decorated from the outside by a neatly embroidered sign "Home Sweet Home" suggesting homely cosiness and domestic bliss, but the domicile eventually turns out to be a sausage factory from the inside with butchered hogs hanging from the bloody ceilings, a murderous cook (who later falls in love with the executioner), and a dark destiny awaiting the poor baby transformed into a pig. (The design reminds of any young adult gothic Tim Burton movie, in particular his *Sweeney Todd*, inspired by a Victorian penny dreadful about a demonic barber and meat pies made of human flesh). The final nightmarish trial scene peaks in a carefully choreographed chaos via a nod to the "Danse infernale" in Stravinsky's *The Firebird*. Individual characters identified by contrasting music present their unrelated solo dances and continue weaving their story fragments, up until Alice knocks them over and they all fall like dominoes—with a reference to a common nonsense-generating plot device of comedies called the "snowball effect" in which a minor chance event induces consequences of incredible proportions (see Bergson 1910). The eerily disembodied Cheshire Cat apparently belongs to the darker undercurrents of Carroll's story, yet its tribute to the Tenniel illustration carries a comforting familiarity, whereas its body parts moved by different dancers allow for an amusing disintegration towards a nonsensical ubiquity (his head in one corner of the stage, his tail in the other) matching the topographical uncertainty implied in the vagueness of his directions ("it doesn't matter which way you go, you are sure to get somewhere, if you walk long enough"). Disorganized and rearranged at whim, the cat embodies the puzzle that can only be answered by the grin remaining behind to make Alice smile, too. The cat's whimsical body movements inscribed in a dynamically renegotiated space mime the fluctuation of the ballet's meanings which depend on the imaginative, associative agency of spectators becoming coproducers of the choreography's significations.

Another feat of the ballet is the unique multimedial combination of image and text (in old and new media alike) within a genre predominated by music and dance. During the initial fall down the rabbit hole (camera bag) in the ballet's frame story, spectators experience a vertiginous feel as Alice plummets surrounded by letters cascading around her in a spiral to spell out the line "curiouser and curiouser" that gets blurred by dropping tea cups. Throughout the play, old-fashioned puppetry gets combined with video animation and projection (designed by Jon Driscoll and Gemma Carrington) to inoculate new media technologies with homages to past decorative arts: shadow animations of Lotte Reininger's fairy-tale films (produced between 1919–1979) as well as 19th century rolling backdrops used in the classic ballet scenery design of choreographer Petipa, regarded as the inventor of modern classic ballet. Alice's shrinking, growings, and metamorphosis are enacted by a clever combination of stage design (larger doors replace tiny ones in the set to make her seem small), puppetry (a gigantic pair of cardboard hands hang over and out of the house that is suddenly too small for her), video projections (the pool of tears floods the stage projected onto a screen where an animated swimmer alternates with the silhouette of the ballerina), props (Alice and Carroll/White Rabbit are sailing in a boat folded from a page of the *Wonderland* novel), and choreography (Alice is spinning around faster and faster and crouching smaller and smaller to evoke the impression of shrinking). As a witty reference to Carrollian language games, the start flag signaling the beginning of the Caucus Race folds uneasily and before the word START reveals the words TART and ART which prove to be of crucial importance in the unfolding story of the ballet adaptation. The intermedial insertion of text into dance may also denote how ballet as a fundamentally non-verbal mode of artistic expression gains ambiguous meanings when interpreted in terms of the linguistic, semantic categories of discourse.

The finale is not only impressively poetic but also pays a clever tribute to Carroll's photographic work intricately interrelated with his literary writings. Alice and Jack return from Wonderland dreams to the waking life of present day reality. In an idyllic scene we spot Alice peacefully resting on a bench reading a book while Jack is sitting by her feet,

Alice in Wonderland, ballet created by Christopher Wheeldon, first performed by the Royal Ballet in London in 2011. Alice and White Rabbit (Jillian Vanstone and Dylan Tedaldi), the National Ballet of Canada, at Lincoln Center, New York, September 9–14, 2014 (courtesy of photographer Bruce Zinger).

gently caressing her. Later they perform a tender *pas de deux* to express their affections for each other in the language of dance. When a photographer walks by, they ask him to take their picture, and then walk away hand in hand toward a well-deserved happy-ending. The passer-by turns out to be a latter day incarnation of Carroll-as-photographer who eventually discovers the book Alice left on the bench, sits down and starts leafing through the novel that spectators surely identify with none other than *Alice's Adventures in Wonderland*. The ballet begins with the storyteller-magician-photographer and ends with the photographer-wanderer-reader Carroll, leaving Carroll-as-writer a textual aporia, a figure dwelling in the realm of the unsaid. In an open ended or cyclical manner, the story ends where it all began, time turns back on itself and all movements stops, since Carroll, all of a sudden, finds himself submerged immobile in the tale he has/will have authored, a *Wonderland* he is destined to create.

The 'Eat Me' cake and the 'Drink Me' potion indubitably belong to iconic markers of Alice's adventures, as the most memorable specimen of the many surprising, sensorially stimulating oddities of Wonderland. Besides contributing to the heroine's magical metamorphosis, making her shrink or grow, they constitute curious culinary composites, gustatory equivalents of the unstable signifiers of literary nonsense which impose a challenge for any interpretive attempts at meaning-fixation. In Carroll's original novel the 'Drink Me!' potion is described as an unusual assortment of flavors of "cherry-tart, custard, pineapple, roast turkey, toffy and hot buttered toast," that Alice finds truly tasty and finishes off in one gulp, while the 'Eat Me' cake is referred to as interchangeable with pebbles. Tim Burton's 2010 film adaptation names the cake and the drink Upelkuchen and Pishsalver respectively, and has the White Queen perform a spectacular recipe of the latter as "a pinch of worm fat, urine of a horsefly, buttered fingers, three coins from a dead man's pocket, and two teaspoons of wishful thinking," pointing towards nonsensical registers. Jan Švankmajer's stop-motion animation adaptation makes menacing meals reach surrealist extremes: Alice slurps viscous jam filled with nails and needles to provoke viewers' gut reactions of food loathing and evoke the "decay at the heart of Wonderland" (Cherry 2002) or to mock the bad taste of his provocative anti-aesthetic agenda.

For Victorian audiences, Carroll's twisted treatment of food and drink offered delight because of the carnivalesque breaking of bourgeois table manners prescribed by the era's popular conduct books (as in the mad tea partiers' systematic violation of dinner etiquette), a release of anxieties concerning food adulteration that became a public health concern of the 1850s' lived realities (fictionalized by the Duchess' contaminating her dishes with sneeze-inducing ground pepper), and child Alice's trust and fantasmatic agency in her appreciation of culinary delights (her readiness to drink a bottle of unidentifiable liquid and her imaginativeness in describing its curious taste). Contemporary readers likely identify Alice's consumption practices with omnivorous delights characteristic of the oral phase of the Freudian account of psychosexual development where the mouth of the infant is her primary erogenous zone; or on the contrary with a natural gourmet's "discriminating palate" (Sweeney 17) a spontaneously 'acquired taste' able to distinguish different layers of flavors and appreciate radically unfamiliar gustatory sensations which are first considered unpleasant by most and usually need substantial exposure to learn to enjoy. Her description of the 'Drink Me' potion's taste reminds Kevin W. Sweeney of a sommelier's "aesthetic evaluation based upon fanciful associations" qualifying "a distinctive style of white wine—a high-extract, large-format Chardonnay, probably a Grand Cru white Burgundy such as a Corton-Charlemagne." The reference to a cherry tart remarks the wine's fruitiness and acidity, while the succeeding complex flavors from custard to roast turkey are commonly identifiable, middle range, projected features of "heavy-extracted, ripe, high-glycerin and pronounced-alcoholic Chardonnays traditionally produced in Burgundy and lately in California" (29).

As Sweeney notes, Alice's words about the little bottle also have a philosophical point, reminding us of the aesthetical tradition that metaphorically associated the critical appreciation of arts and Nature with gustatory experience and "fine taste" (18). Moreover, the little girl's "defamiliarizing description that draws attention to the seemingly idiosyncratic character" of a sensual encounter (Sweeney 17) invites to draw a parallel between the puzzling verbalization of a gustatory experience and the linguistic subversions involved in the workings of literary nonsense. The odd mixture of toffy and turkey flavors is a culinary counterpart of Carrollian portmanteau words like "chortle" a giddy laugh coined from 'chuckle' and 'snort.' Fanciful associations, the wedding of opposites, presenting the familiar in unfamiliar ways to enhance its perception characterize this whimsical mode of writing that pleases the taste buds of language-erudites (sophisticated fans of haute cuisine) and language-gamers (curious, omnivore, orally fixated children) alike.

A humorous extension of Carroll's nonsensical universe for gourmets, *Alice Eats Wonderland* subtitled *An Irreverent Annotated Cookbook Adventure in which a Gluttonous Alice*

Devours Many of the Wonderland Characters (2009), authored by August A. Imholtz and Alison Tannenbaum with original illustrations by A.E.K. Carr, rewrites the storyline of Alice's adventures, giving a new twist to each of the twelve chapters of the original story inspired by children's insatiable voraciousness identified as a decisive character-feature of the protagonist. Besides curiosity, appetite appears as a major instinctive, corporeal drive motivating Alice's actions. Constantly hungry, she often disrupts her journey to find something to eat: right at the beginning she temporarily abandons the pursuit of the white rabbit to run home and get a snack; after gulping down the all too tiny 'eat me' cake, yearns for more, and decides to make some Victorian currant cake for herself; later the White Rabbit being 'dressed' in bourgeois attire makes her stop to think of possible ways of preparing rabbit starting out from Welsh Rarebit to actual Rabbit Pie; and eventually she steals a hedgehog from the Queen's Croquet ground and sneaks back to her kitchen to make a Gypsy-Style Roast Hotchi-Wichi. Throughout her cookbook adventure, Alice learns to prepare, cook, and consume the animal (and vegetable) characters of Wonderland with the help of the recipes' instructions complemented by annotations which inform readers about the natural and social history of the animals, food ingredients and cultural practices thematized by Carroll's fairy-tale fantasy. (For instance, besides the recipes of scones, tart, and pudding made from treacle, the legend about British troops burying barrels of treacle and the popularity of wells with healing water known as *theriaca* (hence treacle) offer Victorian trivia as potential inspiration for make-believe culinary feasts as the nonsensical treacle well in the tea-partying dormouse's tale.) Like the 'Drink Me' potion blending incompatible flavors of pineapple and custard, *Alice Eats Wonderland* presents a curious interdisciplinary composite of odd and exciting bites from a variety of fields, stirring data on the symbolic meanings communicated by Victorian parlor's flower language, butchers' techniques for dissecting meat, the chemical composition of black pepper, the principal anatomical components of the human heart, and—with a nod to Carroll—the mathematical logical explanation for the reappearance of previously consumed animals at the final Wonderland trial.

In the cookbook adventure, grotesque metamorphosis relates to the transformation of animate fauna and flora into edible dishes bordering on the bizarre and macabre as Alice fantasizes about consuming practically all the Wonderland creatures who mock, annoy or bore her. She dreams of Mumbled Rabbit, Pickled Oysters, Pigeon Pie, Stuffed Dormouse introduced to readers in archaic recipes. Her thoughts are playfully associative and increasingly ravenous: cutting her finger with the knife with which she is preparing the currant cakes, brings to her mind "by the curious form of association typical of deans' daughters, the recipe her grandmother had used for blood pudding" (16). A remorseless carnivore with a taste for dark humor she toys with ideas of cannibalism, fantasizing about ways of cooking the anthropomorphic creates of Wonderland, transforming into a dish the baby turned pig, and baking a King Cake and a Queen Cake, too. She allows her imagination run wild towards nonsensical vistas of weird gustative blends, considering culinary portmanteau, pondering how "She heard of an elegant poultry dish called TurDuckEn, which consisted of a stuffed boned chicken inside a boned duck, inside a boned turkey, all roasted together. It would be a little complicated but perhaps she could do something similar with the species at hand, the dodo, the duck, and the mouse, and perhaps create a DoDuckMus?" (23)

Imholtz and Tannenbaum mix historical recipes reaching fantastic gustatory registers (Pig Uterus Sausage from Ancient Rome, Roman Roast Flamingo, including the original recipe in Latin too), exotic delicacies from international cuisine (Silkworm Omelet from China, Iguana Tamales from El Salvador) and British national meals which might surprise American target audiences (marmite soldiers). In the preface, the authors mockingly refuse to take responsibility for any physiological, psychological, political, or religious consequence that may occur as a result of preparing or ingesting their entertaining and educational recipes. During the culinary adventures, the verbalization of extreme palatal sensations exercises our fantasy but also tease our actual taste buds and make us aware of those common synaesthetic perceptions that have gradually become transparent and nearly imperceptible to us because of our habituation to them, like the ordinary experience of "*tasting a recipe as we read* it," "a commutative act between the visual comprehension of abstract language and its carnal meaning" that demonstrates the body's subversive "capacity to function both figuratively and literally" (Sobchack 70). Our eyes comprehend *Alice*'s meals cognitively and also allow for a carnal experience of taste "albeit in a transformed and somewhat diffused act of gustatory sense-making" (Sobchack 70)—that is even more exciting because it makes us sample imaginary savors never experienced before.

The experimental culinary art-project of transforming eating into a surprising adventure is the major aim of British celebrity chef Heston Blumenthal, a pioneer of multisensory cooking, food pairing and flavor encapsulation, as well as an advocate of a new scientific attitude to cuisine called "molecular gastronomy." He embarks to unsettle all established alimentary knowledge and habits so as "to realize the full expressive potential of food and cooking" as a "comprehensive performative art" while combining the finest ingredients, fantastic design and historical tradition with cutting-edge scientific innovations, and (retro)futuristic "new ingredients, techniques, appliances, information, and ideas" (Blumenthal 2006)—a revolutionary agenda reflected in the titles of his TV programs *Kitchen Chemistry* (2002), *Adventures in Search of Perfection* (2004–2007), *Heston's Feasts* (2010), *Heston's Mission Impossible* (2011), or *Heston's Fantastical Food* (2012).

Blumenthal's imaginativeness earned him the label "the Lewis Carroll of cooking whose snail porridge and egg and bacon ice-cream lured a sceptical public through a door into a Wonderland of fantasy food" (Gerard 2009). Series 1 Episode 1 of *Heston's Feasts* recreated famous Victorian period dishes for the ultimate 21st-century banquets, paying a tribute to the Mad Hatter's Tea Party. The chef set out "on a mission to combine myth, science, and history to create a multisensory dining experience," a delicious and spectacular food adventure his guests would remember for their rest of their lives because of its grandiosity, naughtiness and mad surrealism.

The aperitif served in flamingo-shaped glasses was a 'Drink Me' potion that combined the five incongruent flavors of Alice's original drink in a layered way so that guests could never find out what they were drinking because with each new sip they reached a new layer, a different taste of the all too complex gustatory experience. Mock Turtle Soup served in a china cup a watch-shaped, ticking "tea bag"—that actually comprised consommé (beef broth from a cow's head) covered in golden leaf—that dissolved into soup under a cascade of hot water, and had to be poured into a bowl where turnip mousse mimicking an egg, a terrine of pressed, cured pork fat and oxtail, and enoki mushroom were arranged in homage of Wonderland's hookah-smoking caterpillar. An Edible Insect Garden gained inspiration from a Victorian cookbook for the poor to turn creepy crawlies into a feast and included undersoil made of bread, anchovies, and chopped herbs; soil made out of grape nuts, pumpkin seeds and black olives; a gravel path made of fried eel, tapioca, and waffle cones, baby vegetables, potato pebbles, and fried insects—silk moth pupa, crickets and grasshoppers—injected with onion cream and tomato concentrate to "give a realistic ooze when bitten into." The dessert was an absynthe-based gelatin with a giant wobbling fluorescent centerpiece powered by vibrators Victorians invented for the therapeutic treatment of hysteric women.

Blumenthal's trademark new cookery strategically combines taste, smell, spectacle, and sound to transport the diner, through an integrated appeal to the senses and the mind, to another world. His meals exercise imaginative faculties, and, like Humpty Dumpty master of nonsense, invite to think twice and reconsider preconceptions and initial meanings for the sake of entertaining ambiguities. Food is made to seem and taste different than it actually is, calls forth fanciful idiosyncratic associations, memorial fantasmatic agency, and sensorial delights. Eating turns into a magical experience, a real fall down the rabbit hole, where cakes and potions do evoke the illuminating feel of transformation (shrinking and growing!) which allow us to discover adventures beyond our superficially perceived daily reality. As his "Statement on the New Cookery" (2006) claims, Blumenthal's culinary art combines skills of scientists, food chemists, psychologists, artisans, performing artists, architects, designers, and industrial engineers to produce a sensually stimulating adaptation of Wonderland as a *Gesamtkunstwerk* suiting the spirit of the multitalented Victorian don fathering Alice, writer-photographer-mathematician Lewis Carroll.

Epilogue: Celebrating the 150th Anniversary of Wonderland

"We're all mad here!"

This year 2015 marked the sesquicentennial anniversary of the publication of the first edition of *Alice's Adventures in Wonderland,* a time for celebration all over the world for Alice aficionados, Carrollian scholars and fans who take pride and delight in the renewed interest focused on the enigmatic figures of their favorite author and character. In place of conclusion, a brief overview of the anniversary events shed light on the most recent significations attributed to one of the world's best loved stories everyone is familiar with but no one can be certain about fully understanding in its complexity. Post-millennial strategies of telling old stories in new ways to explore hidden meanings, to make sense of nonsense and to wonder—puzzled and amazed alike—reinterpret Wonderland in terms of an increasingly transmediated and international collective experience of enchantment.

A browsing through the newspaper articles and reviews published to commemorate the sesquicentennial anniversary neatly demonstrate the fact that whereas there is no critical consensus concerning the authentic meaning of the novel, the opaque enigmatic status of Carroll, Alice, and Wonderland remain unquestionable. The titles tell it all with headlines like: "After 150 Years We Still Haven't Solved the Puzzle of Alice in Wonderland" (Fimi in *The Conversation*), "Go Ask Alice: What Really Went On in Wonderland?" (Lane in *The New Yorker*), "Who in the World Am I?" (Wood in *The New York Times Sunday Book Review*), "Alice in Wonderland—What Does It All Mean?" (Douglas-Fairhurst in *The Guardian Online*), "The Mystery of Lewis Carroll" (Woolf in *The Public Domain Review*), "A Girl Keeps Growing" (Kennedy in *The New York Times*). Most poignantly, *The New York Times* chose to celebrate Alice day on July 4 with a challenging riddle combining nonsense and logics from master puzzler Raymond Smullyan's *Alice in Puzzle-Land*—as if to insist on the preeminence of questions over answers, in a truly Carrollian manner.

As the above anniversary articles suggest, the fantasy we refer to for the sake of convenience simply as "Alice in Wonderland"—although there is not a book by Carroll under this very title—has become "a folklore, a meme that we love to reproduce" (Fimi), and interpret along the lines of puzzles, misinterpretations, and the mystery of uncertainty. While Carroll "remains to this day an enigmatic figure," a "brilliant, secretive, and complex man" with undecipherable joys and struggles (Woolf 2015), Alice continues her puzzling wanderings through ages, cultures, and media "familiar as a household god but remote as a child star, a prime case of cultural osmosis, having seeped through the membrane of the original book, […] infusing herself into the language, the broader social discourse [and …] the nonsense of our own lives" (Wood BR15). The most popular five elaborate theories believe to find the meaning behind Alice's fantastic excursions in sex, drugs, jokes, food, or dreams (Douglas-Fairhurst 2015), while "supremos of logic and linguistics, photographers, historians of childhood, gender fiends, and chess wonks" all claim to have solved the puzzle of Wonderland (Lane 2015) but their triumph remains delusional, and ever-so elusive Alice has the last laugh.

The Lewis Carroll Society and the Lewis Carroll Society of North America, two of the largest scholarly societies assisted by Carroll scholars, collectors and enthusiasts around the world maintain a website (managed by Mark Richards) that tracked the sesquicentennial events (http://lewiscarrollresources.net/2015/index.html). More than 100 publications (not counting the new literary adaptations) were recorded as perhaps the most obvious anniversary tributes to *Wonderland*. The most noteworthy of these recent book publications[1] can be divided into three distinct categories.

1. Comprehensive collections of Alice material include W. W. Norton's 150th Anniversary Deluxe Edition of *The Annotated Alice* by Martin Gardner (edited, art-directed and introduced by Mark Burstein with over 100 new or updated annotations, more than 100 images, and a filmography of every Alice related film); a Penguin Classics Deluxe collectible, tactile clothbound anniversary edition of *Wonderland* and *Looking-Glass* (designed by Coralie Bickford-Smith, with an introduction by Charlie Lovett); and the original publisher Macmillan's English Explorer editions of the two tales available in print, ebook and audio download, complemented by lots of free online Alice resources for classroom use, self-study, and fun (including lesson plans, a Wonderland creative writing competition, playing cards and a board game applicable as a classroom poster at http://www.macmillanreaders.com/150-years-of-alice), as well as anniversary paraphernalia from the University of Oxford Bodleian Libraries Online Shop (from Alice brooch to fridge magnet to puzzle game).[2] Edward Wakeling's Catalogue Raisonnée of all *The Photographs of Lewis Carroll* as well as *Games, Puzzles, and Related Pieces* collected together for the first time by Christopher Morgan in *The Pamphlets of Lewis Carroll Volume 5* also belong here, along with *Mathematical Wonderlands*, an ebook from *Nature* and *Scientific American* celebrating Carroll as a mathematical gamester and logic puzzler.

2. Revelatory-explicatory works aim to solve the mysteries of bibliogenesis and decode the enigmas of Wonderland, Carroll and Alice either from a biographical perspective (as in Robert Douglas-Fairhurst's *The Story of Alice: Lewis Carroll and the Secret History of Wonderland* and Edward Wakeling's *Lewis Carroll: The Man and his Circle*); or via a close-reading rhetorical focus combined with a cultural critical viewpoint (see *Elucidating Alice: A Textual Commentary on Alice's Adventures in Wonderland* with 600 notes on the text by Selwyn Goodacre and *Alice's Adventures in Wonderland Decoded. The Full Text of Lewis Carroll's Novel with its Many Hidden Meanings Revealed* by David Day).

3. Inventive reimaginings present Alice like you have never seen her before: 2015 saw the publication of the first trade edition with Salvador's Dalí's illustrations by Princeton University Press, Craig Yoe's survey about *Alice in Comicland*, Gregory Maguire's literary vision in a novel called *After Alice*, and no less than three 3-D paper craft books (Maria Taylor's pop-up scenes, Yelena Bryksenkova's fold-out concertina, and Grahame Baker Smith's

pocket book format panorama pops commissioned by the British Royal Mail for a set of special commemorative stamps).

Among the numerous anniversary exhibitions are a few particularly exciting ones. *The Alice Look* exhibition at the V&A Museum of Childhood organized by Queen Mary University of London and curated by Kiera Vaclavik associated "being Alice"—besides a sense of adventure—with the memorable vestimentary fashion clues of the blue dress, the blonde locks with a hair band, and the white apron which all have inspired renown designers, stylists, and photographers. The display traced a "Wonderland aesthetic" distinguished by white rabbits, playing cards, teacups, and pocket watches turned emblematic signifiers, and followed Alice's "evolution from follower-of-fashion to trend-setter" in the international arena of high style through a selection of garments, photographs, rare editions and a brand new commission by Roksanda pattern-cutter Josie Smith. Still in London, the Cartoon Museum of London organized the *Alice in Cartoonland* exhibit curated by Brian Sibley to offer an impressive overview of "Alice's many misadventures at the hands of cartoonists, caricaturists and satirists, animators and graphic artists through 150 years of parodies and pastiches, jibes, jokes and gags aimed at making political points, social comment or just intended to make us laugh," as its website indicates. In the United States,[3] the Morgan Library & Museum's *Alice: 150 Years of Wonderland* organized by Carolyn Vega invited New Yorkers to see Carroll's original manuscript of "Alice's Adventures Under Ground"—the green-morocco-bound, hand-written and -illustrated version he gave as a Christmas present to Alice Liddell—on loan from the British Library. In the center of the show, the manuscript tellingly turned to pages 10 and 11 decorated by Carroll's drawing of an elongated Alice and the passage "Curiouser and curiouser!" was the "sun around which orbit displays of" Carroll's diary entry of 4 July 1862, the day of the legendary boating excursion when the composition of the story began, original drawings and hand-colored proofs of Tenniel illustrations, as well as memorabilia related to the real Alice (Alice Liddell's writing case, prayer book, purse, and Carroll's hand colored photo of her) (Kennedy C19). The British Library's Wonderland exhibit embraced a "counter cultural feel" (Hudson 2015) when it displayed the same original manuscript—that Alice Liddell sold to pay the death duties of her husband, and a group of American anglophiles donated to the British people in recognition of the country's gallantry in World War II; a precious volume the Librarian of Congress brought to Britain on the Queen Mary, sleeping with it under his pillow, and the Archbishop of Canterbury greeted on behalf of the Nation—along with stunning editions by Mervyn Peake, Ralph Steadman, Leonard Weisgard, Arthur Rackham, and Salvador Dali and an array of Alice-inspired material, from computer games to toys, tea caddies, Edwardian films and psychedelic posters, complemented by a bold op art graphic design and fragments of classic illustrations blown up on illuminated panels (Hudson 2015).

The largest commemorative conference event was *Alice Through the Ages: The 150th Anniversary of Alice's Adventures in Wonderland Conference* hosted by Maria Nikolajeva and Zoe Jaques at the Cambridge-Homerton Research and Teaching Centre for Children's Literature and supported by the Lewis Carroll Society. The conference invited innovative papers on Carroll with the aim to seek new understandings of the work by challenging longstanding truisms (such as the text's canonical status at the root of children's fantasy tradition or the relationship between author and illustrator), by focusing on the book's initial production context (including Carroll's biography, cultural milieu and artistic influences), by adopting new theoretical approaches (in the fields of medical humanities, the politics of literature, or cultural iconography among others), or by considering the history of adaptation and its uses in popular culture (Wonderland's influence on design and style). The topics of plenaries highlighted the variety of research themes. Dame Gillian Beer talked about the rhetorical similarities between Alice's polite conversations with Wonderland creatures and Socratic dialogue's attempt to explore others' views of moral, philosophical issues by means of kind questioning. Jan Susina tackled the Walt Disney animation adaptation's efforts in domesticating Carroll's very British humor to satisfy the needs of the American public. Kiera Vaclavik provided an exciting tour in the world of fashion, around Alice's dress, scrutinizing vestimentary attributes as semiological signifiers along with the changing representations and international reception of Alice as a fashion-follower or a trend-setter. As the integral part of a complete Wonderland Week, the academic discussions of the conference were complemented by colorful programs such as a film screening featuring a double bill of the earliest and the latest *Alice* movies, a Looking-Glass Banquet, a theatrical performance portrait of Carroll called *Crocodiles in Cream*, a museum exhibit on Fantastical Victorians, *Cellophony* a new musical version of *Wonderland* composed for a cello octet, a teachers' workshop for using *Alice* in the classroom, and the grand finale of a glorious Wonderland Tea Party. Further surprises included a magician's show, a book fair and the exhibition of some rare editions of Wonderland, along with the integration into a conference site of amazing artwork like a gigantic animatronic hookah-smoking caterpillar mockingly referred to as "Cuthbert, Homerton's guest honor," a grinning Cheshire Cat hiding on a tree top and mome raths hiding under bushes, and William Stok's 24-meter-long drawing of Alice's adventures displayed in the Great Hall. The lasting legacy of Carroll's iconic Wonderland has been defined—on the website's preliminary note—along the lines of a "kind of precocious and charming British childhood that has been celebrated the world over, giving voice to youthful freedom, diversity, imagination, and, most of all, curiosity" and "a little playful nonsense, too."

Perhaps the most impressive and comprehensive accomplishment compiled for the 150th anniversary was the project titled *Alice in a World of Wonderlands: The Translations of Lewis Carroll's Masterpiece* that brought together a three-volume international book project, an exhibition, and a New York based conference as a part of a full week of anniversary events and meetings. Inspired by Warren Weaver's pioneering study, *Alice in Many Tongues: The Translations of Alice in Wonderland* (2006)—that offered a brief history of translations and a bibliography of foreign editions of *Wonderland*—this gigantic book project edited by Jon A. Lindseth (with the assistance of technical editor Alan Tannenbaum) and published by Oak Knoll Press in cooperation with the Lewis Carroll Society of North America, ventured on an amazingly ambitious, large scale realization of Weaver's work. A total of 251 writers volunteered to "back-translate" into English from 174 languages the "Mad Tea Party" chapter from *Wonderland* from the first as well as the most recent edition in each language with footnotes explaining the greatest challenges and the most inventive solutions of the original translators. The back-translations—presented in the second volume—were complemented by four tables recording how the most memorable nonsensical phrases were translated into the various languages, along with the illustrations of the book covers. As the project's website (http://aliceinaworldofwonderlands.com/) claims, "The book is believed to be the most extensive analysis ever done about one English language novel translated into so many languages." One can trace the curious transformations of Wonderland adapted to a flood of languages from Albanian to Zulu, as well as English dialects (including Old English and Cockney), and other alphabets, unusual orthographies, and constructed languages, which face us with Alice in Braille, shorthand, and Esperanto, too. The first volume contains preliminary essays on Alice and in translation by esteemed Carroll specialists such as Morton N. Cohen, Edward Wakeling or Selwyn Goodacre, followed by individual essays authored by the back-translators about the specificities of each language and the most thought-provoking difficulties encountered throughout the original translations and their own back-translations, as well as additional essays on Carrollian comics, Disney's Alice in other languages, fashions of Alice, and Alice illustrations as translation, among others (along with a sixteen-page color section of book covers, numerous illustrations—the project makes a catalogue of 1201 different illustrators of the translated *Alice* books!—informative appendices, notes on contributors, and an index). The third volume offers a bibliographical checklist of more than 7,600 editions of *Wonderland* in 174 languages and over 1,500 editions of *Looking-Glass* in 65 languages.

The book took the notion of transmedia storytelling to a whole new, academic level. Hundreds of contributing volunteers—scholars, academics, fans—scrutinized the many shapes Alice can take in a plethora of languages and representational modes to explore how shapeshifting, a major leitmotif of the tale, emerges on a verbal, discursive plane (in translations and back-translations) as well as on a pictorial plane attesting the imagetextual diversity of the oeuvre (in an impressive collection of illustrations and cover images). The corpus of their findings is a feat of collective intelligence and a communal labor of love carefully edited by Lindseth and shared on multiple media platforms: the scholarly printed book was complemented by the oral lectures of a conference event on the same theme, and the virtual online forum of a finely designed website AliceInAWorldOfWonderlands.com that made public for a wider audience teasers (e.g., the project's significant data funnily referred to as "Bites from the Mushroom"), programs, tables of contents, and an interactive map of languages covered, among others. The overall results showed that the whole is much more than just a sum of its parts. The wondrous variety of nationally or culturally specific figures of speech and imagery, the multitude of inventive verbal (and visual) translations as well as their back translations exhibit the transnational lure of nonsense, the universal urge of meaning generation, and demonstrate just how much metanarrativization (writing about stories, commenting on language) functions as a form of storytelling, too.

Another large-scale collaborative anniversary project called *150Alice: The World's Most Collaborative Artbook*, launched with an online fund-raising on Indiegogo.com (www.indiegogo.com/projects/150alice-the-world-s-most-collaborative-art-book#/story150Alice), brings together 150 graphic artists from 42 countries to create together a unique imagetextual masterpiece. The idea was to cut up the original text into 150 segments—in commemoration of the 150th anniversary—send one to each contributing artist and invite them to imagine the particular piece in their own way. The outcome is one-of-a-kind edition composed of 150 pages of text and 150 vibrant illustrations accompanying each page.[4] The project's self-designation as a "restylization of the original" acknowledges Tenniel's illustrations as integral constituents of the original design, but the transnational showcasing of art styles and pictorial interpretations all over the world is meant to demonstrate the multi-colored heterogeneity of *Wonderland*. Moreover, as it is explained on the website, this large sized album will not only "add color to your living room, and life to your coffee table," but beyond providing delight to children and adult audiences alike, it offers a chance "to give back to society through art" and "to drive forward Lewis Carroll's idea of encouraging art and creativity among children" by using donations and money from the purchases to establish an art school for children in Mongolia. As this wording suggests, the book serves ambiguous purposes. It holds a decorative and an entertainment value, and—despite the text's anti-didacticism—also fulfils an educational role and the ethical moral obligation of charity by highlighting the importance of humanitarian aid, children's right to free play and education, and solidarity found in the common gift of fantasy. Wonderland becomes a utopia turned true, a place where children can gain empowerment by learning, experimentation and a play with their imagination—in an actual art school emerging from within the pages of a book about a fictional universe. This is an authentic celebration of the performative, political potential of make-believing the project immediately ties to the figure of Alice's author. The answer to the organizers' rhetorical question "Now, Lewis Carroll will be pleased, won't he?" cannot be but positive.

A similarly heterogeneous anniversary tribute realized in a different media is an acoustic project simply called *Wonderland* dreamed into being by pianist Ashley Wass and violinist Matthew Trusler. The musicians asked 13 contemporary composers to create short music pieces each inspired by a different section of Carroll's classic (containing a dozen chapters plus a prefatory poem). The commissioned composers were meant to represent different styles and genres in order to reflect the original book's crossover appeal to all age groups united by an intergenerational bonding, a feature assumed to be a decisive reason of *Alice*'s popularity. On the live events of the national and the succeeding worldwide tour, the music gets "transmediated" combined with words and images. The musical compositions are performed in the chronological order of chapters while an actor reads out a script—written by celebrated Louis de Bernières, author of the novel *Captain Corelli's Mandolin*—based on Carroll's original book and meant to tie the melodies together into "a clear and compelling narrative" that is complemented by a projection of Emily Carew Woodard's new illustrations inspired by text and sound alike. The makers also teamed up with the Pharos Arts Foundation and the IMF Cyprus to commission a series of short films to correspond with the Wonderland music, and have authored a personal blog on the website dedicated to the project (http://www.wonderland150.com). All profits from the performances and the sales of the CD—released with Orchid Classics in November 2015—raised money for the Lenny Trusler Children's Foundation dedicated to provide relief to babies, infants and children suffering from serious illness in the United Kingdom and abroad. The project aimed to pioneer in "creating a legacy of new music inspired by children's literature," but also fused words, tunes, images, and film into a singular *Gesamkunstwerk* to raise funds and build public awareness in order to help sick children and to offer therapeutic assistance to parents experiencing the horror of losing a child to illness at an early age.[5]

Via a strange parallel, the foundation fulfils a quasi-ritualistic memorial function similar to that of *Alice*. Lewis Carroll's *Wonderland* was inspired by one specific little girl muse Alice Liddell who became preserved as an eternal child in a literary work meant to fictionally freeze frame the gentle feel of a legendary friendship, while the Lenny Trusler Children's Foundation—and the acoustic *Wonderland* project produced by it—was created by two musician parents so as to keep the memory of baby son who died of a rare kidney disease when he was just two hours old, with the intent to use contemporary classical music to ease the pains of never seeing a child to come of age. The musical adaptation's fundraising for neonatal intensive care and children's hospice supports a practice and philosophy of care that focuses on attending to the emotional, spiritual, psychic needs of terminally or seriously ill or suffering minors and their families. This mission is much in a line with a philosophical idea spelt out by Carroll: "It is one of the great secrets of life that those things which are most worth doing, we do for others."

Hence, the compositions performed by Trusler and Wass highlighted the humanitarian facet of Wonderland, reminding us that Alice's original author was just as much a fantasist master of whimsical nonsense as a philanthropic philosopher. Carroll's "moral crusade concerned with fairness" was recorded in the hundreds of pamphlets[6] he wrote on various ethical issues—in favor of the rights of child actors, against the existence of slavery, the mistreatment of factory workers, the degradation of women, or the abuse of animals. But it also surfaced in his most memorable fictional heroine's empathic relational attitude to the curious creatures she encounters in the dream realms of her own making which constitute twisted replicas of the oddities of our own reality. Alice reveals to us in an entertaining manner how to navigate in a world where we wonder and keep being puzzled at what we do not know, issues of life and death alike.

Like on planet Earth, "life in Wonderland and Looking-Glass Realm is a savage affair, rife with shaken babies, threats of decapitation and vorpal swords" (Lane 2015), however the *Alice* books are also most often still associated with a labor of love Carroll carried out to please a little girl with transforming the potential anxiety caused by rubbery rules between the real and the impossible into a limitless laughter. This infinite joy against all odds and the empowerment by imaginativeness has been reflected in the amazing variety of creative sesquicentennial anniversary festivities such as *The Looking-Glass Cocktail Book* featuring a Mad Hatter (a hot rum punch served on fire at your table) and a White Rabbit (a brandy based cocktail that reminds you of carrots); a performance called Floriferocity where plant collectors ventured to re-imagine the Garden of Live Flowers; or the new musical opera *Wonder.land* that "plays with the idea of what 'falling down a rabbit hole' might mean in today's digital age" (wonder.land) by telling the story of a bullied schoolgirl Aly who finds confidence by virtue of an online alter ego Alice, a brave and beautiful adventuress of an extraordinary virtual world inhabited by the weird Dum and Dee, the creepy Cheshire Cat, and the terrifying Red Queen, strangers she feels curiously familiar with.

Regardless of the media employed or the modes of dis/enchantment elicited by postmillennial adaptations Alice never ceases to put on trial her imaginative agency by boldly facing the Unthinkable and the Unspeakable manifested in many ways in *Wonderland* and beyond the Looking-Glass. Her experimentation, curiosity, and *Wonderlust* remain primary narrative engines and major motivations for aspiring adventurers.

Chapter Notes

Preface

1. A disorder common in children causing distortions in spatial awareness is known as the Alice in Wonderland Syndrome. Brain scans exploring the machinery of language use "Jabberwocky sentences" to prove that meaning and grammar are processed separately in the brain, while post-millennial neuroscientific research verified the White Queen's assumptions about memory's capacity to work backwards and forwards alike by proving that "we imagine the future by pulling apart our recollections and then piecing them together in a montage that might represent a new scenario" (Robson 2015).

Introduction

1. In June 1865 Carroll commissioned Clarendon Press to print and Macmillan to bind 50 copies of his novel and arranged to have a unique gift copy bound in white vellum to be sent for Alice on July 4, 1865. He distributed the other copies to friends in the following days. For an overview of the publishing history of *Alice's Adventures in Wonderland* and *Through the Looking Glass* see Zoe Jaques and Eugene Giddens' 2013 book.
2. *Alice in a World of Wonderlands: The Translations of Lewis Carroll's Masterpiece* edited by Jon A. Lindseth and Alan Tannenbaum (New Castle: Oak Knoll, 2015), published in cooperation with the Lewis Carroll Society of North America and compiled for the 150th anniversary of the publication of *Alice's Adventures in Wonderland*, is the most extensive analysis ever done about one English language novel translated into so many languages. Its three volumes with 251 volunteer writers cover translations of *Alice* in 174 languages. I was in charge of the Hungarian translations.
3. Carroll put an orange in Alice Raikes' right hand, put her in front of a mirror and asked her in which hand she was holding the fruit. The child friend's response—"Supposing I was on the other side of the glass, wouldn't the orange still be in my right hand?"—gave him the idea to locate his heroine's new adventures on the other side of the looking-glass (Douglas-Fairhurst 198).
4. I use the following abbreviations: *Wonderland* stands for *Alice's Adventures in Wonderland* (1865), *Looking-Glass* for *Through the Looking-Glass, and What Alice Found There* (1871), and *Alice* or alternately "the Alice tales" or "the Alice books" for the unit of the two novels recycled in a mixed manner by a multiplicity of adaptations. Wonderland denotes the story world, the elaborate fantasy universe inhabited by Alice throughout her two adventures.
5. Charles Lutwidge Dodgson is referred to in this book as Lewis Carroll as he is discussed in his role as author of Alice's adventures, except in the few occasions when discussing the biographical persona.
6. For convenience's sake I include here brief summaries of the two novels' quite complicated plotlines which might serve as points of reference with regards the adaptations I analyze in depth.

Summary of Lewis Carroll's *Alice's Adventures in Wonderland* (1865):

On a bright summer's day, Alice gets bored in the company of her elder sister, who is reading a book with no pictures or conversations, so she follows a talking White Rabbit with a pocket watch and falls down a rabbit hole to find herself in a curious hall with a row of little doors including one through which she peeps at a beautiful garden she longs to reach. Consuming the contents of a bottle labeled "DRINK ME" makes her shrink so tiny she cannot reach the keys, whereas eating a cake with "EAT ME" written on it in makes her grow to such a gigantic size that her tears flood the hallway. When shrunken again thanks to a fan she picked up, she must swim in the pool of her own tears and meets strange animals equally swept away by the tide who help her to get dry with a dry lecture on William the Conqueror given by the Mouse and a Caucus Race with no winners organized by the Dodo. After she involuntarily scares away the creatures by mentioning her pet cat, she is ordered by the White Rabbit, mistaking her for his maid Mary Ann, to fetch his gloves, and once inside his house grows again, kicks Bill the Lizard who tries to pull her out, and eventually regains her size by eating the pebbles which turn into cakes after the crowd stoned her with them. A blue Caterpillar smoking a hookah makes her realize she no longer knows who she is and advises her on the transformative effects of the mushroom she tastes to experience an extreme elongation of her neck high into the trees where a pigeon mistakes her for a serpent. As a Fish-Footman delivers an invitation to a Frog-Footman for the Duchess, Alice enters the Duchess's house, meets the Cook who is throwing dishes while preparing a too peppery soup that makes everyone sneeze, and she witnesses a baby turning into a pig as well as a Cheshire Cat disappearing to leave only its grin behind. She joins a Mad Tea Party in the company of the crazy March Hare, a sleepy Dormouse, and a Hatter who keeps cracking jokes, unanswerable riddles, and nonsensical stories she fails to understand as Time stands still at an eternal teatime. In the Queen's

Garden she encounters living playing cards preoccupied with painting the white roses red to please the Queen of Hearts obsessed with giving out orders for beheadings. The Queen invites Alice to an increasingly chaotic game of croquet played with live flamingos used as mallets and hedgehogs as balls, and gets annoyed by not being able to have the Cheshire Cat decapitated since only its head is visible. Alice meets the Cat's owner, and the Duchess, fond of moralizing, listens to the story of the Mock Turtle who is sad without a sorrow, and dances the Lobster Quadrille with the Turtle and the Gryphon. She attends a trial where the Knave of Hearts is accused of stealing the Queen's tarts, while most of the creatures she has encountered before reappear in the court room. When she is called up as a witness, Alice starts growing at such a fast pace that the monarchs want to immediately expulse her but far from being intimidated, she rebels against them calling them just a pack of cards. As she tries to fight the cards all swarming upon her she awakens with her head in the lap of her sister who is brushing away dead leaves from her face. Alice realizes that everything was a dream and tells her adventures to her sister who falls asleep and dreams the same dream as Alice, while fantasizing about a grown-up Alice who will eternally preserve her childish spirits.

Summary of *Through the Looking-Glass, and What Alice Found There* (1871):

In the sequel, on a snowy winter evening, Alice is playing with her kittens, the offspring of her former cat, and ponders about the alternate reality on the other side of the mirror she reaches by stepping through the looking-glass. In the reflected version of her home she discovers and decodes a nonsense poem in mirror writing about a beamish knight defeating a monstrous Jabberwock and gets in touch with animated chess figures. In the Garden of Live Flowers the Red Queen impresses Alice by her breathtaking speed and informs her that the country is divided into squares just like a huge chessboard. Alice is invited to take the place of the White Pawn on the second rank and become Queen provided she can reach the eighth square. She spies elephants mistaken for bees, and Looking-Glass insects like the punning-named Rocking-Horse-Fly, Bread-And-Butterfly, and the melancholic little Gnat. She boards without a ticket a train that flies her to the fourth rank along with the passengers thinking in a chorus, befriends a lonely fawn in the woods where things have no name, and gets mocked by the twins Tweedledum and Tweedledee, who recite a long poem about "The Walrus and the Carpenter," philosophically speculate about Alice existing only in the Red King's dreams, and initiate a duel interrupted by a big black crow. The absent-minded White Queen she meets boasts about remembering future events before they have actually happened until she transforms on the fifth rank, after crossing a brook, into a talking knitting Sheep who keeps a shop that quickly metamorphoses into a rowboat and then back. An egg on the shop shelf grows—on the sixth rank, over a brook—into Humpty Dumpty, who is celebrating his Unbirthday, and explains the meaning of Jabberwocky as well as portmanteau word-composite neologisms to Alice before his inevitable fall down the wall. The Lion and the Unicorn arrive to the rescue of Humpty, then fight for the crown, eat bread and plum-cake, and are drummed out of town. The Unicorn mistakes Alice for a fabulous monster but they agree to believe in each other. In the meanwhile, the March Hare and the Hatter of the first book reappear as Anglo-Saxon messengers, Haigha and Hatta. Alice captured by the Red Knight is freed by the White Knight who keeps falling off his horse, raves about his useless inventions and a long song of his own composition and guides Alice, after a final brook-crossing to the safety of the eighth square where she finds herself wearing a crown. Queen Alice takes part in a royal dinner party in the company of the White and Red Queens who examine her with nonsensical questions and moral lessons and further, increasingly foolish guests like talking food that resists to be eaten, moving furniture, bottles turned birds, animals and flowers. As the feast starts to border on chaos, the White Queen disappears in the soup, the Red Queen shrinks and is shaken into a cat by Alice who thus unknowingly puts the Red King into checkmate, wins the game and can finally wake up. In her armchair she wonders that everything may have been the Red King's dream, including herself who is possibly no more than a part of his imagination—an assumption reinforced in the epilogue's suggesting that "life is just a dream."

7. My book treats the two volumes of Alice's adventures as a dialogic unit, and I chose episodes for close reading alternately from *Wonderland* and *Looking-Glass* to support my line of argumentation. Some other critics, like Sundmark (1999), refer to "the Alice books" when discussing the four extant texts—*Alice's Adventures under Ground* (1864), *Alice's Adventures in Wonderland* (1865), *Through the Looking-Glass, and What Alice Found There* (1871) and *The Nursery Alice* (1890)—however, since publication history is not at the primary focus of my analysis, for convenience's sake I use the aforementioned solution.

8. Just how much Alice's identity is grounded in confusion is supported by anecdotal evidence: upon meeting Alice Raikes Carroll supposedly said "So you're another Alice. I'm very fond of Alices. Would you come and see something that is rather puzzling?" (Douglas-Fairhurst 198).

9. J.R.R. Tolkien shares these ideas on fairy tales being particularly suitable for updating or reimagining: in "Tree and Leaf," he writes: "Fairy-stories are by no means the rocky matrices out of which the fossils cannot be prised except by an expert geologist. The ancient elements can be knocked out, or forgotten and dropped out, or replaced by other ingredients with the greatest ease." (32).

10. The situation is even more complex with the rating on contemporary fairy tale-films targeting mixed-media audiences. As Suzanne Enzerink points out, while in the oral folk tradition "many stories now viewed as fairy-tales were first written with an adult audience in mind, and it was only in the 17th century that collections specifically geared towards children became popular. But now, they are remodeled to such an extent that a PG-13 rating (for violence, or more often for the awkwardly termed 'sensuality') will prevent the original, young fairy tale-appreciators from seeing the film versions at all" (Enzerink 2011).

11. "I HAVE reason to believe that *Alice's Adventures*

in *Wonderland* has been read by some hundreds of English Children, aged from Five to Fifteen: also by Children, aged from Fifteen to Twenty-five: yet again by Children, aged from Twenty-five to Thirty-five: and even by Children—for there *are* such—Children in whom no waning of health and strength, no weariness of the solemn mockery, and the gaudy glitter, and the hopeless misery, of Life has availed to parch the pure fountain of joy that wells up in all child-like hearts—Children of a "certain" age, whose tale of years must be left untold, and buried in respectful silence" (Carroll 2010, 1).

12. In *Victorian Afterlife: Postmodern Culture Rewrites the Nineteenth Century* (2000), editors John Kucich and Dianne F. Sadoff's collection of essays presents case studies for "postmodernism's privileging of the Victorian as its 'other'" (xi).

Chapter 1

1. The collection offers a synthesis of Louvel's two most seminal theoretical works which together constitute her poetics: chapters 1, 2, 3, 5 are derived from *L'oeil du texte: Texte et image dans la littérature anglophone* (Toulouse: Presses Universitaires du Mirail, 1998) while chapters 4, 6, 7 were extracted from *Texte/image: Images à lire, textes à voir* (Rennes: Presses Universitaires de Rennes, 2002).

2. This public assumption has been heavily influenced by the collection of essays *Contemporary Fiction and the Fairy Tale* edited by Stephen Benson (Detroit: Wayne State University Press, 2008) that focus on contemporary fiction by erudite authors such as Margaret Atwood, A.S. Byatt, Angela Carter, Robert Coover, and Salman Rushdie, among others, who utilize the tropes, structures, and intertexts of fairy tales in their postmodernist writings.

3. Jaques and Giddens take a similar stance on arguing that "Post-Disney appropriations of Alice enact a binary divide. They can be serious or playful, but rarely both" (217).

4. Jack Zipes's socio-historical overview of the changing functional significance of folk and fairy tales points out that the oral wonder tale storytelling's democratic, ritualistic quest for a communal harmony was gradually lost with the medial shift to written and printed tales that the rising Victorian bourgeoisie supported and exploited for the sake of solidifying its social class status through marginalizing the illiterate from the privileged elite or readers of tales and thereby reaching a "control over imagination and desire within the symbolic order of Western culture." The contemporary Disney Princess Industry's "monologue of self-praise of the ruling classes" masked by the illusory promise to "eliminate social and class conflicts forever" with the help of sugary fantasies seems to be a logical continuation of this self-establishing gesture of the rising middle class (Zipes 1995, 19, 24, 26).

5. Turning the act of *creative imaginative productivity* into a *product* corresponds in Michel de Certeau's terminology with a *tactic* (a spontaneous instance of creative agency operating within the slips of the conventional thought, un/weaving the patterns of everyday life) being framed by and eventually transformed into a *strategy* (a carefully designed institutional ideological practice setting normative conclusions and rules of behavior)— an appropriation Lev Manovich (2008) finds characteristic of new media industries.

6. After the first unsatisfactory printing Carroll commissioned a more commercial printer, Richard Clay of London, to reset the type and print a second edition which, although post-dated 1866, was issued by Macmillan in December 1865, in time for the Christmas trade. Another printing of 3,000 copies was announced by Macmillan in August 1866. The original 2000 condemned copies of the first edition were brought by New York publishing firm D. Appleton, which removed the Macmillan title page, inserted a new title page with the Appleton imprint, used red cloth bindings with a gold stamped vignette on the front cover, and issued the first U.S. edition in early 1866—several months after the second edition was issued in England. See: Schiller and Goodacre, 1990.

7. The mobilization of the story by intermedial means may take place in regular (i.e., non pop-up) picturebooks too. Katalin Szegedi's collages decorating the 2007 Hungarian book edition of *Wonderland* are authentic *Gesamkunstwerk* which transcend the (spatial, temporal, artistic) confines of the page. The delicate aquarelle drawing illustrations of a mischievous, redheaded Alice with a bob cut are embedding emblematic words and text fragments from the original novel in English and Hungarian translation alike, along with Carroll's photographs of Alice Liddell, and found object composites. These include a piece of fur for the Dormouse's hide and real bird feathers on the pigeon's body by courtesy of the artist's sons, a piece of lace from a wedding dress for Alice's clothes, the covering of a box of Cuban cigars inherited from her grandfather for the branch of wood the Cheshire Cat sits on, and neatly carved matches for the White Rabbit's house with a name plate (Dr. Nyuszi Alajos, meaning Dr. Lewis Bunny) cut out from a beer box, and an old family pack of playing cards. All items complement the story with individual histories of their own, in a variety of means and media. Szegedi's cunning devices include the visual evocation of tactile experience (via furs and feathers contained in the collage) and the pictorial representation of unimaginability (the Gryphon is present in his absence, represented by its footsteps in the sand), among others.

8. Technological enhancement of nonsensification is further increased in the sequel, *Alice in New York for iPad2*, a special celebration of the 140th anniversary of *Through the Looking-Glass*, first published in 1871, advertised as "the incredible and the never-before-seen turned real" (*AliceNY* 2011).

9. Patricia Pringle writes about fascination as spatial experience in connection with Victorian stage magic. She quotes Rudolf Rugoff's ideas: "Tiny artworks force us to draw closer … and this forward movement parallels a mental process; the more closely we examine minute details, the less we notice the gulf in size that separates us. The act of paying attention is in itself a kind of magnifying glass … this charges our experience of the object, *imbuing it with an almost hallucinatory acuity* [my italics]… Despite the negligible physicality of tiny work, its effect on us may be surprisingly visceral" (Rugoff 14–15 in Pringle 2004).

10. Sony's recent innovation called Wonderbook, an augmented reality game platform displayed on the home television screen, is spectacularly connected to its analogue equivalent even if it does not have much to do with

print literature. The pad physically "opens" like a book, and the platform's first title release is a Book of Spells (in collaboration with J.K. Rowling) and is advertised as a significant step in the "reinvention of traditional storybooks." However, as Timothy J. Welsh notes, Wonderbook makes use of visual feedback and motion control, which extend the arena of interaction onto the screen and requires no reading or text at all. Thus, the company's presentation of this iBook-cum-3DS device as a *book* appears to be an attempt to justify a sophisticated entertainment technology as a socially beneficial educative medium (see Welsh 2012).

11. According to experimental child psychologist Adriana G. Bus, interactive electronic storybooks for children often include inconsiderate games and animation that interfere with optimal learning conditions and as superficial additional information sources debilitate text comprehension. See Adriana G. Bus and Susan B. Neuman, eds., *Multimedia and Literacy Development: Improving Achievement for Young Learners* (New York: Taylor & Francis Group, 2010).

12. As we can read on Su Blackwell's Homepage: "It is the delicacy, the slight feeling of claustrophobia, as if these characters, the landscape have been trapped inside the book all this time and are now suddenly released. A number of the compositions have an urgency about them, the choices made for the cut-out people from the illustrations seem to lean towards people on their way somewhere, about to discover something, or perhaps escaping from something. And the landscapes speak of a bleak mystery, a rising, an awareness of the air" http://www.sublackwell.co.uk/profile/. For more on book sculptures and an amazing gallery of thought-provoking and beautiful works that transform books into art see: Jason Thompson, *Playing with Books: The Art of Upcycling, Deconstructing, and Reimagining the Book* (Quarry Books, 2010).

13. As Joe Queenan puts it poetically and with a touch of self-irony in his *One for the Books*: "Books as physical objects matter to me, because they evoke the past. A Métro ticket falls out of a book I bought 40 years ago, and I am transported back to the Rue Saint-Jacques on Sept. 12, 1972, where I am waiting for someone named Annie LeCombe. A telephone message from a friend who died too young falls out of a book, and I find myself back in the Chateau Marmont on a balmy September day in 1995. A note I scribbled to myself in 'Homage to Catalonia' in 1973 when I was in Granada reminds me to learn Spanish, which I have not yet done, and to go back to Granada. None of this will work with a Kindle. People who need to possess the physical copy of a book, not merely an electronic version, believe that the objects themselves are sacred. Some people may find this attitude baffling, arguing that books are merely objects that take up space. This is true, but so are Prague and your kids and the Sistine Chapel. Think it through, bozos" (2013).

14. Lessing's time-space notions were criticized as restrictive polarizations by his contemporaries (Johann Gottfried Herder), and most recent iconological revisions alike (W.J.T. Mitchell).

15. This scene, whereby the tale is going to be read just as much as shown to the audience, illustrates the indebtedness of the visual to the textual, and stages an exciting image-text interaction complemented by the auditory component of the voice (and the commemoration of the oral origins of fairy tales) as the story's temporal, eternal charm is guaranteed by its "retell ability," the fact that it can be retold over and over again to a changing audience of eager listeners.

16. Ross reflects on the superficially PC quality of recent Disney movies: the environmentalism of Lion King ruling by divine right, the multiculturalism of Pocahontas drawn to be a "babe," and the mainstreaming of the physically challenged in the Hunchback of Notre-Dame who can hope to achieve in life a second-best cuteness (Ross 2000, 223).

17. "Instead of going forward into maturity, Disney's Alice retreats into perpetual childhood, learning to treasure 'dull reality' rather than the memory of the dream that alone, to Carroll, made reality tolerable. At the end she can't wait to become again the object she sees through the keyhole: inactive—asleep—and ready to be taught, commanded and fed once more" (Ross 2000).

18. Jeff Hong's photo collage project "Unhappily Ever After" (2014–) places Disney animation characters in realistic circumstances of dark modern day scenarios to unfold sociodramas related to social, political, environmental, and economic problems. His Alice is an emaciated junkie lost in the deserted alley of her own addiction with her ominous "drink me" bottle as her sole companion.

19. In 1992 a hedge maze attraction called Alice's Curious Labyrinth opened in Disneyland Paris (Brooker 308–314), and Alice characters play a prominent part in character greetings both in the Magic Kingdom and Epcot Center in Disney World.

20. Nick Willing's 1999 film adaptation adopts a similarly didactic coming-of-age narrative frame, whereby Alice's adventures in Wonderland help her to learn to conquer her anxiety and eventually excel in feminine arts by performing a song of her choice instead of "Cherry Ripe" to entertain guests at a Victorian garden party.

21. Woolverton also wrote the screenplay for Disney's animated feature film *Beauty and the Beast*, co-wrote the screenplay for *The Lion King*, and contributed additional story material to *Mulan*. Burton's more feminist filmic features were due to scriptwriter Caroline Thompson, who wrote the script for *The Addams Family*, *The Nightmare Before Christmas*, *Edward Scissorhands*, and later collaborated on *Corpse Bride* (see Ray 201).

22. "Baring the device" was a self-reflexive metafictional strategy introduced by Viktor Šklovskij and widely used by the Russian Formalists as a contrast to the effect of verisimilitude: instead of reaching beholders' forgetfulness about their encountering an artifact, the aim was to foreground art's being a willed simulacrum incommensurate with life itself.

23. "Narcissistic narrative pleasures," in Linda Hutcheon's original sense, result from challenging canonical authorial privileges and reintrepreting reading as a co-operative experience (see Hutcheon 1984).

24. Zipes points out how the early filmmaker Disney tendentiously "interjects himself into the film he draws as an omnipotent figure capable to create and annihilate fictional universe with his phallic pen." Disney consistently made his team of animators invisible and exploited, like dwarfs toiling down in the mines, while Prince Charming (cinema-author Disney), in his version, kisses Snow White (emblematizing the artwork) to life—much unlike in the original fairy tale, where one of a dwarf's tripping with the glass-coffin rescues the girl making her cough up the poisoned apple (Zipes 1995, 29).

25. Pier's succinct summary relies on the following theoretical texts by Gérard Genette here: *Palimpsests: Literature in the Second Degree* (Lincoln: University of Nebraska Press, [1982] 1997), *Narrative Discourse Revisited* (Ithaca: Cornell University Press, [1983] 1988), and *Métalepse:. De la figure à la fiction* (Paris: Seuil, 2004).

26. The image of the slaying of the Jabberwocky was replaced by a less frightening image of Alice and the White Knight.

27. The initial title *Alice in Wonderland: An Adaptation of Lewis Carrol's* (sic) *The Adventures of Alice in Wonderland and Through the Looking Glass* misspelled Carroll's name (Jaques and Giddens 205).

28. Originally, the Cheshire Cat was supposed to sing a song called "I'm Odd" but was later replaced with "Twas Brillig."

29. This acoustic characterization and the play with accents possibly alludes to the Disney animation's strategic contrasting of Alice's English boarding school accent with the American-accented Queen of Hearts to imply a strong sense of "the Old World meeting the New, and not getting on particularly well" (Jaques and Giddens 207).

30. The notion of "muchness" as an attribute that Burton's Hatter claims Alice has lost originates from Carroll's original Mad Tea Party scene where the Dormouse tells Alice about three little sisters who lived in a treacle-well and learned to draw everything "that begins with an M, such as mousetraps, and the moon, and memory, and muchness [...]."

31. One of Carroll's many *tableau vivant* costume photographs of young girls—entitled "Waiting for the Trumpet" in honor of Tennyson's poem "Sir Galahad" including the line: "A maiden knight; to me is given/ Such bliss, I know not fear."—portrays Rose Lawrie as a maiden-knight dressed in a chain-mail (borrowed from the artist Henry Holiday), equipped with a long sword, and crowned by a Pre-Raphaelitean mane of flowing hair and an androgynous aura of chivalric gallantry and determination—all reminiscent of Tenniel's "beamish" boy-knight illustration and Burton's Amazonian Alice figure. See Roger Taylor and Edward Wakeling. *Lewis Carroll, Photographer*, The Princeton University Library Albums (Princeton: Princeton University Press, 2002).

32. Michael Hancher notes that the *Punch Almanch* for 1865, published about the same time as *Alice's Adventures in Wonderland*, features on its page for July and August an Alice-like figure personifying "the astrological sign Virgo, in the form of a statue of the modest and long-suffering Joan of Arc" (1982, 35).

33. Alice's magical incantation-like monologue in Burton is the following: "I try to believe in as many as six impossible things before breakfast. Count them, Alice. One, there are drinks that make you shrink. Two, there are foods that make you grow. Three, animals can talk. Four, cats can disappear. Five, there is a place called Underland. Six, I can slay the Jabberwocky" (Burton 2010).

34. "I'm just one hundred and one, five months and a day." "I can't believe that!" said Alice. "Can't you?" the Queen said in a pitying tone. "Try again: draw a long breath, and shut your eyes." Alice laughed. "There's no use trying," she said: "one *can't* believe impossible things." "I daresay you haven't had much practice," said the Queen. "When I was your age, I always did it for half-an-hour a day. Why, sometimes I've believed as many as six impossible things before breakfast" (210).

35. Carroll's praise in his diary of Henry Savile Clark's theatrical adaptation of Alice adopts this multifocal view that sees several roles in one figure, when he mentions that Master C. Adeson, whose performance of the Cheshire Cat "was a gem," also excelled previously in the role of the Pirate King in *Pirates of Penzance* (Nichols 42).

36. The same happened with the *Twilight* novel and movie which popularized Shakespeare's *Romeo and Juliet* as the love-story that inspired the first volume of vampire Edward and human Bella's teenage Gothic romance saga authored by one-time fan-fiction writer Stephenie Meyer who, absurdly, brought new readership for the Bard due to a recommendation she made on the cover of her YA bestseller.

37. Scriptwriter Woolverton's memory-morsel concerning her cooperation with director Burton on their adaptation of Alice is clearly suggestive of the difficulty of the clear-cut distinction between verbal and visual creativity throughout co-authorial interactions: "[Burton, a notoriously visual storyteller] didn't talk about images. He really sat down and talked to me like a writer. We looked at the words on the paper. He didn't draw anything in my presence, although I did draw for him, which is crazy" (Callaghan 2011).

Chapter 2

1. The paradox is that even if we idealistically presume that children's fantasy can remain free from these burdens of socialization, and revel in the heterogeneity of being without one's world falling apart, the adult imagination fictionalizing and interpreting it, making sense and nonsense of it, clearly fails to do so.

2. For example, Miramax division Dimension Pictures' Harvey and Bob Weinstein did not allow him to put a huge fake nose on Matt Damon for fear that distorting the handsome face of the lead actor would discourage his fans from watching the movie.

3. Carroll's essay "Alice on the Stage" (1887) claims that "eager enjoyment of Life [...] comes only in the happy hours of childhood, when all is new and fair, and when sin and sorrow are just names, empty words signifying nothing" (Kelly 225).

4. Accordingly, the following fragment of Jeliza-Rose's stream of consciousness can be regarded as a tongue-in-cheek "repetition with a difference": "And Dell would take care of us all. Soon she'd watch our babies while we explored the Hundred Year Ocean. She'd marry my father and become my mother. Then she and Dickens and Cut 'N Style and I would build a castle from mesquite branches and flattened pennies. We'd eat meat and pound cake at every meal. We'd drink juice from gold-plated Dixie cups. 'It's a dream come true,' I said" (126).

5. Her regarding the dangers she faces inconsequential and reevaluating violence in terms of a dark but harmless comedy reminds of safe infantile fears caused by animated cartoon series where cute creatures—like *Tom and Jerry*, and many other MGM features—inflict fatal injuries on one another in slapstick-style, inventively aggressive ways for no particular reason, and, in the next moment, jump up unharmed to start all over again. The infinite, irrational fight of these more "iconic" than real enemies provides safe amusement even to the youngest spectators, because children get a clear sense of the fact

that the dangers are contained make-believe within a fictional universe governed by its own rules of functioning, partly differing (the nonexistence of fatal physical injury) and partly overlapping with ours (the preeminence of mischievous fraternity). The animation's comic quality arises not from its violence but from the inviolability of the antagonists who emerge as playmates, as partners in crime in an ideal world where crime is a meaningless concept. The inviolability of the characters guarantees the tale's authenticity: if Tom or Jerry would suffer or die, one would not accept it to be a real *Tom and Jerry* show anymore.

6. As Bruce Bennett (2006) notes, Gilliam may be "the *noisiest* fantasist going" with "films full of chattering background characters, kabongs and shrieks." *Tideland*'s soundtrack is dominated by sounds of nature, wind blowing, wind chimes tinkling, squirrels chirping, complemented by the minimalist music of "woodwind tootlings that herald magic," and most importantly the focalizer protagonist Jeliza-Rose's own corporeal noises which complement the larger-scale global cacophony with her own microcosmic organic sounds: her enduring giggle reinterpreting horrific events as wonders and her occasional screams, gasps, or sighs of excitement on recognizing their reality, her stomach-growl misread as pregnancy from silly-kissing, and even her ventriloquization of dollheads as imaginary friends/selves.

7. Gilliam's film adapts the same ideas into the junkie father's drug-induced fantasies: "Daddy's gonna stroll down that far subterranean shore, all littered with the flotsam of hopes and dreams. Relics of ancient times. Lonely cenotaphs. Standing along that melancholy tideland."

8. "The end of the world was purple, appearing as an iris or a rose in my dream, blooming with an ear-piercing eruption, the petals suddenly bursting away from the bud like a fire- work. Or was I already half-awake—having just stirred beside my father—when the explosions shook What Rocks so abruptly, so violently, that the table lamp beside my bed fell to the floor; the window near the staircase collapsed in pieces, and all the windows downstairs—I soon discovered—shattered inward, throwing glass over the floorboards. Then with astonishing speed, the ruinous aftermath of the blasts unfolded beyond the farmhouse, cacophonous and jarring-the whine of iron wheels sparking on the tracks, passenger cars tipping this way and that, metal striking metal, the ground quaking—then everything was quiet, enveloped in a brown and white dust which rose into the evening sky like smoke" (Cullin 139).

9. However, this revelation by means of art remains in a sense down-to-earth, non-secular, bitter-sweet, without a promise of eternal happiness. As in most efficient *Alice* adaptations, the classic Carrollian ambiguity prevails: the melancholy encapsulated in a pun in *Sylvie and Bruno* where to "LIVE" appears as an anagrammatic equivalent of "EVIL"—possibly influenced by the Darwinian evolutionary theoretization of the ruthless struggle for survival in a disinterested nature Tennyson calls "red in tooth and claw"—is complemented by *Wonderland*'s more hopeful credo "love makes the world go around"—a sentiment not so much akin to the pedophiliac erotic desire criticized by Kincaid as childish empathy. This idea is strangely reinforced by the Duchess' antididactic mock-moralizing: "if everybody minded their own business, the world would go round a great deal faster than it does" (63). Albeit in a nonsensical, twisted way, the line surveys in philosophical and physical terms human civilization's current state of functioning by highlighting human beings' affinity to *mind* each other, that is to think about each other, to think about each other thinking, caring, in the hope of understanding, against all odds.

10. Unlike the emblematic suffering minors of Victorian fiction, ranging from the Little Match Girl to Little Nell, Alice does not die—and far from it, even flirts with the idea of mortality, cracking death jokes—since, luckily, Carroll immortalizes childhood by another narrative strategy. His heroine is kept small in a literal sense, due to numerous shrinking in Wonderland and her diminution to a white pawn's size beyond the Looking-Glass.

11. Szabó Gendler illustrates the former, imaginable impossibility with the example of *Alice's Adventures in Wonderland*: "even if we do not have a fully comprehensive mental image of the scenario, it is, I take it, true in the Alice-in-Wonderland fiction that the Queen of Hearts, who is a playing card, has ten heart-sporting children; that spade cards are gardeners, whereas club cards are soldiers; that cards ornamented with kings and queens are royalty—and so on. A reader who reported imaginative barriers in the face of such claims would, it seems fair to say, be considered a bit of a bad sport. But note that, in order to understand the Alice story, we must simultaneously exploit a range of conflicting mapping principles each drawing on a different feature of our associational repertoire: people have hands and feet in a roughly diagonal configuration, so the hands and feet of the playing cards are arranged likewise; spades are associated with gardening, so spade-sporting cards are gardeners; children resemble their parents, so heart-sporting cards are the children of the King and Queen of Hearts; kings and queens tend to be friends with other kings and queens, so the King and Queen of Clubs are royal guests. And so on. Moreover, we do this despite the fact that it introduces all sorts of tensions: If the five of spades is an adult, shouldn't the five of hearts be an adult too? If the seven of spades is a gardener, shouldn't the King of Spades be a gardener too? These inconsistencies do not result in imaginative barriers: we are easily able to circumscribe our attention, focusing on one set of similarities in one context, another in another. Nor is there any sense of imaginative impropriety. One may think that monarchy is a distasteful form of government, or object to parades on aesthetic grounds. But none of this seems to get in the way of imaginatively engaging with the *Alice in Wonderland*" (168).

12. For an analysis on how fairy tales fictionalize the infantile fear of being devoured by the mother and the concomitant fantasy to assimilate and annihilate the maternal (i.e., the wicked witch, the bad breast) which is external to the self, see Carolyn Daniel's *Voracious Children: Who Eats Whom in Children's Literature* (2006), that primarily relies on Melanie Klein's child-psychology.

13. Mist also figures in Freud's poetic description of haunting repetition, déjà-vu involved in uncanny experience: "caught in a mist, perhaps, one has lost one's way ... [and] every attempt to find the marked or familiar path may bring one back again and again to one and the same spot" (Freud 1985, 359). Gaiman seems to pay a tribute to this Freudian passage when he describes Coraline

walking in a mist to always arrive back at the house she has walked away from, asking, "how can you walk away from something and still come back to it?" (89) Moreover, the ambiguous dynamics of "walking away from" and "arriving back to" also has exciting implications regarding literary recycling that strives to find the appropriate balance between moving away from and falling back on the original. This movement can certainly be mapped onto the relation of *Coraline* and *Alice*.

14. Further examples include the extended clan-like the Addams Family whose credo "We gladly feast on those who would subdue us" (1991) ironically comments on the aggression lurking under the apparent gentility of family ties; Harry Potter, a Dickensian orphan tormented by a disenchanted "muggle" adoptive family who gains support from friendship instead of kinship bonds; Tim Burton's Corpse Bride literalizing the marital wows "till death do us apart" while spookily confounding marital and familial relations between the living and the (un)dead (Kérchy-Povidisa 2011, 117).

15. This is neatly spelt out in the passage: "She crept back into the silent house, past the closed bedroom door inside which the other mother and the other father— what? She wondered. Slept? Waited? And then it came to her that, should she open the bedroom door she would find it empty, or more precisely that it was an empty room and it would remain empty until the exact moment that she opened the door. "//Somehow that made it easier." (80).

16. Portraying the protagonist from the back is not necessarily disempowering if we think of Tenniel's drawing of the Jabberwock-slaying beamish knight who turns away his/her face from readers but is recognized as clandestine alter ego of Alice because of the flowing hair and the backwards posture echoing other representations of Alice (facing the Cheshire Cat and Humpty Dumpty) elsewhere in the book.

17. American McGee on Burton and Disney's Alice movie: "Alice? She's just along for the ride. An empty bag, blowing in the wind. Things happen to her but never because of her. The story's finale hammers home this point when someone reminds Alice that she literally *doesn't have to do anything*. She just needs to relax and let the Vorpal Blade take care of business. Snore. / For a character whose main obstacle is indecisiveness, you'd expect her final triumph to materialize in a flurry of blades and blood—a definitive signal that this girl isn't just along on someone else's ride. But no. It might have been a Burton film—and I'm certain that left to control the enterprise alone he would have delivered—but more than anything it was a Disney film. Can't be splattering blood all over the place. And god forbid a girl *kick someone's ass*" (2013).

Chapter 3

1. Carroll's views about the age of child-friends changed over time, in an 1877 letter to publisher Macmillan he "put the nicest age at about 17" and later wrote that some of his "dearest child-friends are 30 or more" (Cohen 462). These claims provide textual evidence for Karoline Leech's challenging of Carroll iconic persona as "child-lover."

2. The latter is just one manifestation of a lifetime mania that made him do catalogued records of all minor details of his life as if embarking on a gigantically impossible project to fight with systematic calculations the passing of time, forgetting, and unpredictle, unmasterable chance. A letter-register he started in his late twenties and kept for his entire life to keep track of his "wheelbarrows full" of letters recorded more than 98,000 sent and received.

3. For these see Januszczak and Self in Brooker 49–59, and the chapter "Freudian Interpretations" in Phillips 279–377.

4. Florence Becker Lennon supports the assumption of asexuality describing Carroll as a happy heteroromantic asexual with a pure romantic infatuation for his ideal-child-friend Alice to whom he likely proposed an "honourable marriage" (192) implying a *mariage blanc*, a "white marriage," without consummation.

5. For more, sex-centered Freudian interpretations of Alice see Phillips 279–377; for a detailed analysis of them see "The Freudians and the Apologists" in Leach 69–113.

6. Juliet Hacking's analysis concentrates on one of Carroll's contemporaries, Camille Silvy's *deshabillé* photographs of Mrs. Holford's Daughter (ca. 1860) coming to the rather shocking (and fully speculative) conclusion that these *cartes de visite* might have been advertising images of Victorian sex-traffickers. Hence the woman accompanying the underdressed little girl on the photo might have actually "a brothel-keeper who wished to derive a financial gain from the sale or distribution of photographs of her pretended daughter" (97).

7. See: "Lapide candidiore diem notare" in Catullus, Poem 68, Line 148.

8. "The project was initiated by Olympia, wanting attention, and the arrangement has since developed organically" (Webb 2004).

9. See Belgian surrealist René Magritte's metapicture "This is not a pipe. The Betrayal of Images" thematizing the representational confines of visual and verbal communication and the numerous art historical analysis thereof: e.g., Michel Foucault, *This Is Not a Pipe*, Trans. Ed. James Harkness (Berkeley: University of California Press, 1983).

10. Papapetrou deals with parents projecting their desires on their children already in her earliest photo-series inspired by her daughter ("Olympia's Clothes") where the fetishistic visual catalogue of the toddler's wardrobe incorporates in her maternal art Olympia's presence through her physical absence.

11. How O'Kane's photocollage performs a shadow-dance reanimating ghosts recalls the legend about the origin of art, according to which the first portrait ever was created by "the Corinthian maid," called Dibutades, who was heartbroken for having to say farewell to her lover departing on a journey, so she decided to trace the shadow of the young man's profile cast on the wall, and asked her father, a potter, to press clay on her silhouette drawing and make a bas-relief sculpture that could act as a memento for her during the lover's absence (Warner 159). This story about amorous artistic collaboration to capture and compensate for loss was originally included in Pliny the Elder's *Natural History*, came to be transmitted to painting manuals from antique to present days, and remains an allegory widely referred to by seminal art critics, iconographers, and semioticians.

12. Kali Israel quotes writer Dennis Potter's speaking

of his own experience of childhood assault by an uncle at the age of ten, to argue for the complexity of children's emotional lives even in the case of abuse: "such deeply damaging experiences can generate many kinds of stories, many kinds of containments, and representations that should not be reduced to their traumatic origins" (Israel 263).

13. On Freudian psychoanalysis/ Seduction Theory as a cultural discourse that provides a key to understanding *Lost Girls* see Eric Tribunella's article. "Literature for Us 'Older Children': Lost Girls, Seductions Fantasies, and the Reeducation of Adults," *The Journal of Popular Culture* 45.3 (2012): 628–648.

14. "Throughout much of the novel they prod and eat and frig each other, in and out of dress, to near-distraction, while somehow managing also to regale each other with elaborate, absurdly filthy stories, confessional and reflective tales that constitute their sexual autobiographies" (Hatfield 4).

15. Alice says: "'Fiddlesticks! Why, there is a notable professor of the mind currently practising not far from here, in Vienna. He would find your image of flight perfectly acceptable and indeed appropriate. I have no doubt you are as sane as I. Of course, I did spend a number of years in a sanatorium" (1, 8, 8).

16. Ida Yoshinaga calls attention to the drawbacks of this excessive, somewhat idealistic celebration of sex-magic, claiming that although Gebbie portrays traumatized characters, she keeps the horrifying, abusive acts mostly invisible, de-sensationalized or be-jewelled in guise of exquisite consensual pleasures. Hence the colonialist ideological implications of the relationships are ignored while black bodies are fragmentated, fetishized, and minimalized (411–5).

17. The back cover of the box that houses the three volumes warns: "For Adults Only."

Chapter 4

1. Švankmajer considers himself a poet with an inherently multimedial vocation: "If I should say it in a slightly exaggerated way, I would say I consider myself to be a poet. There is only one poetry, and whichever tools or methods you use, poetics is all one" (Švankmajer 2006 in Vasseleu 2009). "There is just one sort of poetry and the form is not important if it is film, painting, engraving, collage or ceramics. It is professional laziness to use only one form of self-expression. In that respect I consider myself to be a militant surrealist ... for wizards, there is no such thing as just a wall" (Švankmajer in Leclerc and Schmitt 2001, 4.42).

2. The term (*humour noir*) was quite appropriately coined by surrealist theoretician André Breton to designate a genre where the comic effects arise from hopelessness, a skeptical or cynical encounter with taboo topics such as death, decay, physical and mental fragility.

3. René Magritte portrays Alice gigantic, morphing into a tree, for Salvador Dalí she is whirlwind-like, shadowy skipping-roping towards infinity, Max Ernst sees her as a combination of his own double the superior Loplop bird and of fellow artist lover Leonora Carrington, and Dorothea Tanning hears "eine kleine Nachtmusik" while a tentacled sunflower mesmerizes the girl with her hair on end and in flame.

4. However, some of the most memorable figures of the *Toy Story* trilogy are the discarded and ruined, "scary" toys. Grotesque composites made by the naughty neighbor boy, like the doll head on spider legs in the first part, or abandoned toys, like the one-eyed baby doll and the ragged old bear in the third part, serve as villainous counterparts to the plastic heroes and may end up by means of a well deserved punishment on the junk heap that is the natural habitat of the Svankmajerian toy objects. Still, in *Toy Story* plastic toys hold a memorial function as cherished fetishes of childhood clearly surpassing insignificant consumer objects and they may even call forth sensible scenes, the sensorial stimuli of embodied filmic experience as tactile cinema theoretician Vivian Sobchacks suggests by quoting a critique of the film: "A Tyrannosaurus rex doll is so glossy and tactile you feel as if you could reach out and stroke its hard, shiny head.... When some toy soldiers spring to life, the waxy sheen of their green fatigues will strike Proustian chords of recognition in anyone who ever presided over a basement game of army.... [T]his movie ... invites you to gaze upon the textures of the physical world with new eyes. What *Bambi* and *Snow White* did for nature, *Toy Story*, amazingly, does for plastic" (qtd in Sobchack 54).

5. Švankmajer's art is distinguished by specific national characteristics, too. The Czech Surrealist Group has functioned throughout some forty years of the country's totalitarian oppression as "the only alternative to the official cultural wasteland" (Hames 110) imposed by the 1950s' Stalinist regime and the subsequent Soviet invasion of the country in 1968. His paranoid fantasy about Alice's persecutions in Wonderland and her rebellion against absurd authorities can easily be interpreted as a dark parody of the 1950s' cultural repression, political trials, and communist censorship which seriously restricted independent artists' opportunities to shoot and distribute films.

6. "For me, objects are more alive than people, more permanent and more expressive—the memories they possess far exceed the memories of man. Objects conceal within themselves the events they've witnessed. I don't actually animate objects. I coerce their inner life out of them—and for that animation is a great aid which I consider to be a sort of magical rite or ritual" (Švankmajer in Cherry 2002).

7. As the topic's greatest expert cultural historian Horst Bredekamp (1995) pointed out, the Kunstkammer's "programmatic display of oddities" was regarded in its time as a microcosm of the world and a memory theatre that served to illustrate the miraculous yet mechanistic ordering of the universe as well as the patron's creative capacity to comprehend and control this world by microscopically reproducing the totality of its being in his collection. It was a forum where art could collide with nature, fact could fuse with fiction, and Western scientific achievements could take place side-by-side with knowledge brought from non-Western civilizations during the first geographic discoveries.

8. Curiosity Cabinets abound in and out of Švankmajer's filmic oeuvre. In his animation short *Jabberwocky or Straw Hubert's Clothes* (1971) Carroll's mythical monster is impersonated by a wardrobe loitering zombie-like in the woods and opening up to a strange playroom as the hidden elsewhere of any cosy nursery-realm, while the Brothers Quays' duo straightforwardly entitle their

tribute-animation *The Cabinet of Jan Švankmajer* (1984) and portray their major inspiring figure as a professional puppet, a self-made master magician in charge of metamorphic spaces lecturing a disciple about the art of illusion through exploring migrating objects in a bank of drawers.

9. "He's a film-maker in fertile and powerful dispute with his medium: battling against the disembodied immateriality of film with the fleshy sensations he excites, and overturning the deadness of things with his endlessly inventive animation. His films, which combine live action, stop-frame animation, puppetry, drawing and any number of other techniques, divert the medium from its usual naturalistic, documentary tradition of the Lumière brothers and re-route it back into the strong, countervailing current of illusionists, magicians, circus artists, magic lanternists, acrobats, dancers, and all who use tricks and artifice (the tradition of George Méliès)" (Warner 2007).

10. The surrealists' original tactile games—like the one called "Restorer" where participants manually explored an artwork hidden under a cloth to recreate it verbally and visually in their own fashion—were meant to study touch as an imaginative stimulus, fostering associative, irrational thinking.

11. Sobchack's ideas are heavily indebted to French philosopher Maurice Merleau-Ponty's ideas in the *Phenomenology of Perception,* according to which "each organ of sense explores the object in its own way, [and] is the agent of a certain type of synthesis" (223) so that the sensible-sentient lived body "is a ready-made system of equivalents and transpositions from one sense to another. The senses translate each other without any need of an interpreter, and they are mutually comprehensible without the intervention of any idea" (235).

12. Sobchack writes elsewhere of "our common sensuous experience of the movies": "we are in some carnal modality able to touch being touched by the substance and texture of images; to feel a visual atmosphere envelop us; to experience weight, suffocation, and the need for air; to take flight in kinetic exhilaration and freedom even as we are relatively bound to our theater seats; to be knocked backward by a sound; to sometimes even smell and taste the world we see on the screen" (65).

13. As we see Švankmajer's alternating shots between little girl's and doll's mouths, we are reminded of contemporary Canadian artist Diana Thorneycroft's *Doll Mouth Series* (2004) presenting photographic close-ups of plastic baby doll lips, reading the play and possibilites involved in "the visual language of the open mouth" "that part of the body we use to feed ourselves, make love and express joy or rage [...] where language exits [and] all things that relate to existence [b]ut [that] can also be violated and penetrated, sexually, medically, punitively," as the exhibition catalogue claims (Thorneycroft.com).

14. Richardson condemns perhaps a bit too easily linguistic representation as a totally transparent and tyrannic communicational mode, forgetful of the nonsense language games' subversive significations abounding in the source text to Švankmajer's animation adaptation. But he is certainly right about the overwhelming visual provocativeness of *Alice* that predominates the scarcity of the film's spoken discourse nearly always articulated through the title-character's mouth recounting or commenting on the story in a monologue that is consistently left unanswered like the Carrollian mad Hatter's famous riddle "Why is the raven like a writing desk?"

15. Our culture's prioritization of verbality is likely a Judeo-Christian cultural heritage of a biblical origin assuming that the mastery of the word effectuates a transcendental mastery of the world: "In the beginning was the Word, and the Word was with God, and the Word was God."

16. Carroll's most famous homage to Wittgensteinian philosophy is Humpty Dumpty's line "When *I* use a word it means just what I choose it to mean—neither more nor less" (224), a fictional reformulation of the "private language argument" according to which language maps ideas in each person's minds in individual ways. Mental images constitute a private imagery that provides a fundament of meaning we cannot share with each other apart via the communal sign system of language.

17. "'Don't stand there chattering to yourself like that,' Humpty Dumpty said, looking at her for the first time, 'but tell me your name and your business.'

"'My *name* is Alice, but—'

"'It's a stupid name enough!' Humpty Dumpty interrupted impatiently. 'What does it mean?'

"'*must* a name mean something?' Alice asked doubtfully.

"'Of course it must,' Humpty Dumpty said with a sort laugh: '*my* name means the shape I am—and a good handsome shape it is, too. With a name like your, you might be any shape, almost.'" (219).

18. Consequences is an old parlour game in which players write in turn on a sheet of paper, fold it to conceal part of the writing, and then pass it to the next player for a further contribution.

19. As Michelle Ryan-Sautour highlights, Carter's 1993 story-version quoted riddles from Carroll's *A Tangled Tale* (1885), while her 1990 publication adopted conundrums from Raymond Smullyan's *What Is the Name of this Book: The Riddle of Dracula and Other Logical Puzzles* (1986), to which clear answers were provided at the end of the story. (77).

20. The two stances Haughton refers to are: "'No, no! The adventures first,' said the Gryphon in an impatient tone: 'explanations take such a dreadful time'" (109) "but the Red Queen interrupted her impatiently. "That's just what I complain of! You *should* have meant! What do you suppose is the use of a child without any meaning? Even a joke should have some meaning— and a child's more important than a joke, I hope" (265).

21. The quotation continues as follows. "In Eden, to see a thing Yahweh had dreamed and to say its name aloud was to bring it surging into the real. The letter **B**, so solid and threatening, *was* the bee; it was the embodiment of all its potencies. Looking at that letter, that blossom and that bee was like looking into a mirror from which the skin had been peeled away. The page afforded a passage—transcendental and yet altogether tangible.

Much later I learned that for the Kabbalist, **B**eth is female and passive—a little house waiting to be prodded by the thrusting dart of letter **A**. **A**leph, knowing that **B**eth will always be there, her door open in expectancy, boldly confronts the universe: O vigorous, confident, *thrusting* Aleph! (Now I know, too, just how *erotic* the image was—those engorged petals about to be ravished! Perhaps my sensuous life is here somehow reduced to its essential honey!).

Just as once Persian wizards read a sacred text on the bodies of tigers, I had, from that morning, entered into an exulted state from which I was never to entirely recover, expecting, no, *demanding* enchantment each time I opened a book. That letter **B** convinced me of what I think I already knew—that the world is a ceremonial dialogue to be actively engaged, and life's intention the searching out of the fertile passages and places, a fearless looking for the thorny **A** and **B** in everything" (155–156).

22. This analogy is perhaps not too far-fetched since throughout the composition of the Alice songs filled with puns and poetry in homage of Carroll's language-games Waits has admittedly relied on professional carny man Daniel P. Mannix's classic book *Freaks: We Who Are Not as Others* (Powerhouse, 1999). For more on freak shows see Robert Bogdan, *Freak Show: Presenting Human Oddities for Amusement and Profit* (Chicago University Press, 1990), Rosemarie Garland Thomson, *Extraordinary Bodies: Figuring Physical Disability in American Culture and Literature* (New York: Columbia University Press, 1997), Anna Kérchy and Andrea Zittlau, eds. *Exploring the Cultural History of Continental European Freak Shows and Enfreakment* (Newcastle upon Tyne: Cambridge Scholars, 2012).

23. "Fawn: Who are you?
"Alice: I am me.
"Fawn: So am I. I am me.
"Alice: Then we're we.
"Fawn: We are?
"Alice: Don't you see? Here we are, just we two…
"Fawn: I am I, you are you…
"Alice: But what does that mean? And what should we do?
"Fawn: How can we talk if we don't know who we are?
"Alice: How can we know who we are if we don't talk?
"Fawn: What exactly do you mean?
"Alice: I seem to be searching for something.
"Fawn: Yes, I know what you mean.
"Alice: We seem to be searching together.
"Fawn: Together! That's lovely, I think. Don't you?
"Alice: I do! Yes, that's what I meant."

24. A precedent for the identification of a Carroll character by its odd movements figured in Terry Gilliam's 1977 *Jabberwocky* movie in which the director—famously preferring traditional puppetry to cutting-edge special effects—dressed up a live actor in a costume with a freakish long neck, fangs and winglike arms; controlled him like a marionette with poles and lines; and had him walk backward. With this simple solution, widely adopted in Godzilla movies of the 1950s, he could create a "disturbingly real" reproduction of "the monster's jerky, awkward movements" (Nichols 68).

Epilogue

1. For a full list of *Wonderland* anniversary titles compiled by Mark Burstein see Lewis Carroll Society website at http://www.lewiscarroll.org/pdf/2015Books.pdf. I did not deal with relaunchings of former titles here.

2. In celebration of the anniversary, a vintage shop called *Alice Through the Looking Glass* opened in London and is dedicated to selling all things Wonderland and boasting a living white rabbit in it shop window at 14 Cecil Court, WC2N 4HE; alicelooking.co.uk.

3. Other major private collections of Aliceana going on view in the United States in 2015 were Jon A. Lindseth's gifts to Columbia shown in a fall exhibition at the university's Rare Book & Manuscript Library; loans from August and Clare Imholtz at Hornbake Library at the University of Maryland; Byron and Victoria Sewell at the Huntington Museum of Art in West Virginia (with a catalog from Evertype); and Charlie Lovett at the New York Public Library for the Performing Arts at Lincoln Center. Further 2015 U.S. exhibitions included "Peanuts in Wonderland" at the Charles M. Schulz Museum in Santa Rosa, California; 200 items, including Salvador Dalí's illustrations for a 1969 edition of *Wonderland*, a restored 1933 paper filmstrip called "Alice and the Mad Hatter," and a pretend tea party area for children and the young at heart at the Harry Ransom Center at the University of Texas at Austin; and a pop-up exhibition in the Rosenbach Museum & Library, part of the Free Library of Philadelphia. The New York Public Library for the Performing Arts' "Alice Live!" featured works from its dance, theater and music archives and screenings of Alice films (see Levere F4), while the Portland Public Library's "Wake Up Alice!" presented 38 contemporary illustrators reimagining Wonderland.

4. Inky Parrot Press also released a sesquicentennial edition of *Wonderland* with each chapter decorated by a different illustrator.

5. As one of the composers, Roxanna Panufnik, puts it on the project's website: "Being a parent myself, I can only imagine the horror of losing a child to illness at an early age—when I was approached as one of 12 composers to write a short piece on a chapter from *Alice in Wonderland*, I leapt at the chance to be part of something that might contribute towards helping other parents through this nightmare." The 13 composers involved in the Wonderland project are: Panufnik, Mark-Anthony Turnage, Howard Blake, Stuart MacRae, Poul Ruders, Sally Beamish, Carl Davis, Stephen Hough, Richard Dubugnon, Ilya Gringolts, Colin Matthews, Gwilym Simcock, and Augusta Read Thomas.

6. His pamphlet pieces appeared in more than three hundred issues of forty periodicals, using, in addition to his own name and his best-known pseudonym, Lewis Carroll, the pseudonyms B.B., The Lounger, K., R.W.G., Rusticus Expectans, and Dynamite (see Abeles 2001).

Bibliography

Abeles, Francine. *The Political Pamphlets and Letters of Charles Lutwidge Dodgson and Related Pieces: A Mathematical Approach*. Charlottesville: Lewis Carroll Society of North America/University of Virginia Press, 2001.

Adair, Gilbert. *Alice Through the Needle's Eye: A Third Adventure for Lewis Carroll's Alice*. Boston: E.P. Dutton, 1984.

Adams, Jennifer, and Alison Oliver. *Alice in Wonderland. A Baby Lit Colors Primer Board Book*. Layton: Gibbs Smith, 2012.

Adriani, Götz, Winfried Konnertz, and Karin Thomas. *Joseph Beuys: Leben und Werk*. Köln: DuMont, 1984.

Alaniz, José. "Speaking the 'Truth' of Sex: Moore and Gebbie's *Lost Girls*." In *Alan Moore: Portrait of an Extraordinary Gentleman*. Ed. Smoky Man and Gary Spencer Millidge. London: Abiogenesis, 2003.

Atomic Antelope. *Alice for the iPad*. Version 3.01. 2010. https://itunes.apple.com/hu/app/alice-for-the-ipad/id354537426?mt=8.

Atomic Antelope. *Alice in New York for the iPad*. 2011. http://www.AliceNY.com.

Auerbach, Nina. "Alice and Wonderland: A Curious Child." *Victorian Studies* 18.1 (September 1973): 31–47.

Auerbach, Nina. "Falling Alice, Fallen Women, and Victorian Dream Children." *English Language Notes* 20.2 (December 1982): 46–64. In *Romantic Imprisonment: Women and Other Glorified Outcasts*. New York: Columbia University Press, 1986. 149–168.

Auerbach, Nina, and U.C. Knoepflmacher. *Forbidden Journeys: Fairy Tales and Fantasies by Victorian Women Writers*. Chicago: University of Chicago Press, 1993.

Bacchilega, Cristina. *Fairy Tales Transformed? 21st-Century Adaptations and the Politics of Wonder*. Detroit: Wayne State University Press, 2013.

Bacchilega, Cristina. *Postmodern Fairy Tales: Gender and Narrative Strategies*. Philadelphia: University of Pennsylvania Press, 1999.

Bachmann, Beth. "Dodgson Mumbles (After Reviewing the Supreme Court Ruling on Virtual Child Pornography)." In *Alice Redux*. Ed. Richard Peabody. Washington: Paycock, 2005. 193–195.

Baker, Kenneth. "In the Eye of the Beholder: Lewis Carroll Photography Show Raises Difficult Aesthetic Questions." *The San Francisco Chronicle*. 5 August 2002: D-1.

Baker-Smith, Grahame. *Alice's Adventures in Wonderland: Panorama Pops*. The Royal Mail. London: Walker, 2015.

Bakhtin, Mikhail. *Rabelais and his World*. Trans. Helene Iswolsky. Bloomington: Indiana University Press, 1984.

Balay, Anne. "'They're Closin' Up Girl Land': Female Masculinities in Children's Fantasy." *Femspec* 10.2 (July 2010): 5–23.

Barker, Francis. *The Tremulous Private Body: Essays on Subjection*. London: Methuen, 1984.

Barthes, Roland. *Camera Lucida: Reflections on Photography*. Trans. Richard Howard. New York: Hill and Wang, 1981.

Barthes, Roland. *Image Music Text*. Trans. Stephen Heath. London: Fontana, 1977.

Barthes, Roland. *The Pleasure of the Text*. Trans. Richard Miller. New York: Hill and Wang, 1975.

Basic, Zdanko, Harriet Castor, and Lewis Carroll. *Lewis Carroll's Alice's Adventures in Wonderland*. Pop-up book. New York: Barron's Educational Series, 2010.

Bassnett, Susan. *Translation Studies*. London: Routledge, 2002.

Baudrillard, Jean. (1981). *Simulacra and Simulation*. Trans. Sheila Glaser. Ann Arbor: University of Michigan Press, 1994.

Bauman, Bruce. "Lilith in Wunderland." In *Alice Redux*. Ed. Richard Peabody. Washington: Paycock, 2006. 109–113.

Bayley, Melanie. "Alice's Adventures in Algebra: Wonderland Solved." *New Scientist*. 16 December 2009.

Bazin, André. (1946). "The Myth of Total Cinema." Trans. Hugh Gray. *What is Cinema?* Berkeley: University of California Press, 2005. 17–23.

Becker Lennon, Florence. *Victoria Through the Looking-Glass*. New York: Simon & Schuster, 1945.

Beckett, Sandra. *Crossover Picturebooks: A Genre for All Ages*. New York: Routledge, 2012.

Beddor, Frank. *The Looking Glass Wars*. London: Egmont, 2004.

Beer, Gillian. "Alice in Dialogue." Alice Through the Ages: The 150th Anniversary of Alice in Wonderland. Conference Paper. Cambridge University, 2015.

Bélanger, Susan, and Edward Shorter. "Alice in Wonderland in Psychiatry and Medicine." Oxford University Press Blog. 4 July 2012.

Bell, Elizabeth, Lynda Haas, and Laura Sells, eds. *From Mouse to Mermaid: The Politics of Film, Gender, and Culture*. Bloomington: Indiana University Press, 1995.

Benjamin, Melanie. *Alice I Have Been*. New York: Delacorte, 2010.

Benjamin, Walter. (1931). "A Short History of Photography." Trans. Stanley Mitchell. *Screen* 13.1 (1972): 5–26.

Benjamin, Walter. "The Storyteller." In *Illuminations*. Trans. Harry Zohn. Ed. Hannah Arendt. New York: Shocken, 1969. 83–109.

Benjamin, Walter. "The Task of the Translator." In *The Translation Studies Reader*. Trans. Harry Zohn. Ed. Lawrence Venuti. London: Routledge, 2005. 15–23.

Benjamin, Walter. (1936). "The Work of Art in the Age of Mechanical Reproduction." In *Illuminations*. Trans. Harry Zohn. Ed. Hannah Arendt. New York: Shocken, 1969. 217–253.

Benson, Stephen, ed. *Contemporary Fiction and the Fairy Tale*. Detroit: Wayne State University Press, 2008.

Bergson, Henri. (1901). *On Laughter: An Essay on the Meaning of the Comic*. Boston: Atropos, 2010.

Bettelheim, Bruno. *The Uses of Enchantment: The Meaning and Importance of Fairy Tales*. London: Vintage, 1976.

Blackwell, Su. Paper-Sculpture Art Homepage. 2016. http://www.sublackwell.co.uk.

Blake, Kathleen. *Play, Games, and Sport: The Literary Works of Lewis Carroll*. Ithaca: Cornell University Press, 1974.

Bloom, Harold, ed. *Alice's Adventures in Wonderland: Viva Modern Critical Interpretations*. New York: Infobase, 2006.

Blumenthal, Heston. *Heston's Feasts*. Cooking show. Channel Four. 2009–2010.

Blumenthal, Heston, Ferran Adria, Thomas Keller, and Harold McGee. "Statement on the New Cookery." *The Observer*. 10 December 2006.

Bollobás, Enikő. *Egy képlet nyomában: Karakterelemzések az amerikai és a magyar irodalomból*. Budapest: Balassi, 2012.

Bolster, Stephanie. *White Stone: The Alice Poems*. Montréal: Véhicule, 1998.

Bolter, Jay David, and Richard Grusin. *Remediation: Understanding New Media*. London: MIT Press, 2000.

Bower, Dallas, dir. *Alice in Wonderland*. Written by Edward Eliscu, Albert E. Lewin, and Henry Myers. Lou Bunin Productions, 1949.

Bowers, William. "Tom Waits' Alice and Blood Money." *The Pitchfork Review*. 13 May 2002. http://pitchfork.com/reviews/albums/8564-alice-and-blood-money/.

Bradshaw, Peter. "Review of *Alice in Wonderland*." *The Guardian*. 4 March 2010. http://www.guardian.co.uk/film/2010/mar/04/alice-in-wonderland-review.

Bredekamp, Horst. *The Lure of Antiquity and the Cult of the Machine: The Kunstkammer and the Evolution of Nature, Art, and Technology*. Trans. Allison Brown. Princeton: Marcus Wiener, 1995.

Brode, Douglas. *From Walt to Woodstock: How Disney Created the Counterculture*. Austin: University of Texas Press, 2004.

Brooker, Will. *Alice's Adventures: Lewis Carroll in Popular Culture*. New York: Continuum, 2005.

Brooks, Peter. *Body Work: Objects of Desire in Modern Narrative*. Cambridge: Harvard University Press, 1993.

Brooks, Xan, and Henry Barnes. "Review of *Alice in Wonderland*." *The Guardian*. 5 March 2010. http://www.guardian.co.uk/film/video/2010/mar/05/tim-burton-alice-in-wonderland?INTCMP=ILCNETTXT3487.

Bruhm, Steven, and Natasha Hurley, eds. *Curiouser: On the Queerness of Children*. Minneapolis: University of Minnesota Press, 2004.

Bruyn, Dirk. "Chasing Rabbits out of the Hat and into the SHEDding of Childhood: *Alice*." *Senses of Cinema: Cinémathèque Annotations on Film* 20. May 2002. http://sensesofcinema.com/2002/cteq/Švankmajer/.

Bruyn, Dirk. "Re-Animating the Lost Objects of Childhood and the Everyday: Jan Švankmajer." *Senses of Cinema: Cinémathèque Annotations on Film* 14. June 2001. http://sensesofcinema.com/2001/cteq/Švankmajer/.

Bryant, Levi, Nick Srnicek, and Graham Harman, eds. *The Speculative Turn: Continental Materialism and Realism*. Melbourne: re.press, 2011.

Bryksenkova, Yelena. *Alice in Wonderland Unfolded*. Santa Fe: Rock Point, 2015.

Budd, Mike, and Max H. Kirsch. *Rethinking Disney: Private Control, Public Dimensions*. Middletown: Wesleyan University Press, 2005.

Burton, Tim. "Comic-Con: Tim Burton Talks *Alice* and *The Jabberwocky*, Taking on *Dark Shadows*." *HitFix*. 23 July 2009. http://www.hitfix.com/articles/comic-con-tim-burton-talks-alice-and-the-jabberwocky-taking-on-dark-shadows.

Burton, Tim. "Finding Alice Featurette." *Alice in Wonderland*. DVD. Walt Disney Studios Home Entertainment, 2010.

Burton, Tim, dir. *Alice in Wonderland*. Written by Linda Woolverton. Walt Disney Studios Motion Pictures, 2010.

Bus, Adriana G., and S.B. Neuman, eds. *Multimedia and Literacy Development: Improving Achievement for Young Learners*. New York: Taylor & Francis Group, 2010.

Butler, Judith. *Gender Trouble: Feminism and the Subversion of Identity*. New York: Routledge, 1990.

Butler, Rex. "Polixeni Papapetrou." Polixeni Papapetrou's Website. 2001. http://www.polixenipapapetrou.net/text.php?txt=RB_PolixeniPapapetrou&cat=On_Polixeni_Papapetrou.

Bye, Susan. Education Resource Kit: "Approaches to Alice in Wonderland." 2010. http://www.acmi.net.au/global/docs/ed-kit-burton-alice.pdf.

Callaghan, Dylan. "Wonder Woman: An Interview with *Alice in Wonderland*'s Linda Woolverton." Writers' Guild of America, West. 2011. http://www.wga.org/content/default.aspx?id=4004.

Carroll, Lewis. "Alice on the Stage." *The Theatre*. April 1887. Appendix C in *Alice's Adventures in Wonderland*. Ed. Richard Kelly. Peterborough: Broadview, 2011. 223–227.

Carroll, Lewis. *Alice's Adventures Underground*. Manuscript. Add. MS 46700. 1864. British Library Online Gallery Virtual Books. http://www.bl.uk/onlinegallery/ttp/alice/accessible/introduction.html.

Carroll, Lewis. (1865, 1871). *The Annotated Alice. The Definitive Edition*, including *Alice's Adventures in Wonderland* and *Through the Looking-Glass, and What Alice Found There*. Ed. Martin Gardner. London: Penguin, 2001.

Carroll, Lewis. *The Annotated Alice: 150th Anniversary Deluxe Edition*. Eds. Martin Gardner and Mark Burstein. New York: Norton, 2015.

Carroll, Lewis. *The Complete Illustrated Works of Lewis Carroll*. London: Chancellor, 1996.

Carroll, Lewis. *Curiosa Mathematica: A New Theory of Parallels*. London: Macmillan, 1892.

Carroll, Lewis. (1880–1885). *The Mathematical Recreations of Lewis Carroll: Pillow Problems and a Tangled Tale*. New York: Dover, 1958.

Carroll, Lewis. (1890). *Nursery Alice*. London: Macmillan Children's Books, 2010.

Carroll, Lewis. *The Selected Letters of Lewis Carroll*. Ed. Morton Cohen. London: Macmillan, 1989.

Carroll, Lewis. (1889). *Sylvie and Bruno*. Middlesex: Echo Library, 2008.

Carter, Angela. "Alice in Prague or the Curious Room." *Burning Your Boats: The Collected Short Stories*. London: Penguin, 1995. 397–408.

Carter, Angela. "Introduction to the Curious Room." *On Strangeness*. Ed. Margaret Bridges. Tübingen: Gunter Narr Verlag, 1990. 215–217.

Carter, Angela. "Notes from the Frontline." *On Gender and Writing*. Ed. Michelene Wandor. London: Pandora, *1983*. 69–77.

Carter, Angela. *The Sadeian Woman and the Ideology of Pornography*. New York: Pantheon, 1978.

Carter, Angela. "Wolf-Alice." *The Bloody Chamber*. New York: Penguin, 1979. 119–126.

Cartmell, Deborah, I.Q. Hunter, Heidi Kaye, and Imelda Whelenan. *Classics in Film and Fiction*. London: Pluto, 2000.

Casasanto, Daniel, and Katinka Dijkstra. "Motor Action and Emotional Memory." *Cognition* 115 (2010): 179–185.

Catone, Josh. "Why Printed Books Will Never Die." *Mashable*. 16 January 2013. http://mashable.com/2013/01/16/e-books-vs-print/.

Cherry, Brigid. "Dark Wonders and the Gothic Sensibility: Jan Švankmajer's *Něco z Alenky* (*Alice*, 1987)." *KinoEye: New Perspectives on European Film* 2.1 (7 January 2002). http://www.kinoeye.org/02/01/cherry01.php#7.

Childers, Doug. "Dark Secrets Underground: Katie Roiphe's *Still She Haunts Me*." *The Wag: A Magazine for Decadent Readers*. 2001. http://www.thewag.net/books/roiphe.htm.

Chin, Unsuk, music, dir. *Alice in Wonderland*. Written by David Henry Hwang. Munich Opera Festival, 30 June 2007.

Cixous, Hélène, and Marie Maclean. "Introduction to Lewis Carroll's *Through the Looking-Glass* and *The Hunting of the Snark*." Trans. Marie Maclean. *New Literary History* 13.2 (Winter 1982): 231–251.

Clarke, Jeremy. "Jan Švankmajer: Puppetry's Dark Poet." *Cinefantastique* 26.3 (April 1995): 54–57.

Coats, Karen. "Between Horror, Humour, and Hope: Neil Gaiman and the Psychic Work of the Gothic." In *The Gothic in Children's Literature*. Eds. Anna Jackson, et al. New York: Routledge, 2008. 77–93.

Cohen, Morton, and Edward Wakeling, eds. *Lewis Carroll and His Illustrators: Collaborations and Correspondence, 1865–1898*. Ithaca: Cornell University Press, 2003.

Cohen, Morton N. *Lewis Carroll: A Biography*. New York: Knopf, 1995.

Cohn, Dorrit. *Transparent Minds: Narrative Modes for Presenting Consciousness in Fiction*. Princeton: Princeton University Press, 1984.

Collingwood, Stuart Dodgson. (1898). *The Life and Letters of Lewis Carroll*. Charleston: BiblioBazaar, 2008.

Comolli, Jean-Louis. "Machines of the Visible." *The Cinematic Apparatus*. Ed. Teresa De Lauretis and Steven Heath. New York: St. Martin's, 1980. 121–142.

Conboy, Katie, Nadia Medina, and Sarah Stanbury, eds. *Writing on the Body: Female Embodiment and Feminist Theory*. New York: Columbia University Press, 1997.

Cook, John R. *Dennis Potter: A Life on Screen*. Manchester: Manchester University Press, 1998.

Cullin, Mitch. *Tideland*. Chester Springs, PA: Dufour, 2000.

Curtis, Neil, ed. *The Pictorial Turn*. New York: Routledge, 2010.

Czirák, Ádám. *Kortárs táncelméletek*. (*Contemporary Theories of Dance*.) Budapest: Kijárat, 2012.

Dalí, Salvador. *Alice's Adventures in Wonderland*. Princeton: Princeton University Press/National Museum of Mathematics, 2015.

Daniel, Carolyn. *Voracious Children: Who Eats Whom in Children's Literature*. New York: Routledge, 2006.

Davis, Richard Brian, and William Irwin, eds. *Alice in Wonderland and Philosophy: Curiouser and Curiouser*. Hoboken, NJ: John Wiley & Sons, 2010.

Day, David, ed. *Alice's Adventures in Wonderland Decoded: The Full Text of Lewis Carroll's Novel with its Many Hidden Meanings Revealed*. Toronto: Doubleday Canada, 2015.

Debord, Guy. (1967). *The Society of Spectacle*. Trans. Fredy Perlman and Jon Supak. Kalamazoo, MI: Black & Red, 1970.

De Lauretis, Teresa. "Preface." *Alice Doesn't: Feminism, Semiotics, Cinema*. Bloomington: Indiana University Press, 1984. vii.

Deleuze, Gilles. (1969). *The Logic of Sense*. New York: Continuum, 2001.

Del Toro, Guillermo, dir. *Pan's Labyrinth*. Written by del Toro. Estudios Picasso, Warner Bros., 2006.

Del Tredici, David. (1969). *An Alice Symphony*. Text by Lewis Carroll. Tanglewood Music Festival, 1991.

Dierbeck, Lisa. *One Pill Makes You Smaller*. New York: Picador, 2004.

Dimitra, Fimi. "After 150 Years We Still Haven't Solved the Puzzle of *Alice in Wonderland*." *The Conversation*. 3 July 2015. https://theconversation.com/after-150-years-we-still-havent-solved-the-puzzle-of-alice-in-wonderland.

Disham, Lydia. "Alice for iPad Co-Creator Chris Stevens on Risk and Rabbitholes." *InnovationAgents*. 12 October 2010. http://www.fastcompany.com/1694027/alice-ipad-co-creator-chris-stevens-risk-and-rabbit-holes.

Disney, Walt, prod. *Alice in Wonderland*. Directed by Clyde Geronimi, et al. Written by Winston Hibler et al. Walt Disney Studios, 1951.

Disney, Walt, and Ub Iwerks. *Alice Comedies*. 57 episodes. Laugh-O-Gram Films/ Winkler Productions. See The Big Cartoon Database. 1923–27. http://www.bcdb.com/cartoons/Other_Studios/W/M__J__Winkler_Productions/Alice_Comedies/.

Disneyland Park Paris. *Alice's Curious Labyrinth*. Hedge maze operating in Paris since 12 April 1992.

Disneyland Theme Park Dark Ride. *Alice in Wonderland*. Operating in Anaheim, California, since 14 June 1958. WED Enterprises Design. Duration 3:38.

Dixon, Dave. *Curious Alice*. The National Institute of Mental Health, 1968.

Douglas-Fairhurst, Robert. *The Story of Alice: Lewis Carroll and the Secret History of Wonderland*. Cambridge: Harvard University Press, 2015.

Duckworth, A.R. "Influential Theorists: André Bazin and the Myth of Total Cinema." *The Motley View: Journal of Film, Art, Aesthetics*. 6 April 2009.

Ducornet, Rikki. (1994). *The Jade Cabinet*. Normal, IL: Dalkey Archive, 1997.

Dunn, George A., and Brian McDonald. "Six Impossible Things Before Breakfast." *Alice in Wonderland in Philosophy: Curiouser and Curiouser*. Ed. Richard Brian Davis. Hoboken, NJ: John Wiley & Sons, 2010. 61–79.

Du Plessis, Rachel Blau. *Writing Beyond the Ending: Narrative Strategies of Twentieth-Century Women Writers*. Bloomington: Indiana University Press, 1985.

Durchholz, Daniel, and Gary Graff, eds. *Musichound Rock: The Essential Album Guide*. London: Omnibus, 1998.

Dusinberre, Juliet. *Alice to the Lighthouse: Children's Books and Radical Experiments in Art*. New York: St. Martin's, 1999.

Eco, Umberto. *Opera Aperta*. London: Hutchinson Radius, 1989.

Egan, Kieran. "A Very Short History of Imagination." *Imagination in Teaching and Learning: Ages 8 to 15*. New York: Routledge, 1992.

Eklund, Tof. "A Magical Realism of the Fuck." *ImageTexT: Interdisciplinary Comics Studies* 3.3 (2007).

Empson, William. "Alice in Wonderland: The Child as Swain." *Some Versions of the Pastoral*. London: Chatto & Windus, 1935. In *Aspects of Alice*. Ed. Robert Phillips. New York: Vintage, 1977. 344–377.

Ennis, Mary Louise. "Alice in Wonderland." In *The Oxford Companion to Fairy Tales: The Western Fairy Tale Tradition from Medieval to Modern*. Ed. Jack Zipes. Oxford: Oxford University Press, 2000. 10–12.

Enzerink, Suzanne. "Trouble in Wonderland, or the Crisis of the Fairy Tale in Film." *PopMatters*. 30 May 2011. http://www.popmatters.com/column/141301-trouble-in-wonderland-or-the-crisis-of-the-fairytale-in-film/P0/.

Faber, Michel. "Released at Last: Review of *Lost Girls*." *The Guardian*. 5 January 2008. http://www.theguardian.com/books/2008/jan/05/comics.

Fanfiction.net. "Once Upon a Time in Wonderland." Database. 2013.

Fensch, Thomas. (1968). "Lewis Carroll—The First Acidhead." In *Aspects of Alice*. Ed. Robert Phillips. New York: Vintage, 1977. 421–425.

Feyersinger, Erwin. "Diegetic Short Circuits: Metalepsis in Animation." *Animation: An Interdisciplinary Journal* 5 (2010): 279–294.

Fiske, John. "The Cultural Economy of Fandom." In *Adoring Audience: Fan Culture and Popular Media*. Ed. Lisa A. Lewis. New York: Routledge, 1992. 30–50.

Fitzgerald, Michael. *Autism and Creativity: Is There a Link Between Autism in Men and Exceptional Creativity?* Hove and New York: Brunner-Routledge, 2004.

Fleischer, Dave, dir. *Betty in Blunderland*. Fleischer Studios. 1934.

Fleming, Laura. "Expanding Learning Opportunities with Transmedia Practices: Inanimate Alice as an Exemplar." *The Journal of Media Literacy Education* 5.2 (2013): 370–377.

Fordyce, Rachel, and Carla Marello. *Semiotics and Linguistics in Alice's Worlds*. Berlin and New York: Walter de Gruyter, 1994.

Foucault, Michel. *The History of Sexuality, Volume I: An Introduction*. Trans. Robert Hurley. New York: Pantheon, 1978.

Foucault, M. (1967). "Of Other Places, Heterotopias." Trans. Jay Miskowiec. *Foucault.Info*. http://foucault.info/documents/heteroTopia/foucault.heteroTopia.en.html.

Foucault, Michel. *Power/Knowledge: Selected Interviews and Other Writings, 1972–1977*. Trans. Ed. Colin Gordon. New York: Pantheon, 1980.

Francke, Lizzie. "On Gavin Millar's *Dreamchild*." *The Observer*. 6 December 2009.

Frankova, Milada. "Angela Carter's Mannerism in Rudolph II's Curious Room." *Brno Studies in English* 25 (1999): 127–133.

French, Philip. "Review of *Alice in Wonderland*." *The Guardian*. 7 March 2010. http://www.guardian.co.uk/film/2010/mar/07/alice-in-wonderland-review.

Freud, Sigmund. "Fetishism." *The Complete Psychological Works of Sigmund Freud*. Vol. XXI. Trans. James Strachey. London: Hogarth, 1927. 147–157.

Freud, Sigmund. (1905). *Jokes and Their Relation to the Unconscious*. New York: Norton, 1989.

Freud, Sigmund. (1919). "The Uncanny." ("Das Unheimliche.") Trans. Ed. James Strachey. *The Standard Edition of the Complete Psychological Works of Sigmund Freud*. Vol. XVII. London: Hogarth, 1953. 219–252.

Fricke, David. "Review of Tom Waits' *Alice*." *Rolling Stone*. 25 April 2002. http://www.rollingstone.com/music/albumreviews/alice-20020425#ixzz2rshMw3Wg.

Frigerio, Francesca. "Out of Focus: A Portrait of Charles Lutwidge Dodgson, a.k.a. Lewis *Carroll*." In *Strange Sisters: Literature and Aesthetics in the Nineteenth Century*. Eds. Francesca Orestano and Francesca Frigerio. Bern: Peter Lang, 2009. 137–155.

Gaiman, Neil. *Coraline*. London: Bloomsbury, 2002.

Gaiman, Neil. "Introduction." *Coraline and Other Stories*. London: Bloomsbury, 2009.

Garcia, Camille Rose, and Lewis Carroll. *Alice's Adventures in Wonderland*. New York: Harper Design, 2010.

Gardner, Martin, Francine Abeles, Warren Weaver, Gillian Beer, and Lewis Carroll. *Mathematical Wonderlands: Lewis Carroll, The Alice Books, and Beyond*. Nature ebook, 2015.

Genette, Gérard. *Palimpsests: Literature in the Second Degree*. Trans. Channa Newman and Claude Doubinsky. Lincoln: University of Nebraska Press, 1997.

Gerard, Jasper. "Heston Blumenthal: My New Alice in Wonderland Menu." *The Telegraph*. 1 June 2009.

Gernsheim, Helmut. *Lewis Carroll, Photographer*. New York: Dover, 1969.

Gil, José. "The Dancer's Body." Trans. Karen Ocana. In *A Shock to Thought: Expressions after Deleuze & Guattari*. Ed. Brian Massumi. New York: Routledge, 2005. 117–148.

Gilead, Sarah. "Magic Abjured: Closure in Children's Fantasy Fiction." *PMLA* 106.2 (March 1991): 277–293.

Gilliam, Terry. "Ask Terry Gilliam." *Dreams: The Terry Gilliam Fanzine*. June-July 2006. http://www.smart.co.uk/dreams/askterry.htm.

Gilliam, Terry. "An Introduction to Tideland." 2007. http://www.youtube.com/watch?v=aRcvDaw0WB4.

Gilliam, Terry, dir. *Jabberwocky*. Python Films, Umbrella Films. Columbia Warner Distributors, 1977.

Gilliam, Terry, dir. *Tideland*. Written by Tony Grisoni and Terry Gilliam. Recorded Picture Company, 2005.

Giroux, Henry A., and Grace Pollock. *The Mouse that Roared: Disney and the End of Innocence*. Plymouth: Rowman and Littlefield, 2010.

Golasowski, Viviane. "Étude transmédiatique du genre: entre stéréotypes et modernités dans les fictions sérielles se réclamant des contes merveilleux (l'univers de *Once Upon a Time*)." *Colloque Internationale Genre en Séries*. Conference organized by Université Bordeaux Montaigne. 26–27 March 2014.

Goldschmidt, A.M.E. (1933). "Alice in Wonderland Psycho-Analysed." *New Oxford Outlook* 1.1 (May 1933). In *Aspects of Alice*. Ed. Robert Phillips. New York: Vintage, 1977. 279–283.

Goodacre, Selwyn, ed. *Elucidating Alice: A Textual Commentary on Alice's Adventures in Wonderland*. Woodgrove: Evertype, 2015.

Gooding, Richard. "'Something Very Old and Very Slow': Coraline, Uncanniness, and Narrative Form." *Children's Literature Association Quarterly* 33.4 (2008): 390–407.

Grant, Stephanie. *Passion of Alice*. New York: Bantam, 1996.

Gravett, Paul. "Creator Profile: Melinda Gebbie." Paul Gravett's Comics, Graphic Novel, Manga Website Sponsored by Escape Books, 2008. http://www.paulgravett.com/index.php/profiles/creator/melinda_gebbie.

Green, Roger Lancelyn. (1960). "Alice." In *Aspects of Alice*. Ed. Robert Phillips. New York: Vintage, 1977. 13–39.

Greenacre, Phyllis. *Swift and Carroll: A Psychoanalytical Study of Two Lives*. New York: International University Press, 1955. Extract in *Aspects of Alice*. Ed. Robert Phillips. New York: Vintage, 1977. 316–332.

Greenhill, Pauline, and Sidney Eve Matrix. "Envisioning Ambiguity: Fairy Tale Films." In Greenhill and Matrix, eds. 2010. 1–23.

Greenhill, Pauline, and Sidney Eve Matrix, eds. *Fairy Tale Film: Visions of Ambiguity*. Logan: Utah State University Press, 2010.

Grønstad, Asbjørn, and Øyvind Vågnes. "What Do Pictures Want? An Interview with W.J.T. Mitchell." *Image & Narrative*. November 2006. Online Center for Visual Studies: http://www.visual-studies.com/interviews/mitchell.html.

Gubar, Marah. *Artful Dodgers: Reconceiving the Golden Age of Children's Literature*. Oxford: Oxford University Press, 2010.

Guiliano, Edward, ed. *Lewis Carroll: A Celebration: Essays on the Occasion of the 150th Anniversary of the Birth of Charles Lutwidge Dodgson*. New York: Clarkson Potter, 1982.

Guillemin, Grégoire Léon. *The Secret Life of Heroes*. 2013. http://www.greg-guillemin.com.

Hacking, Juliet. "The Eroticised Victorian Child: Mrs. Holford's Daughter." In *Understanding Art Objects: Thinking Through the Eye*. Ed. Tony Godfrey. Farnham: Lund Humphries, 2009. 93–103.

Halberstam, Judith. *Female Masculinity*. Durham: Duke University Press, 1998.

Hamel, Keith James. "Modernity and Mise-en-scene: Terry Gilliam and *Brazil*." *Images: Journal of Film and Popular Culture* 6 25 February 2004). http://www.imagesjournal.com/issue06/features/brazil.htm.

Hames, Peter. "The Core of Reality: Puppets in the Feature Film of Jan Švankmajer." in Hames, ed., 2008. 83–104.

Hames, Peter. "Interview with Jan Švankmajer." In Hames, ed., 2008. 104–140.

Hames, Peter. "Švankmajer's Alice." *Electric Sheep Magazine*. Autumn 2008.

Hames, Peter, ed. (1995). *Dark Alchemy: The Films of Jan Švankmajer*. London: Wallflower, 2008.

Hancher, Michael. "Punch and Alice: Through Tenniel's Looking-Glass." In *Lewis Carroll: A Celebration*. Ed. Edward Guiliano. New York: Clarkson Potter, 1982. 28–38.

Hancher, Michael. *The Tenniel Illustrations to the "Alice" Books*. Columbus: Ohio State University Press, 1985.

Hanke, Ken. *Tim Burton: An Unauthorized Biography of the Filmmaker*. New York: St. Martin's, 2000.

Hanson, Matt. *The End of Celluloid: Film Futures in the Digital Age*. Brighton: Rotovision, 2003.

Hargreaves, Alice Liddell. "Alice's Recollections of Carrollian Days." In *Alice in Wonderland*, 2d ed. Ed. Donald J, Gray. New York: Norton, 1992. 273–278.

Hart, Hugh. "Match Made in *Wonderland*: Danny Elfman's Music, Tim Burton's Freaks." *Wired*. 3 March 2010. http://www.wired.com/underwire/2010/03/alice-danny-elfman/.

Harvey-Brown, Jodi. Book Sculpture Website. 2012. http://www.jodiharvey-brown.com.

Hatch, Evelyn, ed. *A Selection from the Letters of Lewis Carroll (the Rev. Charles Lutwidge Dodgson) to his Child-Friends; Together with "Eight or nine wise words about letter-writing."* London: Macmillan, 1933.

Haughton, Hugh. "Introduction." In *The Centenary Edition of Alice's Adventures in Wonderland and Through the Looking-Glass and What Alice Found There*. London: Penguin, 1998. ix–lxvi.

Heath, Peter. *The Philosopher's Alice: The Thinking Man's Guide to a Misunderstood Nursery Classic*. London: Academy, 1974.

Hello Kitty, and Timeless Tales, vol. 3. DVD. *Hello Kitty in Wonderland*. Sanrio Japan, 2004.

Hennard Dutheil de la Rochère, Martine. "From Bloody Chamber to cabinet de curiosités: Angela Carter's 'Alice in Prague or The Curious Room.'" Wonderlands Conference paper. Université de Lausanne. 9 December 2014.

Hennard Dutheil de la Rochère, Martine. *Reading, Translating, Rewriting: Angela Carter's Translational Poetics*. Detroit: Wayne State University Press, 2013.

Hepworth, Cecil, and Percy Stow, dir. *Alice in Wonderland*. Written by Cecil Hepworth. American Mutoscope and Biograph Company, Edison Manifacturing Company, Kleine Optical Company, 1903.

Herold, Charles. "Game Theory: Down a Rabbit Hole to a Dark Wonderland." *New York Times*, 21 December 2000: G9.

Hill, Dan. Review of Tom Waits' *Alice*. BBC, 2002. http://www.bbc.co.uk/music/reviews/6nvr.

Hollingsworth, Christopher. "Improvising Spaces: Victorian Narrative, Carollian Narrative, and Modern Collage." In Hollingsworth, ed., 2009. 85–101.

Hollingsworth, Cristopher, ed. *Alice Beyond Wonderland: Essays for the Twenty-First Century*. Iowa City: University of Iowa Press, 2009.

Homes, A.M. *The End of Alice*. London: Anchor UK, 1996.

Hong, Jeff. Unhappily Ever After Website. 2014–2015. disneyunhappilyeverafter.tumblr.com.

Hudson, Derek. *Lewis Carroll*. London: Longmans, 1966.

Hudson, Mark. "Alice in Wonderland, British Library, Review: 'Really Fascinating.'" *Telegraph*. 19 November 2015.

Hume, Kathryn. *Fantasy and Mimesis: Responses to Reality in Western Literature*. New York: Methuen, 1984.

Hutcheon, Linda. *Narcissistic Narrative: The Metafictional Paradox*. New York: Routledge, 1984.

Imholtz, August, and Alison Tannenbaum. *Alice Eats Wonderland: An Irreverent Annotated Cookbook Adventure*. Carlisle: Applewood, 2009.

Irigaray, Luce. (1977). "The Looking-Glass from the Other Side." *This Sex Which Is Not One*. Trans. Catherine Porter and Carolyn Burke. New York: Cornell University Press, 1985. 9–23.

Israel, Kali. "Asking Alice: Victorian and Other Alices in Contemporary Culture." *Victorian Afterlife: Postmodern Culture Rewrites the Nineteenth Century*. Eds. John Kucich and Dianne F. Sadoff. Minneapolis: University of Minnesota Press, 2000. 252–288.

Jackson, Anna. 2008. "Uncanny Hauntings, Canny Children." In Jackson, et al., eds., 2008. 157–177.

Jackson, Anna, Karen Coats, and Roderick McGillis, eds. *The Gothic in Children's Literature: Haunting the Borders*. New York: Routledge, 2008.

Jackson, Rosemary. *Fantasy: The Literature of Subversion*. London: Methuen, 1981.

Jackson, Wendy. "The Surrealist Conspirator: An Interview with Jan Švankmajer." *Animation World Magazine* 2.3 (June 1997). http://www.awn.com/mag/issue2.3/issue2.3pages/2.3jacksonŠvankmajer.html.

Jaques, Zoe, and Eugene Giddens. *Lewis Carroll's Alice's Adventures in Wonderland and Through the Looking-Glass: A Publishing History*. Burlington: Ashgate, 2013.

Jenkins, Henry. *Convergence Culture: Where Old and New Media Collide*. New York: New York University Press, 2006.

Jenkins, Henry. "Transmedia Storytelling." Confessions of an Aca-Fan: The Official Weblog of Henry Jenkins. 22 March 2007. http://henryjenkins.org/2007/03/transmedia_storytelling_101.html.

Jenkins, Henry, and David Thorburn, eds. *Rethinking Media Change: The Aesthetics of Transition*. Cambridge: MIT Press, 2003.

Johnston, Andrew. "Wielding a Magic of Uncanny Images: Jan Svankmajer's Film." *The New York Times*, 1 July 2001. http://www.nytimes.com/2001/07/01/movies/film-wielding-a-magic-of-uncanny-images.html.

Joyce, James. "Lolita in Humberland." *Studies in the Novel* 6.3 (Fall 1974): 339–348.

Kaplan, Lisa H. "Soaring to New (?) Heights: Cute, Tough, Geek Girls and Post-Feminist Discourse."

In *It Happens at Comic-Con: Ethnographic Essays on a Pop Culture Phenomenon*. Eds. Ben Bolling and Matthew J. Smith. Jefferson, NC: McFarland, 2014. 53–64.

Keeling, K. Kara, and Scott Pollard. "The Key Is the Mouth: Food and Orality in *Coraline*." *Children's Literature* 40 (2012): 1–27.

Kelly, Richard. "'If you don't know what a Gryphon is': Text and Illustration in *Alice's Adventures in Wonderland*." In *Lewis Carroll: A Celebration*. Ed. Edward Guiliano. New York: Clarkson Potter, 1982. 52–62.

Kelly, Richard. "Introduction." *Alice's Adventures in Wonderland by Lewis Carroll*. Ed. Richard Kelly. Peterborough: Broadview, 2011. 9–51.

Kennedy, Randy. "A Girl Keeps Growing: Looking at the Birth of Lewis Carroll's 'Alice,' 150 Years Old." *The New York Times*. 26 June 2015: C19.

Kérchy, Anna. "Ambiguous Alice: Making Sense of Lewis Carroll's Nonsense Fantasies." In *Does It Really Mean That? Interpreting the Literary Ambiguous*. Eds. Janka Kaščáková and Kathleen Dubbs. Newcastle upon Thyne: Cambridge Scholars, 2011. 104–121.

Kérchy, Anna. *Body-Texts in the Novels of Angela Carter: Writing from a Corporeagraphic Point of View*. Lewiston, Lampeter: Edwin Mellen, 2008.

Kérchy, Anna. "Changing Media of Enchantment: Tracking the Transition from Verbal to Visual Nonsense in Tim Burton's Cinematic Adaptation of Alice in Wonderland." *Americana* 8.1 (Spring 2012).

Kérchy, Anna. "Nonsensical Disenchantment and Imaginative Reluctance in Postmodern Rewritings of Lewis Carroll's Alice Tales." In *Anti-Tales: The Uses of Disenchantment*. Eds. Catriona Fay McAra and David Calvin. Newcastle upon Thyne: Cambridge Scholars, 2011. 62–75.

Kérchy, Anna. "Stammering, Somniloquy and Somatized Semiosis: (Un)making Sense of Nonsense in Lewis Carroll's Alice Tales." In *The Language of Sense, Common Sense and Nonsense*. Eds. Ewa Borkowska, Tomasz Burzynski, and Maciej Nowak. Bielsko-Biala: Wydawnictwo WSEH, 2012. 43–54.

Kérchy, Anna, ed. *Postmodern Reinterpretations of Fairy Tales: How Applying New Methods Generates New Meanings*. Lewiston, Lampeter: Edwin Mellen, 2011.

Kidd, Kenneth. "Down the Rabbit Hole: ImageSexT: A Roundtable on Lost Girls." *ImageTexT: Interdisciplinary Comics Studies* 3.3 (2007). http://www.english.ufl.edu/imagetext/archives/v3_3/lost_girls/kidd.shtml.

Kincaid, James R. "Alice's Invasion of Wonderland." *PMLA* 88.1 (January 1973): 92–99.

Kincaid, James R. *Child-Loving: The Erotic Child and Victorian Culture*. New York: Routledge, 1992.

Kiss, Attila Atilla. *The Semiotics of Revenge: Subjectivity and Abjection in English Renaissance Tragedy*. Szeged: JATE, 1995.

Kiss Attila, and György Szőnyi, eds. "Introduction." *The Iconography of the Fantastic*. Szeged: Jate, 2002. 21–30.

Kitsis, Edward, and Adam Horowitz, et al., dir. *Once Upon a Time in Wonderland*. ABC Studios Fantasy Drama Series, 2013.

Klein, Melanie. *The Psychology of Children*. London: Hogarth, 1932.

Knoepflmacher, U.C. "The Balancing of Child and Adult: An Approach to Victorian Fantasies for Children." *Nineteenth-Century Fiction* 37.4 (March 1983): 497–530.

Kövecses, Zoltán. *Metaphor and Emotion: Language, Culture, and Body in Human Feeling*. Cambridge: Cambridge University Press, 2000.

Kristeva, Julia. *Powers of Horror: An Essay on Abjection*. Trans. Leon S. Roudiez. New York: Columbia University Press, 1982.

Kristeva, Julia. *Revolution in Poetic Language*. Trans. Margaret Waller. New York: Columbia University Press, 1984.

Kucich, John, and Dianne F. Sadoff, eds. *Victorian Afterlife. Postmodern Culture Rewrites the Nineteenth Century*. Minneapolis: University of Minnesota Press, 2000.

Kukkonen, Karin, and Sonja Klimek, eds. *Metalepsis in Popular Culture*. Berlin: De Gruyter, 2011.

Kusama, Yayoi. *Lewis Carroll's Alice's Adventures in Wonderland with Artwork by Yayoi Kusama*. London: Penguin Classics, 2012.

Lacan, Jacques. (1949). "The Mirror Stage as Formative of the Function of the I as Revealed in Psychoanalytic Experience." Trans. Alan Sheridan. *Modern Literary Theory: A Reader*. Eds. Philip Rice and Patricia Waugh. London: Edward Arnold, 1992. 189–195.

Lacombe, Benjamin. *Il était une fois… (Once Upon a Time…) Pop-Up Book*. Paris: Seuil Jeunesse, 2010.

Lacombe, Benjamin. Illustrations for Lewis Carroll. *Alice au Pays de Merveilles*. Trans. Henri Parisot. Paris: Métamorphose/ Soleil, 2015.

Lane, Anthony. "Go Ask Alice: What Really Went on in Wonderland." *The New Yorker*. 8 June 2015. www.newyorker.com/magazine/2015/06/go-ask-alice-a-critic-at-lare-lane.

Leach, Elsie. "Alice in Wonderland in Perspective." In *Aspects of Alice*. Ed. Robert Phillips. New York: Vintage, 1977. 91–92.

Leach, Karoline. *In the Shadow of the Dreamchild: The Myth and Reality of Lewis Carroll*. London: Peter Owen, 2009.

Lebailly, Hugues. "Dodgson and the Victorian Cult of the Child: A Reassessment on the Hundredth Anniversary of Lewis Carroll's Death." *The Carrollian: The Lewis Carroll Journal* 4 (Autumn 1999): 3–31.

Lecercle, Jean-Jacques. *Philosophy of Nonsense: The Intuitions of Victorian Nonsense Literature*. New York: Routledge, 1994.

Leclerc, Michel, and Bertrand Schmitt, dir. *Les Chimères des Svankmajer*. Studo Chalet Pointu, 2001.

Lee, Newton, and Krystina Madej. *Disney Stories: Getting to Digital*. New York: Springer, 2012.

Leibovitz, Annie. "Alice in Wonderland Fashion Editorial." *Vogue USA*. December 2003.

Leitch, Thomas. *Film Adaptation and Its Discontents*. Baltimore: John Hopkins University Press, 2007.

Lessing, Gotthold Ephraim. (1766). *Laocoön: An Essay on the Limits of Painting and Poetry*. Trans. Edward Allen McCormick. Baltimore: Johns Hopkins University Press, 1984.

Lethem, Jonathan. *As She Climbed Across the Table*. New York: Doubleday, 1997.

Levasseur, Aran. "The Literacy of Gaming: What Kids Learn from Playing." *MediaShift: Your Guide to the Digital Media Revolution*. 3 August 2011.

Levere, Jane L. "Stampeding Down the Rabbit Hole." *The New York Times*. 19 March 2015: F4.

Lewis, C.S. (1952, 1966). "Three Ways of Writing for Children." *Of Other Worlds: Essays and Stories*. New York: Houghton, Mifflin, Harcourt, 1994. 22–35.

Lewis, Lisa A. *Adoring Audience: Fan Culture and Popular Media*. New York: Routledge, 1992.

Lim, Keith. Jabberwocky Variations Website. http://www76.pair.com/keithlim/jabberwocky/.

Lindseth, Jon, Allan Tannenbaum, and the Lewis Carroll Society. Alice in 150 Languages. Alice in a World of Wonderlands Website. http://aliceinaworldofwonderlands.com/.

Lindseth, Jon A., and Allan Tannenbaum, eds. *Alice in a World of Wonderlands: The Translations of Lewis Carroll's Masterpiece*. New Castle: Oak Knoll, 2015.

Loeb, Jeph, and Tim Sale. "Madness." *Haunted Knight 2*. New York: DC Comics, 1996.

Louvel, Liliane. *Poetics of the Iconotext*. Ed. Karen Jacobs. Trans. Laurence Petit. Farnham, Surrey, UK, and Burlington, VT: Ashgate, 2011.

Lyotard, Jean-Francois. *The Postmodern Condition: A Report on Knowledge*. Trans. Geoffrey Bennington. Minneapolis: University of Minnesota Press, 1984.

Maguire, Gregory. *After Alice: A Novel*. New York: William Morrow, 2015.

Maltby, Richard. "Nobody Knows Everything: Post-Classical Historiographies and Consolidated Entertainment." *In Contemporary Hollywood Cinema*. Eds. Steve Neale and Murray Smith. New York: Routledge, 1998. *21–46*.

Manning, Kara M. "From Wonderland to Looking-Glass Land." *Victorians Institute Journal Annex* 41 (2013). Nineteenth Century Scholarship Online. http://www.nines.org/print_exhibit/979.

Manning, Kara M. "'That's the effect of living backwards': Technological Change, Lewis Carroll's *Alice* Books, and Tim Burton's *Alice in Wonderland*." *Neo-Victorian Studies* 4.2 (2011): 154–179.

Manovich, Lev. "Assembling Reality: Myths of Computer Graphics." *Afterimage* 20.2 (September 1992): 12–14.

Manovich, Lev. "The Practice of Everyday Media Life." *Lev Manovich's Website*. 2008. http://manovich.net/index.php/projects/the-practice-of-everyday-media-life.

Manovich, Lev. "'Reality' effects in computer animation." *In A Reader in Animation Studies*. Ed. *Jayne Pilling*. London: John Libbey, 1997. *5–16*.

Manson, Marilyn, dir. *Phantasmagoria: The Visions of Lewis Carroll*. Universal Pictures. Production postponed.

Marcus, Laura: "How Newness Enters the World: The Birth of Cinema and the Origin of Man." In *Literature and Visual Technologies: Writing After Cinema*. Eds. Julian Murphet and Lydia Rainford. New York: Palgrave Macmillan, 2003. 29–45.

Marin, Louis. "Disneyland: A Degenerate Utopia." *Glyph* 1 (1977): 61.

Marinovich-Resch, Sarolta. "Interrogating the Iconography of the Female Gothic: The Parody of the Female Gothic." In *The Iconography of the Fantastic*. Ed. Kiss Attila, et al. Szeged: Jate, 2002. 257–268.

Marks, Laura U. *The Skin of the Film: Intercultural Cinema, Embodiment and the Senses*. Durham: Duke University Press, 2000.

Marshall, David P. *New Media Cultures*. London: Hodder Arnold, 2004.

Martellaro, John. "Alice for the iPad: A Charming Must Have." *The MacObserver*. 20 January 2012. www.macobserver.com/tmo/review/alice_for_the_ipad_a_charming_must_have.

Martin, Cathlena. "'Wonderland's become quite strange.' From Lewis Carroll's *Alice* to American McGee's *Alice*." In *Beyond Adaptation: Essays on Radical Transformations of Original Works*. Eds. Phyllis Frus and Christy Williams. Jefferson, NC: McFarland, 2010. 133–143.

Matthews, Jack. *Dreaming Brazil* (essay accompanying Criterion Collection DVD release). 1996.

Mavor, Carol. *Pleasures Taken: Performances of Sexuality and Loss in Victorian Photographs*. Durham: Duke University Press, 1995.

McAra, Catriona. "The Embodied Fairy Tales of Samantha Sweeting." *12th ESSE Conference*, Pavol Jozef Šafárik University, Kosice, Slovakia. 2014. "Witch Milk. Samantha Sweeting's Lactation Narratives." *ASAP/Journal*. 1.2. (2016): 261-285.

McAra, Catriona Fay. "Surrealism's Curiosity: Lewis Carroll and the Femme-Enfant." *Papers of Surrealism* 9 (Summer 2011): 1–25. http://www.surrealismcentre.ac.uk/papersofsurrealism/journal9/.

McAra, Catriona Fay, and David Calvin, eds. *Anti-Tales: The Uses of Disenchantment*. Newcastle upon Tyne: Cambridge Scholars, 2011.

McCallum, Robyn, and John Stephens. "Film and Fairy Tales." In *The Oxford Companion to Fairy Tales: The Western Fairy Tale Tradition from Medieval to Modern*. Ed. Jack Zipes. Oxford: Oxford University Press, 2000. 160–164.

McCaw, Kerrie. "Thinking and Talking to Alice: An Antipodean Adventure." In *Beyond Textual Literacy: Visual Literacy for Creative and Critical Inquiry*. Ed. Mary A. Drinkwater. Oxford: Inter-Disciplinary, 2011. 69–81.

McCloud, Scott. *Understanding Comics: The Invisible Art*. New York: Harper Perennial, 1994.

McGee, American. "Alice Kicking Ass on the Big Screen." Kickstarter. 22 July 2013. https://www.

kickstarter.com/projects/spicyhorse/alice-otherlands/posts/545771F1.

McGee, American. *American McGee's Alice*. Computer game. Rogue Entertainment. Electronic Arts, 2000.

McKean, Dave. Illustrations to Neil Gaiman's *Coraline*. London: Bloomsbury, 2002.

McLeod, Norman Z., dir. *Alice in Wonderland*. Written by Joseph L. Mankiewicz. Paramount Pictures, 1933.

McLuhan, Marshall. *The Gutenberg Galaxy: The Making of Typographic Man*. London: Routedge & Kegan Paul, 1962.

Merleau-Ponty, Maurice. *Phenomenology of Perception*. Trans. Colin Smith. London: Routledge and Kegan Paul, 1962.

Millar, Gavin, dir. *Dreamchild*. Written by Dennis Potter. PfH, Thorn EMI, 1985.

Mitchell, W.J.T. *Picture Theory. Essays on Verbal and Visual Representation*. Chicago: University of Chicago Press, 1995.

Mitchell, W.J.T. "The *Unspeakable* and the *Unimaginable*: Word and Image in a Time of Terror." *ELH* 72.2 (Summer 2005): 291–308.

Mitchell, W.J.T. "Word and Image." In *Critical Terms for Art History*. Eds. Robert Nelson and Richard Shiff. Chicago: University of Chicago Press, 1996. 51–62.

Moore, Alan. "Bog Venus Versus Nazi Cock-Ring: Some Thoughts Concerning Pornography." *Arthur Magazine* 1.25 (2006): 32–39.

Moore, Alan, and Melinda Gebbie. *Lost Girls*. Graphic Novel. Top Shelf, 2006.

Morgan, Christopher, ed. *The Pamphlets of Lewis Carroll, Volume 5: And Games, Puzzles, and Related Pieces*. LCSNA/University of Virginia Press, 2015.

Myers, Lindsay. "Moral Panic and 'Stranger Danger' in Henry Selick's *Coraline*." *The Lion and the Unicorn* 36 (2012): 245–257.

Nabokov, Vladimir. "Interview." *Vogue*. December 1966. http://photographyoflewiscarroll.googlepages.com/.

Neale, Steve, and Murray Smith, eds. *Contemporary Hollywood Cinema*. New York: Routledge, 1998.

Nelson, Olympia. "Dark Undercurrents of Teenage Girls' Selfies." *The Age*. 11 July 2013.

Nice, David. "Alice's Adventures in Wonderland: A Ballet in Two Acts. The Royal Ballet." Booklet accompanying the DVD edition, Royal Opera House, 2011.

Nichols, Catherine. *Alice's Wonderland: A Visual Journey through Lewis Carroll's Mad, Mad World*. New York: Race Point, 2014.

Nichols, Shaun. *The Architecture of the Imagination: New Essays on Pretence, Possibility, and Fiction*. Oxford: Oxford University Press, 2006.

Nickel, Douglas R., and Lewis Carroll. *Dreaming in Pictures: The Photography of Lewis Carroll*. New Haven: Yale University Press, 2002.

Nières, Isabelle. "Tenniel: The Logic Behind His Interpretations of the Alice Books." In *Semiotics and Linguistics in Alice's Worlds*. Eds. Rachel Fordyce and Carla Marello. Berlin and New York: Walter de Gruyter, 1994. 194–209.

Nikolajeva, Maria. "Imprints of the Mind: The Depiction of Consciousness in Children's Fiction." *Children's Literature Association Quarterly* 26 (2002): 174–87.

Nikolajeva, Maria, and Carole Scott. *How Picturebooks Work*. New York: Routledge, 2006.

Nodelman, Perry. *The Hidden Adult: Defining Children's Literature*. Baltimore: John Hopkins University Press, 2008.

Nodelman, Perry. *Words About Pictures: The Narrative Art of Children's Picture Books*. Athens: University of Georgia Press, 1988.

Noheden, Kristoffer. "The Imagination of Touch: Surrealist Tactility in the Films of Jan Švankmajer." *Journal of Aesthetics & Culture* 5 (September 2013). http://www.aestheticsandculture.net/index.php/jac/article/view/21111/29896.

Noon, Jeff. *Automated Alice*. London: Crown, 1996.

O'Kane, David. E-mail correspondence with the artist. 12 December 2015.

O'Kane, David. "Lewis Carroll and Alice." Digital photo collage, 2005. David O'Kane's Website. http://www.davidokane.com/photography%20archive.html.

Olson, Debbie C., and Andrew Scahill, eds. *Lost and Othered Children in Contemporary Cinema*. Plymouth: Lexington, 2012.

150Alice: The World's Most Collaborative Artbook. Beijing: Pickatale, 2015.

O'Pray, Michael. (1995). "Jan Švankmajer: A Mannerist Surrealist." In *Dark Alchemy: The Films of Jan Švankmajer*. Ed. Peter Hames. London: Wallflower, 2008. 40–67.

Oxenbury, Helen. Illustrations to Lewis Carroll's *Alice's Adventures in Wonderland*. Cambridge: Candlewick Press, 2003.

Papapetrou, Polixeni. "Trilogy Inspired by Lewis Carroll's Work: *Phantomwise* (2002), *Dreamchild* (2003), *Wonderland* (2004)." Polixeni Papapetrou's Website. http://www.polixenipapapetrou.net.

Parsons, Elizabeth, Naarah Sawers, and Kate McInally. "The Other Mother: Neil Gaiman's Postfeminist Fairy Tales." *Children's Literature Association Quarterly* 33.4 (2008): 371–389.

Peabody, Richard, ed. *Alice Redux: New Stories of Alice, Lewis and Wonderland*. Arlington, VA: Paycock, 2005.

Perrot, Jean. "'Il était une fois...un pop-up pop surréaliste.' Une lecture de Benjamin Lacombe par Jean Perrot." In Benjamin Lacombe, *Il était une fois... (Once Upon a Time...)*. Paris: Seuil Jeunesse, 2010. 19–20.

Phillips, Adam. *The Beast in the Nursery: On Curiosity and Other Appetites*. New York: Vintage, 1999.

Phillips, Robert, ed. *Aspects of Alice. Lewis Carroll's Dreamchild as Seen Through the Critics' Looking-Glasses*. New York: Vintage, 1977.

Pier, John. "Metalepsis." *The Living Handbook of Narratology*. 2013. http://wikis.sub.uni-hamburg.de/lhn/index.php/Metalepsis.

Pilinovsky, Helen. "Body as Wonderland: Alice's

Graphic Iteration in *Lost Girls*." In *Alice Beyond Wonderland*. Ed. Cristopher Hollingsworth. Iowa City: University of Iowa Press, 2009. 175–199.

Pilinovsky, Helen. "*Salon des Fées*: Cyber Salon: Re-Coding the Commodified Fairy Tale." In *Postmodern Reinterpretations of Fairy Tales*. Ed. Anna Kérchy. Lewiston, Lampeter: Edwin Mellen, 2011. 17–33.

Pilling, Jayne, ed. *A Reader in Animation Studies*. London: John Libbey, 1997.

Popova, Maria. "Between Page and Screen: A Digital Pop-up Book about Love." *BrainPickings*. 30 April 2012. http://www.brainpickings.org/index.php/2012/04/30/between-page-and-screen-siglio/.

Pringle, Patricia. "Seeing Impossible Bodies: Fascination as Spatial Experience." *Scan Journal* 1.2 (2004). http://scan.net.au/scan/journal/print.php?journal_id=34&j_id=2.

Project Gutenberg. E-text of *Alice's Adventures in Wonderland* by Lewis Carroll. http://www.gutenberg.org/ebooks/11.

Pullinger, Kate, Chris Joseph dir.; Ian Harper prod. *Inanimate Alice: A Digital Novel*. 2005. http://www.inanimatealice.com/.

Queenan, Joe. *One for the Books*. New York: Penguin, 2012.

Rabinowitz, Peter J. "'What's Hecuba to us?' The Audience's Experience of Literary Borrowing." In *The Reader in the Text*. Eds. Susan R. Suleiman and Inge Crosman. Princeton: Princeton University Press, 1980. 241–63.

Rackin, Donald. "Book Review of Caroline Leach's *In the Shadow of the Dreamchild*." *Victorian Studies* 43.4 (2001): 650–653.

Radway, Janice. *Reading the Romance: Feminism and the Representation of Women in Popular Culture*. Chapel Hill: University of North Carolina Press, 1984.

Ray, Brian. "Tim Burton and the Idea of Fairy Tales." In *Fairy Tale Film: Visions of Ambiguity*. Eds. Pauline Greenhill and Sidney Eve Matrix. Logan: Utah State University Press, 2010. 198–219.

Ray, Gordon Norton. *The Illustrator and the Book in England from 1790 to 1914*. New York: Dover, 1991.

Ray, Paul C. *The Surrealist Movement in England*. Ithaca: Cornell University Press, 1971.

Reynolds, Kimberley. *Radical Children's Literature: Future Visions and Aesthetic Transformations in Juvenile Fiction*. Houndmills: Palgrave Macmillan, 2007.

Richards, Mark. *Alice's Adventures in Wonderland: 150th Anniversary Homepage*. http://lewiscarrollresources.net/2015/index.html.

Richardson, Michael. *Surrealism and Cinema*. New York: Berg, 2006.

Robson, David. "Five Things *Alice in Wonderland* Reveals about the Brain." *BBC Future*. 25 February 2015. http://www.bbc.com/future/story/20150225-secrets-of-alice-in-wonderland.

Roiphe, Katie. *Still She Haunts Me*. London: Hodder, 2001.

Roof, Judith. *Come, as You Are: Sexuality and Narrative*. New York: Columbia University Press, 1996.

Rose, Jacqueline. *The Case of Peter Pan: The Impossibility of Children's Fiction*. Philadelphia: University of Pennsylvania Press, 1984.

Rosenwald, Michael. "Serious Reading Takes a Hit from Online Scanning and Skimming, Researchers Say." *The Washington Post*, 6 April 2014.

Ross, Deborah. "Escape from Wonderland: Disney and the Female Imagination." *Marvels & Tales* 18.1 (2004): 53–66.

Ross, Deborah. "Home by Tea-Time: Fear of Imagination in Disney's *Alice in Wonderland*." In *Classics in Film and Fiction*. Ed. Deborah Cartmell, et al. London: Pluto, 2000. 207–229.

The Royal Ballet. *Alice*. Choreography Christopher Wheeldon, music Joby Talbot, orchestrated by Christopher Austin and Talbot. Royal Opera House, London, 28 February 2011.

Rudd, David. "An Eye for an I: Neil Gaiman's *Coraline* and Questions of Identity." *Children's Literature in Education* 39 (2008): 159–68. *English, Film and Media and Creative Writing: Journal Articles*. Paper 1. (2008): 1–17.

Rushdie, Salman. "Salman Rusdhie Talks with Terry Gilliam." *The Believer Magazine*, March 2003. http://www.believermag.com/issues/200303/?read=interview_gilliam.

Russell, P. Craig. *Coraline: A Graphic Novel*. New York: HarperCollins, 2008.

Russo, Mary. *The Female Grotesque*. London: Routledge, 1995.

Ryan, Marie-Laure, ed. *Narrative Across Media: The Languages of Storytelling*. Lincoln: University of Nebraska Press, 2004.

Ryan-Sautour, Michelle. "The Alchemy of Reading in Angela Carter." In *Angela Carter: New Critical Readings*. Eds. Sonya Andermahr and Lawrence Phillips. New York: Continuum, 2012.

Ryder, Christopher. "Alice in Wonderland—Press Conference with Tim Burton." Collider.com. 23 July 2009. http://www.collider.com/2009/07/23/alice-in-wonderland-press-conference-with-tim-burton/.

Sabia, Joe. "The Technology of Storytelling." *Ted Talks*. May 2011. http://www.ted.com/talks/joe_sabia_the_technology_of_storytelling.html.

Sabuda, Robert. *Alice's Adventures in Wonderland: A Pop-Up Book Adaptation of Lewis Carroll's Classic*. New York: Little Simon & Schuster, 2003.

Salisbury, Mark. *Alice in Wonderland: A Visual Companion*. New York: Disney, 2010.

Salisbury, Mark. "Tim Burton and Johnny Depp Interview for Alice in Wonderland." *The Daily Telegraph*. 2 February 2010.

Sanchez, Sergi. "Terry Gilliam's *Tideland*: Alice in Nightmareland." *Fipresci: The International Federation of Film Critics*. 2005. http://www.fipresci.org/festivals/archive/2005/san_sebastian/tideland_ssanchez.htm.

Sandifer, Philip. "Review of *Lost Girls* by Alan Moore

and Melinda Gebbie." *ImageTexT: Interdisciplinary Comics Studies* 3.1 (2006).

Sandifer, Philip, ed. "ImageSexT: A Roundtable on *Lost Girls*." *ImageTexT: Interdisciplinary Comics Studies* 3.3 (2007).

Schanoes, Veronica. "Fearless Children and Fabulous Monsters: Angela Carter, Lewis Carroll, and Beastly Girls." *Marvels & Tales* 26.1 (2012): 30–44.

Schilder, Paul. (1938). "Psychoanalytic Remarks on *Alice in Wonderland* and Lewis Carroll." In *Aspects of Alice*. Ed. Robert Phillips. New York: Vintage, 1977. 283–293.

Schiller, Justin G., and Selwyn H. Goodacre. *Alice's Adventures in Wonderland: An 1865 Printing Re-Described*. New York: Battledore, 1990.

Schwenke-Wyile, Andrea. "New Old Media and Metamorphoses: Playing with Paper and Movable Graphic Metaphors." *Children's Literature and Media Culture IRSCL Conference*. Maastricht, 10–14 August 2013.

Scottish Ballet. *Alice*. Choreographer Ashley Page, stage designer Antony McDonald, musical score Robert Moran, video design Annemarie Woods, lightning Peter Mumford. Theatre Royal Glasgow, 12 April 2011.

Scottish Ballet. *Alice Ballet Souvenir Programme*. Glasgow: Scottish Ballet, 2011.

Selick, Henry, dir. *Coraline*. Focus Features, Laika Entertainment, Pandemonium, 2009.

Séllei, Nóra. *Tükröm, Tükröm... Írónők önéletrajzai a 20. század elejéről*. Debrecen: Kossuth University Press, 2002.

Shuttleworth, Sally. *The Mind of a Child: Child Development in Literature, Science, and Medicine, 1840–1900*. Oxford: Oxford University Press, 2010.

Sigler, Carolyn. "Wonders Wild and New: Lewis Carroll's Alice Books and Postmodern Women Writers." In *Twice-Told Children's Tales: The Influence of Childhood Reading on Writers for Adults*. Ed. Betty Greenaway. New York: Routledge, 2005.

Sigler, Carolyn, ed. *Alternative Alices: Visions and Revisions of Lewis Carroll's Alice Books*. Lexington: University Press of Kentucky, 1997.

Silverstein, Shel. *Where the Sidewalk Ends: The Poems and Drawings of Shel Silverstein*. New York: Harper & Row, 1974.

Skinner, John. (1947). "From Lewis Carroll's *Adventures in Wonderland*." In *Aspects of Alice*. Ed. Robert Phillips. New York: Vintage, 1977. 293–308.

Smith, Zack. "P. Craig Russell: Adapting *Coraline* and More." Newsarama.com. 19 August 2008.

Sneddon, Laura. "Stripped: Melinda Gebbie—*Lost Girls*, Pornography & Censorship." The Beat: The News Blog on Comics Culture. 9 September 2013. http://comicsbeat.com/stripped-melinda-gebbie-lost-girls-pornography-censorship/.

Sobchack, Vivian. *Carnal Thoughts: Embodiment and Moving Image Culture*. Berkeley: University of California Press, 2004.

Sorfa, David. "The Object of Film in Jan Švankmajer." *KinoKultura: New Russian Cinema* 4 (2006).

Spar, Debora L. *Ruling the Waves: Cycles of Discovery, Chaos, and Wealth from the Compass to the Internet*. New York: Harcourt, 2001.

Sparks, Beatrice, ed. Anonymous. (1971). *Go Ask Alice*. New York: Simon Pulse, 2006.

Springer, Claudia. "The Seduction of the Surface: From Alice to Crash." *Feminist Media Studies* 1.2 (2001): 197–213.

Stafford, Mark, and Virginie Sélavy. "Interview with Jan Švankmajer." *Electric Sheep Magazine* (14 June 2011).

Stam, Robert. "Introduction: The Theory and Practice of Adaptation." *Literature and Film: A Guide to the Theory and Practice of Film Adaptation*. Eds. Robert Stam and Alessandra Raengo. Malden: Blackwell, 2008. 1–53.

Stanhope, Zara. "Serious Play: On Polixeni Papapetrou's *Dreamchild*." Exhibition catalogue for *Dreamchild*, Johnston Gallery, Monash University, 18 August-18 September 18 2005. Polixeni Papapetrou's Website. http://www.polixenipapapetrou.net/text.php?txt=ZS_SeriousPlay&cat=On_Dreamchild_2003.

Staples, Terry. "Alice in Wonderland, Film Versions." In *The Oxford Companion to Fairy Tales: The Western Fairy Tale Tradition from Medieval to Modern*. Ed. Jack Zipes. Oxford: Oxford University Press, 2000. 12–13.

Steel, Jayne. "'I can't go on, I must go on': How Jeliza-Rose Meets Alice and the Dark Side of Childhood in Terry Gilliam's *Tideland*." In *Lost and Othered Children in Contemporary Cinema*. Eds. Debbie C. Olson and Andrew Scahill. Plymouth: Lexington, 2012. 19–47.

Stern, Jeffrey. "Lewis Carroll the Surrealist." In *Lewis Carroll: A Celebration*. Ed. Guiliano Edward. New York: Clarkson Potter, 120–141.

Stevens, Chris. "Making Alice for the iPad." *The Literary Platform*. 14 April 2010. http://www.theliteraryplatform.com/2010/04/making-alice-for-the-ipad/.

Street, Douglas, ed. *Children's Novels and the Movies*. New York: Ungar Film Library Press, 1984.

Stubbs, Phil. "Terry Gilliam Chats about Finishing *Tideland* and *The Brothers Grimm*." Dreams: The Terry Gilliam Fanzine. August 2005. http://www.smart.co.uk/dreams/tgint05.htm.

Sundmark, Björn. *Alice in the Oral-Literary Continuum*. Lund Studies in English 97. Lund: Lund University Press, 1999.

Susina, Jan. "Down the Rabbit Hole: Disney's Alice in Wonderland." Conference lecture. Alice Through the Ages: The 150th Anniversary of Alice in Wonderland Conference. Cambridge University. 2015.

Susina, Jan. *The Place of Lewis Carroll in Children's Literature*. New York: Routledge, 2010.

Susina, Jan. "'Why is a raven like a writing-desk?' The Play of Letters in Lewis Carroll's Alice Books." *Children's Literature Association Quarterly* 26.1 (Spring 2001): 15–21.

Sutherland, T.T. *Disney: Alice in Wonderland (Based on the Motion Picture Directed by Tim Burton)*. New York: Disney Press, 2010.

Švankmajer, Jan. "An Alchemist's Nightmares: Extracts from Jan Švankmajer's Diary." *Kinoeye* 2.1 (2002). http://www.kinoeye.org/index_02_01.php.

Švankmajer, Jan. "Animating the Fantastic." *Afterimage* 13 (Autumn 1987): 4–67.

Švankmajer, Jan. *Hmat a Imaginace, Taktilní experimentace, 1974–1983.* Prague: Kozoroh, 1994.

Švankmajer, Jan. "Out of My Head." *The Guardian.* 18 October 2001.

Švankmajer, Jan, dir. *Alice (Něco z Alenky).* Channel Four Films, 1987.

Švankmajer, Jan, dir. "The Jabberwocky or Straw Hubert's Clothes." Krátký Film Praha, 1971.

Sweeney, Kevin W. "Alice's Discriminating Palate." *Philosophy and Literature* 23.1 (1999): 17–31.

Sweeting, Samantha. Artist's website, 2014. http://www.samanthasweeting.com/.

Sweeting, Samantha. "Through the Looking-Glass: Interview." *Filler Magazine* 6.2 (Summer 2015). http://fillermagazine.com/culture/gallery/though-the-looking-glass-samantha-sweeting/.

Szabó Gendler, Tamar. "Imaginative Resistance Revisited." In *The Architecture of the Imagination.* Ed. Shaun Nichols. Oxford: Oxford University Press, 2006. 149–173.

Szabó Gendler, Tamar. "The Puzzle of Imaginative Resistance." *Journal of Philosophy* 97.2 (2000): 55–81.

Szecskó, Tamás. "Alice Illustrations." In *Alice Csodaországban.* Trans. Dezső Kosztolányi and Tibor Szobotka. Budapest: Móra, 1958.

Szegedi, Katalin. Illustrations to Lewis Carroll's *Alice Csodaországban.* Trans. Zsuzsa and Dániel Varró. Budapest: General, 2007.

Szőnyi, György Endre. "Radical Continuities: Hypertextual Links to a Textual Past." *Semiotische Berichte* 1.4 (2003): 227–242.

Tait, Vanessa. *The Looking Glass House.* Fairfax: Corvus, 2015.

Talbot, Bryan. *Alice in Sunderland: A Graphic Novel.* London: Jonathan Cape, 2007.

Tantimedh, Adi. "Finding the Lost Girls with Alan Moore." *Comic Book Resources. 25 May 2006.* http://www.comicbookresources.com/?page=article&id=7151.

Taylor, Maria. *Alice in Wonderland: With 3-Dimensional Pop-Up Scenes.* New York: Tango, 2015.

Taylor, Roger, and Edward Wakeling. *Lewis Carroll: Photographer.* The Princeton University Library Albums. Princeton: Princeton University Press, 2002.

Telotte, J.P. "Disney's Alice Comedies: A Life of Illusion and the Illusion of Life." *Animation: An Interdisciplinary Journal* 5.3 (November 2010): 331–340.

Tenniel, John. (1865, 1871). Illustrations to *Alice's Adventures in Wonderland* and *Through the Looking-Glass, and What Alice Found There* in *The Annotated Alice.* Ed. Martin Gardner. London: Penguin, 2001.

Thomas, Karima. "Angela Carter's Adventures in the Wonderland of Nonsense." In *Rewriting/Reprising in Literature: The Paradoxes of Intertextuality.* Eds. Claude Maisonnat, Josiane Paccaud-Huguet and Annie Ramel. Newcastle upon Thyne: Cambridge Scholars, 2009. 35–43.

Tiffin, Jessica. *Marvelous Geometry: Narrative and Metafiction in Modern Fairy Tale.* Detroit: Wayne State University Press, 2009.

Tiffin, Jessica. "Metafiction." "Tim Burton." In *The Greenwood Encyclopedia of Folktales and Fairy Tales.* Ed. Donald Haase. Westport: Greenwood, 2008. 622, 148.

Tolkien. J.R.R. (1947). "On Fairy Stories." *Tree and Leaf.* Boston: Houghton Mifflin, 1964. 9–45.

Townsend, Bud, dir. *Alice in Wonderland: An X-Rated Musical Fantasy.* Cruiser Productions, 1976.

Townshend, Dale. "The Haunted Nursery: 1764–1830." In *The Gothic in Children's Literature.* Eds. Anna Jackson, et al., New York: Routledge, 2008. 15–39.

Tribunella, Eric L. "Literature for Us 'Older Children': Lost Girls, Seductions Fantasies, and the Reeducation of Adults." *The Journal of Popular Culture* 45.3 (2012): 628–648.

Uhde, Jan. "Jan Švankmajer: Genius Loci as a Source of Surrealist Inspiration." In *The Unsilvered Screen: Surrealism on Film.* Eds. Graeme Harper, Rob Stone. London: Wallflower, 2007. 60–72.

Uhde, Jan. "Jan Švankmajer: The Prodigious Animator from Prague." *Kinema.* Spring 1994. http://www.kinema.uwaterloo.ca/article.php?id=363.

Vasseleu, Catheryn. "The Švankmajer Touch. (Animation Studies-Animated Dialogues, 2007)." *Animation Studies Online Journal* (9 July 2009): 91–101. http://journal.animationstudies.org/cathryn-vasseleu-the-svankmajer-touch/.

Venuti, Lawrence. "Adaptation, Translation, Critique." *Journal of Visual Culture* 6.1. (2007): 25–43.

Waits, Tom. "Mule Variations Q&A with Journalist Rip Rense." 1999 interview excerpts supplied by Epitaph Records. http://www.theexcuse.com/excuse/interviews/tomwaits/.

Waits, Tom, Robert Wilson, and Paul Schmidt, after Lewis Carroll. *Alice.* Thalia Theater, Hamburg. Brooklyn Academy of Music, New York. 13 October 1995. Lyrics of art musical available on Tom Waits' website. http://www.tomwaits.es/alice_obra.php. Music album: Tom Waits and Kathleen Brennan. *Alice.* Epitaph Records. 2002. 48:23.

Wakeling, Edward. "Lewis Carroll and His Photography: Mystic, awful was the process." A talk given at various venues after the publication of *Lewis Carroll, Photographer. The Lewis Carroll Site.* 2003. Available: http://www.wakeling.demon.co.uk/page3-real-lewiscarroll.htm.

Wakeling, Edward. *Lewis Carroll: The Man and His Circle.* London: I.B. Tauris, 2015.

Warner, Marina. "Dream Works. [On Jan Švankmajer]" *The Guardian,* 16 June 2007.

Warner, Marina. "The Soul of the Toy." *The Journal of Aesthetic Education* 3.2 (Summer 2009). 3–18.

Warner, Marina. "'Stay this moment.' Julia Margaret Cameron and Charles Dodgson." *Phantasmagoria: Spirit Visions, Metaphors and Media into the*

Twenty-First Century. Oxford: Oxford University Press, 2006. 205–220.
Warner, Marina. *Stranger Magic: Charmed States and the Arabian Nights.* Cambridge: Belknap, 2012.
Warren, S., J.S. Wakefield, and L.A. Mills. "Learning and Teaching as Communicative Actions: Transmedia Storytelling." *Cutting-Edge Technologies in Higher Education* 5.2 (2013): 67–94.
Wass, Ashley, and Matthew Trusler, music. Louis de Bernieres, script. Emily Carew Woodard, illustrations. *Wonderland.* 2015. http://www.wonderland150.com.
Watt, Mike. *Fervid Filmmaking: 66 Cult Pictures of Vision, Verve, and the Self-Restraint.* Jefferson, NC: McFarland, 2013.
Waugh, Patricia. *Metafiction: The Theory and Practice of Self-Conscious Fiction.* London: Methuen, 1984.
Weaver, Warren. *Alice in Many Tongues: The Translations of Alice in Wonderland.* Mansfield Centre: Martino, 2006.
Webb, Vivienne. "Mystical Places." Polixeni Papapetrou's website. http://www.polixenipapapetrou.net/print.php.
Weber, Max. (1905). *The Protestant Ethic and the Spirit of Capitalism.* London: George Allen, 1976.
Weiss, Margaret, ed. *Fantastic Alice: New Stories from Wonderland.* New York: Ace, 1995.
Wells, Paul. "Animated Anxiety: Jan Švankmajer, Surrealism and the 'Agit-Scare.'" *KinoEye* 2.16 (21 October 2002). http://www.kinoeye.org/02/16/wells16.php#11.
Wells, Paul. "Body Consciousness in the Films of Jan Švankmajer." In *A Reader in Animation Studies.* Ed. Jayne Pilling. London: John Libbey, 1997. 177–195.
Wells-Lassagne, Shannon, and Ariadne Hudelet, eds. *Screening Text: Critical Perspectives on Film Adaptation.* Jefferson, NC: McFarland, 2013.
Welsh, Timothy J. "Wonder, Book?" *Modern Narrative, New Media, Mixed Reality.* 5 December 2012. http://www.timothyjwelsh.com/tag/augmented-reality/.
Williams, Linda. "Film Bodies: Gender, Genre, and Excess." *Film Quarterly* 44.4 (Summer 1991): 2–13.
Williams, Linda. *Hard Core:. Power, Pleasure, and the "Frenzy of the Visible."* Berkeley: University of California Press, 1999.
Willing, Nick, dir. *Alice.* Written by Willing. Original television mini-series for Syfy channel, two episodes, 180 minutes, original run: 6–7 December 2009.
Willing, Nick, dir. *Alice in Wonderland.* Babelsberg International Film Produktion, Hallmark Entertainment, NBC Studios, 1999.
Wojcik-Andrews, Ian. *The Children's Film.* New York: Garland, 2000.
Wolff, Janet. *The Aesthetics of Uncertainty.* New York: Columbia University Press, 2008.
Wonder.land. Music by Damon Albarn. Book and lyrics by Moira Buffini. Directed by Rufus Norris. Designed by Rae Smith. Manchester International Festival. Palace Theater, 2–19 July 2015. London National Theatre, November 2015. http://www.nationaltheatre.org.uk/shows/wonder.land.
Wong, Mou-Lan. "Generations of Re-Generation: Re-Creating Wonderland through Text, Illustration, and the Reader's Hands." In *Alice Beyond Wonderland.* Ed. Cristopher Hollingsworth. Iowa City: University of Iowa Press, 2009. 135–155.
Wood, Michael. "Who in the World Am I? On 'The Story of Alice: Lewis Carroll and the Secret History of Wonderland.'" *The New York Times Sunday Book Review.* 14 June 2015: BR15.
Woolf, Jenny. *The Mystery of Lewis Carroll.* New York: St. Martin's, 2010.
Woolf, Jenny. "The Mystery of Lewis Carroll." *The Public Domain Review.* 1 July 2015. http://publicdomainreview.org/2015/07/01/the-mystery-of-lewis-carroll/.
Woolf, Virginia. "Lewis Carroll." *The Moment and Other Essays.* New York: Harcourt Brace, 1948, republished in *Aspects of Alice.* Ed. Robert Phillips. New York: Vintage, 1977. 47–50.
Wu, Yan, Kerry Mallan, and Roderick McGillis, eds. *(Re)Imagining the World: Children's Literature's Response to Changing Times.* New York: Springer, 2013.
Wullschläger, Jackie. "Lewis Carroll: The Child as Muse." In *Inventing Wonderland: The Lives and Fantasies of Lewis Carroll, Edward Lear, J.M. Barrie, Kenneth Grahame, and A.A. Milne.* New York: Simon & Schuster, 1995. 29–65.
Yoe, Craig. *Alice in Comicland.* San Diego: IDW, 2014.
Yoshinaga, Ida. "A Transmedial Narratological Reading of Racialized and Colonial Sexual Fantasies in the Libertarian Feminist Graphic Novel, Alan Moore and Melinda Gebbie's *Lost Girls.*" In *Postmodern Reinterpretations of Fairy Tales.* Ed. Anna Kérchy. Lewiston, Lampeter: Edwin Mellen, 2011. 403–411.
Zipes, Jack. "Breaking the Disney Spell." In *From Mouse to Mermaid: The Politics of Film, Gender, and Culture.* Ed. Elizabeth Bell, Lynda Haas, and Laura Sells. Bloomington: Indiana University Press, 1995. 21–43.
Zipes, Jack. *Breaking the Magic Spell: Radical Theories of Folk and Fairy Tales.* London: Heinemann, 1979.
Zipes, Jack. *The Enchanted Screen: The Unknown History of Fairy-Tale Films.* New York: Routledge, 2011.
Zipes, Jack. *Fairy Tale as Myth/Myth as Fairy Tale.* Lexington: University Press of Kentucky, 1994.
Zipes, Jack. *Fairy Tale as the Art of Subversion: The Classical Genre for Children and the Process of Civilization.* New York: Routledge, 2006.
Zipes, Jack. "Foreword. Grounding the Spell: The Fairy Tale Film and Transformations." In *Fairy Tale Film: Visions of Ambiguity.* Eds. Pauline Greenhill and Sidney Eve Matrix. Logan: Utah State University Press, 2010. vii-ix.
Zipes, Jack. *The Irresistible Fairy Tale: The Cultural and Social History of a Genre.* Princeton: Princeton University Press, 2012.

Zipes, Jack, ed. *The Oxford Companion to Fairy Tale: The Western Fairy Tale Tradition from Medieval to Modern.* Oxford and New York: Oxford University Press, 2000.

Zipes, Jack, ed. *Victorian Fairy Tales: The Revolt of Fairies and Elves.* New York: Routledge, 1991.

Žižek, Slavoj. *The Sublime Object of Ideology.* London: Verso, 1989.

Žižek, Slavoj. *Welcome to the Desert of the Real! Five Essays on September 11 and Related Dates.* London: Verso, 2002.

Zolkover, Adam. "King Rat to Coraline: Faerie and Fairy Tale in British Urban Fantasy." In *Postmodern Reinterpretations of Fairy Tales.* Ed. Anna Kérchy. Lewiston, Lampeter: Edwin Mellen, 2011. 67–83.

Index

ADAIR, Gilbert 5
adaptation 3–27; adaptogenic 7; appropriation 9, 115, 124, 131, 231; creative reanimation 9; creative revision 13; expansion 9, 20–22, 31, 42, 115, 148; fidelity 11, 13, 28, 47, 57, 107, 194; reappropriation 8, 22, 207; repurposing 9, 31, 49, 70, 166, 206; screen bleed 22
affective meaningfulness 38, 43, 75 81, 90, 120, 121, 128, 137, 145, 175, 195, 205; emotional productivity 38, 49, 61, 78, 90, 95, 97, 119, 121, 123, 128, 145, 153, 173, 181, 204, 210, 236
After Alice 12, 222
alchemy 5, 6, 90, 168, 175–181, 188–189, 192, 195, 199; esoterism 25, 24, 135, 175, 178, 188, 193; hermeticism 175–176
Alice Comedies 23, 55–57
Alice Eats Wonderland 217–219
Alice for the iPad 21, 41–50
Alice in Wonderland. An X-Rated Musical Fantasy 131
The Alice Look 223
Alice on the Stage 8, 80, 233
Alice Redux 11, 131
Alice Through the Ages 16, 223
Alice's Adventures Under Ground 7–8, 33, 223
Alternative Alices 11
Angst Alice 12
animal 12, 64, 80, 207–211
animation: anatomo- 179; anxiety 171; digital 71; Pixar 173; stop-motion 106, 168, 171, 173, 177; tactile 181
The Annotated Alice 6, 46, 50, 222
Automated Alice 12

Bacchilega, Cristina 4, 19, 23, 115
ballet: Royal Ballet 211–216; Scottish Ballet 11, 22, 25, 140–142
Barthes, Roland 29, 130
Basic, Zdanko 39–41
Bassnett, Susan 10
Bazin, André 66
Beer, Gillian 16, 224
Beggar Maid 128–130, 132, 137, 138, 139, 145
Benjamin, Walter 9, 10, 21

Beuys, Joseph 210–211
biofiction, biografiction 26, 133–140, 149, 150, 167, 201
Blackwell, Su 35, 45–46, 232
Blake, Kathleen 12
Blumenthal, Heston 219–220
body art 206, 209; Abramovic, Marina 210; Schneeman, Carolee 207; *see also* Beuys, Joseph; Sweeting, Samantha
body-text 163, 206; anatomo-(in)animation 179; anatomization of the subject 167; bodily aphasia 179; body genre 166, 179; body-in-becoming 184; carnal art 206–221; carnal residue 214; corpography 207; corporeal reaction 138, 150, 155, 164, 166, 167, 178, 179; cultured embodiment 214; disembodiment 17, 57, 104, 126, 158, 185, 211, 215, 237; embodied cognition 38; embodied imagination 98, 178; embodied language 20, 99, 166, 181, 191, 201, 237; embodied memories 46, 155; embodied nonsense 7, 23, 26, 28, 85, 167, 190, 191–196, 200, 206; embodied reading experience 31, 33, 38, 43; embodied spectatorship 168–187, 236; embodied storytelling 25, 160, 207, 214; embodied writing 134, 205; somatization of semiosis 21, 61, 88, 167, 206; somato-sensory receptivity 185; tactile dialogue 180; tremulous private corporeality 205, 214; *see also* Kristeva, Julia; voice
Bolster, Stephanie 138–140
Bolter, Jay David 9, 21, 32, 44
book sculpture 45–47
Brennan, Kathleen 26, 167, 200; *see also* Waits, Tom
Brooker, Will 2, 4, 13, 16, 53, 116, 117, 118, 127, 131, 132, 156, 232, 235
Brooks, Peter 21, 61, 88, 167, 206
Burstein, Mark 222, 238
Burton, Tim 5, 10, 13, 14, 21, 22, 23, 24, 27, 28, 30, 39, 51, 54, 60–74, 116, 121, 141, 146, 168, 200, 214, 217, 232, 233, 235
Bus, Adriana G. 232

carnivalesque 19, 36, 101, 107, 126, 155, 174, 189, 192, 201, 202, 217; Bakhtin, Mikhail 19; grotesque 4, 19, 26, 30, 57, 58, 66, 69, 79, 81, 103, 107, 115, 119, 126, 153, 156, 166, 168, 169, 172, 178; masquerade 4, 5, 123
Carroll, Lewis *see* Dodgson, Charles Lutwidge
Carter, Angela 5, 131, 159, 166, 167, 187–196, 199, 200, 231, 237
Castor, Harriet 39–41
CGI 3D 1, 14, 20, 21, 23, 27, 31, 32, 60, 64, 66, 68, 70, 71, 73, 117, 141
child: *femme enfant* 131, 151, 172, 188, 207; friend 32, 125, 143, 148, 184, 198, 229, 235; loving 126, 127, 132, 141, 158; martyr 86; orphan ingénue 86, 130; puer aeternus 86, 131, 142; young adult 14, 40, 107, 109, 114, 121, 214; *see also* children's gothic; children's literature; Dreamchild
children's gothic 18, 24, 95, 96, 101, 103, 105, 106, 109, 193; funcanny 18, 114
children's literature 15, 16, 18, 25, 27, 42, 44, 94, 98, 154, 156; girl's adventure story 24, 95, 102; impossibility of children's fiction 157; pre-readers 8, 16, 40, 49; young adult literature 40, 95; *see also* picturebook
Chin, Unsuk 17
cinema: auteurial 64, 66; buddy comedy 173; embodied cinema 168–187, 236; fairy-tale film 14, 29, 215, 230; family adventure romance 14, 25, 114, 118; fantasy thriller 24, 75, 86; total cinema 66; *see also* Burton, Tim; CGI; Gilliam, Terry; Millar, Gavin; Švankmajer, Jan
cinesthetic spectator: coenaesthesia 166, 183; *see also* Sobchack, Vivian
Cohen, Morton N. 3, 14, 74, 126, 127, 138, 225, 235
Cohn, Dorrit 24, 98
common sense 18, 76, 78, 82, 85, 127, 178, 188, 191, 195, 196, 202, 203; consensus reality 4, 76, 77, 80, 85, 96, 101, 107, 109, 119

253

Index

computer game 11, 24, 27, 49, 114–121
Coraline 5, 11, 22, 24, 94–113, 234, 235
Craig, Russell 24, 96, 109–113
Creativity and Perversion 192
crossover fiction 15, 16, 119, 122, 226; dual spectatorship 14; family entertainment 16, 54; intergenerational quality 14, 16, 26, 130, 157, 167, 201, 226; mixed-age audience 14, 16
cultural anxiety 5, 23, 132, 191
curiosity 4, 11, 16, 17, 18, 21, 52, 53, 105, 121, 170, 176, 184, 188, 189, 190, 196, 218, 224, 227; epistemophilia 172, 190; scopophilia 30, 32, 127, 144
curiosity cabinet 26, 167, 188, 189, 197, 199, 236

Darwin, Charles 12, 21, 58, 114, 234
death joke 8, 18, 115, 116, 165, 174, 202, 204, 208, 211, 234, 236; memento mori 208
De Creeft, José 27
déja vu 36, 70, 189, 234; déja lu 189, 194; jamais vu 182
destabilization; deconstruction: demythologizing business 25, 103, 153, 159, 189; identity crisis 4, 5, 11, 60, 89, 96, 100, 103, 112, 148, 177; uncertainty 7, 8, 18, 40, 58, 63, 70, 78, 81, 83, 100, 104, 117, 134, 139, 174, 185, 201, 215, 221; unreliability 28, 31, 58, 89, 100, 103, 133, 134, 157, 191, 197; vulnerability 45, 77, 81, 97, 109, 116, 123, 128, 131, 136, 150, 153, 163, 167, 170, 185, 191, 205, 210, 213; *see also* ambiguity
deviantart.com 22, 62, 73, 102
dialogism 98, 122, 127, 154, 163, 172, 177, 180
digital media 4, 21, 22, 23, 32; collage 145–148, 172; computer digitalization 64–74, 123; culture 20, 227; novel 20, 22, 23, 41–50; Sony Wonderbook 231–232
disability 118, 202, 238; Asperger's 127; freak show 167, 201–202, 238
disbelief 5, 17, 28, 61, 80, 83, 99, 112, 196; skepticism 28, 62, 68, 76, 99, 120, 236; *see also* imaginative resistance
Disney, Walt 5, 13, 22, 23, 27, 28, 30, 31, 39, 50–57, 58–60, 64, 69, 74, 115, 119, 124, 168, 180, 200, 210, 224, 225, 233, 235; dedisneyfication 17; Disney Princess Industry 30–31, 53, 54, 231; Disney touch 181; disneyfication 23, 50, 54, 66; Disneyland 67, 117, 176, 232
Dodgson, Charles Lutwidge 3, 4, 11, 53, 74, 116, 117, 125, 126, 128, 131–140, 144–147, 154, 189, 198, 199, 201, 203–207

Douglas-Fairhurst, Robert 221, 222, 229, 230
dream 11, 13, 92–94; daydream 18, 48, 64, 75–81, 87, 98, 108, 111–115, 118, 130, 151, 152, 187; dreamscape 6, 86, 168, 180, 189, lucid dream 83, 89, 170, 222; eerie state of consciousness 84, 117; nightmare 62, 67, 72, 75, 84–87, 92, 93, 94, 99, 100, 107, 109, 113, 114, 116, 132, 148, 154, 161, 168, 169, 174, 200, 214, 215, 232; reverie 4, 83, 147; sleep paralysis 89, 109, 153
Dream Child 6, 77, 79, 80, 127, 139, 197, 201, 204; *Dreamchild* 25, 138, 143, 148–154; dreamgirl-child 24, 75–77, 200
Ducornet, Rikki 196–199
Dunn, George 91
Dusinberre, Juliet 12
dystopia 12, 79

e-book application 41–50; see also *Alice for the iPad*
Eco, Umberto 29
enchantment 1, 3, 4, 9, 11, 13, 16, 18, 19, 24, 28, 29, 31, 63, 65–74, 84, 108, 118, 136, 139, 145, 150, 161, 166, 177, 179, 197, 199, 202, 205, 221, 227; disenchantment 3, 19, 24, 29, 31, 63, 65–74, 115, 136, 149, 154, 157, 235, 238; re-enchantment 3, 23
The End of Alice 132
epistemological crisis 2, 15, 24, 27, 29, 72, 76, 128, 166, 167, 176, 182, 188–195; corporeal turn 191; embodied epistemology 182, 186; linguistic turn; paradigm shift 27, 50, 191; pictorial turn 27, 28, 71; speculative turn 166, 176
erotica 7, 25, 119, 125–165, 167, 180, 181, 190, 191, 193, 197, 207, 234, 237; fetish 16, 130, 146, 150, 151, 175, 192, 236; Lolita 53, 115, 131, 153; moral pornography 131, 159; petit mort 164; pro-porn feminism 25, 131, 154; sexual autobiography 155, 158, 164, 236; sexual healing 158, 160; sexualization of the author 79, 125–130; virginal sexuality 207; visual promiscuity 145
ethics of enchantment 1, 5, 17, 19, 24, 76, 90, 91, 98, 101, 160, 226, 227; charity 226; empathy 16, 24, 37, 43, 76, 79, 86, 91, 92, 116, 136, 139, 165, 211, 227, 234; environmentalist morality 207, 232; hope 18, 30, 92, 96, 120, 234; reciprocity 127, 183; relational model of identity 2, 17, 80, 81, 85, 88, 89, 92, 93, 119, 183, 205, 227

fairy tale 4, 13, 14, 18, 29, 36, 41, 45, 52, 65, 71, 89, 95, 96, 114, 130, 137, 173, 178, 187, 207, 231; anti-tale 62, 114; cautionary tale 100,

101, 154; oral tradition 7, 8, 9, 13, 14, 36, 47, 51, 61, 96, 151, 184, 185, 217, 230, 231, 232
fall down the rabbit hole 9, 11, 18, 37, 41, 82, 91, 97, 115, 127, 137, 169, 194, 201, 215, 220, 227; fall asleep 56, 83, 89, 115, 141; fall from innocence 99, 158, 173; fall in language 194–197; fall in/out of love 133, 135, 210; fall into the story 133, 140, 210
fandom 9, 20, 22, 25, 121–125; Comic-Con 122; cosplay 21, 25, 27, 107, 115, 123–124; fanfiction 121–124; Fanfiction.net 121–122; *see also* Fiske, John; Radway, Janice
Fantastic Alice 11
fantastification 28, 65–71, 83, 87, 116, 154, 156, 175,
feminism 6, 21, 25, 54, 62, 63, 68, 94, 101–106, 119–121, 124, 130–133, 145, 154, 157–159, 179, 207, 232; female grotesque 103; feminine mode of life-writing 134; gender trouble 53, 104; heterosexual romance 54, 94, 101, 105, 119, 120, 122; libidinal writing 132, 160; masculine hegemony 103–104; moral pornography 131, 159; patriarchy 24, 30, 51, 54, 77, 94, 101, 120, 123, 132; phallogocentrism 101, 132, 191; pro-pornography 25, 131, 154; tomboy 54, 94, 103, 104, 130; queer 122, 157; writing beyond the ending 101
fictional reality 1, 25, 35, 40, 43, 48, 50, 62, 63, 65, 67, 80, 90, 91, 92, 93, 116; alternate reality 23, 62, 101, 160, 230; fantasy realm 1, 63, 67, 76; fictive world 22; storyworld 2, 8, 9, 21, 22, 31, 63, 90, 97, 107, 121, 229; *see also* consensus reality
Fiske, John 121, 123
food of Wonderland 96, 108, 184, 217–220, 222, 240; Blumenthal, Heston 219–220; cannibalism 13, 97, 108, 138, 174, 184, 200, 218; culinary portmanteau 218; fear of being eaten 97, 184; gustatory nonsense 184, 216–218; voracious children 234
Foucault, Michel 31, 159, 235; ars erotica 159; incitement to discourse 158; scientia sexualis 159; technology of power 30, 52, 89, 103, 115, 146, 183; transgression 31, 158, 180, 190; truth production 167, 189, 203
Freud, Sigmund 6, 18, 79, 126–128, 212, 235; death drive 116, 171; dream; joke 19; Oedipalization 157; orality 217; polimorphous perversity 104; primal scene 137; seduction theory 157–158, 236; talking cure 136, 159; uncanny 81, 95, 97, 105, 174, 180, 234

Index

Gaiman, Neil 5, 11, 22, 24, 95–113, 158, 234
game 17; cards 35, 36, 39, 40, 71, 90, 114, 117, 169, 172, 214, 222, 223, 231, 234; chess 4, 20, 73, 114, 222; computer 114–121; language 4, 7, 13, 19, 20, 24, 27, 31, 40, 60, 61, 74, 141, 168, 193, 203, 214, 215, 217, 237, 238; playable media 27–50; spatial 46, 32–41; *see also* play
Garcia, Camille Rose 16
Gardner, Martin 3, 6, 20, 50, 58, 222
gaze 35, 36, 56, 71, 85, 112, 128, 130, 134, 136, 141, 147, 149, 150, 180, 207; amorous 136, 152; furtive glance 136; invisibility 12, 67, 83, 113, 134, 136, 137, 148, 194, 198, 213, 232, 236; male 144, 145; maternal 144; museal 190; narcissism 55, 82, 130, 144, 150, 175, 232; scopophilia 30, 32, 127, 144; to-be-looked-at-ness 137, 145, 149; visibility 28, 36, 46, 67, 71, 74, 81, 83, 94, 112, 124, 135, 145, 147, 149, 158, 172, 184; voyeurism 28, 32, 37, 128, 144, 148, 149, 150, 187, 190
Gebbie, Melinda 154, 236; *see also* Moore, Alan
Genette, Gérard 41, 55, 57; hypertext 41, 42, 50; hypotext 8, 13, 40, 187, 189; paratext 13, 40, 41, 45, 51, 134, 138, 143, 187; *see also* metalepsis
Giddens, Eugene 2, 5, 9, 223, 229, 231, 233
Gilliam, Terry 22, 24, 51, 75–94, 168, 234; Brazil 79; The Brothers Grimm 79; The Imaginarium of Dr. Parnassus 79; Jabberwocky 175; Tideland 75–94
Go Ask Alice 132
Goodacre, Selwyn 222, 225, 231
graphic novel: *Alice in Cartoonland* 223; *Alice in Comicland* 222; *Alice in Sunderland* 12, *Batman* 131; *Coraline* 109–113; *ImageSexT* 157, 160; *Lost Girls* 154–165
Greenhill, Pauline 10, 13, 14
Grusin, Richard 9, 21, 32, 44
Guillemin, Grégoire 17

Hancher, Michael 9, 33, 69, 70, 113, 233
happily ever after 30, 81, 118, 120, 122, 232
haptic visuality 182; haptic aurality 25, 166, 183; somatic cinema 182–184, 236; tactile dialogue 180; tactile dissonance 168; tactile epistemology 182; tactile fantasy 181; tactile memory 181
Harvey-Brown, Jodi 46–47
Heath, Peter 3, 14
Heiterkeit Alice 12
Hello Kitty 27

Hennard Dutheil de la Rochère, Martine 10
Hepworth, Cecil 13, 27
Hollingsworth, Cristopher 2
Hong, Jeff 232
The Hunting of the Snark 132
Hutcheon, Linda 8, 9, 10, 13, 19, 21, 29, 232; *see also* metafiction

iconic turn, pictorial turn 23, 27–28, 71
iconotext 1, 2, 19, 23, 28, 35; ekphrasis 134; iconotextual counterpoint 35; iconotextual poetics 1, 2, 19, 23, 35; imagetext dynamics 23, 25, 28, 29, 32, 33, 36, 40–45, 48, 51, 58, 70, 73, 74, 160, 163, 165, 197, 207, 225; montage-verbiage technique 194; voyure 28; *see also* Louvel, Liliane; Mitchell, W.J.T.; Nikolajeva, Maria
ideology criticism 55, 67, 81, 133, 163, 178; sociocriticism 4, 14, 24, 27, 130
imagination: collective fantasy 87; commodification of fantasy 15, 23, 30, 31, 50, 67, 72, 115, 118, 153; creative imaginative productivity 2, 18, 23, 30, 31, 50, 57, 79, 134, 153, 172, 173, 176; crib talk 82; embodied imagination 178; erotic imagination 155; false memory 158; female fantasizing 23, 50, 52; girlish fantasy 18, 75, 94–113; homo imaginans 24, 76; imagination against all odds 80, 130, 227; imaginative reluctance 75, 77, 80, 84–94, 116; imaginative resistance 24, 90; imaginative willingness 19, 63, 67, 72, 116; infantile imagination 24, 35, 84, 85, 86, 169; libidinal fancy 157; metafantasy; mind voyaging 114; tactile fantasy 181; therapeutic fantastification 87; trance-like consciousness 84; trusting fantasizing 80, 92, 119; Wonderlust 227; *see also* disbelief; dream; Szabó Gendler, Tamar
Imholtz, August 217–219
impossibility 11, 24, 63, 72, 74, 80, 91, 105, 134, 153, 203, 210, 234; aporia 137, 216; ethical 24; logical 91; representational deadend 205; unimaginable 7, 19, 23, 24, 35, 58, 60, 67, 71, 74, 76, 79, 87, 88, 99, 100, 108, 134, 136, 161, 166, 167, 168, 198, 211, 231; unknowable 4, 6, 85, 133, 188; unnamable 38; unsaid 46, 88, 124, 134, 135, 148, 150, 159, 198, 216; unseen 46, 57, 83, 97, 117, 138, 147, 187; unspeakable 7, 26, 35, 61, 74, 75, 91, 98, 107, 108, 109, 111, 116, 134, 136, 139, 158, 160–167, 184, 191–198, 205, 206, 207, 227; unspoken 55, 89, 99, 100, 134, 137, 150; unthinkable 1, 90, 114, 208, 227; *see also* nonsense

Inanimate Alice 48–49
interactivity 11, 12, 16, 20, 22, 23, 33, 49, 66, 114, 117
interdisciplinarity 1, 2, 18, 206, 207, 218
intermedial shift 1, 4, 23, 34, 36, 51, 63, 74, 117 *see also* media change
interpretation: hypermetaphorization 192; knowing reader 9, 198; literal 5, 7, 10, 33, 69, 87, 88, 89, 112, 119, 147, 155, 196, 219, 324, 235; metaphorical 5, 6, 10, 19, 21, 26, 88; overliteralization 90; rhetorical 5, 29, 32, 50, 55, 193, 195, 222, 224, 226
intertextuality 3, 5, 8, 9, 10, 11, 23, 29, 35, 36, 46, 67, 68, 69, 86, 113, 132, 156, 164, 186, 187, 189, 196, 199, 231; commercial 67; *see also* metafiction; parody
iPad application 41–50

Jabberwock 12, 51, 57–64, 72, 80, 95, 99, 116, 117, 119, 122, 141, 161, 235; Jabberwocky 8, 19, 23, 28, 57–64, 68, 70, 87, 137, 161, 175, 202, 203, 233, 236, 238; Jabberwocky sentences 229
Jade Cabinet 26, 167, 196–199
Jaques, Zoe 2, 5, 9, 223, 229, 231, 233
Jenkins, Henry 21–23, 29, 32, 72

Kafkaesque 15, 175
Kidd, Kenneth B. 25, 156, 157
Kincaid, James 18, 77, 234
kinesthetic tactile interactivity 8, 20, 25
Kövecses, Zoltán 38
Kristeva, Julia: abjection 81; revolutionary poetic language 29, 61, 191, 197; semiotic 191
Kusama, Yayoi 16

Lacombe, Benjamin 23, 35–36
Lambton worm 12, 58
language: Babel 195; game 4, 7, 13, 19, 20, 24, 27, 31, 40, 60, 61, 74, 141, 168, 193, 203, 214, 215, 217, 237, 238; lingua adamica 167, 195, 197; *see also* nonsense; portmanteau; poststructuralist language philosophy; voice
Leach, Karoline 126, 127, 138
Lethem, Jonathan 12
Lewis, C.S. 6
The Lewis Carroll Society 222, 238
The Lewis Carroll Society of North America 222, 223, 224, 229
Liddell, Alice 4, 6, 7, 8, 13, 69, 116, 125, 128, 129, 131, 133–140, 144, 146, 148–154, 186, 201, 207, 212, 223, 226, 231; *see also* "The Beggar Maid"
Lindseth, Jon 224, 225, 238
literacy 49; bi-literate brain 49; hyperliteracy 178; multimedia 1;

social-emotional 49; visual 19, 28, 68, 69, 71
The Looking Glass House 13
Lost Girls 154–165
Louvel, Liliane 19, 23, 28, 29, 231

MacDonald, George 7
madness 18, 24, 81, 82, 91, 114–124, 139, 188, 202, 213; dementia 114, 149, 153
magic lantern show/slides 31, 65, 119, 140
Maguire, Gregory 12, 222
Malice Alice 12
Manning, Kara 13, 65, 73
Manovich, Lev 65, 67, 231
Many Worlds Postulate 24
Marks, Laura 182–183
Matrix, Sidney 13, 14, 65
McDonald, Brian 91
McGee, American 114–121
McLuhan, Marshall 23
media change 1, 7, 10, 11, 23, 24, 28, 32, 64, 72, 107, 109, 168; *see also* intermedial shift
Meggendorfer, Lothar 34, 44
memory 9, 38, 46, 60, 69, 70, 86, 102, 116, 133, 141, 147, 151–160, 165, 167, 173, 175, 177, 180–182; 186, 190, 191, 196, 197, 199, 201, 205, 207, 210, 214, 220, 227, 232; misremembering 26, 133, 151, 167; nostalgia 42, 44, 46, 67, 79, 117, 120, 128, 133, 141, 149, 170, 212
Merleau-Ponty, Maurice 237
metafantasy 1, 18, 29, 100; metaimagination 29, 46, 50, 98, 109, 114
metafiction 1, 4, 5, 23–31, 32, 41, 48, 50, 51–58, 61, 63–64, 66, 67, 69, 79, 82, 100, 141, 145, 155, 158, 160, 163, 171, 172, 184, 186, 190, 197, 204, 232; alienation 29, 54, 71, 117, 145, 174, 178, 179, 185; self-reflectivity; metarepresentational recognition 61
metalepsis 23, 28, 55, 56
metamediality 1, 2, 18, 19, 23, 27–29, 32, 184
Millar, Gavin 25, 148–154
Miller, Hillis 8
Mitchell, WJT 23, 28, 29, 71, 72, 232
Moore, Alan 154–165; *see also* Gebbie, Melinda
mother: bad 76, 83, 87, 91, 92; maternal gaze 142–145, 150, 151, 212; monstrous 24, 94–113, 235; reading 15, 58
multimedial 1, 2, 19, 21, 22, 41, 45–50, 60, 64, 148, 155, 174, 180, 184, 212, 215, 236; mixed media 29, 31, 71, 230; plurimedial 19, 49
multisensorial 20, 25, 42, 45, 142, 166, 178, 182, 184, 186, 219; synesthesia 206
music 22, 26, 31, 58, 67, 81, 167, 183, 191, 197; The Beatles 200; Cel-lophony 224; Del Tradici, David 200; Elfman, Danny 67; Jefferson Airplane 140, 171, 200; Lavigne, Avril 69; Manson, Marilyn 131, 200; Moran, Robert 140; musical 22, 23, 31, 51–53, 131; NIN 115; soundtrack 234; Roxy Music 132; Stravinsky, Igor 160, 215; Talbot, Joby 211; Tchaikovsky, Pyotr Ilych 214; Trusler, Matthew 226; Waits, Tom 199–206; *Wonder.land* 227

networked society 22
new media 2, 4, 16, 20–24, 31, 33, 41, 42, 44, 50, 70–73, 106, 118, 122, 212, 215, 231
Nichols, Catherine 7, 17, 19, 77, 90, 233, 238
Nikolajeva, Maria 24, 35, 97–99, 223
nonsense 5, 13, 17, 19, 20, 21, 23, 27, 31, 40, 48, 51–53, 64, 70, 72, 74, 78, 87, 90, 103, 121, 126, 132, 139, 141, 151, 152, 178, 186, 207, 211, 215, 218, 221, 224, 225, 227, 231; acoustic 108; affective 135; embodied 7, 85, 167, 191, 193, 200, 206; erotic 136, 161, 163; ethical 90–91; gendered 165; gustatory 184, 216–218; hypermetaphorization 192; imaginative 7, 84, 91; kinetic 26, 167, 206, 213, 217; literary 5, 7, 51, 58, 68, 70, 86, 125, 167, 184, 187–199. 202, 213, 214, 217; logical 91; ludic 192; meaninglessness 7, 74, 81, 101, 108, 148, 165, 202, 203, 204; miscomprehension 14, 82, 152, 193; multisensorial 166; nonsense as fantasy; nonsense as tragedy 87; nonsensification 43, 61, 68; ordinary 91; oxymoron 29, 136; technologically enhanced 31, 43, 64, 231; visual/ocular 23, 28, 64, 68, 69, 70, 194; *see also* common sense; nonsensification; portmanteau
Noon, Jeff 5, 12
The Nursery Alice 8, 15, 27, 33, 48, 230

object-oriented ontology 25, 166, 171, 176, 181; fetish object 16, 130, 146, 150, 151, 175, 192, 236; found object 166, 168, 173, 174, 181, 184, 189, 194, 231
O'Kane, David 145–148
Once Upon a Time (in Wonderland) 24, 118–123
One Pill Makes You Smaller 139
open text 12, 29, 32, 49, 152, 159, 164, 194, 206, 211, 216; fluid text 8; producerly text 121
otherness 24, 40, 54, 68, 81, 93, 103, 132, 202; alterity 202; cultural diversity 40
Oxenbury, Helen 16

Papapetrou, Polixeni 18, 25, 142–145, 146, 235

parkour 22, 142
parody 9, 10, 11, 27, 41, 53, 58, 81, 87, 101, 104, 107, 117, 190, 200, 214, 223, 236; irony 53, 108, 232; pastiche 4, 8, 69, 117, 155, 187, 194, 223
Passion of Alice 132
pathology 17, 86, 88, 115, 126; Alice in Wonderland Syndrome 229; necrophilia 78, 90, 171, 177; pedophilia 25, 78, 86, 90, 125–133, 145, 156, 234; *Wonderland Club* 132
Peabody, Richard 11, 131–132
Peter Pan 5, 35, 119, 122, 155–157, 158, 161
Phillips, Robert 24, 32, 96, 235
Philosopher's Alice 14
photography 125–148; animal 207–210; child nude 7, 131, 128–130, 135, 145; corpography 207; digital collage 145–148; freeze-frame 85, 107, 135, 136; optical toy 13, 65; photographic metaphor 135, 136, 139; punctum 130, 173; spirit 147; still life 135; tableau vivant 21, 128, 130, 144, 146, 147, 207, 233, *see also* "The Beggar Maid"
pictorial turn 23, 27, 28, 71
picture poem 20
picturebook 3, 8, 28, 16, 32–41, 48, 49, 143, 231
Pilinovsky, Helen 12, 30, 52, 103, 131, 154, 156, 158, 165
play: doll 12, 75, 76, 78, 81, 83, 87, 89, 93, 104, 106, 132, 136, 169, 173, 176, 178, 180, 182, 185, 188, 191, 192, 210, 213, 236; hide and seek 137, 139, 140, 147, 195; ludic energy 6, 29, 35, 43, 64, 88, 128, 130, 139, 144, 147, 192, 194, 203; magical toys 168; playground 45, 83, 147, 175, 211; pretense 18, 49, 77, 80, 82, 87, 88, 98, 130, 139, 171, 210; toy 34, 65, 95, 103, 115, 127, 166–173, 182, 198, 203, 208; *Toy Story* 173, 236 *see also* game; puppetry
poor girl fiction 24, 86, 88
pop-up book 3, 11, 16, 21, 23, 28, 32–41, 43, 44, 46, 222, 231, 238
portmanteau 28, 58, 70, 123, 136, 168, 184, 193, 194, 199, 217, 230; culinary 218
postsemiotics 2, 71
produser, prosumer 44–45; cultural consumer 50; DIY 25; *see also* fandom
pro-print-and-paper arguments 44–47
psychedelic 16, 68, 117, 140, 170, 200, 204, 210, 223; hallucinogenic 6, 69, 171, 183, 204, 210
psychogeography 21, 43, 46, 55, 115, 155, 170, 199, 212; heterotopia 93, 202
psychonarration 24, 98, *see also* Cohn, Dorrit

Punch 7, 32, 70, 233
puppetry 25, 68, 81, 153, 168–187, 189, 208, 210, 211, 212, 215, 237, 238
puzzle 8, 12, 49, 56, 203, 215, 221, 237; mathematics 3, 6, 125, 126, 127, 140, 168, 188, 195, 218, 220, 222; Smullyan, Raymond 221, 237

Quay brothers 168, 236

Rackham, Arthur 67, 69, 210, 223
realism 21, 39, 42, 52, 57, 63, 65, 80, 87, 109, 118, 167, 175, 181, 182, 220, 232; anti- 71, 161; capitalist 67; hyper- 24, 71, 146; magical 26, 78, 85, 160; photo- 31, 68, 72; pseudo- 35, 67; socio- 86, 88, 89; speculative 176; total cinematic 66; *see also* surrealism
Reiniger, Lotte 215
remediation 2, 10, 13, 21, 32, 44; *see also* Bolter, Jay David; Grusin, Richard
retro–Victorian 7, 85
Reynolds, Kimberley 5
Roiphe, Katie 133–140
Rose, Jacqueline 77, 157
Ryan, Marie-Laure 19
Ryan-Sautour, Michelle 187, 189, 196, 237

Sabuda, Robert 36–38
Saville Clarke, Henry 31
Selick, Henry 22, 24, 96, 106–109, 168
sesquicentennial anniversary 221–228
Sigler, Carolyn 4, 5, 6, 11, 15, 148; Alice type story 10
simulation 15, 24, 26, 28, 38, 43, 44, 78, 123, 133, 146, 147, 172, 203, 207, 208, 213; Baudrillard, Jean 28, 78, 146, 189; photoshop 146; simulacra 145, 232; *see also* CGI 3D
Smith, Kiki 210
Sobchack, Vivian 25, 169, 179, 183, 219, 236, 237; *see also* cinesthetic spectator
society of spectacle 28, 78
somatization of semiosis 21, 61, 88, 167, 206
Something from Alice 168–187
spin-off 25, 115, 118
Springer, Claudia 15
Stam, Robert 9, 13, 21

Steadman, Ralph 17, 223
steampunk 12, 114
Still She Haunts Me 133–140
Stok, William 224
storytelling 9, 14, 17, 21, 25, 32, 36, 41, 44, 45, 47, 51, 56, 65, 99, 112, 120, 125, 130, 132, 138, 149, 155, 156, 159–165, 167, 176, 197, 199, 207, 216, 225, 231, 233; Scheherazade 154, 165
Stow, Percy 13, 27
Sundmark, Björn 8, 11, 15, 17, 230
surrealism 6, 16, 25, 35, 57, 70, 88, 108, 140, 141, 167–184, 188–190, 194, 217, 219, 235, 236, 237; *An Andalusian Dog* 88, 186; automatic writing 189, 192; Bunuel, Luis 88, 168, 175, 186; Czech surrealism 175, 181, 186, 236; Dali, Salvador 69, 88, 168, 175, 186, 188, 222, 223, 236, 238; Duchamp, Marcel 174; exquisite cadaver 193–194; found object 166, 168, 173, 174, 181, 184, 189, 194, 231; montage-verbiage technique 194; paranoid-critical method 67, 188, 189; *see also* Švankmajer, Jan
Susina, Jan 15, 32, 33, 34, 41, 42, 50, 53, 74, 128, 224
Švankmajer, Jan 168–187
Švankmajerova, Eva 18, 25, 166, 172, 181; *see also* Švankmajer, Jan
Sweeting, Samantha 206–211
Szabó-Gendler, Tamar 24, 77, 90, 234
Szegedi, Katalin 231

tactility 4, 20, 29, 33, 37, 42, 206, 208, 211; animation 181; cinema 180–187, 237; dissonance 168; fantasy 181; game 237; memory 181; reading 20, 32–41, 42, 95, 231; *Touch and Imagination* 181; *see also* Švankmajer, Jan
Tait, Vanessa 13
Talbot, Bryan 12
Tatar, Maria 14, 41
taxidermy art 76, 80, 89, 92, 168, 176, 207, 208, 210
Ted Talks 44
Telotte, J.P. 57
Thomson, Gertrude 27, 48, 127
Thorneycroft, Diana 237
Through the Looking-Glass and What Alice Found There 2, 3, 7, 8, 11, 20, 57, 58, 80, 93, 133, 156, 190, 222, 225, 229, 230, 234

Tideland 24, 51, 75–94, 234
Tiffin, Jessica 30, 54, 65, 68, 69
Tolkien, J.R.R. 19, 230
translation 10, 224, 225, 229
transmedia 2, 3, 19, 21, 22, 27–74, 115, 142, 166, 181, 206, 211, 221; plurimedial 19; storytelling 2, 21, 22, 25, 49, 166, 225; transmediation and transmediatization 22, 24, 31, 221, 226
trauma 1, 11, 24, 25, 61, 77, 86, 87, 91, 92, 95, 97, 106, 114, 115, 116, 118, 120, 132, 135, 148, 154, 155, 158, 159, 164, 165, 170, 175, 180, 190, 205, 236; trauma as tragedy/fantasy 88

Vaclavik, Kiera 223, 224
Venuti, Lawrence 10
voice: embodied 25, 141, 167, 185; incarnated 26, 61, 167, 191, 206; lingua adamica 167, 195, 197, materialized metaphor 26, 77, 79, 88, 167, 187, 191, 206; polyphony 18, 28, 83; somniloquy 82; sound montage 168, 180, 183, 184; talking to oneself 82, 99, 106, 113; tongue 89, 163, 182, 184, 185, 204; transverbal 20, 26, 82, 97, 98, 108, 109, 111, 139, 158, 163, 164, 165, 167, 186, 191, 192, 195, 197, 202, 206; visual-vocal 185; vocality 20, 58, 82, 167, 168, 199

Waits, Tom 199–206
Wakeling, Edward 222, 225
Warner, Marina 4, 65, 84, 130, 147, 173, 175, 179, 235, 237
Weaver, Warren 224
Weiss, Margaret 11
White Stone. The Alice Poems 138–140
Williams, Linda 179
Wittgenstein, Ludwig 193, 237
The Wizard of Oz 5, 69, 107, 155, 161, 165
The Wonderland Postage Stamp Case 8, 33, 37
Woolf, Virginia 12, 14, 134, 139, 221

young adult 14, 40, 95, 107, 109, 114, 121, 214

Zipes, Jack 2, 4, 13, 15, 18, 23, 29–30, 50, 52, 53, 54, 55, 63, 64, 171, 173, 231, 232
Zizek, Slavoj 44, 87–88

www.ingramcontent.com/pod-product-compliance
Lightning Source LLC
Chambersburg PA
CBHW081547300426
44116CB00015B/2787